The Nature of Religious Language

The Nature of

RELIGIOUS LANGUAGE

A Colloquium

Edited by Stanley E. Porter

ROEHAMPTON INSTITUTE LONDON PAPERS, 1

Sheffield
Academic Press

Copyright © 1996 Sheffield Academic Press

Published by Sheffield Academic Press Ltd
Mansion House
19 Kingfield Road
Sheffield, S11 9AS
England

Printed on acid-free paper in Great Britain
by Bookcraft Ltd
Midsomer Norton, Bath

British Library Cataloguing in Publication Data

A catalogue record for this book is available
from the British Library

ISBN 1-85075-580-9
ISBN 1-85075-783-6 pbk

CONTENTS

FOREWORD

The papers collected together in this volume originated at a conference on the nature of religious language, held at Roehampton Institute London in February 1995. The idea to hold such a conference came from Father Michael Hayes, the Chaplain of Digby Stuart College, one of Roehampton's constituent colleges. Michael's idea was taken up enthusiastically by the Faculty of Arts and Humanities which, in conjunction with the Roehampton Chaplaincy and the Centre for Advanced Theological Research, agreed to sponsor the event. I would like to thank him and the other members of the Faculty who organized the conference and this publication (Professor Stanley E. Porter, Head of Theology and Religious Studies, Professor Ann Thompson, Head of English, and Reeva Charles, the Faculty Administrative Officer) for all their enthusiasm and hard work.

Although, in the end, the conference concentrated only on Christian language, it nevertheless covered a wide range of issues and ideas. It soon became clear that the phrase 'religious language' could and should mean many things. We found ourselves dwelling on and then drawing distinctions between, for example, the language of God and the language of Jesus; the language of organized religion, the language of religious experience and the language of religious people; the language of priests and the language of the laity; the language of men and the language of women; the languages of different classes within our culture; the languages of different periods within our culture. Above all, we were obliged to ask 'Is there a kind of language or language use which is specifically *religious*, as opposed to *everyday* or *literary*?'

Contributors to the Conference included Ewan Clayton, one of the lecturers on Roehampton's Calligraphy and Bookbinding degree programme, who mounted a small exhibition of calligraphy on religious themes. Another was Judith Peacock, an Art student who is engaged in a MPhil/PhD project on the design of religious vestments and who also mounted an exhibition of her work. So, as well as being asked by various speakers to consider what happens to religious subject matter when it is mediated by speech, writing, print, translation or television, we were also confronted with religious subject matter expressed in part or whole through the non-verbal visual arts.

Ultimately, some of us at least found ourselves asking the old question, 'Isn't religion and religious experience concerned with things that defeat language?' But, that didn't stop us talking, and, as this volume reveals, writing about it.

Neil Taylor, Dean of Arts and Humanities
Roehampton Institute London

ABBREVIATIONS

AB	Anchor Bible
ABRL	Anchor Bible Reference Library
AGJU	Arbeiten zur Geschichte des antiken Judentums und des Urchristentums
ANTJ	Arbeiten zum Neuen Testament und Judentum
ATR	*Anglican Theological Review*
AUSS	*Andrews University Seminary Studies*
AV	Authorized Version
BETL	Bibliotheca ephemeridum theologicarum lovaniensium
Bib	*Biblica*
CBQMS	*Catholic Biblical Quarterly* Monograph Series
CRINT	Compendia rerum iudaicarum ad Novum Testamentum
DJD	Discoveries in the Judaean Desert
ExpTim	*Expository Times*
HNT	Handbuch zum Neuen Testament
HSM	Harvard Semitic Monographs
ICC	International Critical Commentary
JAAR	*Journal of the American Academy of Religion*
JBL	*Journal of Biblical Literature*
JSNTSup	*Journal for the Study of the New Testament*, Supplement Series
JTS	*Journal of Theological Studies*
NovT	*Novum Testamentum*
NTS	*New Testament Studies*
PG	J. Migne (ed.), *Patrologia graeca*
REB	Revised English Bible
SBL	Society of Biblical Literature
SBLDS	SBL Dissertation Series
SBLSP	SBL Seminar Papers
SBT	Studies in Biblical Theology
SJT	*Scottish Journal of Theology*
SNTSMS	Society of New Testament Studies Monograph Series
TDNT	G. Kittel and G. Friedrich (eds.), *Theological Dictionary of the New Testament*
TEV	Today's English Version
TrinJ	*Trinity Journal*
TS	*Theological Studies*

VT	*Vetus Testamentum*
WBC	Word Biblical Commentary
WUNT	Wissenschaftliche Untersuchungen zum Neuen Testament
ZTK	*Zeitschrift für Theologie und Kirche*

LIST OF CONTRIBUTORS

Beverley Clack, Roehampton Institute London, England

David Daniell, University College, London

Craig A. Evans, Trinity Western University, Langley, BC, Canada

J. Stephen Fountain, University of Glasgow, Scotland

Gerald Hammond, University of Manchester, England

David Hilborn, The City Temple United Reformed Church, London

Katharine Hodgkin, University of East London, England

David Jasper, University of Glasgow, Scotland

Kevin McCarron, Roehampton Institute London, England

Michael Nevin, Roehampton Institute London, England

Pat Pinsent, Roehampton Institute London, England

Stanley E. Porter, Roehampton Institute London, England

Philip Richter, Roehampton Institute London, England

Linda Thomas, Roehampton Institute London, England

John O. Thompson, University of Wales at Cardiff

Suzanne Trill, The Queen's University of Belfast, Northern Ireland

INTRODUCTION

Stanley E. Porter

How does one introduce sixteen different essays, each one creating its own literary and linguistic world and—in keeping with the subject of this volume—reflecting its own theology? It is not an easy task to capture the essence of what links all of these essays together, apart from the obvious fact that they all address one or more issues related to the way that language is used in various religious contexts. It is almost as difficult to capture the essence of each of the individual essays, since they roam over a broad range of topics as well as areas of scholarly expertise. This is not only their challenge but their reward, since the volume encompasses a dazzling array of topics and approaches. The topics include ancient, modern and early modern texts, and the approaches range from the historical to the theological to the literary.

When the tenor of discussion of the conference from which these papers emerged and their individual contributions are considered, there are two primary focuses that seem to unite the essays. They are concerned with either theological or literary issues related to the nature of religious language. The essays are presented here according to these two categories. Within these two categories there is a further division between those papers delivered as plenary papers and those designed for smaller parallel sessions. The plenary papers were designed to address some of the major areas of discussion to be focused upon during the conference. The rest of the papers reflect the particular interests of those who wrote them for smaller discussion groups. Although there is great diversity in these shorter papers, they too share the two major themes of being concerned with either theology or literature.

Part I contains papers concerned with theology and religious language. The first three papers, all delivered in plenary sessions, address biblical problems. As a linguist and theologian, I have long been interested in how linguistic matters have a bearing on interpretation of the

Bible. In my essay, 'Problems in the Language of the Bible', I do not single out the Bible as the problem but address various items of discussion where scholars have often been misled in their interpretation because of failure to consider linguistic issues. The several topics briefly introduced are the languages of the Bible, especially Greek, the supposed differences between Hebrew and Greek mindsets as seen in their differences in language, the issue of corporate personality and the individual, theological lexicography, and whether grammar is theory-neutral. This is a quick survey, but it does raise what I consider to be some recurring challenging questions.

The second paper is a detailed and focused study of an issue of theological interest but addressed from the standpoint of the historian. Professor Craig Evans of Trinity Western University in Canada looks at the evidence regarding who Jesus thought he was, according to the evidence of the New Testament and other contemporary literature. Shifting the emphasis from the Greco-Roman world, where previous discussion has often focused, Evans introduces evidence from the Old Testament, Rabbinic literature, pseudepigrapha, and especially the Dead Sea Scrolls, to shed light on the historical Jesus. Evans is convinced that this material is crucial to understanding the New Testament, especially a passage such as Mk 14.55-65, and what Jesus appears to be saying regarding the 'son of man seated at the right hand of Power and coming with the clouds of heaven'. The deification of Christ found in the rest of the New Testament appears to have had its origins in the words and activities of Jesus himself.

In the final of the plenary papers in this part, Professor David Daniell, emeritus professor of University College, London, explores a very straightforward thesis regarding 'Translating the Bible'. He argues that the ability to translate the Bible into language that speaks in the current idiom is an art that seems to have been lost. Rather than adopting one of the standard explanations for such a failure, such as the degeneration of English (something Daniell roundly rejects), he analyses what he considers the model translation by William Tyndale. As the editor of Tyndale's Bible, as well as his recent biographer, Daniell has a familiarity with Tyndale's text that surely is unparalleled, and he makes a strong case for Tyndale's version being one of the great translational feats. Citing examples from a number of recent translations, including the TEV, REB, and AV, Daniell repeatedly shows (often quite humorously) that apart from a few occasions, to his mind Tyndale preserves what is required in a translation, that is, that it be accurate, make sense, deal boldly with difficulties, have an exceptionally wide range of expression and find the proper register. We are left with respect for Tyndale but also a concern for what has gone on in recent Bible translation.

In the shorter papers, John O. Thompson raises a number of provocative questions in dealing with televangelical language. For example, he wonders why are so many repulsed by such broadcasting, what ways do these speakers come across, what does it mean to sound Christian, and the like. He then tries to get at answers by analysing several poignant examples. Philip Richter offers a sociological analysis of the 'Toronto Blessing', a charismatic religious phenomenon that has recently swept through a number of North American and British churches, resulting in various forms of overt religious expression. His sociological approach relates their practices with other forms of religious expression. In a paper that explores attempts to bridge the gap between theology and literature by means of language, Stephen Fountain takes a detailed look at Thomas Altizer's thought in the light of postmodernist categories. This results in a re-analysis of writing and reading, the already and the not-yet, in terms of redefined theological categories. Beverley Clack offers a feminist critique of the concept of God. Rejecting the referential theory of God, she argues that language about God reflects human ideals and values, thus introducing the concept of 'thealogy' as a different model of discussion of the divine. Linda Thomas enters the debate over exclusive language in the context of recent developments in the Anglican and Roman Catholic churches. From the perspective of pragmatics in recent linguistic research, David Hilborn analyses the performative characteristics of liturgical language. His study involves analysis of actual samples gathered from a number of churches in the Reformed tradition throughout Britain, and draws telling comparisons between current and previous liturgical practice. Michael Nevin explores the concept of analogy in the work of Thomas Aquinas and Wolfart Pannenberg. In the end, Nevin finds Pannenberg's use of the concept of analogy problematic, and reinforces a Thomistic notion.

The essays in Part II are concerned with literature in the context of religious language. In his plenary paper, David Jasper of the Centre for the Study of Literature and Theology of the University of Glasgow introduces the second major theme found in these papers by offering a discussion of the thought of Samuel Taylor Coleridge. In an essay that is very complimentary of Coleridge, Jasper defines and defends Coleridge's notion that words are 'Living Powers'. He is concerned to show that Coleridge's notion, although consonant with the Romantic thought of Coleridge's era, was more than that. It was an attempt to come to terms with the nature of religious language as poetic. Fending off the rise of critical thought, which he saw as flattening the language of the Bible, Coleridge looked at the origins of religious language in the individual human mind. This poetic origin of religious language, Jasper tells us, provided a basis for religious language that appears to have been lost in modern religious discourse.

The final plenary essay, by Professor Gerald Hammond of the University of Manchester, continues the literary theme by exploring what Hammond sees as the rise and fall of religious language in the early modern period. In 'In the Belly of the Whale', Hammond explores the possibilities of religious language at the time of the Reformation. What began as a Reformation ideal to revolutionize the English language so that religious language might form the basis of all language decayed into a false language that maintained its spiritual tone but betrayed a lack of religious content. To develop his argument, Hammond draws attention to a number of significant examples, including Tyndale's preface to and translation of the book of Jonah, as well as texts from Herbert, Marvell, Skelton and Pepys. He thereby traces the rise and fall of religious language from a place of centrality to a marginalization such that it is virtually meaningless, expressing intentions never meant to be kept and being utilized in a jargonistic and cantish fashion.

Among the shorter papers, several are concerned with the same era as Hammond, that is, the early modern period. Katharine Hodgkin, following up earlier research on Dionys Fitzherbert and taking us to primary texts, raises the question of whether this woman was experiencing some form of mental crisis (as her contemporaries thought) or whether she was in the midst of a spiritual crisis (as she attempts to argue in her own account). The essay raises intriguing questions regarding the nature and interpretation of religious discourse, both then and now. Suzanne Trill explores the nature of gendering of language. Whereas she recognizes how language has often been used to deny women a place in the Church, in this essay she shows how some women writers of the early modern period utilized psalms in various ways to assimilate them to their own experience, use them for their own ends, and articulate their own experiences. In the final paper concerned with the early modern period, Pat Pinsent shows how the apparent formal religious belief and affiliation of various poets of the time is reflected in their treatment of Holy Communion. She does this by examining both well-known and lesser-known writers of the period. In the final essay, Kevin McCarron brings us to the twentieth century and William Golding's *The Paper Men*. Rejecting the critical consensus regarding this 1984 novel, McCarron argues that it is unique among contemporary novels in its dramatization of the indivisible nature of good and evil, resulting in a sophisticated theological allegory.

In all, these papers offer a number of different interpretations of a range of issues, issues that obviously fascinate and have attracted those who have written upon them. They also suggest a number of issues that are still unresolved about the nature of religious language, from its early usage in the biblical texts to its recent use in contemporary writing and religious discourse, as well as many points in between. Some of the essays are forward looking, suggesting new and bold analyses for future research into their problematic areas. A number of the essays, however, are nostalgic, looking back at earlier periods that seemed in some ways less complex and less ambiguous, perhaps even in which language itself seemed to be more straightforward and there was more hope about its use than some seem to find today. Whatever the case, these essays represent serious thinking on a number of issues of the day on the nature of religious language.

Part I

THEOLOGY

Problems in the Language of the Bible: Misunderstandings that Continue to Plague Biblical Interpretation

Stanley E. Porter

1. Introduction

The nature of religious language is to be problematic. This century has made the problematic character of religious language a particularly relevant observation because of a variety of developments. One has been the phenomenal increase in primary materials available for comparison. These include the publication of a huge number of Greek papyri that have shed light upon numerous aspects of New Testament study,[1] and the discovery and decipherment of a number of Semitic language sources that have informed study of the language of the Old Testament and increased knowledge of the New Testament milieu.[2] These discoveries have had the overall effect of helping to establish the larger context into which to position the biblical text. From another angle, it has been in this century—especially in the work of the logical positivists and the linguistic analysts—that a particularly large number of philosophical questions have been raised about religious language. These questions include such basic questions as whether God exists, whether it is even meaningful to speak of God, and the like. As important as the first category of discoveries has been, it is the second that has come to dominate much popular understanding of the problematic nature of religious language. This is despite the fact that much of the general knowledge associated with these viewpoints does not in fact reflect current philosophical thought on the topic. The failure of the verification principle in

---

1. See E.G. Turner, *Greek Papyri: An Introduction* (Oxford: Clarendon Press, 1968), pp. 17-41; cf. W.F. Howard, *The Romance of New Testament Scholarship* (London: Epworth Press, 1949), pp. 111-37.
2. See R.E. Brown, *Recent Discoveries and the Biblical World* (Dublin: Veritas, 1983). The most well-known discoveries have been those connected with Qumran.

positivist thought,[3] and a clear retrenchment, even from such an out-spoken critic as Ayer, as well as numerous differences of professional opinion between Ayer and others, such as Carnap and Wittgenstein, and even Ayer's own change of views,[4] and a recent surge of interest in non-foundationalist thought,[5] has left this a very lively area of discussion in which it is once more plausible to speak of believing in God's existence.[6] Although I would welcome the opportunity to pursue this topic further, it would take me well beyond my longstanding interest in matters biblical. Much of the recent discussion of philosophical issues connected with biblical studies, apart from very specialist circles, works from the apparently settled belief that the major facts or issues regarding the biblical text are resolved. This view has been undoubtedly perpetuated by severe neglect and disregard of the ancient languages. Without access to the original text, it is difficult to appreciate even some very basic issues of interpretation and understanding. What I would like to address, therefore, are several issues where there still seem to be a number of misunderstandings regarding the nature of understanding the Bible, all ultimately focused upon matters of language. This is undoubtedly not a complete picture, but it will attempt to give an idea of some of the issues that still befuddle biblical interpreters. It seems to me that issues of biblical interpretation will always need to be important when considering the issue of the nature of religious language, and hence it is incumbent upon us to have at least a working knowledge of how to approach some of these issues.

3.   On this difficulty, see W.T. Jones, *A History of Western Philosophy. V. The Twentieth Century to Wittgenstein and Sartre* (New York: Harcourt Brace Jovanovich, 2nd edn rev., 1975), esp. pp. 220-22, 245-48.

4.   Cf. A.J. Ayer, *Language, Truth and Logic* (New York: Dover, 1952), pp. 115-16; R. Carnap, 'The Elimination of Metaphysics through Logical Analysis of Language', in A.J. Ayer (ed.), *Logical Positivism* (New York: Free Press, 1959), pp. 78-80; L. Wittgenstein, *Tractatus Logico-Philosophicus* (trans. D.F. Pears and B.F. McGuinness; London: Routledge & Kegan Paul, 1961), p. 74 proposition 7; and Ayer, 'Editor's Introduction', in Ayer, *Logical Positivism*, pp. 15-16.

5.   E.g. A. Plantinga and N. Wolterstorff (eds.), *Faith and Rationality: Reason and Belief in God* (Notre Dame: University of Notre Dame Press, 1983).

6.   V. Brümmer, *Theology and Philosophical Inquiry: An Introduction* (Philadelphia: Westminster Press, 1982).

2. *The Languages of the Bible*

In this first section, I would like to focus upon the language of the New Testament, that is, the kind of Greek that is found in the New Testament. Of course, the Old Testament is written in Hebrew and in a few sections in Aramaic. Hebrew has been a longstanding focus of discussion because it was the language of the ancient Israelites, and has been a part of an enduring fascination with the question of what was the original or earliest human language. After all, Adam and Eve spoke with each other and to God in the Garden of Eden, so they must have spoken in some language. There could be few more basic questions regarding the nature of religious language than to discover the language that God used.

One of the earliest attempts to discover the most ancient language, and hence the most ancient peoples, is recorded in Herodotus (2.2).[7] He relates the story of an Egyptian king, Psammetichus, who in the seventh century BCE decided to do an experiment to discover the original language. He reportedly took two new-born children and put them into solitary confinement under the care of a shepherd, who was ordered not to speak a word to the children or to say anything in their presence. The king thought that when the children did speak they would speak the world's first language, since they would be untainted by any 'modern' language. After two years, the children started to make a particular noise, which was later thought to be the Phrygian word for 'bread'. Thus, Phrygian, the king concluded, must have been the oldest language. In fact, it appears that the noise that the children were making resembled the bleeting of sheep (*blekos*), not surprising if they had been reared by a shepherd.

James IV of Scotland supposedly carried out a similar experiment in around 1493, but this time with different results. This time the children reportedly spoke very good Hebrew. As late as 1797, when a wild boy was found in France, a boy who had supposedly had no contact with humanity, many expected him to be able to speak Hebrew or some ancient language. They were no doubt disappointed to discover that he could speak no language at all. It was once a common expectation of the time that Hebrew, being the oldest language, or so it was supposed,

7.   This and the following stories are all taken from D. Crystal, *Linguistics* (Harmondsworth: Penguin, 1971), pp. 46-48.

would prove to be the progenitor of all other languages. Not all have been so willing to accept this, however. A Swedish scholar believed that in the Garden of Eden Adam spoke Danish, the serpent French and God Swedish. A German scholar, on the other hand, argued—perhaps not surprisingly—that German was the oldest language. His logic was that the first language must have been the most perfect, and since German was superior to other languages, it must have been first. Hence German was the language that Adam spoke. German was able to avoid the effects of Babel because the ancient forebearers of the Germans had not participated in the Tower's construction. Later God caused the Old Testament to be translated into Hebrew from German. Although no one takes such findings seriously any more, it is obvious that various agendas have been instrumental in the discussion. The same has been true in discussing the Greek of the New Testament.

Discussion of the nature of the Greek of the New Testament has a long history, if not always a particularly enlightened one.[8] The discussion can be divided into four approaches. The first approach characterized the Greek of the New Testament as a special kind of Semitic Greek. This kind of Greek, because it was thought to be found only in the Greek of the New Testament and the Septuagint, the Greek translation of the Old Testament out of Hebrew, was seen to be quite different from the Greek of the classical authors and even from that of the other literary writers of the Hellenistic period. It was thought to be less refined and even simplistic in its grammar, and odd in its use of words. Consequently, lexicographers published lists of words used in the Greek Bible that were unparalleled in meaning in secular Greek of the time and to their minds provided evidence that the Greek of the Bible constituted its own dialect, with words used in unique senses.[9] This kind of attitude predominated in opinion regarding the Greek of the New Testament for over two hundred years, from the first significant studies of Semitic influence on

---

8. See S.E. Porter, *Verbal Aspect in the Greek of the New Testament, with Reference to Tense and Mood* (Studies in Biblical Greek, 1; New York: Peter Lang, 1989), pp. 11-17; *idem*, 'Introduction: The Greek of the New Testament as a Disputed Area of Research', in S.E. Porter (ed.), *The Language of the New Testament: Classic Essays* (JSNTSup, 60; Sheffield: JSOT Press, 1991), pp. 11-37.

9. See, e.g., J.H. Thayer (ed.), *A Greek–English Lexicon of the New Testament being Grimm's Wilke's Clavis Novi Testamenti* (New York: American Book, corr. edn, 1889), pp. 693-98.

the New Testament published in the seventeenth century, until the turn of the twentieth century.

In the middle of the nineteenth century a number of important archaeological discoveries were made, including vast quantities of papyri in Egypt. These papyri were discovered in what amounted to the rubbish heaps of ancient civilizations.[10] Digging in this garbage did not turn up soft drink cans and glass bottles but numerous papyrus fragments. These fragments contained different kinds of texts. Some were a range of important fragments of classical authors, which were of interest to classical philologists. To my mind every bit as important, if not more so, were the numerous ephemeral documents or non-literary or documentary papyri.[11] These texts themselves are varied, from simple personal notes to financial receipts and various legal documents. The ideal climatic conditions of Egypt had enabled these specimens to be preserved for as much as two millennia. Although a few other papyri have been discovered elsewhere, such as in the Palestinian desert,[12] these discoveries in Egypt remain the most important. Around the turn of the century the dissemination and publication of these papyrus texts had reached such a significant level that one could appreciate their importance. Although several earlier scholars had speculated that a more thorough knowledge of the actual language of Hellenistic Greek speakers would see greater similarities between the Greek of the Bible and that of the times,[13] it was Adolf Deissmann in Germany and James Hope Moulton in England who were two of the first to appreciate the new papyrus finds. Deissmann's major contribution among many was to see that numerous words that had been thought to be used in unique senses in the New Testament and Septuagint could in fact be paralleled in these non-literary papyri. What began as over seven hundred supposedly

10. In fact, J.H. Moulton named one of his books on the subject, *From Egyptian Rubbish-Heaps* (London: Kelly, 2nd edn, 1917).

11. A handy collection of the different kinds of papyri is found in A.S. Hunt and C.C. Edgar (trans.), *Select Papyri* (2 vols.; Cambridge, MA: Harvard University Press, 1932, 1934).

12. E.g. N. Lewis, *The Documents from the Bar Kokhba Period in the Cave of Letters: Greek Papyri* (Jerusalem: Israel Exploration Society, 1989).

13. For example, E. Mason in the preface to his translation of Winer's grammar (referred to in J.R. Harris, 'The So-Called Biblical Greek', *ExpTim* 25 [1913], pp. 54-55) and J.B. Lightfoot in lectures delivered in 1863 (referred to in J.H. Moulton, *Prolegomena*, vol. 1 of *A Grammar of New Testament Greek* [Edinburgh: T. & T. Clark, 3rd edn, 1908], p. 242).

unparalleled words in the Greek Bible was reduced by Deissmann to under fifty words with senses unparalleled in the papyri, representing the popular language of the day.[14] Moulton performed a similar task in the area of Greek grammar. Whereas a number of grammatical phenomena of the Greek New Testament had often been cited as unparalleled in classical writers (although these generalizations were not completely accurate), Moulton was able to show that many of these were in fact part and parcel of the writing of the common people.[15] The Greek may not always have been elegant, but it did reflect the writing of the times by those who were attempting to communicate, not to create polished literary prose.

Although the position of Deissmann and Moulton has continued to be highly influential, especially among linguists who investigate the language of the New Testament, it was soon challenged by a position that maintained that at least the Gospels and the first part of the book of Acts had been heavily influenced by Aramaic. This theory was a natural one, since although Jesus may have spoken Greek and Hebrew he probably predominantly spoke Aramaic. This introduces issues of translation, but it does so at the earliest stages of transmission of the biblical account. Scholars began to propose various degrees of translation to be found in the Gospels. Some of the early proponents of this theory argued that one or more of the Gospels that we now have only in Greek were later translations of documents originally written in Aramaic or possibly Hebrew.[16] The argument was that some of the Greek found in the New Testament was sufficiently crude that it had to reflect a literalistic translation of an underlying Semitic original. Although this kind of theory was more widely held earlier in the century, it later became more common to argue that the Gospels themselves were Greek documents although they may contain words of Jesus translated from Aramaic, either by the Gospel writer or by his source.[17] This theory helped to

14. See especially G.A. Deissmann, *Bible Studies* (trans. A. Grieve; Edinburgh: T. & T. Clark, 2nd edn, 1903) and *Light from the Ancient East* (trans. L.R.M. Strachan; repr. Grand Rapids: Eerdmans, 1979).

15. See especially Moulton, *Prolegomena*. But see also his work in lexicography, encapsulated in Moulton and G. Milligan, *Vocabulary of the Greek Testament* (London: Hodder & Stoughton, 1914–29).

16. See, e.g., C.C. Torrey, *Our Translated Gospels: Some of the Evidence* (London: Hodder & Stoughton, 1936).

17. See, e.g., M. Black, *Aramaic Approach to the Gospels and Acts* (Oxford: Clarendon Press, 3rd edn, 1967); M. Wilcox, *The Semitisms of Acts* (Oxford:

account for some unusual Greek in some of the words of Jesus, some of which found parallels in other Semitic literature of the time. However, the number of plausible instances of this kind of word for word translation became decreasingly slim, so that in more recent times, even advocates of a form of the Aramaic hypothesis have argued that the Gospels cannot be seen as translated documents in any meaningful sense. They are Greek documents, in that Jesus' words though perhaps originally Aramaic have been sufficiently re-written and interpreted in Greek by the Gospel writers or their precursors.[18]

The fourth position to mention is one that has aroused more controversy than any other of late, and it is in essence a form of the earlier Holy Ghost Greek hypothesis. In its current form, this theory is a revival of the nineteenth-century theory that there was a Jewish-Greek dialect in use in Palestine in the first century. The American scholar Henry Gehman and the British scholar Nigel Turner have been advocates of this theory. Since hypotheses regarding Semitic influence and conformity to the standards of Greek, whether classical or as found in the papyri, are inadequate to explain the Greek of the New Testament, Turner concludes that only the supposition of such a dialect explains the language found in the Greek Bible.[19] Gehman considered this dialect a temporary linguistic condition brought about by Jews passing from Semitic to Greek language (his work concentrated upon the Septuagint), but Turner considered that the period was not transitional but that the language was an actual language in use by a significant population.[20]

It is not appropriate here to evaluate all of these theories, but allow me to suggest a couple of points. First, regarding the origins of language,

Clarendon Press, 1965); *idem*, 'The Aramaic Background of the New Testament', in D.R.G. Beattie and M.J. McNamara (eds.), *The Aramaic Bible: Targums in their Historical Context* (JSOTSup, 166; Sheffield: Sheffield Academic Press, 1994), pp. 362-78.

18. One of the most balanced positions is found in J.A. Fitzmyer, 'The Languages of Palestine in the First Century A.D.', in his *A Wandering Aramean: Collected Aramaic Essays* (Missoula, MT: Scholars Press, 1979), pp. 29-56.

19. See, e.g., H. Gehman, 'The Hebraic Character of Septuagint Greek', *VT* 1 (1951), pp. 81-90; and among many others, N. Turner, 'The Language of Jesus and his Disciples', in his *Grammatical Insights into the New Testament* (Edinburgh: T. & T. Clark, 1965), pp. 174-88.

20. See N. Turner, 'The "Testament of Abraham": Problems in Biblical Greek', *NTS* 1 (1954–55), pp. 219-23.

most linguists are pessimistic that we can know much about the origins of language, especially since Chomsky's theory of the brain being hard-wired for language has fallen on hard times philosophically and linguistically.[21] It is interesting to note that ancient peoples acknowledge that the phenomenon of language and its diverse varieties is an issue to consider—witness the incident at the Tower of Babel—but linguists do not think that these early stories provide more than mythical interpretations to account for experience. As a result many linguists bracket out such issues, although a number look either to child language or animal behaviour as a possible way forward.[22] Perhaps of some relevance will be some recent work in psycholinguistics, regarding how the brain produces and processes language.[23] We are a long way from solving such issues, however.

Secondly, the issue of the nature of the Greek of the Bible is a question of a different type. In the next section I will discuss some of the possible reasons for misconstruals of the relations between Semitic and Greek language-speakers. Much of the discussion regarding the Greek of the Bible has suffered from a failure to utilize firm sociolinguistic criteria in making an assessment.[24] For example, one cannot simply compare Greek with Aramaic, in the light of what is known now regarding the local languages of the eastern Mediterranean world. Semitic languages were local indigenous languages within the larger milieu of Greek as the prestige language. Further to be considered is that Greek may well have been a second language for many Palestinians. Whereas their idiolects may have evidenced influence of both languages, these would not have been permanent so as to create the kind of dialect posited by Gehman and Turner.[25] Regarding the Greek of the New Testament, however, it is probably the case that its two major writers, Paul and 'Luke', were native Greek speakers.

21. J.R. Searle (ed.), 'Symposium on Innate Ideas', in *The Philosophy of Language* (Oxford: Oxford University Press, 1971), pp. 121-44.

22. See J. Aitchison, *The Articulate Mammal: An Introduction to Psycholinguistics* (London: Hutchinson, 2nd edn, 1983), pp. 29-58.

23. See A.R. Damasio and H. Damasio, 'Brain and Language', *Scientific American* (September 1992), pp. 63-71.

24. See, e.g., R. Hudson, *Sociolinguistics* (Cambridge Textbooks in Linguistics; Cambridge: Cambridge University Press, 1980); Porter, *Verbal Aspect*, pp. 147-56.

25. Regarding multilingualism in ancient Palestine, see S.E. Porter, 'Jesus and the Use of Greek in Galilee', in B. Chilton and C.A. Evans (eds.), *Studying the Historical Jesus: Evaluations of the State of Current Research* (Leiden: Brill, 1994), pp. 129-33.

Thirdly, whereas much of the discussion has traditionally concentrated upon the lexicon (and it is admitted that the lexicon is most easily influenced in such an environment, especially where technical or theological vocabulary is involved), to determine influence upon a language one must consider grammatical structure, and it is here that there has been little substantiation that the Greek of the Bible has a different grammatical structure than other Greek. The distinct tendency is for the non-prestige language to be influenced by the prestige language, not the other way around. Such is the apparent case with the influence of Greek upon Semitic verb structure.[26]

Fourthly, how one characterizes a language is important. In evaluating Greek, the standards of classical literary Greek have often been used, with the Greek of the Hellenistic period especially in non-literary texts seen to be inferior. This fails to account for several factors, including the fact that the classical literary texts are themselves highly stylized and unrepresentative of the language of the people (there was probably a significant difference between the spoken language and the language of literary texts and inscriptions),[27] the fact that languages are changed over the course of time by their users, and the fact that many have been hesitant to admit that the text of the Bible as a religious document may not convey its truths in pristine language.

Fifthly, often discussion of this issue has failed to define crucial terminology, such as 'dialect', 'language', and 'register'.[28] Varieties of register or style, that is, how language is used in specific generic contexts, do not constitute new languages, at least in a meaningful sense for such a discussion. The language of the Hellenistic world was a surprisingly dialectless language created out of the widespread dissemination of Greek by Alexander and his successors when used by a relatively mobile and fluid population. Thus the theory of Deissmann and Moulton, reasserted again recently by a number of scholars, appears to be the most satisfactory accounting of the nature of the Greek of the New

---

26. See C. Rabin, 'Hebrew and Aramaic in the First Century', in S. Safrai and M. Stern (eds.), *The Jewish People in the First Century* (CRINT, 1.2; Assen: Van Gorcum, 1976), p. 1024.

27. See K. Dover, 'The Colloquial Stratum in Classical Attic Prose', in G.S. Shrimpton and D.J. McCargar (eds.), *Classical Contributions: Studies in Honour of M.F. McGregor* (Locust Valley, NY: Augustin, 1981), p. 16.

28. See Porter, *Verbal Aspect*, pp. 152-54; cf. Hudson, *Sociolinguistics*, pp. 21-72.

Testament, although one can also see that such a simple question as this is not without problems.

3. *Hebrew versus Greek Mindsets*

One of the abiding problems in discussing the nature of the language of the Bible is with regard to supposed differences between Hebrew and Greek mindsets. This is often linked to supposed differences between the grammars of their languages. Major discussion of this issue occurred in the early 1960s and has continued since that time in a variety of specialist publications. What is distressing, however, is that much of the debate appears to be unknown by those outside such circles.[29]

The problem is essentially this. Some have argued that there is a close relationship between language and thought-patterns, which is true also of the minds of Greek and Hebrew speakers.[30] The Greeks are stereotypically depicted as static and contemplative, the Hebrews as dynamic; the Greeks as abstract and the Hebrews as concrete in their thinking; the Greeks as dualistic and the Hebrews as monistic in their view of the person. Although there may be some truth to such stereotypes (I am admittedly sceptical), such characterizations become problematic when statements such as these regarding contrasts in thought-patterns are given their basis in the grammar of the language. For example, these contrasts can supposedly be seen between the Hebrew verbal system (establishing their dynamism) and the noun-based structure of Greek (illustrating their static nature). The Hebrews supposedly had a special understanding of time reflected in their verbal system, such that the future has the same certainty as the past. Hebrew word order was verb-subject, placing the action first in the sentence. The Hebrews thus had a clear sense of history, with only two verb tenses available, present and past-future, whereas the Greeks did not have such a clear sense but were

29. I made an attempt to bring these issues to the fore in S.E. Porter, 'Two Myths: Corporate Personality and Language/Mentality Determinism', *SJT* 43 (1990), pp. 299-306, which provides the basis of the following remarks.

30. The classic works—but by no means the only—in this regard are T. Boman, *Hebrew Thought Compared with Greek* (trans. J.L. Moreau; London: SCM Press, 1960), esp. pp. 17-23, 123-92; O. Cullmann, *Christ and Time* (trans. F.V. Filson; London: SCM Press, 1951); and more recently M.R. Wilson, *Our Father Abraham: Jewish Roots of the Christian Faith* (Grand Rapids: Eerdmans, 1988). This kind of thinking characterized the biblical theology movement. See B.S. Childs, *Biblical Theology in Crisis* (Philadelphia: Westminster Press, 1970), pp. 44-47.

given to nuance, purportedly because of their numerous verb tenses; Greek was a language of elaboration, subtlety and richness. This list could be extended, but provides enough so that the stereotype is illustrated.[31]

One might be tempted to regard such a characterization as particularly naive, were it not that this kind of perspective was derived from principles laid down in the nineteenth century, especially by the German nationalistic scholar Wilhelm von Humboldt, founder of the University of Berlin.[32] His ideas were developed in this century most notably in the work of Edward Sapir and his student Benjamin Lee Whorf, probably under the influence of the American anthropologist Franz Boas.[33] They made popular a combination of linguistic relativity and linguistic determinism that has become known as the Sapir–Whorf hypothesis. As Whorf says, his research indicated

> that the background linguistic system (in other words, the grammar) of each language is not merely a reproducing instrument for voicing ideas but rather is itself the shaper of ideas, the program and guide for the individual's mental activity, for his analysis of impressions, for his synthesis of his mental stock in trade... We dissect nature along lines laid down by our native languages... We cut nature up, organize it into concepts, and ascribe significances as we do, largely because we are parties to an agreement to organize it in this way—an agreement that holds throughout our speech community and is codified in the patterns of our language. The agreement is, of course, an implicit and unstated one, BUT ITS TERMS ARE ABSOLUTELY OBLIGATORY; we cannot talk at all except by subscribing to the organization and classification of data which the agreement decrees.[34]

31. See J. Barr, *The Semantics of Biblical Language* (Oxford: Oxford University Press, 1961), pp. 8-106; cf. *idem*, *Biblical Words for Time* (London: SCM Press, 2nd edn, 1969 [1962]).

32. For assessment of these positions, and many of the examples used below, see J. Lyons, *Language and Linguistics: An Introduction* (Cambridge: Cambridge University Press, 1981), esp. pp. 302-12, cf. 312-29; and A.C. Thiselton, *The Two Horizons* (Grand Rapids: Eerdmans, 1980), pp. 133-39.

33. E. Sapir, *Language: An Introduction to the Study of Speech* (New York: Harcourt Brace, 1921); B.L. Whorf, *Language, Thought and Reality* (Cambridge, MA: MIT Press, 1956); and F. Boas, *Handbook of American Indian Languages* (Washington, D.C.: Smithsonian Institute, 1911).

34. Whorf, 'Science and Linguistics', in *Language, Thought and Reality*, pp. 212-14.

The hard form of this theory is the one that is often found in popular knowledge, as well as biblical studies. It simply states that in our thinking we cannot experience anything apart from the categories and distinctions encoded in our language. These categories in a given language are unique to that system and incommensurable to those of any other system.[35]

There are several important responses that can and should be made to such an analysis. First, one needs to address the stereotypes themselves. The above description of the differences between Hebrew and Greek language are subject to numerous qualifications. For example, the contrasts are made without concern for controls on the method employed. There is no linguistic methodology in evidence; therefore, it is difficult to say what counts as evidence from the languages involved. When some recent work on Greek and Hebrew linguistics is brought into the picture, the difficulties increase. The majority of Hebrew scholars who have considered the problem of Hebrew verbal structure argue for an aspectual system, that is, a system in which Hebrew verbs are used according to a view of the kind of action rather than time of action. This makes it difficult to characterize the Hebrew language as conveying a clear sense of history on the basis of its two verb tenses, since the time-based nature of the tenses has been eliminated. More importantly still, recent work in Greek verbal structure has concluded that the Greek verbal system is also aspectually-based, rather than time-based. Languages such as Greek and Hebrew use various deictic indicators to establish temporal reference, not tense forms alone.[36] Similarly, in Japanese temporal reference is not established according to verbal usage (and the Japanese verbal system is similar to Hebrew and Greek in this regard), and this despite the fact that Japanese society is usually characterized as very time-oriented.[37] This kind of evidence further vitiates deterministic connections between language and mindset, as well as sharp contrasts between the Hebrew and Greek mindsets on the basis of language.

The second area to be addressed is in terms of the Sapir–Whorf hypothesis. There have been studies that indicate that language users

35. Lyons, *Language*, pp. 304-305.

36. See Barr, *Semantics*, pp. 72-85; Porter, *Verbal Aspect*, pp. 157-59 on Hebrew and *passim* on Greek.

37. E.A. Nida, 'The Implications of Contemporary Linguistics for Biblical Scholarship', *JBL* 91 (1972), p. 83.

tend to remember and adapt their memories to correspond to the things for which there are words and expressions already available in their language. This seems quite understandable. However, the lexicon of a language does not correspond in a one-to-one relation with things in the world around. Thus we get such noteworthy and well-known examples as the following: Eskimo has several words for snow, Australian Aboriginal languages have several words for different kinds of sand, some Chinese varieties have several words for rice, Hungarian has different words for elder and younger brother, and Russian has different words for dark and light blue (kinship terms and colour-terms are particularly significant for these kinds of differences among languages). In each of these examples, English only has a single word (sometimes the languages above do not have a single word for the general concept). Does that pose an insuperable difficulty for expression? English speakers apparently do understand the complexities of such distinctions, despite their lack of the same linguistic resources. Whereas their expressions may not be as elegant as in some languages, useful means of expression are found. For example, skiers may refer to powdery snow or powder; beach-goers speak of white sand or rocky sand; cooks may serve wild rice, white rice or brown rice; relatives speak of elder and younger brothers; and artists use dark and light blue. More complex expressions may even take on the status of a single lexical item, such as 'wild rice'. There are examples that move in the opposite direction as well. For example, an American-Indian language, Zuni, does not differentiate yellow and orange, and research has indicated that there is a difficulty for Zuni speakers in expressing a distinction that an English speaker readily makes, although the Zuni apparently perceives that there is a difference in the two shades of colour.

Furthermore, some of the research that Whorf did to substantiate his theory has been called into question. For example, he argued that since the Hopi language did not have a time-based tense structure the Hopis perceived of the world differently from those who did, such as many Indo-Europeans.[38] But Whorf was not able to substantiate what that difference in behaviour was. There may be a parallel with certain Aboriginal languages that lack numerals higher than four. Some have interpreted this to mean that the Aboriginals are limited in their concept of number, yet when Aboriginals learn a language such as English which

38. Whorf, 'Some Verbal Categories of Hopi', in *Language, Thought and Reality*, pp. 112-24.

has numerals higher than four, they show no greater lack of numericity than native English speakers. This numerical limitation is apparently confined to the convention of language, not mentality. Similarly, I would be hesitant to argue that since English no longer has a gender system English speakers, including Americans, have, using Nida's words, 'lost interest in sex',[39] or that all French people are preoccupied with sex because they make every noun to be either masculine or feminine. And the Germans have a neuter gender for such words as 'young girl'. Perhaps worst of all, Malay has only one word for both brother and sister, although all indications are that Malayans can distinguish the two. This is not to deny cultural differences between speakers of various languages. British culture of the late twentieth century is different from French culture. But it is also apparently true that British culture of the late twentieth century is quite a bit different from British culture of two hundred years ago. Many who speak the same language have different cultures as well, for example, German speaking groups in continental Europe, or British culture of the South and North. What is clear is that the differences in culture bear no necessary correlation with the languages that are spoken by members of these various cultural groups, and certainly their languages are in no way deterministic of their thinking.

The ability to perform translation is a case in point. Although it is undeniable that a translation is never the same as the original, most translators would agree that in most instances what has been said in one language can be said in another. Difficulties can be confronted in various ways, including use of loan words or loan translations, or even various periphrastic constructions. Numerous difficulties apparently successfully overcome include the lack of an article in Latin and Greek having only one form of article, not the definite and indefinite articles of English. While some language may make expression of some concepts easier than others, a correlation between differences in language and mentality cannot be demonstrated.[40]

4. *Corporate Personality and the Individual*

Related to the distinction between language and mentality determinism is a similar kind of stereotype that has plagued study of the Bible, and that

---

39. Nida, 'Implications of Contemporary Linguistics', p. 83.
40. Lyons, *Language*, p. 311.

is that the Semitic peoples viewed personality in terms of corporate identity, as opposed to the Greeks who viewed personality individualistically.[41] This may not seem like a problem related to the language of the Bible but may seem more like a problem of ancient psychology or sociology. It is true that the concept of corporate personality is connected to these topics, but discussion of this issue is also part of problems regarding the language of the Bible. The basis for the belief comes from a particular way of reading the Bible, as the primary means of access to the thinking and behaviour of the ancient Israelites, and has had serious implications for subsequent interpretation of various incidents in the Bible. Consequently this issue has had a role to play in creating problems in the language of the Bible.

The concept of corporate personality had its chief origins in the work of the theologian H. Wheeler Robinson. Robinson's view of the ancient Israelite concept of human personality was predicated upon his view of 'primitive psychology', which included such ideas as a quasi-physical soul, the access of personality to external influences apart from the senses, and lack of a sense of individuality. It is the lack of a sense of individuality that he labeled 'the idea of corporate personality', in which people were categorized as members of various groups such as tribes, clans or families—not on the basis of their being individuals bound together by consciousness. As a result of this corporate personality, Robinson maintained, one can understand such biblical episodes and passages as blood revenge, the sin of one being visited upon the larger group to which this one belongs (e.g. Achan in Joshua 7), the use of 'I' in the Psalms when a larger group appears to be implied (such as Israel), and the servant songs of Isaiah (e.g. ch. 53).[42]

Some have simply asserted that, despite appearances, all of the instances above reflect not a corporate sense of personality but individuality similar to the modern conception.[43] But this does not seem to be a

41. See Porter, 'Two Myths', pp. 289-99, which provides the basis of the following remarks. This concept too was part of the biblical theology movement. See Childs, *Biblical Theology*, p. 46.

42. See, e.g., H. Wheeler Robinson, 'The Hebrew Conception of Corporate Personality' (1935) and 'The Group and the Individual in Israel' (1937), repr. in *Corporate Personality in Ancient Israel* (Philadelphia: Fortress Press, 1964).

43. The following points of criticism draw upon J.W. Rogerson, 'The Hebrew Conception of Corporate Personality: A Re-Examination', *JTS* NS 21 (1970), pp. 1-16; *idem*, *Anthropology and the Old Testament* (The Biblical Seminar; repr. Sheffield: JSOT Press, 1984), esp. pp. 46-65.

sufficient explanation. A number of dimensions to Robinson's study require re-assessment, so as to illuminate this problem. There are three major points of criticism of his schema. First, Robinson's characterization of the primitive personality has been called into question on methodological and evidential grounds. It is unclear what are the limitations of culture and what are genuine elements of primitive psychology. This has not been quantified, if it can be proven to exist at all. Furthermore, even if the concept of a primitive personality could be adequately defined there is the serious question of whether the ancient Israelites are best considered as primitives. On the basis of their legal, literary and other accomplishments, it would be highly dubious to do so. Secondly, in Robinson's attempt to describe the ancient Israelites he appealed to parallels with modern Bedouin. This kind of use of parallels is not uncommon when studying ancient cultures, but one must use it carefully. Rogerson has indicated that there has been much anachronistic analysis of the ancient world on this basis. For example, the indications regarding the Patriarchs is that they were not similar to modern Bedouin but were semi-nomadic peoples not living in the deep desert for extended periods of time but on the outskirts of civilization, as witness their various confrontations with city-groups. Thirdly, again as Rogerson has pointed out, for Robinson and his followers, the term corporate personality is being used in at least two ways. On the one hand it is used to refer to corporate representation and on the other to refer to a psychical unity. The latter has become the dominant way in which it was used by Robinson and those who have followed him.

This distinction between corporate representation and corporate unity helps to understand the biblical episodes cited above. The ancient Israelites apparently had a concept of corporate representation. This concept of corporate representation, far from being confined to the ancient Israelites, is one that is found in other cultures, such as the ancient Greek, as well as in modern life. For example, the contemporary person may see his own fortunes rising and falling in relation to his favourite sports team, or view the Prime Minister (or leader of the opposition) as speaking and acting on behalf of the nation or a group within it, without necessarily any loss of the sense of the individual. This appears to be the sense in which Paul uses 'in Christ' language in his epistles. He characterizes human existence for the believer as being within the sphere or under the authority of Christ.[44] This language

44. See S.E. Porter, *Idioms of the Greek New Testament* (Biblical Languages:

would apparently have been readily understandable to a Hellenistic audience that was long-familiar with similar images. For example, in Sophocles's *Oedipus the King*, the king enters and speaks to a priest, who responds:[45]

> You too have seen our city's affliction, caught in a tide of death from which there is no escaping—death in the fruitful flowering of her soil; death in the pastures; death in the womb of woman; and pestilence, a fiery demon gripping the city stripping the house of Cadmus to fatten hell with profusion of lamentation... Now, Oedipus great and glorious, we seek your help again. Find some deliverance for us by any way that god or man can show. We know that experience of trials gives strength to present counsel. Therefore, o greatest of men, restore our city to life (ll. 22-30, 40-47).

Oedipus's brother-in-law, Creon, returns from the oracle with a message: 'There is an unclean thing, born and nursed in our soil, polluting our soul, which must be driven away, not kept to destroy us' (ll. 97-98). Oedipus is told upon further enquiry that what is needed is 'The banishment of a man, or the payment of blood for blood. For the shedding of blood is the cause of our city's peril' (ll. 100-101). Though most are familiar with the tragic tale that unfolds, how many realize that the plot of this play is predicated upon a clear case of corporate representation? Line 314 summarizes this orientation: 'for we are in you', Oedipus says with reference to the city being in the hands of Teiresias the prophet, similar to the way that the city is in his hands. This story is strikingly reminiscent of the story of Achan in Joshua 7, in which a man violates divine precept and those close to him suffer. But Sophocles's Oedipus is even more perplexing in that an entire city must suffer for deeds committed by a man estranged from either city he could have called home, rather than just his family paying the penalty. In any case, one cannot draw upon the supposed idea of corporate personality as a means of contrasting ancient Israelite with Greek culture or as a means of simplistically resolving several exegetically difficult passages in the Bible.

Greek, 2; Sheffield: JSOT Press, 2nd edn, 1994), p. 159.

45. The translation is from E.F. Watling (trans.), *Sophocles, The Theban Plays: King Oedipus, Oedipus at Colonus, Antigone* (Harmondsworth: Penguin, 1947), pp. 26, 28.

5. *Theological Lexicography*

There are a number of issues that are related to the study of the lexicon that raise problems concerning the language of the Bible. Rather than survey the entire field of biblical lexicography, however, I would like to address several issues that often seem to emerge when the biblical text is discussed.[46] The first is etymology. True etymologies are to be distinguished from folk etymologies. True etymologies are a useful part of historical linguistics, that is, in tracing the origins and development of a word. They may even have some bearing upon the question of meaning. Unfortunately, much of what we know about Greek is of the folk etymology sort. Occasionally one hears statements to the effect that it is too bad that we do not understand the Greek language as Plato or Aristotle or other 'real Greeks' did. I am not so sure that this is desirable. Plato in his 'Cratylus' 399C, full of all sorts of reflections on language, contains this etymology of the word ἄνθρωπος (man). He says that it comes from the verb ἀναθρεῖ (look up) and ὄπωπε (he has seen), because it is only man who looks up and has seen. This is sheer fancy.

Nevertheless, there is a persistent tendency to use etymologies in an irresponsible way. As recently as 1974, one scholar stated, 'In investigating the history of any word it is essential that we begin with its etymology [so far, acceptable though not recommended, but now things take a turn] and take its etymological meaning as the basic one. For if words mean anything at all [this is a point that needs definition], then the radical words, of whose elements a compound word is constituted, must surely disclose the fundamental meaning of that word.'[47] A nice idea (I here play intentionally on the Latin meaning of the word that *nice* is derived from, ignorant), but one that is highly problematic when one considers how people use language, apart from consideration of any principles of linguistic study. Not only are many etymologies unknown both now and to native users (remember Plato's view of ἄνθρωπος), but etymologizing overlooks the fact that apart from a very small group that may study such things these kinds of histories of words are

46. A fuller form of this essay is to be found as ch. 4 in S.E. Porter, *Studies in the Greek New Testament: Theory and Practice* (Studies in Biblical Greek, 6; New York: Peter Lang, 1996), pp. 49-74.

47. C.C. Caragounis, '*Opsonion*: A Reconsideration of its Meaning', *NovT* 16 (1974), p. 36.

unknown to the users of the language. If only those who knew the histories of their words could use those words we, like people of any language at any time, would be reduced to speechlessness.

Explanations for why a particular word is used in the Greek of the New Testament are often devised on the basis of the Septuagint. For example, some have argued (see below) that ἐκκλησία (church) is used to translate the Hebrew *qahal*, since it comes from *qol*, meaning 'voice, call' (with the possibility of the influence of the sounds [k] and [l], an unlikely suggestion), and since the Greeks had no word for religious community. This is an interesting idea, but it tends to make ἐκκλησία into a technical theological term on the basis of the Septuagint, one that finds it difficult to explain not only Mt. 16.18 and 18.18 (two different kinds of religious community) but Acts 19.32, where it refers to a hostile crowd. More likely is the fact that ἐκκλησία is used because it was a word for 'gathering for a purpose', an instance of which might have been a Christian one.

The above deficiencies in traditional lexicography reflect a particular kind of biblical lexical study, theological lexicography. This may seem an archaic concept, but it was institutionalized in two programmatic lectures delivered at Cambridge in 1937 by Gerhard Kittel.[48] Essentially theological lexicography is an attempt to describe words and their histories, especially those words with theological significance. The significance lies in the use of words that are tied to definite historical events to which they bear witness. In other words, words are thought to bear witness to facts, with the facts behind these events, or the fundamental events, being even more significant than the words themselves. Language then exists not as a self-referring system but as a crystal through which to make concepts visible. For Kittel, genuine lexicography is the study of this relationship. For this purpose, the language that is analysed is the language of the New Testament treated as a distinct language heavily influenced by Semitic thought. Its development is seen to be completely distinct from that of other Greek and not to follow the kinds of patterns

48. G. Kittel, *Lexicographia Sacra* (London: SPCK, 1938) from whom the following examples are taken. Of course, Kittel's work and approach were severely criticized by Barr, *Semantics,* esp. pp. 206-62. See also M. Silva, *Biblical Words and their Meaning: An Introduction to Lexical Semantics* (Grand Rapids: Zondervan, 1983), pp. 22-28; P. Cotterell and M. Turner, *Linguistics and Biblical Interpretation* (London: SPCK, 1989), pp. 106-28. Theological lexicography was also part of the biblical theology movement. See Childs, *Biblical Theology,* p. 47.

seen in the development of other languages. As evidence of this, δόξα is said to have become an entirely new word in the New Testament, changing from its classical meaning 'opinion' to 'glory of God'.[49] The distinctives of secular Greek, as opposed to biblical Hebrew, are, in the minds of theological lexicographers, intimately connected to the particular ways of thinking of these people, as noted above. The discipline of New Testament studies has in the past been and in fact continues to be dominated by theology, and in particular theological lexicography, and I would say often at the expense of informed linguistic study. Numerous questionable assumptions and methods have been perpetuated under the veneer of lexicography, when what is really meant is theology. In some cases, the standard reference tools used in New Testament studies were written before the advent and certainly before the development of modern linguistics. Of course, they cannot be held blameworthy for not using a not-yet-developed method, but neither should they be exalted or at the least held immune from criticism on that same account.

Several of the assumptions of theological lexicography that have bearing upon serious lexicography warrant mention. Even those who do not share the agenda of the biblical theology movement can often be found subscribing to some of their ill-conceived tenets. For example, the idea of words bearing witness to facts was already disputed in philosophical thinking by Frege, who showed that there is no necessary correlation between the word and the thing. It was he who made the fundamental distinction between sense and reference.[50] It is important to note that it is not a word that refers, but a language-user who uses a word to refer, otherwise it is simply an item in the lexical store.

The reliance upon etymology has been discussed above, but a classic instance that has died hard is Jeremias's thoughts regarding use of *abba*.[51] Jeremias argued that it was a vocative form, probably going back to childish babble. The same word, according to Jeremias, was used

---

49. There are several problems with this analysis. First, the disjunctive thinking is evident—words being either pagan or Christian. Secondly, the semantic development of the word is neglected, from 'opinion' to 'high opinion' to 'glory'. Thirdly, the word is not used in the New Testament only of divine glory (Mt. 6.29) but retains other senses. Fourthly, often the word is modified to indicate the divine ascription. On the concept of so-called Christian words, see S.E. Porter, 'Is *dipsuchos* (James 1,8; 4,8) a "Christian" Word?', *Bib* 71 (1990), pp. 469-73.

50. See Jones, *History of Western Philosophy*, V, pp. 148-50.

51. See, e.g., J. Jeremias, *New Testament Theology* (trans. J. Bowden; London: SCM Press, 1971), pp. 61-68; see also Kittel, *Lexicographia Sacra*, pp. 14-16.

by adults and children, so by the time of Jesus it had become an adult word, and thus, on the basis of its origin in child-language, was one that meant 'daddy'. All of this has been called into serious question.[52] The speculation on the origins of the sounds in childish babble is dubious (as is the idea that 'pa' and 'ma' are childish references to parents), besides the fact that it has no apparent relevance for the developed use of the word. This crucial link gone, Jeremias's case collapses. Besides the fact that many of Jeremias's examples are too late to be of relevance to study of the New Testament, the fact that children and adults use the word does not necessarily imply an intimate use, especially when there are many contexts where this kind of address is totally lacking. In the New Testament, the word *abba* is always glossed by ὁ πατήρ ('father'; Mk 14.36; Rom. 8.15; Gal. 4.6), never a diminutive. The article probably indicates emphatic usage, not modified by 'my' or another term of familiarity. The reliance upon a dubious etymology probably led Jeremias astray.

Concerning word and concept, this kind of confusion still abounds, for example when an author refers to the 'Johannine concept of logos' or the 'concept of διακονέω'.[53] The important consideration here is that there may be many words that go to forming the Greek concept of love, ἀγάπη being only one of them. In fact, the Greek concept of something might even be represented by a scene in which there is no common lexical item. This is closely related to the problem of studying words in isolation, as if the individual words have theological meaning. Barr is right when he states that 'It is the sentence (and of course the still larger literary complex such as the complete speech or poem) which is the linguistic bearer of the usual theological statement, and not the word (the lexical unit)...'[54] In the extreme, there have been those who have wanted to write theologies of the prepositions, besides such problems as understanding the use of ἐκκλησία, and words for love. It is true that there are some important uses of the preposition ὑπέρ in the New Testament, but it seems to me that the significance is more fully

52. See J. Barr, 'Abba isn't Daddy', *JTS* 39 (1988), pp. 28-47.
53. The examples here are simply too numerous to mention, and to single out one or two would be unfair.
54. Barr, *Semantics*, p. 263. Barr presciently foreshadows the recent development of discourse analysis. See S.E. Porter and D.A. Carson (eds.), *Discourse Analysis and Other Topics in Biblical Greek* (JSNTSup, 113; Sheffield: Sheffield Academic Press, 1995).

appreciated when it is realized that substitutionary uses were part and parcel of common Greek usage, seen in instances in the papyri when, for example, one person writes 'for' another,[55] than in some sanctified use of ὑπέρ that must neglect all of the more humdrum uses. From a linguistic standpoint these non-theological uses (if the term may be used) are every bit as important in establishing the usage of the word as the special instances. But the tendency has been to then read the theological sense into all of the uses, or to commit 'illegitimate totality transfer' to use Barr's phrase. Similarly, Fee, in his recent work on the Holy Spirit, understands the use of πνεῦμα in Rom. 1.9 as referring both to Paul's human spirit *and* to the Spirit of God at work in his own spirit.[56]

Furthermore, this view takes an anthropomorphic or mystical view of language. Kittel says that the language of the New Testament has a single purpose, that is, the expression of what has taken place. Kittel gives the idea that his is a kind of lexicography that is internal to the language and has penetrated to its core. He wants to link language to theology. But Kittel has language acting of its own accord, apart from the users of the language. Perhaps the writers wished to express this single purpose, but surely it was not the language itself. Where does this language live, where is it located and how does it accomplish its purposes? Deissmann's and Moulton's view is much more convincing when they find the vocabulary and syntax part of the common language, applied to tasks by its users. Kittel ends up making language (to say nothing of theology) what it clearly is not or at least is not meant to be, and that is something that exists in isolation apart from language users. For Kittel, because 'yoke' (ζυγός) is used of Christ's yoke, it must be a theological term, which will come as a surprise to many a beast of burden. Of 1 Thess. 1.5ff. Kittel says that logos in 1.6 is 'Word' (capital W), when the article could simply indicate 'this word' and refer to v. 5. Of εὐαγγέλιον he argues that since εὐαγγελίζομαι translates *basar* it must represent procession of God, neglecting the fact that *basar* means bringing news good *or* bad in the Old Testament and minimizing the fact that in the inscriptions from Priene the word refers to good news of the emperor, such as his birthday.[57]

55. See Porter, *Idioms*, pp. 176-77.
56. G.D. Fee, *God's Empowering Presence: The Holy Spirit in the Letters of Paul* (Peabody: Hendrickson, 1994), p. 458.
57. Kittel, *Lexicographia Sacra*, pp. 20-30 *passim* for examples.

6. *Grammar as Theory-Neutral*

Having spoken about the nature of lexicography as creating its own problems in the study of the Bible, it is perhaps fitting at this point to say something about grammar as well.[58] There has been a persistent neglect of Greek grammar in the study of the language of the Bible, leading to many problems in its interpretation. The role of knowledge of the language should be much greater than simply correcting a few abuses carried to the extreme, or being able to look up a few words in a lexicon. In 1975, Lars Rydbeck, a Greek grammarian specializing in the Hellenistic era, commented on the current state of neglect of research into New Testament Greek grammar by stating that 'today research into post-classical Greek in general and New Testament Greek in particular has come almost to a standstill'. He cites a number of reasons, including that 'there is a prevalent but false assumption that everything in New Testament Greek scholarship has been done already'.[59] People who make these kinds of statements—and they have been addressed to me— are usually of the opinion that the major problems of Greek grammar were solved in the nineteenth century by the New Grammarians, thinking (wrongly as it happens) that they were dependent upon the Hellenistic Greek grammarians themselves.

There seem to be at least three reasons for this thought that every-thing has been done already. One is that there is widespread lack of knowledge regarding the history of discussion of Greek grammar. For example, those who think that one should pay closer attention to the Greek grammarians themselves, since they if any should know the linguistic character of their own language, are perhaps unaware that the Greek grammarians themselves were divided on the issues (as well as other issues, such as questions of authorship of the documents involved). Dionysius Thrax had a time-based model of Greek verbs, but ended up putting the aorist, imperfect, perfect and pluperfect all in the same cate-gory of past-tense verbs, as if there was no further distinction to be made. The Stoic grammarians took a view that the tenses were related not only by time but more importantly by kind of action. Hence they

---

58. See S.E. Porter, 'Greek Language and Linguistics', *ExpTim* 103 (1991–92), pp. 202-208, which provides the basis for the following remarks.

59. L. Rydbeck, 'What Happened to New Testament Grammar after Albert Debrunner?', *NTS* 21 (1974–75), p. 427.

recognized formal similarities between the present and imperfect, and the perfect and pluperfect, but also the aorist and the future.[60] A second reason for neglect is that there is a lack of knowledge of various models of language that have been employed in modern study of Greek. There have been at least four major schools of thought on verb structure in the last two centuries alone. The third reason for neglect is the failure to be aware of the recent use of Greek linguistics to inform discussion. There is often a time-lag between disciplines, such that current activities in one discipline cannot always be known to those in other disciplines. This has been unfortunate, because much recent work in theoretical linguistics can be useful for the study of the biblical languages, and has been applied in some areas. A brief survey of some of the recent thought may help to set this problem in its proper perspective.

The verb lies at the heart of serious analysis of the Greek language. And it is to the verb structure that many have turned in attempting to describe the language adequately. Part of this fascination with the study of the Greek verb comes from the fact that the verb can be used in so many different constructions, and that the information conveyed by its morphology is quite complex, including tense/aspect, voice, mood/attitude, and often person and number. Hence sometimes a verb takes on characteristics of an adjective or a noun, or even functions adverbially, besides serving more regular verbal functions in finite and infinitive constructions.

The three schools of thought regarding the verb each have various characteristics worth noting. The first dominated the discussion throughout much of the nineteenth century, and has been characterized as the rationalist school of thought. This analysis of verb structure, dominated by the German scholar G.B. Winer,[61] whose grammar went through eight editions and is still widely used as a reference tool, argues that virtually every use of a verb tense follows a logically derived function, often in conjunction with its specified name. Thus present tense verbs refer to present time and future verbs refer to future time. The aorist and the imperfect are past-time verbs. The system is entirely logical and well laid out so far as a rational scheme is concerned. But what of apparent anomalies to the system, such as the widespread use of the

---

60. See Porter, *Verbal Aspect*, pp. 18-22.

61. G.B. Winer, *A Treatise on the Grammar of New Testament Greek Regarded as a Sure Basis for New Testament Exegesis* (trans. W.F. Moulton; Edinburgh: T. & T. Clark, 3rd edn, 1882).

present tense in historical contexts, or gnomic uses of the tenses, or non-past time uses of the aorist tense? Although Winer acknowledges the use of the historic present in the Gospels, he is hard-pressed to explain what is happening in the language. Whereas many scholars today would disagree with such a rigidly imposed model, it is not clear that many of them have another model to put in its place, and plenty of exegesis of the text of the New Testament is decided according to the equation of tense and time mentioned above. Many apparently find that this is a comfortable model since it is apparently quite similar to English (whether English is as time-based as some suppose is another issue for discussion).

A second school of thought regarding Greek verb structure changes the emphasis from one of time to kind of action, that is, that verbs in Greek are based upon *Aktionsart* or a supposedly objective description of action. According to this system, a present-tense verb represents linear action, an aorist punctiliar action, and a perfect a combination of the two, the continuing result of a past action. This analysis of Greek verbs derives from comparative philological work of last century, especially as it became increasingly obvious that Greek had a common genetic relationship with other Indo-European languages. Most discussion of Greek grammar has halted at this stage, and the primary reason for this appears to be that several of the most influential grammarians of this century utilize this model. For example, Karl Brugmann in 1885 apparently introduced the language of *Aktionsart* into the grammatical discussion of Greek, and this was perpetuated not only in the four editions of his grammar but in its thorough revision in the 1930s and 1950s by Schwyzer. In New Testament study, the grammar of Friedrich Blass, first published in 1896, and translated into English several times, most recently in 1961 from the tenth German edition; the grammar of Moulton, who introduced the term *Aktionsart* into English in 1906; and the massive grammar of A.T. Robertson, all have continued this tradition.[62]

62. K. Brugmann, *Griechische Grammatik* (Munich: Beck, 1885); E. Schwyzer, *Griechische Grammatik auf der Grundlage von Karl Brugmanns Griechische Grammatik* (2 vols., second vol. edited by A. Debrunner; Munich: Beck, 1939, 1950); F. Blass, *Grammatik des Neutestamentlichen Griechisch* (Göttingen: Vandenhoeck & Ruprecht, 1896), translated from the 10th edn as F. Blass and A. Debrunner, *A Greek Grammar of the New Testament and Other Early Christian Literature* (trans. R.W. Funk; Chicago: University of Chicago Press, 1961); Moulton, *Prolegomena*; A.T. Robertson, *A Grammar of the Greek New Testament in the Light of Historical Research* (Nashville: Broadman, 4th edn, 1934).

In 1972, Frank Stagg published an important article that signalled a marked step forward in discussion of Greek verb structure. In the article he shows that categories of *Aktionsart* proved to be an inadequate analytical tool for discussing a number of examples in the Greek New Testament. For example, it is obvious that in some instances a present-tense verb is not used for linear action (e.g. Lk. 19.13) or an aorist is not used for punctiliar action (e.g. Jn 2.20 or 2 Cor. 11.24-25) or a perfect tense is not used of an action with abiding results (e.g. Jn 1.15).[63] Through these examples, Stagg was able to show that many interpreters had been misled in their analysis of the Greek text by relying upon an outmoded conceptual framework. This work paved the way for the third model of verb structure.

The third model is in some ways a logical result of the work of Stagg, and is gaining more and more insight. Relying upon much recent work in modern linguistics, many recent interpreters have turned to the category of verbal aspect to describe the function of the Greek verbs. Many have not yet appropriated what is happening in this area, since much of this work is relatively recent, the first monograph on the subject of verbal aspect written in English only appearing in 1976, and the first in English devoted to the Greek of the New Testament in 1989.[64] The semantic category of verbal aspect is used to describe the speaker or writer's subjective view of a process or event. Although there are variations upon this position, those who hold to it believe that temporal categories are not of primary importance in the use of the verb. Many who have discussed Greek verb structure have been fooled by the traditional names of tenses, which are often based upon typical functions of the tenses concerned and do not capture the full range of functions. While it is tempting to see the typical function that lies behind the tense name as the function, this can be quite misleading, even in such a language as English, where a simple sentence such as 'I am reading this paper' can be used of now or tomorrow.

---

63. F. Stagg, 'The Abused Aorist', *JBL* 91 (1972), pp. 222-31.

64. B. Comrie, *Aspect: An Introduction to the Study of Verbal Aspect and Related Problems* (Cambridge Textbooks in Linguistics; Cambridge: Cambridge University Press, 1976); Porter, *Verbal Aspect, passim*; soon followed by B.M. Fanning, *Verbal Aspect in New Testament Greek* (Oxford: Clarendon Press, 1990); and now K.L. McKay, *A New Syntax of the Verb in New Testament Greek* (Studies in Biblical Greek, 5; New York: Peter Lang, 1994). For further discussion, see S.E. Porter and D.A. Carson (eds.), *Biblical Greek Language and Linguistics: Open Questions in Current Research* (JSNTSup, 80; Sheffield: JSOT Press, 1993), pp. 18-82.

Rather than focusing upon temporal relations, proponents of verbal aspect have had to come up with various other means of describing the relations among the tenses. One that has proved very useful is the concept of planes of discourse, in which the focal planes attached to the tenses serve to set actions in visual perspective. Thus the aorist tense as the background tense serves as the backbone of narrative, or can be used to fill in background detail in a description. The present tense as the foreground tense serves to highlight and bring to the fore various actions in narrative, or can be used to create a description. The perfect tense as the frontground tense serves to highlight or bring actions to the immediate forefront of attention. Thus in a description such as Rom. 5.1-2, the aorist participle ('having been justified') provides the background for the foregrounded hortatory present-tense projection, 'let us have...' The frontgrounded perfect tense is used to describe the stance of believers ('we possess' access).

7. *Conclusion*

In conclusion, let me simply draw out two points that merit attention. The first is that problems of religious language oftentimes start with problems regarding the Bible and its language. I have tried to point out several areas where persistent misunderstanding has had interesting and quite often misleading results. These results affect not only biblical inter-pretation but other disciplines that rely upon some understanding of the Bible. Secondly, there are still many issues to resolve in the study of the Bible, especially in relation to its language. This may seem rather frus-trating, since so much effort has already gone into this area that we would like to think that we can move on. But language is fundamental to understanding. And with increased understanding, new models and approaches, all of these throw up new information for consideration.

THE HISTORICAL JESUS AND THE DEIFIED CHRIST:
HOW DID THE ONE LEAD TO THE OTHER?

Craig A. Evans

1. *Introduction*

In Christian theology no topic has encountered more difficulties and generated more controversy than Christology and attempts to find the appropriate language whereby it might be expressed.[1] Orthodoxy maintains that Jesus was fully human and fully God; the latter reality from eternity past, the former from biological conception. The creeds, of course, represent admixtures of history, exegesis, theological speculation, and affirmations of faith. But if we limit our inquiry to historical exegesis, asking what the historical Jesus in all probability said and did, the discussion takes on a very different complexion.

No one doubts the humanity of Jesus (though this was an item of debate in the early centuries of the Church). No one doubts his biological conception (though the question of the immaculate conception has generated a fair amount of discussion). But did Jesus think of himself as God? If not as God, did Jesus think of himself as in some sense divine? If he did not, why did his followers apply such language to him? It is with these questions that this paper is concerned. It is not intended to be a theological paper, but it does hope to contribute to Christology through the door of Jesus research. It is an attempt to throw some light on a historical and exegetical question. If I may be permitted to reduce all of the above questions to one only, it would be this: At what point in history did the deification of Jesus begin, in the time of Jesus or in the time of the early Church?

---

1. Perhaps the most famous illustration is found in the fourth-century controversy over Christ's nature. Advocates for the view that Christ's nature was the *same* (i.e. *homoousios*) as God's prevailed over those who advocated the view that it was only *similar* (i.e. *homoiousios*). Thus, as was commented upon long ago, the Church very nearly split over an iota, the smallest letter in the Greek alphabet.

For much of the twentieth century, scholars have argued that the deification or divinization of Jesus was foreign to early Jewish Christianity. It took place, we have been told, in the Greco-Roman world as part of an apologetic effort to make the Christian proclamation attractive and convincing to Hellenism. It was further assumed that this effort reflected Hellenistic Judaism's tendency to divinize its heroes and exaggerate miracle stories that may have been associated with them.[2] This assumption grew out of a 'divine man' hypothesis that the comparative religions school thought best explained the origin and development of New Testament Christology and many of its supporting miracle stories.[3]

Roman emperors and the Greek despots before them were hailed in the language of deification. Inscriptions and non-literary papyri, as well as literary sources, offer numerous illustrations. Inscriptions are particularly significant because of their public function. A few samples will suffice to give us a sense of the range of such acclamation in late antiquity.

A third-century BCE inscription from Halicarnassus is in honor of Πτολεμαίου τοῦ σωτῆρος καὶ θεοῦ ('Ptolemy, savior and god'). The famous Rosetta Stone bears the inscription of a later Ptolemy (196 BCE), who is described as Βασιλεὺς Πτολέμαιος αἰωνβίος...ὑπάρχων θεὸς ἐκ θεοῦ καὶ θεᾶς ('King Ptolemy, the everliving...being a god [born] of a god and a goddess'). A first-century BCE inscription from Ephesus describes Julius Caesar as τὸν ἀπὸ "Αρεως καὶ 'Αφρο-δε[ί]της θεὸν ἐπιφανῆ καὶ κοινὸν τοῦ ἀνθρωπίνου βίου σωτῆρα ('the manifest God from Mars and Aphrodite, and common Savior of human life').[4] An inscription found over a door of a Temple of Isis on the island of Philae refers to Ptolemy XIII (62 BCE): τοῦ κυρίου βασιλ[έ]ος θεοῦ ('of the lord king god'). Another inscription comes from Alexandria and refers to Ptolemy XIV and Cleopatra (52 BCE): τοῖς κυρίοις θεοῖς μεγίστοις ('to the lords, the greatest gods'). An inscription from Priene refers to the birthday of Augustus as

2.   As representative of this tendency, see R. Bultmann, *Theology of the New Testament* (2 vols.; New York: Charles Scribner's Sons, 1951–55), II, pp. 128-33.

3.   See R. Bultmann, *The History of the Synoptic Tradition* (Oxford: Basil Blackwell, 2nd edn, 1968), pp. 240-41 and supplemental note on p. 428.

4.   Compare Titus 2.13: ἐπιφάνειαν τῆς δόξης τοῦ μεγάλου θεοῦ καὶ σωτῆρος ἡμῶν 'Ιησοῦ Χριστοῦ ('the manifestation of the glory of our great God and Savior Jesus Christ').

[ἡ γενέθλιος] τοῦ θεοῦ ('the birthday of god'). The same inscription refers to Augustus as τοῦ θηοτάτου Καίσαρο[ς] ('of the most divine Caesar'). An inscription from Pergamum reads: [Αὐτοκράτ]ορ[α Κ]αίσαρα [θ]εοῦ υἱὸν θεὸν Σεβαστὸ[ν] [πάσης] γῆ[ς κ]αὶ θ[α]λάσσης [ἐ]π[όπ]τ[ην] ('The Emperor, Caesar, son of god, the god Augustus, the overseer of every land and sea'). A marble inscription from Magnesia reads in reference to Nero: Γερμανικὸν τὸν υἱὸν τοῦ μεγίστου θεῶν Τιβερίου Κλαυδίου Καίσαρος Σεβάστου Γερμανικος σου Αὐτοκράτοροῦ ('Germanicus the son of the greatest of the gods, Tiberius Claudius; Caesar Augustus Germanicus your Emperor').[5] Finally, another inscription from Halicarnassus refers to Augustus as: Δία δὲ πατρῷον καὶ σωτῆρα τοῦ κοινοῦ τῶν ἀνθρώπων γένους ('Hereditary God and Savior of the common race of humanity').[6]

There is no question that for the Christian presentation of Jesus as a savior of any consequence for the Greco-Roman world there would have been a need at least to equal these royal acclamations. But does this need explain the *origin* of the deification of Jesus? Was the Christian Messiah presented as a Hellenistic 'Divine Man' (θεῖος ἀνήρ) only later, whereas in its earliest formulations in Jewish Palestine the language of deification was absent?[7]

Scholarship in the last twenty years has seriously called the Divine Man hypothesis into question.[8] Not only is the supposed category of

5.   See A. Deissmann, *Light from the Ancient East* (New York: Harper & Row, 1922), pp. 344-54.

6.   See W. Foerster, 'Σωτήρ', *TDNT*, VII, p. 1012.

7.   Underlying some of the scholarly discussion of this problem is a questionable distinction between 'Jewish' Palestine and the 'Hellenistic' Diaspora. This distinction sometimes fails to appreciate the degree of Hellenization of Palestine itself, as well as Hellenism's indebtedness to ideas emanating from the old Persian Empire, of which post-exilic Israel was a part. Thus it is uncritical to assume that early Christian theology needed to emigrate from Palestine before it could encounter Hellenism. On this problem, see the concise treatment by M. Hengel, *The 'Hellenization' of Judaea in the First Century after Christ* (London: SCM Press; Philadelphia: Trinity Press International, 1989).

8.   See D.L. Tiede, *The Charismatic Figure as Miracle Worker* (SBLDS, 1; Missoula, MT: Scholars Press, 1972); C.H. Holladay, *Theios Aner in Hellenistic Judaism: A Critique of the Use of This Category in New Testament Christology* (SBLDS, 40; Missoula, MT: Scholars Press, 1977); E.V. Gallagher, *Divine Man or Magician? Celsus and Origen on Jesus* (SBLDS, 64; Chico, CA: Scholars Press,

Divine Man itself an artificial construct, Israel's ancient Scriptures and later messianic traditions themselves conceive of a divinized Messiah. There really was no need for early Christians, who as Jews would have been familiar with these traditions, to import such a concept from Hellenism. In Israel's Scriptures the anointed king is regarded as God's son: 'The kings of the earth set themselves...against the Lord and His Messiah...You are My son, today I have begotten you' (Ps. 2.2, 7); 'I will be his Father, and he shall be My son' (2 Sam. 7.14; cf. 1 Chron. 17.13; Ps. 89.26); 'The Lord says to my lord: "Sit at my right hand..." ' (Ps. 110.1);[9] 'Solomon sat on the throne of the Lord as king' (1 Chron. 29.23). The sonship of the king and the fatherhood of God were integral components of Jewish messianology long before the ministry of Jesus. These texts and others from the Old Testament contributed to messianizing speculations in the intertestamental period. To the writings of this period we now turn.

2. *Divine Attributes in Messianic Traditions in the Time of Jesus*

There are several messianic traditions from the intertestamental period that are potentially relevant for our study. Not all of these traditions necessarily contributed to Jesus' thinking or to the christologies of the New Testament. These traditions, however, help us appreciate the diversity of messianic speculation and the potential for deification of a messianic figure.

Daniel 7. The divine or supernatural potential of a messianic figure is seen in a passage such as Daniel 7, which describes the appearance of a 'son of man' who 'comes with the clouds' and receives authority and dominion.[10] A few of the most important lines are as follows:

1982); B. Blackburn, *Theios Aner and the Markan Miracle Traditions* (WUNT, 2.40; Tübingen: Mohr [Siebeck], 1991).

   9.   On the importance of this text for understanding ancient ideas of the king as God's associate, even co-regent, see M. Hengel, ' "Setze dich zu meiner Rechten!" Die Inthronisation Christi zur Rechten Gottes und Psalm 110,1', in M. Philonenko (ed.), *Le Trône de Dieu* (WUNT, 69; Tübingen: Mohr [Siebeck], 1993), pp. 108-94, esp. pp. 153-61.

   10.   Daniel is found in the Old Testament, of course. But the book as we have it originated in the second century BCE, in response to the Maccabean struggle with Antiochus IV. It is therefore treated along with other writings of the intertestamental period.

> 9. As I looked, thrones were placed and one that was ancient of days took his seat; his raiment was white as snow, and the hair of his head like pure wool; his throne was fiery flames, its wheels were burning fire.

> 13. I saw in the night visions, and behold, with the clouds of heaven there came one like a son of man [כבר אנש], and he came to the Ancient of Days and was presented before him.

> 14. And to him was given dominion [שלטן] and glory [יקר] and kingdom [מלכו], that all peoples, nations, and languages should serve him; his dominion is an everlasting dominion, which shall not pass away, and his kingdom one that shall not be destroyed.

In my judgment, this is one of the most important passages for understanding the Christology of Jesus. The one 'like a son of man' in this vision should be understood as either a human being or a heavenly being (an angel?) who is human-like.[11] The expression, 'son of man', is not in itself a technical title, but a Semitic way of referring to the human class. In some instances it may function more or less as an equivalent for the first person pronoun (cf. Mt. 10.32 ['I'] = Lk. 12.8 ['the son of man']), but the most common function is generic. The one 'like a son of man' stands in contrast to the terrible beasts described in the first eight verses of Daniel 7.

This human-like being, unlike the boastful beasts, is brought before the Ancient of Days (God) and receives dominion, glory, and kingdom. Not only does this being stand before God's throne, he enters God's presence 'with the clouds of heaven'. Such a remarkable description offered subsequent interpreters a scene rich with exploitable interpretative potential.

Indeed, in the opinion of some, the scene was too rich with potential. Debating the question as to what the plural 'thrones' in v. 9 referred, Rabbi Aqiba (died c. 135 CE) suggested that one was for God and the other was for 'David', by which he probably meant the Messiah. We are told that Rabbi Yose rebuked the famous authority: 'Aqiba, how long will you profane the Shekinah?' (*b. Sanh.* 38b). The suggestion that a human being could sit on a throne next to God Himself was shocking. But Yose does not explain who the one 'like a son of man' is in vv. 13-14. Aqiba's interpretation has the advantage of identifying the

---

11. The latter interpretation has been advanced by J.J. Collins, *The Apocalyptic Vision of the Book of Daniel* (HSM, 16; Missoula, MT: Scholars Press, 1977), pp. 141-46. Collins points to *1 En.* 46.2, which describes the face of the son of man as angelic.

mysterious being (which evidently he understood to be a descendant of David) and of offering at the same time an explanation of the plural reference to the thrones in v. 9. Yose's negative reaction is grounded in the belief that a mere mortal cannot stand, and certainly cannot sit, in the presence of God. But what if the one 'like a son of man' is not a mere mortal? The one 'like a son of man' of Daniel 7 invited ancient interpreters to assign to him attributes that transcend those of ordinary human beings.

We find an impressive example of this in *1 Enoch* 37–71 (or the *Similitudes of Enoch*),[12] where we are told that the 'son of man' had the countenance of 'holy angels' (46.2), that he was given the name 'Before-Time' and was so named in God's presence (48.2), and that he was concealed in God's presence prior to the creation of the world (48.6; 62.7). He is also called the 'Chosen One' (48.6), 'Elect One' (49.2; 51.4; 52.6; 53.6; 55.4; 61.8; 62.1) and 'Messiah' (48.10; 52.4). We are told that the day is coming when 'all the kings, the governors, the high officials, and those who rule the earth shall fall down before him on their faces, and worship and raise their hopes in that Son of Man; they shall beg and plead for mercy at his feet' (62.9).[13]

Some of these ideas, such as being named and concealed in God's presence prior to creation, suggest that the one 'like a son of man' is no mere mortal. Indeed, when we are told that those of the highest of humanity fall down and worship before the throne of the 'son of man', we have what seems to be encroachment on prerogatives reserved for God Himself. Aqiba might have endorsed such an interpretation, but Yose would have had none of it.

The mysterious figure of Daniel 7 also influenced *4 Ezra* 13. The allusions are plain enough.[14] In v. 3 Ezra tells us that he looked and beheld a man flying 'with the clouds of heaven'. This man carves out for himself a large mountain made 'without hands' (vv. 6, 36), which is

12. The indebtedness of the *Similitudes* to Daniel 7 is clearly seen in *1 En.* 46. The *Similitudes* probably date to the second half of the first century CE. For discussion, see J.C. VanderKam, *Enoch and the Growth of an Apocalyptic Tradition* (CBQMS, 16; Washington: Catholic Biblical Association, 1984).

13. Translation by E. Isaac, '1 (Ethiopic Apocalypse of) Enoch', in J.H. Charlesworth (ed.), *The Old Testament Pseudepigrapha* (2 vols.; Garden City, NY: Doubleday, 1983, 1985), I, p. 43.

14. A. Lacocque, 'The Vision of the Eagle in 4 Esdras, a Rereading of Daniel 7 in the First Century C.E.', in K.H. Richards (ed.), *Society of Biblical Literature 1981 Seminar Papers* (SBLSP, 20; Chico, CA: Scholars Press, 1981), pp. 237-58.

an unmistakable allusion to the messianic mountain of Dan. 2.35, 44-45. The seer also tells us that this 'man' is 'he whom the Most High has been keeping for many ages' (v. 26). He is none other than God's 'son' (vv. 32, 52), whom no one can see, 'except in the time of his day' (v. 52).

In a recent assessment of scholarship concerned with Daniel's 'son of man' John Collins draws our attention to several important points of agreement in the interpretation that the *Similitudes* and *4 Ezra* 13 give to Daniel 7.[15] Among these there are three that are especially pertinent: (1) Both the *Similitudes* and *4 Ezra* 13 understand the one 'like a son of man' of Daniel 7 as an individual. This observation argues against modern interpretations which view this figure as a symbol for the nation of Israel. (2) Both the *Similitudes* and *4 Ezra* 13 understand the one 'like a son of man' in a messianic sense.[16] (3) Both the *Similitudes* and *4 Ezra* 13 understand the one 'like a son of man' as a heavenly, even pre-existent, being.[17]

This combination of the messianic and heavenly is especially pertinent to the concerns of this paper. Before moving on to other texts, it is worth noting that the idea of a being possessing divine prerogatives, subordinate of course to God, is also attested in the Jewish tradition. The roots of such a concept are found in the Old Testament itself. In Exod. 7.1 we have a remarkable passage: 'And the Lord said to Moses: "See, I make you God to Pharaoh [MT: נתתיך אלהים לפרעה; LXX: δέδωκά σε θεὸν Φαραώ]; and Aaron your brother shall be your prophet"'. In his interpretation of this passage Philo is careful to explain that Moses did not really become God (*Det. Pot. Ins.* 44 §§161-62). But elsewhere the famous Alexandrian Jew suggests that the *logos* is 'the second God [τὸν δεύτερον θεόν]' (*Quaest. in Gen.* 2.62 [on Gen. 9.6]; cf. *Somn.* 1.39 §230; *Fug.* 18 §97). Perhaps the strangest passage of all is found in *3 Enoch*, a pseudepigraphon attributed to Rabbi Ishmael. Although the work as we have it dates from the fifth century, it contains many early traditions, some of which may derive from Palestine. Ishmael discovers that the archangel Metatron is none other than Enoch who because of his righteousness was elevated to the 'heavenly height', was given the

---

15. J.J. Collins, 'The Son of Man in First-Century Judaism', *NTS* 38 (1992), pp. 448-66.

16. For further support of this point, see W. Horbury, 'The Messianic Associations of the "Son of Man"', *JTS* 36 (1985), pp. 34-55.

17. For his several conclusions, see Collins, 'The Son of Man', pp. 464-66.

'name of the Creator', and was installed as 'a prince and a ruler' over the angels of heaven (*3 En.* 4).

Thus, we find from Exodus 7 to *3 Enoch* 4 a range of Jewish Palestinian interpretative tradition, out of which Christian messianology, complete with tendencies of deification, could spring. There is no need to look for non-Jewish myths to explain it. The variety of this interpretative tradition can be illustrated with many more examples that predate Christianity.

Psalms of Solomon. The *Psalms of Solomon* 17–18 speaks of the coming of the Messiah, in fulfillment of the promise to David (17.4, 21), who will rule over Israel and 'judge the tribes' and 'distribute them upon the land' (17.26, 28). We are also told that the Messiah's 'words will be as the words of the holy ones' (17.43). 'Holy ones' here probably refers to angels. What is of especial interest is that twice the Messiah is referred to as the 'Lord Messiah': 'their king shall be the Lord Messiah [κύριος χριστός]'; 'under the rod of discipline of the Lord Messiah [κυρίου χριστοῦ]' (17.32; 18.7). The second passage could be translated 'under the rod of discipline of the Lord's Messiah'. But in light of the first passage, it probably should also be understood as 'Lord Messiah'.[18] This way of referring to the Messiah does not necessarily convey the sense of divinity. I doubt very much if the Greek author intended to imply that the Messiah was God or was Yahweh. The usage may have reflected the conventions of the Greco-Roman world, in which we often find reference to 'Lord Caesar'. But the usage nevertheless could have contributed to the possibility of seeing divine qualities invested in the Messiah figure.

4QFlorilegium. Several writings from Qumran contribute to possibilities of conceiving of the Messiah as quasi-divine. 4QFlor 1.10-14 interprets 2 Sam. 7.11-14, which speaks of the Davidic heir as God's 'son', in a messianic sense: 'this is the Branch of David who is to take his stand at the end of days'. This text does not suggest that the Messiah is divine, but it is important because it gives an explicitly messianic, pre-Christian interpretation to an important Old Testament 'son' passage.

18. On the originality of the reading, 'Lord Messiah', in the Greek and Syriac versions, see R.B. Wright, 'Psalms of Solomon', in Charlesworth (ed.), *Old Testament Pseudepigrapha*, II, pp. 667, 669.

1QSerek, Appendix a. In what is probably an echo of Ps. 2.2-7, 1QSa 2.11-12 speaks of the last day, 'when God will have begotten the Messiah among them'. Although 'begotten' seems to be the best reading, some scholars have argued for other readings. But their arguments are not persuasive.[19] Given the language of Ps. 2.2-7, in which God says to His Messiah, 'Today I have begotten you', the traditional reading of 1QSa is not problematic. This text is important because it shows that Psalm 2 was interpreted in a messianic, eschatological sense in the time of Jesus, and in circles not limited to Christianity. We now have two Old Testament 'son' passages that are interpreted in a messianic sense in writings that antedate those of the New Testament.

4Q521. Recently published materials from Qumran's fourth cave have some relevant examples to offer. According to 4Q521 1 ii 1, 'heaven and earth will obey His Messiah'. John Collins has recently argued convincingly that 4Q521 is describing the works of the Messiah.[20] What could link this text to Davidic tradition is the statement in 4Q522, in which a Davidic heir is told that 'Heaven will dwell with him forever'. In any event, the declaration that heaven and earth will obey the Messiah is a remarkable statement and could suggest that the Messiah will possess powers far beyond those of a mere mortal.

4Q246. 4Q246 2.1 predicts the coming of one who will be called 'son of God (ברה די אל)' and 'son of the Most High (בר עליון)'. Although Joseph Fitzmyer has his doubts,[21] the text is probably messianic.[22] The text is in all likelihood a logical extension of Old Testament passages such as 2 Sam. 7.11-16 and Ps. 2.7, in which God speaks of himself as 'Father' of David and his royal heirs. The text may also bear some relationship to Daniel.[23] The importance of 4Q246 is seen in that we have messianology

19. For discussion, see C.A. Evans, *Jesus and His Contemporaries: Comparative Studies* (AGJU, 25; Leiden: Brill, 1995), pp. 94-98.

20. J.J. Collins, 'The Works of the Messiah', *Dead Sea Discoveries* 1 (1994), pp. 98-112.

21. J.A. Fitzmyer, '4Q246: The "Son of God" Document from Qumran', *Bib* 74 (1993), pp. 153-74 (+ pl.).

22. For discussion, see J.J. Collins, 'The *Son of God* Text from Qumran', in M.C. De Boer (ed.), *From Jesus to John: Essays on Jesus and New Testament Christology in Honour of Marinus de Jonge* (JSNTSup, 84; Sheffield: JSOT Press, 1993), pp. 65-82; Evans, *Jesus and His Contemporaries*, pp. 107-11.

23. S. Kim (*'The "Son of Man"' as the Son of God* [WUNT, 30; Tübingen:

that speaks of 'son of God' and that derives from Jewish, Palestinian sources, not from Greco-Roman.[24]

4Q369. In what is probably another prophecy, 4Q369 1 ii 5-7 describes a 'first-born son', a 'prince and ruler' whom God will instruct 'in eternal light'. The ending of the first column suggests that what follows in the second column is a prophecy of some sort. If so, the prophecy either concerns the historical David, who in Ps. 89.20, 26-27 is called God's 'first-born', or refers to a Davidic heir, perhaps *the* Davidic heir, the Messiah. I incline to the latter option because of the reference to being instructed 'in eternal light' and because of the eschatological orientation of the first column of fragment 1.[25]

4Q536. 4Q536 3 i 10-11 may also be relevant. The fragmentary text reads: 'But all of his plans will succeed, because he is the Elect One of God. His birth and the spirit of his breath [are of God].' The last words, 'are of God', are no more than a conjecture, but Fitzmyer and others suspect that this or something like it is probably how the text should be restored.[26] The words are reminiscent of Isa. 11.1-2 ('There shall come forth a shoot from the stump of Jesse... And the Spirit of the Lord shall rest upon him'), another well known messianic text. Note that reference to birth and spirit cohere with Luke's infancy narrative: 'The Holy Spirit will come upon you...therefore the child to be born will be called holy' (Lk. 1.35). The epithet, 'Elect One of God', is reminiscent of the messianic traditions already observed in *1 Enoch*.

In sum, we find that the Old Testament itself speaks of God as a 'Father' to His 'son' the Messiah (2 Sam. 7.14; cf. 1 Chron. 17.13; Ps. 2.27; 89.26) and describes a mysterious human-like figure who

Mohr (Siebeck), 1983], pp. 20-24) has suggested that because 4Q246 may be part of an interpretative elaboration of Daniel, we may have evidence here of an identification of the Danielic 'son of man' as the 'son of God' and 'son of the Most High' prophesied in the Qumran fragment.

24. The presence of 'son of God' in 4Q246 provides evidence against F. Hahn (*The Titles of Jesus in Christology* [New York: World, 1969], pp. 291-93) who at one time maintained that such language could only have derived from non-Palestinian sources.

25. For discussion, see Evans, *Jesus and His Contemporaries*, pp. 136-37; *idem*, 'A Note on the "First-Born Son" of 4Q369', *Dead Sea Discoveries* 2 (1995), pp. 185-201.

26. For discussion, see Evans, *Jesus and His Contemporaries*, pp. 111-13.

enters heaven and approaches the very throne of God and receives authority (Dan. 7.9-14). Elaborating on this tradition, the *Similitudes of Enoch* describes the rulers of the earth worshipping at the feet of the 'son of man', who is also called 'Messiah' and 'Elect One'. Second-century rabbinic interpretation entertained the notion that David (or the Davidic Messiah) would sit on a throne next to God. The *Psalms of Solomon* refer to the Messiah as the 'Lord Messiah'. Qumranic interpretation views 2 Sam. 7.11-14 and Ps. 2.7 as messianic, as seen in 4QFlor and 1QSa. The most recently published scrolls further add to this picture. 4Q521 speaks of heaven and earth obeying God's Messiah, who in 4Q246 is called 'Son of God' and 'Son of the Most High'. 4Q369 in all probability is referring to the Messiah, when the text speaks of a 'first-born son' whom God will instruct 'in eternal light'. 4Q536 probably also refers to the Messiah, whose birth is in some sense from God. This sampling of pre-Christian texts and traditions suggests that deification of a messianic figure would not be especially innovative in a Palestinian setting. To recognize a messianic figure as God's 'son' and emissary from heaven would not require Greco-Roman influence.[27]

In recent years scholars engaged in Jesus research have been more willing to affirm that Jesus in all probability viewed himself as Israel's Messiah (however that should be defined[28]), or at least was willing to accept recognition as such from his followers.[29] But the question of the origin of his deification is often ignored.[30]

---

27. As Hengel (*The 'Hellenization' of Judaea*, p. 55) puts it: 'Even a christology of pre-existence and of the Son of God is intrinsically not "Hellenistic" nor even "un-Jewish" nor "un-Palestinian"'. See also the succinct summary in M. Hengel, *The Son of God: The Origin of Christology and the History of Jewish-Hellenistic Religion* (London: SCM Press; Philadelphia: Fortress Press, 1976), pp. 41-56.

28. On the diversity of messianic views in the time of Jesus, see J. Neusner *et al.* (eds.), *Judaisms and their Messiahs* (Cambridge: Cambridge University Press, 1987); J.H. Charlesworth (ed.), *The Messiah: Developments in Earliest Judaism and Christianity* (The First Princeton Symposium on Judaism and Christian Origins; Minneapolis: Fortress Press, 1992).

29. See the convenient summary of scholarship on this question in B. Witherington, *The Christology of Jesus* (Minneapolis: Fortress Press, 1990).

30. For one of the better exceptions, see P. Benoit, 'The Divinity of Jesus in the Synoptic Gospels', in Benoit, *Jesus and the Gospel* (2 vols.; New York: Herder and Herder, 1973), I, pp. 47-70. Also noteworthy is the study by P.B. Payne, 'Jesus' Implicit Claim to Deity in His Parables', *TrinJ* 2 (1981), pp. 3-23.

3. *Divine Prerogatives in the Words and Activities of Jesus*

Scholars often point to the various ways in which Jesus expressed his authority. For some Jesus' authority points to messianic self-understanding,[31] for others it indicates a divine self-understanding.[32] In my view, Jesus' assumption of authority provides very little evidence of divine self-understanding,[33] at least little evidence that is not ambiguous. In Jesus' day there were many figures, some prophetic, some militaristic, some charismatic, who in various ways claimed authority, even divine authority.[34] Claims of authority point to a sense of mission, but in what they are based is not always clear.

The ambiguity of the meaning of claims to authority can be seen in the exchange with the religious authorities (Mk 11.27-33). The religious authorities ask Jesus: 'By what authority are you doing these things, or who gave you this authority to do them?' (v. 28). Jesus' counter-question, 'Was the baptism of John from heaven or from men?' (v. 30), implied that Jesus' own authority was 'from heaven'. But the claim to have authority from heaven is not to claim that one is divine. Obviously Jesus believed that John's baptism was from heaven, but that does not mean that he thought that John possessed divine qualities. Jesus' strong sense of authority tells us only that like many of Israel's prophets Jesus sensed that his authority to speak and act ultimately derived from God. Of course, a sense of authority would be consistent with a belief of

31. As seen in the work of some of Bultmann's pupils; cf. E. Fuchs, 'Jesu Selbstzeugnis nach Mt 5', *ZTK* 49 (1952), pp. 14-34; repr. in Fuchs, *Zur Frage nach dem historischen Jesus* (Gesammelte Aufsätze, 2; Tübingen: Mohr [Siebeck], 1960), pp. 100-25; E. Käsemann, 'Das Problem des historischen Jesus', *ZTK* 51 (1954), pp. 125-53; repr. in Käsemann, *Exegetische Versuche und Besinnungen* (2 vols.; Göttingen: Vandenhoeck & Ruprecht, 1960–64), I, pp. 187-214; ET: 'The Problem of the Historical Jesus', in Käsemann, *Essays on New Testament Themes* (SBT, 41; London: SCM Press, 1964), pp. 15-47. Both works focus on the 'antitheses' of Matthew 5.

32. As is argued by Benoit, 'The Divinity of Jesus', pp. 69-70.

33. See the somewhat dated but still helpful study on authority in D. Daube, *The New Testament and Rabbinic Judaism* (Jordan Lectures in Comparative Religion, 2; London: Athlone Press, 1956), pp. 206-23.

34. See Evans, *Jesus and His Contemporaries*, pp. 53-81. Josephus is not sparing in his criticism of these would-be deliverers calling them imposters, false prophets, and tyrants. He also speaks disparagingly of their demand for absolute obedience and their followers' willingness to give it; cf. *War* 4.9.4 §510; 5.7.3 §309.

divinity, but authority by itself does not necessarily indicate the presence of a sense of divinity.

It has been suggested that the accusation that Jesus threatened to destroy the Temple and in three days raise up a new one, not made by human hands (Mk 14.58), a threat that in some form probably was uttered by Jesus, may have hinted at divine authorization or representation.[35] But here again we probably have no more than authority to speak and act in the same way the prophets of old possessed authority to speak and act. Jesus' threat (or prophecy) that the Herodian Temple would be destroyed and replaced by a new structure is consistent with a sense of divinity but is not in itself decisive evidence of such a sense.

There are more convincing examples of expressions of authority that indicate that Jesus may have thought of himself as divine or as a divine representative in a way that transcends the self-understanding of a prophet.

Jesus' pronouncements of the forgiveness of sin were regarded by some as blasphemy (cf. Mk 2.1-12; Lk. 7.36-50). Jesus' statements probably should not be understood as examples of the Divine passive: 'Your sins are forgiven (by God)'. If this is what he meant, why would his antagonists cry out, 'Blasphemy!' (Mk 2.7; Lk. 7.49)? The response, 'Who can forgive sins but God alone?' (Mk 2.7), tells against the interpretation that Jesus' words merely approximated those of the priest in his cultic function of offering up sacrifice for atonement. If this was all that Jesus' words meant, then we should have expected a reply like 'Who can forgive sins but the priests?'.[36] Thus, Jesus' absolutions could very well be evidence of a sense of divine function, if not identity.

Several sayings in which Jesus claims to be 'stronger' or 'greater' than various significant figures or institutions probably also contributed to early Christianity's deification of Jesus. When accused of casting out

35. See E.E. Ellis, 'Deity-Christology in Mark 14:58', in J.B. Green and M. Turner (eds.), *Jesus of Nazareth: Lord and Christ. Essays on the Historical Jesus and New Testament Christology* (Festschrift I.H. Marshall; Carlisle: Paternoster Press; Grand Rapids: Eerdmans, 1994), pp. 192-203.

36. This point is very much debated among interpreters. For summaries of the discussion, see R.A. Guelich, *Mark 1–8:26* (WBC, 34A; Dallas: Word, 1989), pp. 85-87; R.H. Gundry, *Mark: A Commentary on His Apology for the Cross* (Grand Rapids: Eerdmans, 1993), pp. 112-13, 117-18. Gundry's conclusion is consistent with the one that I have taken. He states: 'Blasphemy is too strong a charge for Jesus' merely taking a prophetic prerogative of reporting God's forgiveness' (pp. 117-18).

demons by the authority of Satan, Jesus replies: 'When a strong man [Satan], fully armed, guards his own palace, his goods are secure; but when one stronger [Jesus] than he assails him and overcomes him, he takes away his armor in which he trusted, and divides his spoil' (Lk. 11.21-22 = Mt. 12.29; cf. Mk 3.27).[37] The saying implies that Jesus thought of himself as stronger than Satan. On other occasions Jesus is said to have claimed that he was 'something greater than the Temple' (Mt. 12.6)[38] and that his preaching and wisdom were greater than those of Jonah and Solomon (Mt. 12.38-42 = Lk. 11.29-32).[39] Jesus' much-debated interpretation of Ps. 110.1 (Mk 12.35-37) may also have been meant to imply that as Messiah he was greater than a mere 'son of David'. Jesus asks how the Messiah can be called 'son of David' in view of the fact that David addressed him as 'Lord'.[40] The implication of Jesus' question may have been that the 'Lord Messiah' should be called 'son of God', instead of 'son of David'. Finally, in his saying, 'the son of man is lord of the Sabbath' (Mk 2.27-28), Jesus may have even claimed that his authority transcended that of the sabbath itself.[41] Given the deep respect with which the sabbath was held by Torah-observant Jews such a statement is truly remarkable, even when we recall that the 'son of man' in Dan. 7.14 was given 'authority' and 'dominion'.

The son of man imagery of Daniel 7 also in all probability lies behind another unusual statement: 'Every one who will acknowledge me before humans I will acknowledge before my Father in heaven; but whoever should deny me before humans, him I shall deny before my Father in

---

37. We have in this saying an instance of multiple attestation, in that the saying is found in Mark and in Q. Some think that Luke has preserved the oldest version of the saying; cf. J.A. Fitzmyer, *The Gospel according to Luke* (2 vols.; AB, 28, 28a; Garden City, NY: Doubleday, 1981–85), II, pp. 918-19, 922-23; J.S. Kloppenborg, *Q Parallels* (Sonoma: Polebridge Press, 1988), p. 92. Kloppenborg thinks that Matthew has edited his Q source according to what he finds in Mark.

38. Mt. 12.5-7 is unique to Matthew and betrays several Mattheanisms. For this reason R.H. Gundry (*Matthew: A Commentary on His Literary and Theological Art* [Grand Rapids: Eerdmans, 1982], pp. 223-24) sees it as an elaboration on the argument found in vv. 1-4. He may be correct, but we could have a fragment of a genuine halakic dispute between Jesus and the religious authorities of his day.

39. In support of the authenticity of this material, see N. Perrin, *Rediscovering the Teaching of Jesus* (New York: Harper & Row, 1976), pp. 194-95.

40. See the exposition in Gundry, *Mark*, pp. 718-19. On the authenticity of the passage, see Gundry, *Mark*, p. 722; Fitzmyer, *Luke*, II, p. 1310.

41. On the authenticity of the passage, see Gundry, *Mark*, pp. 144-45, 148-49.

heaven' (Mt. 10.32-33 = Lk. 12.8-9; cf. Mk 8.38).[42] As the 'son of man' of Daniel 7 Jesus envisions the time of judgment, when the court sits (cf. Dan. 7.9-10, 26). As the representative of the 'saints', Jesus will identify those who are worthy of inheriting the kingdom which has been promised to them (cf. Dan. 7.18, 22, 27).

A Danielic theme may lie behind Lk. 10.21-22 (= Mt. 11.25-27), where Jesus thanks (ἐξομολογεῖσθαι) God that he has revealed (ἀποκαλύπτειν) divine truths to 'babes' (νήπιοι), rather than to the wise (σοφοί) and learned (συνετοί). Indeed, from them he has hidden (ἀποκρύπτειν) them.[43] Werner Grimm has argued that Jesus polemicized against the Danielic view that wisdom was exclusively for the learned and the professional (cf. Dan. 1.17-20; 2.20-23).[44] Compare the prayer of Daniel: God 'gives wisdom to the wise [σοφοί] and prudence to those who have understanding [σύνεσις]...he reveals [ἀποκαλύπτειν] deep and hidden [ἀπόκρυφα] matters...I thank [ἐξομολογεῖσθαι] You, God of our fathers...' (Dan. 2.21-22). Jesus' saying reverses the role of the wise man and, as such, is reminiscent of Wis. 10.21, where we hear that 'Wisdom opened the mouth of the dumb, and made the tongues of babes [νήπιοι] eloquent'.[45]

The very style of Jesus' teaching and ministry may have prompted his earliest followers to view him as Wisdom incarnate.[46] Frustrated with his

42. This tradition has multiple attestatiion, being found in Q and in Mark. On its authenticity, see D.C. Allison and W.D. Davies, *The Gospel according to Saint Matthew* (2 vols.; ICC; Edinburgh: T. & T. Clark, 1988–91), II, pp. 214-15. Fitzmyer (*Luke*, II, p. 958) regards the tradition as authentic, but dismisses the reference to 'son of man' as a Lukan addition.

43. Bultmann (*History of the Synoptic Tradition*, p. 160), among others, accepts the authenticity of Mt. 11.25-26. More recently, Fitzmyer (*Luke*, II, p. 870) has opined: 'I am inclined to regard the substance of these sayings as authentic'.

44. W. Grimm, *Jesus und das Danielbuch* (ANTJ, 6.2; Frankfurt am Main: Peter Lang, 1984), pp. 48-49, 97-100.

45. The reversal of another Danielic theme is seen in the much-debated Mk 10.45: 'The son of man has not come to be served but to serve and to give his life as a ransom for many'. Compare this to Dan. 7.14: '...and all nations, tribes, and languages shall serve him'. In the Greek, different verbs are used, but in the original Aramaic form of his utterance Jesus may have used פלח ('to serve', 'to worship'), the word found in Aramaic Dan. 7.14. Recall *1 En.* 62.9: 'all the kings...shall fall down before him on their faces, and worship and raise their hopes in that Son of Man; they shall beg and plead for mercy at his feet'.

46. See B. Witherington, *Jesus the Sage: The Pilgrimage of Wisdom* (Edinburgh: T. & T. Clark, 1994), pp. 147-208.

people, who criticized John the Baptist for being an ascetic and criticized him for freely eating and drinking with people (Mt. 11.7-19 = Lk. 7.24-35), Jesus asserted that 'Wisdom is justified by her children' (Mt. 11.19 = Lk. 7.35, following Luke). Matthew reads 'deeds',[47] thus implying that the works of Jesus are the works of wisdom. Luke's reading ('children') implies that Jesus and John are the children of wisdom.[48] This version, which is probably the original, is reminiscent of Sir. 4.1: 'Wisdom exalts her sons and assists those who seek her'. Several have pointed out that in the Q material Jesus appears as God's Wisdom.[49]

Perhaps the most intriguing saying in the dominical tradition is the one in which Jesus speaks as Wisdom personified: 'Come [δεῦτε] to me [πρός με] all who labor [κοπιᾶν] and are heavy laden, and I will give you rest [ἀναπαύειν]. Take my yoke [ζυγός] upon you and learn from me, for I am meek and lowly in heart, and you will find rest [ἀνάπαυσις] for your souls [ψυχή]. For my yoke [ζυγός] is easy and my burden is light' (Mt. 11.28-30).[50] We are reminded of Wisdom's summons: 'Come to me [πρός με]' (Sir. 24.19; cf. Prov. 9.5); 'Come [δεῦτε], therefore, let us enjoy the good things...' (Wis. 2.6); 'Come [δεῦτε], O children, listen to me, I will teach you the fear of the Lord' (LXX Ps. 33.12 [34.11]). Especially interesting is Sir. 51.23-27: 'Draw near to me [πρός με], you who are untaught... Put your neck under the

---

47. Commentators think Matthew's reading follows Q.

48. Fitzmyer, *Luke*, I, p. 679.

49. See J.S. Kloppenborg, *The Formation of Q: Trajectories in Ancient Wisdom Collections* (Studies in Antiquity & Christianity; Philadelphia: Fortress Press, 1987), pp. 171-263; R.A. Piper, *Wisdom in the Q Tradition: The Aphoristic Teaching of Jesus* (SNTSMS, 61; Cambridge: Cambridge University Press, 1989).

50. A few scholars have regarded Mt. 11.28-30 as authentic dominical tradition, cf. E. Klostermann, *Das Matthäusevangelium* (HNT, 4; Tübingen: Mohr [Siebeck], 4th edn, 1971), p. 102; A.M. Hunter, 'Crux Criticorum—Matt. 11.25-30', *NTS* 8 (1962), pp. 241-49; S. Bacchiocchi, 'Matthew 11.28-30: Jesus' Rest and the Sabbath', *AUSS* 22 (1984), pp. 289-316; J.P. Meier, *A Marginal Jew: Rethinking the Historical Jesus* (2 vols.; ABRL; New York: Doubleday, 1992-94), II, pp. 335, 387 n. 174. Others have contested this view, cf. Gundry, *Matthew*, p. 219; C. Deutsch, *Hidden Wisdom and the Easy Yoke: Wisdom, Torah and Discipleship in Matthew 11.25-30* (JSNTSup, 18; Sheffield: JSOT Press, 1987), p. 51; Allison and Davies, *The Gospel according to Matthew*, II, p. 293. If the substance of Mt. 11.28-30 does indeed go back to Jesus, there can be little question that the tradition has been heavily edited (cf. Allison and Davies, *Matthew*, II, pp. 287-91). But if inauthentic, Mt. 11.28-30 does reflect aspects of Jesus' manner of speaking and acting as Wisdom's envoy.

yoke [ζυγός], and let your soul [ψυχή] receive instruction; it is to be found close by. See with your eyes that I have labored [κοπιᾶν] little and found for myself much rest [ἀνάπαυσις].'[51] These sayings hint that Jesus may have understood himself as God's Wisdom (or as Wisdom's messenger). This suspicion is confirmed when he claims to be 'greater than Solomon' (Lk. 11.31 = Mt. 12.42), Israel's famous patron of Wisdom.[52] In light of these passages and others Martin Hengel has concluded that Jesus understood himself as the messianic teacher of wisdom, indeed as Wisdom's envoy.[53]

The significance of this wisdom element in Jesus' lifestyle and self-reference lies in the observation that Wisdom personified was viewed as a way of speaking of God. Spirit, Wisdom, and Word were three important abstractions that often in late antiquity functioned as hypostases, carrying on the divine function on earth. Among other things, this way of speaking and conceptualizing enabled the pious to affirm the transcendance of God, on the one hand, and the emenance of God, on the other. In Jewish thinking of the first century, Jesus' speaking and acting as though he were God's Wisdom would have made a significant contribution to early Christology, out of which ideas of deification would have readily and naturally sprung. The Christology of the fourth Gospel is indebted to Wisdom traditions.[54] To a certain extent Pauline Christology is indebted to Wisdom traditions. This is seen in the apostle's assertion that 'Christ (is) the power of God and the wisdom of God' (1 Cor. 1.24; cf. 1.30: 'Christ Jesus, whom God made our wisdom').

---

51. See J.D.G. Dunn, *Christology in the Making: A New Testament Inquiry into the Origins of the Doctrine of the Incarnation* (London: SCM Press, 1980), pp. 163-64.

52. Bultmann (*History of the Synoptic Tradition*, pp. 112-13) accepts the saying as authentic. Meier (*A Marginal Jew*, II, pp. 689-90) makes the point that there is no evidence that the early Church showed a tendency to enhance or exploit a Solomon typology.

53. M. Hengel, 'Jesus als messianischer Lehrer der Weisheit und die Anfänge der Christologie', in *Sagesse et Religion: Colloque de Strasbourg, Octobre 1976* (Paris: Bibliothèque des Centres d'Études Supérieures Spécialisés, 1979), pp. 147-88, esp. pp. 163-66, 180-88. See also Witherington, *The Christology of Jesus*, pp. 51-53, 221-28, 274-75; B.L. Mack, 'The Christ and Jewish Wisdom', in Charlesworth (ed.), *The Messiah*, pp. 192-221, esp. pp. 210-15.

54. See M. Scott, *Sophia and the Johannine Jesus* (JSNTSup, 71; Sheffield: JSOT Press, 1992). Statements such as, 'He who has seen me has seen the Father' (Jn 14.9), are illustrative of wisdom Christology.

Perhaps the most important element in Gospel traditions is the various references to Jesus as the 'son', 'son of God', or 'son of the Most High'. Sometimes these references come from traditions whose claim to historicity is not strong. For example, at the baptism and the transfiguration a heavenly voice addresses Jesus as 'My beloved son' (Mk 1.11; 9.7 and parallels). Another problematic example is the confession of the Roman centurion, who proclaims, shortly after Jesus died: 'Truly this man was the son of God' (Mk 15.39). Interpreters suspect that Mark, or a Christian apologist before him, has placed these words on the lips of the Roman officer as part of the Gospel's Christology and apologetic. Matthew's enrichment of Mark's story of the stilling of the storm provides another example. The frightened disciples recover their senses enough to shout out in a manner that reminds us of the centurion: 'Truly you are the son of God' (Mt. 14.33). This revision, as well as the one involving Peter's confession at Caesarea Philippi (cf. Mk 8.29 = Mt. 16.16: 'son of the living God'), is guided by Matthew's wish to enhance Christology and at the same time to put the disciples, who so often fail in the Markan narrative, in a better light.

But other traditions cannot be easily dismissed. The cries of the demonized (Mk 3.11 = Lk. 4.41: 'You are the son of God!'; Mk 5.7: 'Jesus, son of the Most High God') are in all probability rooted in authentic tradition.[55] These epithets remind us of 4Q246, where we find reference to one who will be called 'son of God' and 'son of the Most High'. Two other references have a reasonable claim to authenticity, though some have challenged them. Jesus asserts that no one knows the eschatological hour, 'not even the son, only the Father' (Mk 13.32).[56] In one of the wisdom passages already mentioned Jesus affirms that 'no one knows the Father except the son' (Mt. 11.27).[57] These references to 'son', especially in contrast to the 'Father', should be understood as a shortened form of 'son of God'. To be called 'son of God', as opposed

55. It has to be admitted that these cries complement Markan Christology; cf. Guelich, *Mark*, pp. 148-49. On the possibility of the authenticity of the tradition, see Gundry, *Mark*, pp. 158-59.

56. On the authenticity of this passage, see Gundry, *Mark*, pp. 747-48, 792-95; *idem*, *Matthew*, p. 492; Meier, *A Marginal Jew*, II, p. 347. Gundry comments: 'That Mark does not exclude Jesus' ignorance of the exact time bears tribute to Mark's respect for the tradition' (*Mark*, pp. 747-48).

57. On the authenticity of this passage, see Gundry, *Matthew*, p. 218; A.E. Harvey, *Jesus and the Constraints of History* (London: Gerald Duckworth, 1982), pp. 160-73.

to 'prophet of God' (cf. Ezra 5.2; Lk. 7.16)/'prophet of Yahweh' (1 Sam. 3.20) or 'man of God' (cf. 1 Kgs 17.24), carries with it the implication that one shares in the divine nature. This is the implication of the inscriptions seen above, where various kings and despots call themselves 'son of God' and 'God'. There is no reason to think that Jesus' Jewish contemporaries, who were themselves very much part of the Greco-Roman world,[58] would have thought of these expressions in terms significantly different from those held by Gentiles. This is not to say that the epithet 'son of God' necessarily implied divinity, for it could be honorific or mystical (as I think we have it in the case of certain Jewish holy men who were supposedly addressed by heaven as 'my son').[59] But such an epithet, given its usage in late antiquity, would have contributed to belief in Jesus' divinity.

Perhaps the most important example is found in the passage that describes Jesus' hearing before Caiaphas and members of the Sanhedrin (Mk 14.55-65). Searching for an incriminating charge the High Priest asks Jesus: 'Are you the Christ, the son of the Blessed?' (Mk 14.61).[60] Jesus replies: 'I am; and you will see the son of man seated at the right hand of Power and coming with the clouds of heaven' (Mk 14.62). Caiaphas accuses Jesus of 'blasphemy' (Mk 14.63). Jesus' answer was not blasphemous for affirming that he is the Christ (or Messiah) nor was it in all probability a blasphemy for affirming that he was the 'son of God', since sonship was probably understood by many to be a concomitant of messiahship (as seen in Ps. 2.2, 7). Jesus' blasphemy lay in his combination of Ps. 110.1 ('sit at my right hand'[61]) and Daniel 7 ('son of man coming with the clouds of heaven'). This must be explained.

The juxtaposition of these Scriptures suggests to me that Jesus interpreted Dan. 7.9 much as Aqiba is said to have done: 'one for the Holy One, blessed be He, and the other for David'. That is, Messiah was to sit on a throne next to God, or at God's right hand (as Psalm 110

58. Again, Hengel's discussion in *The 'Hellenization' of Judaea* is apposite.

59. Jewish legends relate a story about God addressing Hanina ben Dosa: 'My son Hanina' (cf. *b. Ta'an.* 24b; *b. Ber.* 17b).

60. 'The Blessed' is a circumlocution for 'God' (cf. *m. Ber.* 7.3) and is probably an abbreviated form of the longer phrase, 'the Holy One blessed be He'. This epithet is ubiquitous in rabbinic literature.

61. Gundry (*Mark*, pp. 915-18) could be right in his suggestion that Jesus' own words were 'seated at the right hand of Yahweh' and that in the 'public' version of Jesus' offense, the circumlocution 'Power' was introduced (as prescribed in *m. Sanh.* 6.4; 7.5).

requires).[62] As Hengel has shown, sitting at God's right hand may actually have implied that Jesus was asserting that he would sit at God's right hand *in God's throne* (recall 1 Chron. 29.23: 'Solomon sat on the throne of the Lord as king'). Such an idea is not only part of primitive royal traditions in the Old Testament but can even be found in the New Testament in reference to the resurrected Christ: 'I will grant him who conquers to sit with me on my throne, as I myself conquered and sat down with my Father on his throne' (Rev. 3.21). When we remember that the throne of Dan. 7.9 had burning wheels, we should think that Jesus has claimed that he will sit with God on the Chariot Throne and will, as in the vivid imagery of Daniel 7, come with God in judgment. This tradition, which I do not think early Christians understood well nor exploited, is authentic and not a piece of Christian confession or scriptural interpretation.[63]

That Jesus referred to himself as 'son of man' in his reply to Caiaphas, as well as in many other sayings, is most probable, and that this self-designation was at times meant to recall the figure in Daniel 7 also seems probable.[64] Bruce Chilton explains that whereas 'son of man' is generic, the consistent appearance of the article (ὁ υἱὸς τοῦ ἀνθρώπου) in the dominical tradition denotes specificity.[65] He believes that this pattern derives from Jesus' references to *the* 'son of man', that is, to the one depicted in Daniel 7.[66] Given what was observed above with respect to the interpretation of the 'son of man' in the *Similitudes of Enoch*, Jesus' frequent use of this epithet is significant. As Messiah and as the 'son of man' of Daniel 7, who is able to approach God, to whom authority and kingdom were to be given, and who is permitted to sit at God's right hand, Jesus has claimed a share of God's authority.[67]

62. See Evans, *Jesus and His Contemporaries*, pp. 204-10.

63. For further discussion, see Evans, *Jesus and His Contemporaries*, pp. 210-11, 431-33.

64. See R.N. Longenecker, *The Christology of Early Jewish Christianity* (SBT, 17; London: SCM Press, 1970), pp. 82-93; D.R.A. Hare, *The Son of Man Tradition* (Minneapolis: Fortress Press, 1990), pp. 257-82.

65. The articular usage of the dominical tradition contrasts with what we find in LXX Dan. 7.13 or Ps. 79.17 (υἱὸς ἀνθρώπου).

66. B.D. Chilton, 'The Son of Man: Human and Heavenly', in F. Van Segbroeck *et al.* (eds.), *The Four Gospels 1992* (3 vols.; BETL, 100; Leuven: Leuven University Press, 1992), I, pp. 203-18.

67. On the importance of the linkage of Ps. 110.1 and Dan. 7.9-14, see Hengel, ' "Setze dich zu meiner Rechten!" ', pp. 158-61.

This explicit claim, however, has been adumbrated in various ways throughout his public ministry.

4. *Conclusion*

The New Testament's deification of Jesus Christ, as seen especially in the theologies of Paul and the fourth evangelist, has its roots in the words and activities of the historical Jesus. These words and activities in important places reflected the language and expectations of some Palestinian Jews of his time. Some of the deification language of the New Testament may very well reflect the Greco-Roman culture of its time, but it is surely mistaken to contend, as some have in the past and some still do today, that the deification of Jesus owes its origin primarily, even exclusively, to the non-Jewish world.[68]

68. Two recent books should be mentioned that deal with aspects of the problem addressed in this essay. The first is by L.W. Hurtado, *One God, One Lord: Early Christian Devotion and Ancient Jewish Monotheism* (Philadelphia: Fortress Press, 1988). Hurtado believes that early Christian worship of Jesus provided a major impetus toward his deification. The second book is by P.M. Casey, *From Jewish Prophet to Gentile God* (Cambridge: James Clarke; Louisville: Westminster/John Knox, 1991). This largely unsatisfactory book fails to take into account adequately the Jewish materials (and fails to interact with Hurtado's work as well). Casey, like so many alluded to at the beginning of this essay, assumes that the New Testament's deification of Jesus must be rooted in non-Palestinian, non-Jewish sources and environments.

TRANSLATING THE BIBLE

David Daniell

The main thrust of what I want to say is that translating the Bible is an art that we seem to have lost, for mysterious reasons.

I am talking, of course, about translating the Bible into English. There are 6528 distinct languages in the world, and some or all of the Bible is now translated into 1739 of them. Though I shall need to mention other languages—Hebrew, Greek, Latin, German, French, Spanish, Italian—I want to stay with English. (Some other modern languages, like Russian, are exceptionally interesting in the matter of Bible translation. The Russian Orthodox Church keeps tight hold of an archaic version in a language [Slavonic] which many people cannot understand. It is as if the Authorised Version in this country were in Welsh, and those who tried to introduce good modern English versions into services were liable to victimization.) But not only is English our own language: it is the world language of communication, and of first importance of all languages spoken on earth. Yet straight away we run into something strange. The English language, because of its earlier making, is unusually responsive, having three or four words for nearly the same thing from Saxon, from French, from Latin and from more exotic imports, all of which allow for remarkable sensitivity. Think of the shadings in, and differences between, these words for almost the same thing: from Saxon 'holiness'; from French 'sacredness'; from Latin 'sanctity'; and—a Maori word which arrived in the 1850s, now fashionable—'mana'. Moreover, English has never been in better shape. It is vividly alive in all its many forms. Always flexible in vocabulary, grammar and syntax, always welcoming, able to adapt, alert to instance changes and fine differences, able to express everything from the most technical scientific jargon (a word I use positively) to the most Jamesian of delicate feelings. You will see that I do not belong to those who write to the *Daily Telegraph* about the appalling destruction of our precious heritage under the influence of

(a) Americanisms (b) trendy teachers (c) non-Anglo-Saxon immigrants (d) television (e) the other 'meeja' (f) social workers (g) the decline of Latin in schools (h) loss of respect for elders and betters (i) young people today. English in 1995 is in terrific shape. It can use anything, and does. It is healthier than ever before, alive and kicking in mainstream, dialects, pidgins and creoles, across the world.

Furthermore, our knowledge of the languages of the Bible, Hebrew, Aramaic, Greek, and of the transmission of the texts, has never been greater. Some of the oldest fortresses of difficulty in understanding the meaning of some Hebrew phrases have fallen. (Sadly, the great phrase in Job 19.20, 'I am escaped with the skin of my teeth', is now 'I gnaw my underlip with my teeth'.) I remind you that *hapax legomena* (words which only occur once) in the Hebrew Scriptures often remain impenetrable because Hebrew to a large extent only exists in the Scriptures, and peculiarities of Temple furnishings, or the wildlife which the Lord permits or does not permit to be eaten, or of items of daily life like a workman's tools, are likely to remain baffling. The Dead Sea Scrolls— and let us not forget something rarely mentioned in the acrimonious debate about them, that the caves contained scrolls in Greek—begin to shed light. And my good friend Professor Carsten Peter Thiede is quite rightly challenging the dating of known papyrus fragments—the three in Magdalen College Oxford are only the most famous—with important results for understanding the original contexts, and therefore meaning, of New Testament documents.[1]

With all this—with English wonderfully vigorous, alive and free, with refined knowledge of the original texts before undreamed of—*why can't we translate the Bible into English*? We can't. We seem to have lost the knack, or lost our nerve. Why, at Gen. 31.28 does Laban say to Jacob, in the very newest 'official' translation, published jointly by OUP and CUP (the first time such joint publishing has happened), the *Revised English Bible* of 1989, why does Laban say to Jacob 'In this you behaved foolishly'? Who speaks like that now, or spoke like that in 1989? It's a vacuous, vapid, prissy phrase in itself. But from *Laban*, and at that point? Perhaps the REB committee was influenced by what King James's translators made of it. You will recall that after the initial request in January 1604, the work on what became AV didn't really start until

---

1. C.P. Thiede, 'Papyrus Magdalen Greek 17…A Reappraisal', *Zeitschrift für Papyrologie und Epigraphik* 105 (1995), pp. 13-21.

1607 or 1608, when 6 companies began, two in Westminster, two in Oxford, two in Cambridge, the Bible divided between them. The first half of the Old Testament was translated by the first Westminster company. That company was—as they all were—a mixed bag, and not necessarily good Hebraists. The best Hebraists in England, Hugh Broughton and Andrew Willett, had been ignored, Broughton because he was thought to be too noisy, and not 'one of us'; when AV came out he got his revenge in a letter to King James venomously pointing out some of the more spectacular errors.[2] He would have made AV's poems and prophets a great deal better than they are. Anyway, the Westminster company at Gen. 31.28 made Laban say 'thou hast now done foolishly in so doing' which is pretty poor in its repetition of 'done' and 'doing' and, again, the cloudy adverb 'foolishly'. The point of all this is that the first man ever to translate Hebrew into English, 78 years before in 1530, when only very few people in England knew Hebrew—it is only slightly bending it to say that both were Cambridge men called Wakefield—and when no-one in England was the slightest bit interested in translating Hebrew into English, this first translator, William Tyndale, who learned his Hebrew in two years on the continent, translated and printed the result in Antwerp while in hiding and in fear for his life, he had translated here at Gen. 31.28 'Thou wast a fool to do it'. Perfect: for the Hebrew, and in English. Why change it? That is a serious question, and leads in to most of what I want to say.

English in 1600 was spoken by 6 million people. It is now spoken by 600 million people. In the 1520s it was a struggling language in an island off the shelf of Europe, barely known outside that island. The first printed catalogue of the library of the University of Oxford, later the Bodleian, printed in 1605, contained over 6000 items.[3] Of these 6000, only 58 were in English. Martin Luther neither knew Tyndale's brilliant solutions to translation problems, nor had any cause to know English. The modern spread of English has been complete. It is now automatically used by Japanese salesmen, Korean air-line pilots, Brazilian computer-buffs and even Zairian school-teachers. We forget that in 1530 when Tyndale translated, English was as irrelevant to European culture

2.   See H. Wheeler Robinson (ed.), *The Bible in its Ancient and English Versions* (Oxford: Clarendon Press, 1940), pp. 189, 199, 206 and especially 209.

3.   *The First Printed Catalogue of the Bodleian Library 1605, a Facsimile* (Oxford: Clarendon Press, 1986).

and learning as Scots Gaelic is today. We know the names of over a thousand printers in Europe in 1500: England had two, neither much good. The great Erasmus, who spent three happy and productive periods at this time in England, coaching Lord Mountjoy, teaching in Cambridge, listening, learning, lecturing, talking, enjoying the hospitality of warm households, neither spoke nor wrote a word of English. Yet Tyndale translated Hebrew into an English which has not only survived, but is clearly often superior to what we get now for Bible translation.

Here is Tyndale in that bit of the Laban story. You will recall that Laban, who was not a nice man, was the brother of Isaac's wife Rebekah; they, Isaac and Rebekah, were the parents of Jacob. Uncle Laban had tricked Jacob into seven years of service for the wrong daughter, and then seven further years for the right one. Laban was a trickster, and he wanted to keep Jacob, who had an effective and mighty personal God, in his power. While Laban was away shearing his sheep, Jacob sneaked off secretly with all his family and flocks. Laban's daughter Rachel, incidentally, she for whom Jacob had effectively served fourteen years, took with her the *teraphim*, the family household gods: we shall come back to that in a moment. Laban pursued them, and overtook them. Here is Tyndale:

> Then said Laban to Jacob: why hast thou done this unknowing to me? and hast carried away my daughters as though they had been taken captive with sword? Wherefore wentest thou away secretly unknown to me and didst not tell me, that I might have brought thee on the way with mirth, singing, timbrels and harps, and hast not suffered me to kiss my children and my daughters. Thou wast a fool to do it, for I am able to do you evil. But the God of your father spoke unto me yesterday saying take heed that thou speak not to Jacob ought save good. And now though thou wentest thy way because thou longest after thy father's house, yet wherefore hast thou stolen my gods?[4]

Now here is the same passage in REB:

> Laban said to Jacob, 'What have you done? You have deceived me and carried off my daughters as though they were captives taken in war. Why did you slip away secretly without telling me? I would have set you on your way with songs and the music of tambourines and harps. You did not even let me kiss my daughters and their children. In this you behaved

---

4. *Tyndale's Old Testament...in a Modern-Spelling Edition and with an Introduction by David Daniell* (New Haven and London: Yale University Press, 1992), p. 52.

> foolishly. I have it in my power to harm all of you, but last night the God
> of your father spoke to me; he told me to be careful to say nothing to you,
> not one word. I expect that you really went away because you were home-
> sick and pining for your father's house; but why did you steal my gods?

Yes, we can understand it. 'You did not even let me kiss my daughters
and their children' is better immediate sense than Tyndale's 'hast not
suffered me to kiss my children and my daughters'. But something is
very wrong. Tyndale the pioneer, working with less than adequate
Hebrew grammar and lexicon, not to speak of printed text, gives us
some sense of the voice of Laban as something to be afraid of; overlaid
in an oily way by his assurance of an instruction from God to be nice to
his son-in-law—Jacob and his God were necessary to Laban's continued
welfare. 'Thou wast a fool to do it, for I am able to do you evil' is in
every way better English than 'In this you behaved foolishly. I have it in
my power to harm all of you...' The woolly 'have it in my power' is an
attempt to get at an idea of having in hand in the original Hebrew,
reflected in both the Greek Septuagint and the Latin Vulgate, though
Luther, on whom Tyndale to some small extent depended in his Old
Testament translating, changes the 'have in hand' notion: *und ich hatte,
mit Gottes hulfe, wohl so viel Macht, dass ich euch konnte Uebels
thun*... Perhaps Luther's curious substitution of 'with God's help'
suggests some problem with Laban's power, which the REB committee
wanted to keep, with the roundabout 'have it in my power'. But this is
not the place for such refinement. In this drama, Laban's smiling words
conceal brutal iron: Tyndale knows this, and has 'I am able to do you
evil'. I prefer that even to AV's rather good 'It is in the power of my
hand to do you hurt'. Twelve words against Tyndale's seven. And
Tyndale cuts through the abstract of 'power' in 'my hand' to the simple
'I am able' which is all it needs. Similarly, which do you prefer for the
same idea, REB's 'carried off my daughters as though they were cap-
tives taken in war' or Tyndale's 'taken captive with sword'? The
specific 'sword' is surely right there in English, for an original which
suggests battle. What is the difference between Tyndale's 'And now
though thou wentest thy way because thou longest after thy father's
houses' and REB's 'I expect that really you went away because you
were homesick and pining for your father's house'? That is a real
question. Such language as the 1989 version would not have produced
Shylock's sinister story, so remarkably catching the specious devices,
this time of Jacob with Laban (though in another story). Shakespeare

heard a voice in the telling which he wanted for the self-justifying Shylock. Emrys Jones, in the chapter in his *The Origins of Shakespeare* on the importance of schoolboy rhetorical exercises founded by Erasmus, wrote 'without Erasmus, no Shakespeare'.[5] I have a file at home labelled 'without Tyndale, no Shakespeare'. At this stage, I'll say no more. But what is wrong with 'I expect that really you went away because you were homesick...' as the voice of Laban at this moment in a Bible story? Fine, there is a sort of hesitation, but it is all caught by Tyndale's one word 'though'—'And now though thou wentest thy way...' It is not just that the modern version lacks *gravitas*, making Laban sound like an inadequate—and patronising—personal counsellor. It is not that older forms ('thou wentest', 'thou longest') sound heavier—as if the patriarchs, to be patriarchal, should speak in Gothic. It is something else.

Let us come at this another way. Some verses later, Laban brutally searches for the missing *teraphim*, the household gods, invading Jacob's tent, and Leah's tent, and the tent of the two servant girls ('maidens' to Tyndale: 'slave-girls' to REB, surely with unpleasant overtones) and not finding them. Rachel, however, put them in the camels' straw and sat on them, and when Laban forced himself into her tent, she excused herself from getting up with a blunt explanation. In Tyndale, 'my lord, be not angry that I cannot rise up before thee, for the disease of women is come upon me'. We do not believe her, of course, but Laban after a ruthless search of the tent does not find the *teraphim*, and soon disappears from the Bible. But do we have any doubt what Rachel's explanation is? Menstruation as a disease is not the best modern thinking, nor is her incapacity to stand up at all modern. Tyndale may be politically incorrect and dated, but he's surely clear. AV has 'the custom of women is upon me', which is vaguer but acceptable, though an older shade of 'custom'. REB produces something which is absolutely not English. True, it is not French or German or Sanskrit: but does anybody actually say things in English like this? 'Rachel said, "Do not take it amiss, father, that I cannot rise in your presence: the common lot of women is upon me".' A matter as socially sensitive as the vocabulary available at a point like this can help with what register a Bible translation should be in, as I hope to show.

First of all, a translation has to be accurate. We must not be led to

5.   E. Jones, *The Origins of Shakespeare* (Oxford: Clarendon Press, 1977), p. 13.

think that Rachel is about to give birth. Such accuracy, properly a matter of course, is not all that common. Some translators select. Whether or not the Apocrypha is included in the Bible is a question nearly 2000 years old. I have at home a 1983 *Reader's Digest Bible* in English which carefully takes out all the off-putting bits like chapter and verse numbers, and most of Leviticus, Chronicles, the Epistle to the Hebrews and similar difficult books. Tyndale and the early sixteenth-century English reformers died for the *whole* Bible in everyone's hands. Yet Martin Luther himself wanted a two-tier Bible, with some of the Old Testament on a lower shelf, and in the New Testament, James, Jude and Revelation downgraded. Some translators paraphrase, and get it wrong. My favourite example out of thousands concerns the *Good News Bible* (TEV) of which the New Testament was first published in America in 1966 as *Today's English Bible*. It is now very widely used.

The opening words of the fourteenth chapter of John's Gospel express something of great importance to Christ and his disciples. He had been with them for some years, and now he had to tell them that he was going away—he was going to be killed. In spiritual terms, he was reassuring them that his death would be revelatory: 'I go to prepare a place for you'. That reassurance was given them, like everything in the Fourth Gospel and the Epistles of John, with deceptive simplicity: a child can understand the words: the significance needs a spiritual lifetime. The chapter opens in Greek with five words containing two elements: your hearts, and the injunction not to let them be troubled. Tyndale gave us 'Let not your hearts be troubled...', which is exactly correct, to the Greek and to the spiritual quality. A troubled heart—as opposed, for example, to a disturbed mind—is a particular thing, and it is what the Greek says, and Tyndale's words have rung down the centuries at that point, as at so many (it is one of the frequent places where the Catholic New Jerusalem Bible, for example, follows Tyndale). It is English at a slightly heightened register, but still spoken English, belonging to a recognizable human relationship. Once in a lifetime perhaps—certainly once in Jesus' lifetime—those words are, were, needed to be spoken. Today only the 'let not' feels archaic, and possibly not even that. The TEV has '"Do not be worried and upset" Jesus told them'. That is wrong on every single count: for the Greek, for the occasion, for the register; and John's spiritual perception is simply wiped out—the words belong to cheering the disciples up when they had missed a bus. Tyndale is accurate, clear and original in a spoken, crafted English which still, for the occasion, feels modern. To lose 'a troubled heart' as a concept is a terrible loss indeed. At moments of great decision, of vocation even, or of bereavement, 'worry' is devilishly trivial. The great vocations have come to men and women with troubled hearts.

Of course, there is worse. The references in Mark 13 and elsewhere to the coming of the Son of Man appear in a very new New Testament as 'the coming of the human one...the human one will come in clouds...' and so on. This is *The Language-Inclusive New Testament*, probably to be published later in this year, 1995, by OUP no less. It removes all discrimination on grounds of race, sex, gender and even right-or-left-handedness. In this 'version' Jesus refers throughout the Gospels not to God the Father but to God the Fathermother—with strange results. 'All who take the sword shall perish by the sword', Jesus now says at a high point in the Passion story. 'Do you think that I cannot appeal to my Fathermother who will at once send me more than twelve legions of angels?' (Mt. 26.53). The man behind this, Burton Throckmorton, claims it is bringing the translation up to date, lest the Bible gather dust as being not relevant. But he is wildly and wonderfully heretical, and just plain wrong to boot. All the New Testament Greek texts, all of them, from the earliest papyri to the great fourth-century uncials and cursives and thereafter, without exception, give Jesus referring to God as *patēr*, father.

First, accuracy comes from very great technical knowledge, not only of Greek for the New Testament and Hebrew for the Old Testament, but Hebrew for the New Testament as well, as Tyndale was the first to discover. His prologue to his revision of the New Testament in 1534 begins with a technical account of finding inside the New Testament Greek, Hebrew,

> whose preterperfect tense and present tense is oft both one and the future tense is the optative mode also, and the future tense is oft the imperative mode in the active voice, and in the passive ever.[6]

That is the fourth sentence of an introduction to what was effectively the first printed New Testament in English.

This is now commonplace. As should be the ability to look for solutions to problems in versions in Latin, German, French, Spanish, what-

---

6. *Tyndale's New Testament...in a Modern-Spelling Edition and with an Introduction by David Daniell* (New Haven and London: Yale University Press, 1989), p. 3.

ever—as very clearly Tyndale did. There's a whole new continent of work to be done, never yet touched (though I've seen it in the distance), on Tyndale getting help from French, Italian and Spanish versions, and the great six-volume Complutensian Polyglot from Spain. We are told that he spoke eight languages like a native, by a German scholar who seems to have thought Tyndale's native tongue was German.[7]

Secondly, the translation must make sense. Here our first translator William Tyndale scores ninety-nine out of a hundred. He translated half the Old Testament and the New Testament twice, and I have worked with these translations for eight years now and I cannot recall more than a very few moments where he fails to make good sense, even in those stupefyingly impossible accounts of Temple fitments in the later chapters of Exodus and 1 Kings 6 and 7 and 2 Chronicles 3 and 4. This again is not something to take for granted, as there is a tradition in the translation of Hebrew Scriptures (as in fact with Scriptures of other faiths) that the aim is to be as philologically exact as possible, and trust that some sort of sense will come through, which it often doesn't. It is that tradition that gives us the woolly bits of AV's prophets, and even poetic books—Tyndale was killed before he could get to them. My AV fell open at Hab. 1.9: 'they shall come all for violence: their faces shall sup up as the east wind, and they shall gather the captivity as the sand'. I don't know what that means. The idea is that as it is a divine book, getting down exactly what each word means will allow for divine help in understanding. The theory doesn't work. The AV prophets are full of a sort of holy rubbish like that.

But Tyndale faces a profounder problem, which I will tackle in two parts: first, what to do when the original is severely lacking: and secondly, how to make a translation not only clear but memorable. I shall focus on a fine and haunting phrase, 'Gold, silver, ivory, apes and peacocks'. This wonderfully evocative set of words, well worthy of Keats or Tennyson in its physical richness, reached the wider world through the 1611 AV, the King James Bible. It is from 1 Kings 10. Like so much else—like 90% of the King James New Testament as calculated by Bishop Westcott in 1868, and over 50% of the first half of the Old Testament—the words were written by William Tyndale, here in what is without doubt his translation of the Hebrew Old Testament, printed in 'Matthew's' Bible after his death, in 1537.

7.   See J.F. Mozley, *William Tyndale* (London: SPCK, 1937), p. 67.

1 Kings 10 is the chapter in which the Queen of Sheba arrives to visit King Solomon and is amazed by his wisdom, which includes the *range* of his wealth. She herself brought wonderful sweet odours and precious stones: he already had for his royal and religious buildings harps and psalteries and singers, as well as a great deal of gold and an ivory throne, and cedar-wood and silver and splendid clothes. The climax of the account is the regularity of the imports of wealth. Tyndale translates:

> And as for silver it was nothing worth in the days of Solomon. For the sea ships which the king had in the sea, with the ships of Hiram, came every third year laden with gold, silver, ivory, apes and peacocks.[8]

It's the apes and peacocks that are the surprise, the special touch of exoticism, creatures of movement and colour, characterizing wealth indeed.

The two main translations of the Old Testament made into English 150 years before Tyndale, in the 1380s, from the Latin of the Vulgate, the manuscript versions associated with John Wyclif—which Tyndale probably did know, incidentally—have variations on something like this:

> and brought from thence gold, and silver, and teeth of olifauntis, and apis, and pokokis.

The Wyclif versions are translating, very literally, the Latin of the Vulgate, of course, whereas Tyndale has gone one thousand two hundred years behind Jerome's Latin to the original Hebrew: the first Englishman to do so—and he did it so well that thousands of his phrases, like this one, have survived—not least in John Masefield's famous poem 'Cargoes', learned by heart at junior school by several generations of British children, including me:

> Quinquereme of Nineveh from distant Ophir
> Rowing home to haven in sunny Palestine,
> With a cargo of ivory,
> And apes and peacocks,
> Sandalwood, cedarwood, and sweet white wine.

Notice that Tyndale does in six words—gold, silver, ivory, apes and peacocks—what the Wyclif versions need eleven for: gold, and silver, and teeth of elephants, and apes, and peacocks. They are simply following the Vulgate,

---

8. *Tyndale's Old Testament*, p. 479.

aurum et argentum et dentes elephantorum et simias et pavos.

We have good evidence that Tyndale, alongside his Hebrew text and Hebrew grammar, worked with the Vulgate, the Septuagint (LXX)—the ancient Greek translation of the Hebrew—and Martin Luther's German translation from the Hebrew, this part published in 1524. Significantly, this has here

und brachte Gold, Silber, Elfenbein, Affen und Pfauen.

The missing out of the conjunctions 'and', and giving 'ivory' (*Elfenbein*) for 'teeth of elephants' gave Tyndale what he wanted—we can see him frequently using Luther in all his biblical translations, though he just as frequently goes his own way.

Tyndale clearly had the Septuagint in front of him throughout his Old Testament work: the LXX sometimes makes clear troubling confusions in the Hebrew. Here it says something interestingly different:

chrusiou kai arguriou kai lithōn toreutōn kai pelekeetōn.

'gold and silver and stones cut into relief with aces'.

There are only two possibilities: either the LXX translator had in front of him a different Hebrew text from the one Jerome, Luther and Tyndale used, which is unlikely: or he was simply guessing. That is not only likely, but probable, as the poor old LXX translator was reduced to doing that fairly frequently. The specialness of Hebrew includes the fact that it doesn't much exist outside the Scriptures. So a peculiar word remains peculiar, until chance or a neighbouring language throws up a clue. (The classic illustration of the LXX translator in difficulties is in Isaiah 3, where there are in the Hebrew twenty-one items of women's clothing, and the LXX translator had not the slightest idea what they were, and was reduced to saying some were green and some were blue... Those Hebrew words were every one of them *hapax legomena* and therefore present extreme difficulties in knowing what on earth they are.) The problem is still with us, as any commentary will show: or it can be seen by comparing modern translations which all represent the cream of modern Hebrew scholarship—and all frequently say something different.

The Hebrew at this point in 1 Kings 10 can be best expressed, as it sat on the page in front of the LXX translator, as 'gold, silver and three funny things'. The first of the funny things is a compound beginning 'teeth', though of what is not known. The other two are quite unknown.

All three words in the Hebrew are *hapax legomena*. Jerome in the fourth century rightly prided himself on his scholarship, and in the centuries after the Septuagint enough work had been done with languages related to Hebrew to make modern scholars moderately certain that we have here some kind of monkeys, though the peacocks may turn out to be baboons. Solomon's navy (an exotic force indeed) bringing gold and silver also brought teeth of something, and it is a reasonable inference that they were of elephants. The ships may yet turn out to have brought 'gold, silver, possibly ornaments made of some kind of teeth and perhaps some furry animals'—but a translator simply cannot say that. What he or she has to do is make the best available guess, and hit hard and clearly. The kingdom of God is not going to fail to come if the translator prints apes and peacocks when it should be little bears and baboons. And that is not a cheap point. Tyndale would rightly have been horrified by the modern fundamentalist positions that think that every syllable of the King James Bible has to be the divine word of God. This is only a bad extension of the position in his day, so lamented by Erasmus, that said that the Vulgate could not be wrong in any way. The very latest of such legalism, which must seem to us all the very opposite of Christianity, is arising with a dogma based on 1 Corinthians 13, 'when that which is perfect is come', 'that which is perfect' being the King James Version, usually in those circumstances called 'The Saint James Version'.

But it hasn't explained everything to say that Tyndale merely followed Luther in giving ivory and omitting the conjunctions. Even when he does, he is conscious of the crafts of language, the devices available to him in English, and uses them as a conscious craftsman would. He would be alert to the effect of the heavier German 'Elfenbein, Affen und Pfauen' becoming the lighter, and rhythmically different, 'ivory, apes and peacocks'. He might well have considered 'ivory, monkeys and birds'—monkeys, though different creatures, have still wonderful poetic possibilities, as in Shylock's great cry in the *Merchant of Venice*,

> Out upon her...it was my turquoise; I had it of Leah when I was a
> bachelor; I would not have given it for a wilderness of monkeys. (III.i.108)

So Tyndale, who wanted above all to be clear and memorable, stayed with Jerome's creatures. Tyndale's Hebrew by that stage was good enough for him to know that Jerome was probably right. What he wanted was the pattern of the consonants and vowels in English (perhaps triggered by Luther's fs in 'Elfenbein, Affen und Pfauen'), where the o and i of gold and silver chime with 'ivory', and the y and the o of 'ivory' chime with 'peacocks', and the two ps relate to their vowels in a balance, 'apes' and 'pea-', and the dactyl of 'ivory' led to the single strokes of 'apes and', and then the falling vowels and firm ks of 'peacocks' make a cadence—something Tyndale is uniquely good at doing, incidentally. There may be a deeper point altogether, though I only brush this lightly. The dipole of ivory and apes may just touch a more unconscious area of satisfaction, remembering the long history of the two: the gates of ivory from classical times were those that brought art as dreams, illusions and fantasies: the gates of horn, art as recording social and moral existence, or mimesis—something implied in the very word aping. That is fanciful, but I have found Tyndale's Bible translations always forward-looking in rather mad but deeply suggestive ways, even to the point of constructing the outline of *Hamlet* from the first book of Samuel, with a mad prince and a ghost and a call to avenge and lots more.

To be accurate, to make sense, to deal boldly with difficulties—these are emerging as the criteria for translating the Bible. There is another: to be ready to write differently, to have a wide range of effects. The 66 books of the Bible have 66 different styles (not quite, as in the New Testament the four Johannine books are similar: but then, there are three writers in 'Isaiah'). The 66 books make a library, a *biblia* of great variety, from the raw Hebrew of the Fall to the strange spare narrative of Abraham and Isaac, the genealogies, the legendary stories of the patriarchs, the sophisticated court narratives of Joseph—and we are not yet even out of Genesis. We add the prehistoric victory song of Deborah, the lists and the laws, stories of Saul, the grand sagas of Elijah and Elisha, through all the kinds of poetry to Psalms and prophets: and in the New Testament the handed-down, polished accounts of the doings and teachings of Jesus, the pellucid prose of the parables, the strength of the Passion-narratives, the journal-entries that make up the last part of Acts, all the intricate thinking in Hebrew-in-Greek of Paul at the frontiers of religious experience, the meditations of John, the hallucinations of the Apocalypse—a good translator has to understand and reflect the differences in tone. A bad translator makes it all sound the same, a charge that can be levelled at the Latin Vulgate, and most certainly at the bland recent English versions we are learning to call the 'have-a-nice-day' Bibles. So the wash of Latinity that King James for his own political reasons wanted to be spread over Tyndale, and to some extent got, both distances and flattens the text, making everything closer to one sonorous tone, so that the kaleidoscope of the Pentateuch can appear in one sombre colour, and Paul, a brilliant mind, can sound musty and old-fashioned—and thus safer.

Let me give three illustrations, all from Tyndale, of such contrast: first from Genesis 3, the Fall story, where the succession of paratactic phrases beginning with 'and' gives a tragi-comic inevitability—there are no contingencies of 'when' here—and allows the woman a sort of garrulity which plays right into the serpent's hands in his easy dismissiveness.

> But the serpent was subtler than all the beasts of the field which the Lord God had made, and said unto the woman. Ah sir, that God hath said, ye shall not eat of all manner trees in the garden. And the woman said unto the serpent, of the fruit of the trees in the garden we may eat, but of the fruit of the tree that is in the midst of the garden (said God) see that ye eat not, and see that ye touch it not: lest ye die.

> Then said the serpent unto the woman: tush ye shall not die: But God doth know, that whensoever ye should eat of it, your eyes should be opened and ye should be as God and know both good and evil. And the woman saw that it was a good tree to eat of and lusty unto the eyes and a pleasant tree for to make wise. And took of the fruit of it and ate, and gave unto her husband also with her, and he ate. And the eyes of both them were opened, that they understood how that they were naked. Then they sewed fig leaves together and made them aprons.

> And they heard the voice of the Lord God as he walked in the garden in the cool of the day. And Adam hid himself and his wife also from the face of the Lord God, among the trees of the garden. And the Lord God called Adam and said unto him where art thou? And he answered: The voice I heard in the garden, but I was afraid because I was naked, and therefore hid myself. And he said: who told thee that thou wast naked? hast thou eaten of the tree, of which I bade thee that thou shouldest not eat? And Adam answered: The woman which thou gavest to bear me company, she took me of the tree, and I ate. And the Lord God said unto the woman: wherefore didest thou so? And the woman answered, the serpent deceived me and I ate.[9]

If, as most modern translations do, you 'brighten' the syntax here, avoiding the parataxis (for no good reason), the result is simply a suburban woman out shopping:

9.   *Tyndale's Old Testament*, p. 17.

> The woman looked at the tree: the fruit would be good to eat: it was pleasing to the eye and desirable for the knowledge it would give. So she took some...[10]

Contrast that with the bright tone of this from 1 Kings 10 in Tyndale: still paratactic phrases, and a woman speaking, but rhythmically quite different.

> And when the Queen of Sheba had seen all Salomon's wisdom and the house that he had built, and the meat of his table, and the sitting of his servants, and the standing of his servitors and their apparel, and his butlers and his sacrifice that he offered in the house of the Lord, she was astonished. Then she said to the king: the word I heard in mine own land of thy deeds and wisdom, is true. Howbeit I believed it not, till I came and saw it with mine eyes. And see, the one half was not told me: for thy wisdom and goodness exceedeth the fame which I heard. Happy are thy men: and happy are these thy servants which stand ever before thee and hear thy wisdom. And blessed be the Lord thy God which had a lust to thee, to set thee on the seat of Israel, because the Lord loved Israel for ever, and therefore made thee king, to do equity and righteousness.[11]

And again this from 1 Kings 18: reported speech again, but now epic drama.

> And when Ahab saw Eliah (Elijah), he said unto him: art thou he that troubleth Israel? And he said: it is not I that trouble Israel, but thou and thy father's house... And Eliah came unto all the people and said: why halt ye between two opinions? If the Lord be very God, follow him: or if Baal be he, follow him. And the people answered him not one word.[12]

Note the running rhythms hitting the buffers with the final three thumps—'not one word'. Note too the way the spoken rhythms are made by the physical, elemental words like 'halt'—'why halt ye...' The Jerusalem Bible of 1966 has here, 'Elijah stepped out in front of all the people. "How long", he said, "do you mean to hobble first on one leg, then on the other?".' This is in fact philologically correct, and at the same time has lost all the epic impact of Tyndale's question. Tyndale has found in the Saxon word 'halt' the perfect answer, as it says in one strong word to hobble first on one leg and then the other with the added splendour of ambiguity in 'halt', that is, not only limping but making no movement at all, stuck between opinions, hobbling on the

10. *Revised English Bible* (1989).
11. *Tyndale's Old Testament*, p. 478.
12. *Tyndale's Old Testament*, p. 492.

fence, as you might say. Perfect for a memorable challenge by God's prophet to a nation.

In 1534, no-one else was writing like that in English—and no-one until Shakespeare sixty years later could touch that range of expression.

So a translator of the Bible has to be accurate, to make sense, to deal boldly with difficulties, to have an exceptionally wide range of expression: yet there is more. The ancient debate about translation, older than Cicero, taken up by Jerome and the translators under Wyclif, debated in the long preface to AV—roughly, should translation be word-for-word or sense-for-sense—a matter of the greatest importance in dealing for example with technical books like classical medical or agricultural treatises, and especially sacred texts—conceals in fact a basic question about register. There are those who want the Bible in what can be called 'stained-glass' English—carefully remote from the everyday as befits a sacred text, distant, not soiled by the realities of everyday life. There are others who say that as the New Testament is about incarnation, the closer to the everyday world the Word of God is, the better. Both positions produce difficulties. I can point to Bible translations which become carefully vague whenever human functions below the waist are mentioned, to the point of failing to communicate anything, even though the Hebrew Scriptures are vivid with human physicality. Martin Luther has been famously vilified for his remark that the incarnation doesn't mean much unless it says that the Holy Spirit is with us even in the privy.[13] But to come back to Rachel sitting on the *teraphim* to keep them from her father. What do you do? There should be some sense that real human beings are present, but if a translator made Rachel say at that moment, 'Sorry I can't get up, Dad, I've started a period' we should rightly object, on several grounds. I have found that Tyndale has grasped the nettle. What you do is be direct, using everyday speech but in a slightly heightened form. Thus in Genesis 38 Judah says to Tamar 'let me lie with thee', which AV turns to 'let me come in unto thee'. Tyndale has Solomon fall in love with many women, and sleep with them, where AV has him 'cleave' to them. I could give a hundred such illustrations. 'Sleep with' is right, and surprisingly modern. At one end of the scale a four-letter word, though swiftly informative, is absolutely wrong; equally wrong, at the other, is the phrase perpetrated at Genesis 38 by the New World Bible Translations Committee 1984 (Jehovah's

---

13. See H.A. Oberman, *Luther, Man between God and the Devil* (New Haven: Yale University Press, 1989; London: Fontana, 1993), p. 155.

Witnesses) which had Judah say to Tamar 'Allow me, please, to have relations with you'. Astonishingly, she did, 'so that she became pregnant by him'. It sounds pretty impossible. The direct simplicity of, say, 'sleep with' may also be a way in.

Tyndale's solution of slightly heightened direct speech is akin to the language of proverbs. Both recognize a certain specialness implied in the use. Both have their feet in the everyday world. One doesn't say 'I love you' to the check-out girl, and that particular simple, direct speech is special. But one does on the right occasion say 'I love you' and not 'Permit me if you will to adumbrate some quality of amorousness towards your goodself'. Proverbs, like 'I love you', live in the real world: 'Cast not a clout till May be out', or 'Measure twice and cut once', or 'Look before you leap' are short, simple, direct, just above the everyday colloquial. Like 'Judge not, that ye be not judged', or 'Ask and it shall be given you: seek and ye shall find: knock and it shall be opened unto you' of Jesus in Matthew 7. Like, indeed, so much of Jesus' sayings in Tyndale, carried through into the AV and thence to the world. Like 'And God said, let there be light: and there was light': before Tyndale's 1530 Pentateuch, the only alternatives in England (it is hard for us to grasp) were *Fiat lux: at facta est lux* or the Wyclif version 'Be made is light: and made is light'. That little volume of Genesis, like all Tyndale's publications a pocket-book, smote its readers between the eyes.

Not enough work has been done on proverbs in the early modern period. The work of the Whitings in 1968 gave us, as their book is entitled, *Proverbs, Sentences and Proverbial Phrases from English Writings mainly before 1500*[14] and at a rough count contains 6000. Erasmus's *Adagia* of 1499 went on to accumulate more and more adages—though all in Latin, of course. There was—and still is—a strong overlap between use of Bible texts among Christians, and use of proverbs. Many of Tyndale's phrases have become proverbial—'with God all things are possible', 'we live and move and have our being', 'be not weary in well doing', 'fight the good fight', 'am I my brother's keeper?', 'the salt of the earth', 'the signs of the times', 'where two or three are gathered together', 'the burden and heat of the day', 'they made light of it', 'the spirit is willing, but the flesh is weak', 'eat, drink

---

14. B.J. and H.W. Whiting, *Proverbs, Sentences and Proverbial Phrases from English Writings mainly before 1500* (Cambridge, MA: Harvard University Press, 1968).

and be merry', 'clothed and in his right mind', 'scales fell from his eyes', 'full of good works', 'a law unto themselves', 'the powers that be', 'filthy lucre', 'let brotherly love continue', 'the patience of Job'.

If these are not proverbs, it is thought, they must be Shakespeare. They are all Tyndale, translating the Bible, and I could go on and give hundreds more. Hardly a week goes by without me seeing a heading in a newspaper in which some sub-editor has caught, presumably unknowingly, a phrase of Tyndale. This is telling us a great deal about Bible translation. The sudden tremendous rush of interest in Tyndale's Bible translations in the last year must be because people have found him expressing their spiritual experience in an older but more direct register, hard-hitting like proverbs, made of short units, with Saxon vocabulary and the basic subject-verb-object syntax which is the Anglo-Saxon legacy. The point is driven home when the Jerusalem Bible of 1966 has, for 'the powers that be', 'the existing authorities'.

I have time for two more points before I close with two longer quotations. First, the old idea held by our grandfathers that Tyndale was some quaint vessel of God, a simple soul, without artistry, through whom God by a miracle poured his word, simply does not stand up. Tyndale was, I am coming to understand, the leading scholar of his age—bold words, when one thinks of Erasmus or Luther or Melanchthon, but a belief I can now justify. Moreover, he was a craftsman working in a tradition, both old and new, of rhetorical skills, the art of putting words in order. Erasmus, in his little schoolbook about rhetoric, the *De Copia* of 1512 (which, incidentally, Tyndale knew), has a famous exercise in which he demonstrates how to express the sentence 'Your letter has given me great pleasure' 150 ways. A Tudor schoolboy worked with the technicalities of putting words in order with the excited delight that long ago my schoolfriends gave to designing engines, and with which modern children now bring to computers. Tyndale knew what he was doing, in giving us our Bible language not in 'literary' form, not aureated with Latin curlicues of dependent clauses, but in the Saxon short straight units so visible in proverbs.

Because proverbs are memorable. When copies are scarce, the Bible must be memorable. It must be memorable anyway, because that's how so much of it was written, to be remembered, memorized. Almost all the sayings of Jesus fall into an Aramaic form designed to be heard once and remembered. This doesn't come through the Latin Vulgate, but it is detectable in the Greek, as Tyndale discovered. Tyndale is unforgettable.

Think of the Christmas stories—in Luke 2 'And there were in the same region shepherds abiding in the field watching their flock by night... But the angel said unto them: Be not afraid. For behold, I bring you tidings of great joy...for unto you is born this day in the city of David, a saviour which is Christ the Lord.' That is Tyndale—taken straight into AV and far beyond.

Tyndale's ear for rhythm makes a separate set of lectures for another time. Above all, he knew that to be memorable you had to attend to the cadence, the fall of the sounds at the end of the phrase. I go into this a bit in my Tyndale books.[15] 'And all that heard it, wondered at those things which were told them of the shepherds. But Mary kept all those sayings, and pondered them in her heart.' 'And when they had brought their ships to land, they forsook all, and followed him'. 'For this thy brother was dead, and is alive again; was lost, and is found'.

I could go on. It is time to finish. With our huge scholarship and uniquely vigorous English, I do not know why we can only produce translations of the Bible which patronize their readers. A Bible translation, we learn from Tyndale, needs to be accurate, to make sense, to deal boldly with difficulties, to have a wide range of expression, to be crafted to that slightly heightened register of everyday speech where proverbs are at home, to be memorable through rhythm and cadence. Everyday speech, note. There will be some specifically religious words, like salvation or righteousness or justification, but not very many in fact. The rest belong to everyday.

Here, to finish, are two passages from the Passion story. Note the Saxon simplicity. Note also, incidentally, the high proportion of monosyllables. In the first, I find only four Latin words, out of a paragraph of 150 words.

> Then went Jesus with them into a place which is called Gethsemane, and said unto the disciples, sit ye here while I go and pray yonder. And he took with him Peter and the two sons of Zebedee, and began to wax sorrowful and to be in an agony. Then said Jesus unto them: my soul is heavy even unto the death. Tarry ye here and watch with me. And he went a little apart, and fell flat on his face, and prayed saying: O my father, if it be possible, let this cup pass from me: nevertheless, not as I will, but as thou wilt. And

---

15. *Tyndale's New Testament*, pp. xix-xxii; *Tyndale's Old Testament*, pp. xviii-xxi; D. Daniell, *William Tyndale: A Biography* (New Haven and London: Yale University Press, 1994), pp. 137-42, 303-304, 350-54.

he came unto the disciples, and found them asleep, and said to Peter: what, could ye not watch with me one hour? Watch and pray, that ye fall not into temptation. The spirit is willing, but the flesh is weak.[16]

The simplicity of effect is appropriately stark, as in 'flat on his face'. AV took the 'flat' out, though Tyndale had caught the full force of the Greek verb *epesen*. AV added 'indeed' to Tyndale's 'the spirit is willing', following the Vulgate's Latin, and again misrepresenting the Greek.

Finally, from Luke 23. This is, as usual with Tyndale, English with little Latin in vocabulary and none in word-order:

And it was about the sixth hour. And there came a darkness over all the land, until the ninth hour, and the sun was darkened. And the veil of the temple did rent even through the midst. And Jesus cried with a great voice and said: Father, into thy hands I commend my spirit. And when he had thus said, he gave up the ghost.[17]

16. *Tyndale's New Testament*, p. 57.
17. *Tyndale's New Testament*, pp. 129-30.

VOICE GENRES: THE CASE OF TELEVANGELICAL LANGUAGE

John O. Thompson

I

In speaking of televangelism, the nettle that must be grasped at the start is that the phenomenon exists for us in a strongly polarized judgmental field, a field of a 'we–they' sort. Writing to a mixed academic and general audience in the UK, I can surely count on 'us' *recoiling* somewhat from the broadcasting genre in question, can I not? Certainly when religious broadcasting issues are discussed in Britain, trouble is always taken to distinguish anything that is proposed from 'USA-style' Christian television or radio.[1]

A quick, provisional breakdown of the reasons for our recoil might look like this: the televangelical style is disliked for being American/ populist/right-wing; for being kitsch; for being hucksterish/'big business'; and for being dumb. Given these perceived characteristics, it is small wonder if a 'we' can be constituted, bringing together believers and non-believers alike, whose instinct is to see this particular version of the propagation of the Word as a suitable candidate for being looked down on, in any of a range of modes of dismissal from amused condescension to committed hostility.

No sooner is this spelt out, however, than 'we' are clearly in trouble, given that the 'they' to whom televangelism speaks is no inconsiderable number of people, and 'our' value system, Christian and/or Enlightenment, suggests that systematically looking down on people, on 'their' beliefs and the genres and styles that sustain their beliefs, is not a very good idea.

The approach I propose in the following discussion, while not aiming to shield American televangelism from criticism along the standard lines,

---

1.   Most recently this has been evident over the launch (still forthcoming as of this writing) of London Christian Radio.

proposes a less immediately judgmental, more prosaically observational, study of what is actually going on when the Word, or something claiming to be such, is taped and transmitted in this manner.

II

How do you, or should you, 'sound Christian'? A sensible first reaction to the question would be to dismiss it: why should there be any such thing as 'sounding Christian'? You speak on the basis of, underlyingly, a genetic capacity for language; on top of that, you speak as you've learned to speak, and (on top of that in turn) as you've chosen to speak. Why, within these parameters, should you not speak about your religion as you would speak about any other matter? There is, or there need be, no more a phenomenon of 'sounding Christian' than of 'sounding Atheist'.

However, if the question is rephrased 'How do (or did) *they* sound Christian?', a more descriptive/analytical task is signalled. For it is clear—and knowing this is part of any speaker–hearer's competence— that there have been and are, distinguishably separated off from the tones of the everyday, *genres of delivery* which declare what is being said to be religious language.

Anthropology is full of accounts of how in particular cultures speech to do with sacred things differs from speech to do with profane things. And, while anthropology may once have had a tendency to exaggerate the stability of the 'traditional' societies it anatomized, the notion of there being provisionally stable, 'fitting' *differences* between language about the quotidian and language about the divine is not apt to give us difficulty.

However, when it comes to the sound of televangelism, it seems hard to feel that this is simply the sound of 'the tribe's tradition', therefore to be respected (while, as 'development' relentlessly melts into air the erstwhile solidity of that tradition, we mourn it as well). There seems to be about televangelical discourse, qua *religious* language, something irreducibly unstable, unfitting—and, at the same time, monstrously successful. This is not a 'Disappearing World' phenomenon; and, perhaps by the same token, neither does it seem to be (for 'us') immediately respect-worthy. But why would respect be withheld?

Bernard Shaw's much-quoted apothegm, 'it is impossible for an Englishman to open his mouth without making some other Englishman despise him', is generally remembered as a remark about class and regional dialects and the evaluative cruelties they generate.[2] Adverse judgment, however, is a further, non-necessary step starting from a more fundamental truth: it is impossible for us to open our mouths without making others *differentiate us as they categorize us.* (Categorization and differentiation, of course, imply one another.)

Perhaps, then, we should look first for the signs of differentiation in manners of speaking first, and then ask which of these differentiations get used in determining or in backing-up respect/contempt/judgments (by whom, at what time, in what place, under what circumstances...). And, behind the signs of differentiation, we might look for the genesis of particular differentiations and the motives for them.

III

Before moving to some examples of televangelical talk,[3] I want to illustrate the very great, and very little understood, *general* pressure within the media towards *differentiation by vocal delivery* along generic lines. The basic point is this: on television, but also on radio, in the cinema and on the pages of newspapers and magazines, a large repertoire of *distinguishing modes of delivery* exist, so that, almost independently of what is actually 'being said' semantically in the sentences produced, the hearer/reader is able to tell what kind of discourse he or she is dealing with.

I could evoke any number of cases of this—think, for instance, of that most curious delivery that was once used to deliver the scripts of newsreels on both sides of the Atlantic, or of the 'sound' of the sentences

2.   G.B. Shaw, *Pygmalion* (Harmondsworth: Penguin, 1941 [1914]), 'Preface', p. 5. Shaw's actual point is an odder one: that it is the lack of an alphabet with letter-sound equivalences of an 'agreed' value which means that 'no man can teach himself what [English] should sound like from reading it'; consequently, 'it is impossible...', and so on. While for our current purposes it is the saying-as-it-has-been-understood rather than the saying-in-its-original-context that is useful, the Shavian interest in making available an exit from being despised (as an 'accented' speaker) via a self-teaching programme facilitated by spelling reform is not without relevance to the 'self-help' (or 'growth') element in televangelism's appeal.

3.   The examples of American religious television I will be working with were collected for me in the December 1994–January 1995 period in the San Francisco area by Nancy Roberts and Robin Beeman, to whom many thanks.

that emanate from the pages of the tabloid press—but it may be best to discuss a subtler instance.

In a mid-eighties advertisement for soap powder, a little scenario is set up, of the most typical kind: a woman approaches another woman, offering her a chance to try out the soap powder, not her regular brand; the housewife at first demurs but then tries the product and is 'converted'. Here is the final bit of dialogue.

Daz Spokesperson	Tricia,[4] we persuaded you to try Daz in the hot whites wash.
Consumer	I was absolutely amazed. This sheet, for instance, my eldest son is very fond of playing ghosties with it and dragging it all over the floor, and it's come out beautifully white. And these pillow-slips: my youngest son has had a cold, and you try giving him medicine at two o'clock in the morning and it goes everywhere but in their mouth, but Daz has brought it out beautifully white. And being that much cheaper, it does save me money.
DS	So will you swap your packet of Daz for two packets of your old powder?
C	No, I'm going to stick with Daz.
DS	Try biological Daz yourself in a hot whites wash. Most women agree: Daz gives unbeatable white at a price that's right.

What is not predictable, just reading the words on the page, is how the vocal styles of the two women differ. *C* delivers her lines with 'naturalistic', conversational intonation:[5] what she says is unlikely to be unrehearsed, but it is spoken with a convincing air of spontaneity ('recognised' by *DS* with a little laugh at its most vivid moment, the mention of the son 'playing ghosties' with the sheet). *DS*, however, speaks in a distinctly different 'this is an advertisement' tone. Such a tone is arguably required by her last lines, spoken directly to the audience and involving the clearly non-conversational rhyming jingle of the final sentence. What is more puzzling is why she should adopt it in

---

4.   Or so it sounds on the tape, though the Consumer has just been identified via subtitle as 'Mrs Susan Davies, Sydenham'.

5.   Strictly speaking, the Consumer does herself sound a bit less than spontaneous, but that conversational spontaneity is to be seen as being aimed at is not in doubt. It may well be, following the logic of my subsequent discussion, that a mild degree of 'failure' here might be felt to be user-friendly by viewers of the ad.

conversing with *C*. It seems to be felt that it would be less fitting for her to change deliveries than for her to keep to 'advertising' delivery at the cost of lack of conversational verisimilitude; equally, keeping the whole thing conversational and eliminating the final lines to the audience would take the ad 'out of genre' unacceptably.

DS's delivery is equivalent to the small-print message 'ADVERTISE-MENT' that is required to appear in print media when the layout of an advertisement is such that an unwitting reader might confuse it with 'real' editorial content.[6] The televisual equivalent might well be, quite generally, not a subtitle but a tone of voice. And viewers might well, while believing themselves to be mildly scornful of the 'obvious' this-is-an-ad sound, actually find the ad's self-proclamation as such an orienting, comforting aspect of it.

Observing this, one might be tempted to hypothesize that, similarly, a distinctive delivery (or a whole series of deliveries, themselves differenti-ated) serving as a metamessage 'this is religious' might be cognitively useful for the viewer, even if the viewer rather ungratefully then took the delivery as a sign of crassness.

IV

Before considering three examples of clearly 'marked' televisual reli-gious language, it will be useful to establish, as a base-line, the 'zero-degree' case.

As an example of American religious television illustrating an uninflected, equal conversational interchange despite religion being one

---

6.   While I was writing this paper, the *Evening Standard* printed (p. 14 of its 10 February 1995 issue) an obituary of *Star Trek's* Captain Kirk on the occasion of the release of the film *Star Trek: Generations* ('Boldly gone: World mourns as Enterprise Captain James T. Kirk dies on final voyage'). It begins, 'Captain James T. Kirk, the man who saved the world and in doing so, saved the whale, is dead', and ends, 'He never married, though he had a son, David, who was tragically assassinated by a Klingon'. The layout of the piece does not contain any metamessage such as 'JOKE' or 'WHIMSY'. This demonstrates a considerable, but no doubt justified, confidence in most readers' cultural competence at picking up at once what is going on. (The *Evening Standard* does not have a regular obituary column, however: compare the effect if the same text had been inserted, in the normal way, in the obituary column of one of the 'quality' papers.) The Kirk obituary is, by the way, juxtaposed with a small item of real news, involving real death: 'Chaos as driver dies on bridge'.

of the topics, take Gary McSpadden interviewing singer Bob Carlyle on 'Stage Door'. McSpadden interviews his guest as an informed, friendly, sensible interlocutor; this is not just 'conversation in front of a camera', since such interchanges are themselves governed by conventions so that they can be 'for the viewer' rather than simply for the participants, but it is standard, competent chat-show performance on the part of both, save for the religious content. Thus, McSpadden asks Carlyle, 'In terms of what you see happening in your ministry, your career, what presses you on?', and Carlyle replies:

> Oh, I think more than anything else, Gary, the idea that God is—even now at this point in my life I can see even more clearly than ever before how God has pursued me, and nurtured me, and loved me through all of this; and it's that passion—and I don't want to sound cliché-ish but it really is true—it's that passion of knowing that I'm loved unconditionally by the Lord, and that he continues to allow me to sing and write songs that affect people's lives: that just, that just charges my batteries unbelievably.

Carlyle's delivery of this is serious and sincere (where 'seriousness' and 'sincerity' no doubt have their own semiotic dimensions), but it is not set apart from his delivery of other sorts of observations about his life and his music.

McSpadden can follow this up immediately with the question: 'Influences on your life, in terms of music and then spiritually?', with Carlyle replying first 'Well, musically, I kind of cut my teeth on the early R-and-B stuff...' before going on at a further prompt to say 'Well, I think more than anything the influences my father had on me growing up have brought me where I am today', and developing the link between his very good relationship with his father and his subsequent relationship with God. The double 'influences' question gets answered without the slightest change of tone between its two halves.

This is not exceptional television; its unexceptionality is precisely the point. It is only the content of what Carlyle is saying that sets it apart from mainstream television: on mainstream television, God would not pursue people, and the concept—virtually a technical concept in televangelical discourse—of 'unconditional love' would not be evoked.

V

Charles Stanley, speaking to a large audience, with a choir arrayed behind him, expounds the doctrine of God's unconditional love:

And you see, it is by loving each other that God uses all of us to meet each other's needs: emotional needs, material needs, physical needs, learning to love Him and receive it, loving ourselves: you see, the reason we don't love each other much is because we are so entangled with getting ourselves and our own sense of self-worth and value straightened out, we don't have any time to give—you see—we don't have anything to give away. If you don't love yourself, you don't have anything to give. Here's what it's like. It's like, here's your heart; and when you received the Lord Jesus Christ, God came into your life, and the love of God's in there. Now, if my whole life is wrapped up in getting, in getting me straightened out and checking out my sense of self-worth and my value and—'I don't, I don't like myself', I don't, I don't have anything to give away. Because it's all locked up. But when the Spirit of God sets me free, when I am liberated by the Spirit of God, and he begins to work in my heart, what happens? Then I am no longer the important one; but now what happens is, my life is open to others and the love of God comes gushing out all over everybody around me, and you see, that is the goal of God. He says, he says you are to love one another, that's the way the Church functions best. He says, now this love is to be all-inclusive—You remember when Jesus said in the Sermon on the Mount and people say, 'Well, I believe in the Sermon on the Mount'... Well, how many of your enemies do you love? 'I don't love any of my enemies'. Well, you don't believe in the Sermon on the Mount. He says we are to love our enemies, if we're only to love our friends, he says then you're no more than a Pharisee, we're to love our enemies, and he says we're to love our neighbours...

This is a relatively brief stretch of Stanley's speech, artificially detached from the impressively continuous flow of the whole discourse, which iterates and tirelessly reiterates the argument that only someone with healthy self-love can love others, and only the unconditionality of God's love can ground such self-love. The argument itself places Stanley, and other televangelists developing this position, in close-enough relationship to a body of discourse ranging from 'New Age/"Growth"' workshops to managerial staff-development techniques—with, of course, the difference that secular versions of these 'technologies of the self' see the building of self-esteem as achievable without God.

Lengthy continuous speech is itself not 'normal television', and other aspects of Stanley's presentation make it immediately recognizable as religious. The voice is urgent, with a gestural vocabulary to match. It can move into mimicry, as in a 'funny voice' adopted for 'I don't love any of my enemies'. It can also incorporate a quaver of emotion, as it does when, later, Stanley recounts a personal experience of suddenly and surprisingly feeling love for a fellow minister (but a liberal!)[7] whom he had not thought he liked.

Especially striking here is a moment of metaphor, starting at 'It's like this: here's your heart'. The words themselves are striking ('the love of God comes gushing out all over everybody around me'), but they are complemented by a gestural image, with Stanley's hands first knotted together and then unfolded and put in motion to represent 'gushing out'. The effect is to propose a very *concrete* image of love and the heart. Once again one can ask: where else in everyday television is such a development of arms and eyes allowed?

Kenneth Copeland sits at a table, a kitchen table (complete with salt and pepper shakers), with a book in front of him: not the book he will urge us to buy, later,[8] but The Book, the Bible. He is 'speaking to' a text, rather as a jazz musician might develop a melody; the text is from the beginning of Matthew 22, the parable concluding 'For many are called and few be chosen' in Tyndale's translation, though he also has in mind the parallel passage in Luke 14, from which he takes the phrase 'highways and hedges' to play with.

Copeland's delivery is much more stylized than Stanley's. He punctuates his speech with 'Amen'. While Stanley's accent is mildly southern, Copeland's is more pronouncedly so, and more 'rural'. He paraphrases in a punchy manner which it would be possible to read as condescending but which is crucially saved from this by something in the delivery style which can only be described as 'eccentric'. Having got himself slightly muddled, 'getting ahead of myself', Copeland retells the last bit of the parable thus:

7.   Since it is probably part of 'our' image of televangelism that, in its conservatism, it is confrontational and discriminatory, it is only right to register that Charles Stanley's discourse is reconciliatory and universalist. Whether there is any 'tactical' subtext to his rendering of his reconciliation to a liberal is not something I am in a position to evaluate; but the experience of repeatedly viewing this particular broadcast has led me to be inclined to take what Stanley says as being what he feels.

8.   The putative 'huckster/big business' side of the Copeland broadcast deserves a more detailed textual analysis than can be provided here. The overall shape is this: after an advertisement for the Copelands' book, delivered in standard voice-over 'this-is-an-advertisement' intonation, Copeland himself returns to the screen, still sitting at his table, to explain to the viewer why buying the book would be a Good Thing. There does seem to be a certain softening of the force, and the eccentricity, of delivery when selling is involved, while at the same time the *accusation* of hucksterism is 'unashamedly' provoked.

> ...But he [the 'man which had not on a wedding garment'], he was not
> there for the same purpose, and he was not anointed, he, he had on no
> wedding garment, and the king [C. prolongs the word, with falling, 'sing-
> song' intonation over the 'i'] had all of him he could take [C. chuckles],
> 'Boy', he said, 'throw him [dramatic arm movement] out the back door!
> And out there where it's dark, let him sit out there and chew on his
> tongue.' Amen. Now...

The king's aggression is taken over by Copeland, sitting slightly hunched
forward, eyes making direct contact with the camera to startling effect at
times. At the same time, he seems somehow to retreat into the world of
the story; 'let him sit out there and chew on his tongue' is almost
thrown away, a musing on the scene the biblical account evokes. The
eyes and the mouth are both mobile, but hardly *smoothly* so, in a generally 'set' face; similarly, gestures are abrupt, even jerky. Awkwardness
and passion register.

Copeland turns out to be someone who works in mimicry using
'funny voices' for those in error more spectacularly (in the particular
examples I'm working with) than Stanley.

> One thing we have to be really, really careful of is making light of what
> God did in Jesus for us. 'Oh Lord, you know I'm just so unworthy—O
> God, I don't deserve Heaven—Oh Lord, yes, Amen, I'm just so unworthy,
> I'm just a little worm': you're making light of the blood, you're making
> light of the name of Jesus, you're making light of the body that was
> broken for you, you're making light—'But, but, I didn't intend to make
> light—' I know you probably didn't intend to do it, but you cannot receive
> from God, making light of this gospel. You cannot receive from God,
> making light of what Jesus did for you on the Cross. 'Well, you know
> how it is, brother, I mean uh, whuw, it looks like the whole world's going
> to Hell in a handbasket'. Well, the whole world's not going to Hell, we're
> reaching out to the world, the Bible said the whole world would be filled
> with his glory. 'Well, I mean, I didn't mean it'. Well, stop saying that junk
> if you don't mean it.

Copeland here satirizes, pointedly and successfully, both a 'dumb-
humble' approach to God and a 'dumb-gloomy' approach. He is about
to move into an apocalyptic reading of what is in store for us in these
last days, but by using one 'funny voice' (not-too-bright) for an unthink-
ingly pessimistic view and another for a defeatist, abject view, he distinguishes his own position from those he mocks, and in an entertaining
way. It is interesting to note that the 'little worm', as Copeland renders
him, looks *up* as he humiliates himself. Copeland himself looks up at

times, in his own serious address to God, but he is prepared to mock looking-up as savagely as any unbeliever might in order to make his point.

Dean and Mary Brown, on 'Music that Ministers', intermix loopiness and back-chat with religious speech and song in a manner which, at a first or even a second glance, might disconcert. The couple address us from a set which simultaneously declares itself to be 'living-room' (shelves, pictures on walls) and 'stage' (huge flower arrangements, overall sense of performing space). 'We have a great day planned for you', Dean enthusiastically begins, and speaks of the day's guest per-formers: 'a special guest...by special demand—great demand'. But then Mary continues, with even greater enthusiasm: 'But a *more* special guest, in even *greater* demand for this guest to be here—it talks about him in the 91st Psalm, the 14th verse...' She reads from a small Bible.

God as the guest of the television hosts, then; but what guest on 'everyday television' has ever been introduced by (constituted by?) reading from a book? (Books, via the appearance of their authors engaged in book *promotion*, of course do feature importantly on chat shows, and it may be worth giving some thought to the relationship between sacred and secular implied in the contrast between 'new book*s* without end' and the inexhaustible One Book.) Mary continues after reading the text in question, 'I tell you, that gives us an overwhelming sense of—the awe and wonder at God's *continued* provision for us [Dean: 'Yes!']. Thank God he is a provision, a fortress in the time of trouble, he's going to deliver us, he'll protect us—that's your [God's] promise...' This is delivered in a manner that (starting from an already high base) grows in force, 'exaltation': it is a lead into something, and that something turns out to be a Dean and Mary rendition of 'A Mighty Fortress Is Our God'.

The transition is very striking, because Dean and Mary are good singers, and the hymn, in itself a distinguished marriage of religious lan-guage and melody, responds wonderfully to a spirited, robust delivery. A possible experience of the transition (my own, I should say) is from kitsch into quality. (I would imagine that the programme's intended audience would experience something more continuous; as might, in negative mode, a thoroughly unsympathetic viewer.)

The last line of 'A Mighty Fortress' is: 'His kingdom is for ever'. Having concluded the singing with a mighty 'Amen', the Browns make the word 'forever' linger as spoken, reiterating it between them oddly;

and even as Mary moves on to describe what is to happen on the rest of the programme—'We're going to talk about and we're going to worship that almighty and forever God'—Dean echoes her echo of the song: 'He *is* an almighty and a forever God'. They invite viewers to sit down for the rest of the programme, and themselves sit down: this becomes the occasion for a bit of by-play about Mary's not sitting on her glasses; it turns out she has pairs of glasses all over the house ('$7 at the drugstore', she assures us, lest this look like a sign of wealth); Dean's mention of this prompts her to counter-tease, 'And guess who wears them sometimes!' Dean responds to this charge of ocular cross-dressing slightly sheepishly: 'Well, some days I do, some days I can't see, but I believe God's going to heal me. But anyway...' The phrase about God's healing is thrown away, not emphasized; there is an eerie air of its being a joke, and Mary certainly utters a little laugh. Here, as elsewhere with the Browns, a sense is generated of their speech running away with them, not being under full control. 'But anyway', Dean continues, moving back into verbal focus, 'I'm thankful for the kingdom of God and the fortress and the deliverer that he is'. Mary continues: 'And he's always, always and for sure'. ('Always' takes over from 'forever' now, while 'for sure' is delivered idiomatically, with the intonation it has in America when it is used to mean 'Yes', even though it is also stressed so as to bring out the 'surety' of God.) She continues, 'Lord, remind us, every person that listens today [note that she speaks of listening, not of watching or viewing], remind us that you are—*always* there. Where we can't see you, when it's dark, when it's night inside of us, that you're always there. When circumstances are overwhelming, that you're not overwhelmed, God, that you're present, and you're always there...' The transition from the jokiness of 'And guess who wears them sometimes' to the seriousness of 'when it's night inside of us' is carried through seamlessly, but what allows the transition is a sustained tone of excitement and of, again, *eccentricity*. As with Kenneth Copeland, a sense of foolishness opening onto the grand Folly of Erasmus is felt, though Dean and Mary are certainly more friendly-seeming eccentrics than Copeland is. (By the same token, Copeland is certainly more 'heavyweight' in effect than the dizzyingly lightweight Browns.)

VI

Mark Crispin Miller has proposed, in a classic article,[9] that American television increasingly tends towards a kind of closure, a self-referentiality which leaves less and less space for any acknowledgment of the non-televisual; the latter becomes acknowledged only as material for 'derision'. Religious television, as represented by the examples we have looked at, both stands apart from and participates in the dynamic that Miller has identified.

In stylizing themselves so unmistakably, the televangelists accept a 'place' in the overall system of television which allows viewers to categorize them and thus feel at home with television as usual. However, their place is a deviant one in its emphasis on the non-televisual, both in the reference 'upward' to the divine, directly and via the Book, and in the reference 'outward' to concrete effects for the audience and concrete manners of participation which the audience can avail itself of.[10] This makes for a more 'open' televisual texture than usual, which may paradoxically account for both a general initial impression that this is not 'quality' television and a tendency for the material to stand up rather well when repeatedly viewed (as for this article).

Much more needs to be done to specify the 'televangelical voice' than I have attempted here. What already begins to emerge, however, is a tension between *familiarity* with the divine, as an ongoing, everyday part of the life of the believer, and the more traditional sense of *distance* from the divine which is what distinguishes faith from secularity in the first place. Delivery stylization both incorporates signs of that distance, in harking back to earlier preaching styles and in registering God gesturally as 'elsewhere' (above, inside), and annuls that distance, as the televangelist uses television to 'come close' (with God) to his or her audience. The instability of the various compromises between familiarity and distance is what keeps televangelism both 'vulgar' and fascinating.

9.   M.C. Miller, 'Deride and Conquer', in T. Gitlin (ed.), *Watching Television* (New York: Pantheon, 1987), pp. 183-228.
10.   For an excellent study of the way in which Pat Robertson's broadcasts are only part of a much wider 'support network' for his audience, see S.M. Hoover, *Mass Media Religion* (Newbury Park, CA: Sage, 1988). Hoover brings out, incidentally, how Robertson's comparative closeness to non-religious televisual norms satisfies viewers who are aware of being marginalised in accepting other religious television as 'theirs'.

CHARISMATIC MYSTICISM: A SOCIOLOGICAL ANALYSIS OF THE
'TORONTO BLESSING'*

Philip Richter

1. *Introduction*

'No cameras, no recorders'[1] reads the sign on the door of a south-west London church. Not surprisingly, many of the people currently worshipping there at Sunday services and week-day meetings would not wish to be captured on film or tape. For some it would be too embarrassing and liable to serious misinterpretation. Rolling about the floor, laughing hysterically, or staggering around as if drunk are not features that would normally be associated with church-going in Britain. But, since the 'Toronto Blessing' hit these shores, these and other unusual phenomena have become commonplace at a large number of churches throughout Britain and across different denominations. Although centred outside the mainstream churches, particularly within the 'House Church' or 'New Church' movement, Vineyard Churches and the older pentecostal churches (Fearon 1994: 10), the Toronto Blessing has also affected individual churches within the main denominations. The Toronto Blessing is being reported within the Baptist, Methodist, Salvation Army, Roman Catholic and even Anglican Church, particularly where local churches have already previously been open to Charismatic Renewal. By October 1994 it was estimated that as many as 3000 churches had been affected (Fearon 1994: 146). Perhaps the most publicized Anglican venue has been Holy Trinity Brompton (HTB) in central London. The *Church Times* reported queues two-hours long for the Sunday evening

* This is an expanded version of my chapter in S.E. Porter and P.J. Richter (eds.), *The Toronto Blessing—Or Is It?* (London: Darton, Longman & Todd, 1995), pp. 5-37.

1.   The sign on the door of Queen's Road Church, Wimbledon, reads, in full: 'No cameras or recorders to be used in the meetings. Thank you.'

service last summer at HTB, with up to two thousand people attending (Fearon 1994: 4).

This paper looks at the Toronto Blessing through the eyes of a sociologist. Whilst the opinions of those who have received the Blessing will be taken seriously, the intention here is to put the Blessing into a wider context using tools from the world of sociology. There is no intention to 'explain away' the phenomena. Questions as to the truth, or otherwise, of the Blessing properly lie beyond the sphere of the sociologist.

Religious experiences are categorized by sociologists into four main types: confirming, responsive, ecstatic and revelational (Glock and Stark 1965). The latter types are least frequently found within mainstream religion. The average mainstream churchgoer may from time to time have an awareness of the divine, helping to *confirm* the validity of his or her beliefs. There may even be a sense that the awareness is mutual and that the divine has *responded* in some way. Much less common is the *ecstatic* experience of intimate relationship with the divine and the *revelational* experience in which the person is given messages or a commission by the divine. The Toronto Blessing stands out from ordinary religious experience in being predominantly ecstatic, and in some cases revelational, in form.

The physical characteristics of the Toronto Blessing, which are treated as 'manifestations of the Holy Spirit', are many and varied. Not every feature will be found in every church affected. Typically, you might expect to find the following features:

Bodily weakness and falling to the ground. After a time of what is termed 'ministry'—special prayer by the leader or members of the leadership team—the church will often resemble a surreal battlefield, with scores of people lying on the floor. Some will be lying peacefully, some will be rolling or flailing about, some will be moving their bodies rapidly and rhythmically, even erotically,[2] some will be making judo-like chopping actions with their fore-arms, some will be twitching, some will be sobbing, some will be laughing hysterically. Their 'carpet experience', as its devotees sometimes euphemistically term it, begins when the person starts to sway, falls, or their legs weaken and crumple, and they drop back into the arms of strategically-placed 'catchers'. This is described by recipients as 'falling under the weight of God's glory', being 'overcome by the Spirit' so that they may 'rest in the Spirit'.

2.   Fearon 1994: 10; sexual arousal has in the past been known to be connected with religious ecstasy (Glock and Stark 1965: 52).

Whilst they are on the floor people often report that they feel physically anaesthetized, weighted-down or, sometimes, weight*less*, unable to get up, sometimes for hours, even when they try. They are generally aware of all that is going on around them. The experience is generally pleasurable[3] and the person will often report later that they felt as if a high-voltage electrical charge or 'light' was sweeping through their body, making them 'tingle all over'.

Shaking, trembling, twitching and convulsive bodily movements. Before or after the person falls, or independently of this, their body may twitch or shake uncontrollably. Sometimes this may resemble an epileptic seizure. Indeed children from affected churches in Toronto have been sent home with notes to their parents suggesting that their children be investigated for potential epilepsy![4] The 'Toronto Twitch', often experienced in the stomach region, can occasionally be quite painful, and has been compared to labour pains, although it can be controlled and directed outwards to shake the hands instead. One man at Airport Vineyard Church, Toronto, proudly wears a T-shirt with the legend: 'I'm a JERK FOR JESUS!' (Chevreau 1994: 215).

Uncontrollable laughter or wailing and inconsolable weeping. The Blessing has been associated with extremes of laughter as well as the weeping that might be expected as part of intense Christian religious experience. The laughter ranges from polite giggles to roaring, hysterical, uncontrollable fits of mirth, such as a young child might display when tickled. This 'gut-busting' convulsive laughter disconnects the person from what is going on around them.

Apparent drunkenness. Some people just feel a little giddy, others lose control of their limbs, as if drunk, and are unable to walk in a straight line or even stand, whilst being otherwise fully conscious. The Blessing has been described as drunkenness 'without the hangover and without the expense'.[5] Sometimes people have had to be carried out to their cars after the church service has finished. This drunkenness has reputedly happened in public places, such as restaurants where people have slid off their chairs and rolled about on the floor—and been asked to leave—as well as within the church or home context. This is not the drunkenness of oblivion, but mind and body are temporarily disconnected.

---

3. The experience is not always pleasurable: see Chevreau 1994: 160; MacNutt 1994: 38.
4. Eleanor Mumford: talk at HTB, 29 May 1994.
5. Testimony at Queen's Road Church, Wimbledon, 5 October 1994.

Animal sounds. Sometimes the Blessing involves a person making animal sounds. People have roared like lions, barked like dogs, brayed like donkeys, or even imitated Donald Duck! It has been suggested that the sounds have a physiological source in the 'Toronto Twitch'.

Intense physical activity. People occasionally start running energetically around the church, jogging on the spot, bouncing up and down as if they are on a pogo-stick, even pretending to be 'red-indians' or racing cars![6]

The external physical characteristics of the Blessing do not exhaust its meaning for the individual or church concerned, indeed these are surface phenomena generally reflecting what is reported to be a deeply meaningful, ecstatic[7] religious experience. It may well be accompanied by insights into the future, announcements from God, deep insight into their, or another's, problems,[8] visions (sometimes of hell), and 'out of the body' mystical experiences.

Sometimes the Blessing may be received without extraordinary outward signs. The worshipper may simply raise their hands and feel an immense sense of peace (Fearon 1994: 2).

2. *The Background to the Blessing*

Churches most likely to be affected by the Blessing are those of a pentecostal or charismatic flavour. Pentecostalism as a mass movement began in the first decade of the twentieth century. It stressed the present availability of direct, powerful experience of the Holy Spirit, together with gifts and signs of the Spirit, such as speaking in tongues, miracles, healings and exorcism. By the mid 1920s Classical Pentecostalism gave birth to the Assemblies of God and the Elim Church (presently numbering over 75,000 members). Pentecostalism took a new and surprising turn in the 1960s, when it began to affect all the major denominations, in the form of the Charismatic Renewal. Previously it had been Protestant,

6.   Other very occasional effects include temporary paralysis, blindness, dumbness or deafness, vomiting or hyperventilating (*Renewal*, December 1994: 17).

7.   The 'sense of being engulfed by divine love usually accompanied by extraordinary sensory manifestations and psychic states akin to loss of consciousness or seizures' (Glock and Stark 1965: 54).

8.   The term 'prophecy' is used to describe these first three phenomena (Roberts 1994: 159, 160).

fundamentalist and sectarian, drawing mostly upon the working class. Now (Neo-)Pentecostalism began to attract the middle-class intelligentsia and to take root more widely, even within the Roman Catholic Church. Unlike Classical Pentecostalism the Renewal Movement did not split off from mainstream churches, but remained within as a springboard for change. Charismatic Renewal expressed many of the, increasingly inward-oriented, counter-cultural values of the late 1960s, including a thirst for authentic experience and supra-rational illumination, not tied to out-dated dogmas and centred in the spontaneity of the present moment.[9]

Since the peak of the Renewal Movement, in the late 1970s,[10] an independent network of newly-formed evangelical-Protestant charismatic churches known originally as 'house churches' or 'restorationist churches' has developed, partly as a response to the perceived growing theological liberalism of parts of the Charismatic Renewal Movement and the waning of its initial impetus.[11] Now describing themselves as 'new churches', these churches or 'fellowships' often meet in hired halls for their exuberant, Spirit-centred, 'happy clappy' style of worship. Influential leaders within this 'new churches' network include Terry Virgo, Bryn Jones, John Noble and Gerald Coates. The 'new church' movement has also been influenced by such figures as the American ex-Quaker, charismatic leader John Wimber, with his stress on 'power encounter' with God's present-day 'signs and wonders'. John Wimber's seven 'Vineyard Fellowships' are now an important feature of the charismatic landscape in Britain. It has been estimated that the membership of the 'new churches' grew in the 1980s from about 250,000 to over 350,000, although they may have peaked in the early 1980s.[12] In the meantime, Charismatic Renewal has entered a new phase within the mainstream churches; its worship has become less emotionally volatile and it has broadened its historical focus to include, for instance, Christian mysticism.[13] Recently there have been attempts to forge stronger links

9.   Although the religious context of the Charismatic Renewal prevented it from becoming purely narcissistic: counter-cultural values were set in a distinctive theological and social context. See Neitz 1987: 227-46.

10.   See Walker 1983: 95, 96; cf. Walker 1989: 294 n. 5.

11.   Its roots also include Classical Pentecostalism, Brethrenism, and the Catholic Apostolic Church (Walker 1989: 263).

12.   See Walker 1991: 13; Davie 1994: 62.

13.   This is sometimes termed the 'recovery of disciplines': Church of England 1991: 20, 23, 27.

between existing evangelical churches and the 'new churches', spear-headed by Clive Calver of the Evangelical Alliance, and 'new churches' themselves have patched up many of their erstwhile differences (D. Roberts 1994: 34; Fearon 1994: 214-15).

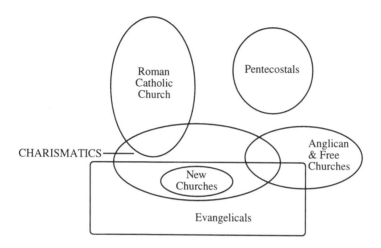

Figure 1. The Charismatics (size of circles does not indicate numbers)

The immediate pre-history of the Toronto Blessing revolves around the figure of 33-year-old, South African-born international Pentecostal evangelist, Rodney Howard-Browne, whose ministry has been widely associated with outbreaks of holy laughter. Howard-Browne was a seminal influence[14] on the leadership of the Airport Vineyard, Toronto and on Randy Clark, the visiting speaker who acted as catalyst for the first outbreak of the Toronto Blessing at Airport Vineyard Church in January 1994. As early as April 1993 people had been travelling from the UK to witness Howard-Browne's extraordinary meetings (D. Roberts 1994: 17).

Most of the features of the Toronto Blessing have been reported within charismatic churches and meetings previously. They are not entirely new phenomena, although the intensity, frequency and spread of these features is said to be unparalleled in recent times. Also the phenomenon seems to have become more 'democratic', less dependent on the ministry of a specific leader of worship and more associated with a 'ministry team'.

14. See Chevreau 1994: 23-25.

The so-called 'Third Wave of the Spirit'[15] in the mid-1980s, particularly associated with John Wimber's international 'power ministry', manifested itself in falling,[16] uncontrollable laughter,[17] shaking, weeping,[18] and bouncing.[19] Indeed the 'Wimber Wobbles' predated the 'Toronto Trots' by ten years,[20] Wimber having first encountered such phenomena in 1979.[21] Wimber's Vineyard Churches have been no strangers to the phenomena of the Blessing in the last decade. Similar manifestations were reported at weekly prayer meetings at Digby Stuart College, south-west London, seven years ago: 'people were bouncing, convulsing, trembling, laughing, crying, and falling over'.[22] 'Slaying in the Spirit' was already prevalent in the Charismatic Renewal in the mid-1970s[23] and was well known to Classical Pentecostalists.[24] George Canty, an Elim leader, has drawn parallels with the 'glory fits' in early Pentecostal cottage meetings.[25]

3. *The Spread of the Blessing*

How has it spread? Its proponents have spoken of the Blessing as a movement of the Spirit, spreading spontaneously from Toronto 'like a virus'.[26] In fact its spread can be explained by more mundane factors reflecting an increasingly 'globalized' world. Modern electronic communications, in the form of national and international phone calls,[27]

---

15.   The first wave was Classical Pentecostalism and the second wave was the Charismatic Renewal.

16.   Lawrence 1992: 120, 121.

17.   Springer 1987: 119, 190. MacNutt notes that laughter was less common than tears at this time (1994: 79).

18.   D. Lewis, *Christian Herald*, 15 October 1994: 3.

19.   Springer 1987: 120 ('like a recently landed fish').

20.   D. Lewis, *Christian Herald*, 15 October 1994: 3. See also MacNutt 1994: 2.

21.   MacNutt 1994: 115.

22.   *The Tablet*, 20 August 1994: 1056.

23.   See Walker 1983: 97.

24.   Poloma and Pendleton (1989: 421) reported that 47% of the membership of the Assemblies of God reported they had been slain.

25.   *Direction* No. 65, October 1994: 41.

26.   Sometimes the Blessing bypassed Toronto altogether and arrived, for instance, via exposure to the ministry of Assemblies of God international evangelist, Claudio Freidzon (Fearon 1994: 95).

27.   Some of the relevant numbers are listed in Chevreau 1994: 175, 183.

faxes, and E-Mail[28] have played a significant part. Magazine articles, for instance in the evangelical magazine *Alpha*, newspaper and TV coverage, and popular paperbacks[29] have helped its spread. Transatlantic air travel by large numbers of church leaders from Britain to see the phenomenon at first hand has also played an important role: Airport Vineyard is literally just at the end of the runway! By September 1994 over 4000 pastors, spouses and leaders had visited, and made their 'pilgrimage', from North America, Great Britain, Chile, Argentina, Switzerland, France, Germany, Scandinavia, South Africa, Nigeria, Kenya, Japan, New Zealand, Australia.[30] British visitors to Airport Vineyard, Toronto have usually brought the Blessing with them on their return to Britain.[31] Eleanor Mumford, wife of the south-west London Vineyard pastor, enthused HTB with the Blessing on 29 May 1994, after her return from Toronto. The tape of her talk has been itself widely circulated.[32] Certain churches have become 'epicentres' of the Blessing, to which curious leaders and members of other churches have flocked for special week-night or late-Sunday-evening meetings dominated by testimony about and experience of the Blessing, with up to 500-600 present (1200 at HTB). The arrival of the Blessing generally depends on the presence and initiative of sympathetic leaders within a church. Leaders themselves, already charismatics or evangelicals, may well have often first come across the phenomenon through their own churches' network[33] or at one of the epicentres. The Tuesday morning 'Leaders Prayer Meetings' during summer 1994 at one such epicentre, Queen's Road Church, Wimbledon, were attended by over 200 leaders per week,

28. See Chevreau 1994: 198.

29. For instance, Chevreau 1994; MacNutt 1994 (especially the new prologue); Roberts 1994; Fearon 1994.

30. See Chevreau 1994: 17.

31. In particular, the Spring 1994 visits of Norman Moss (Queen's Road, Wimbledon), Alan Preston (Church of Christ the King, Brighton), Elli Mumford (South-West London Vineyard) and Bishop David Pytches (St Andrews, Chorleywood) were subsequently extremely influential within the UK (Roberts 1994: 66).

32. The mere playing of the cassette over church PA systems has in some cases led to people 'keeling over' (D. Roberts 1994: 12). Excerpts can be found in Fearon 1994: 102-105.

33. For instance, the Pioneer, New Frontiers, or Covenant networks, which were substantially involved (Fearon 1994: 124).

from all over Britain and Europe. The Blessing was well on show at last summer's large evangelical charismatic gatherings, such as New Wine at Shepton Mallet, attracting 7000, and HTB's Week at Morecambe Bay.

4. How is the Experience Shaped?[34]

Labelling the Experience

The experience labelled 'The Toronto Blessing' has been interpreted by participating churches in broadly similar ways, although the phenomena could be subject to quite different interpretations: John and Charles Wesley, for instance, interpreted spontaneous uncontrollable laughter as the 'buffeting of Satan' (John Wesley's Journal: 9 May 1740 and 21 May 1740) and as a terrorizing experience.[35] It appears that in some cases, at least, the raw experience[36] precedes any knowledge of the Blessing and that in these instances it is not a learned behaviour, but instead attributable to psychological causes.[37] An incident connected with the ministry of USA faith healer, Kathryn Kuhlmann, earlier this century is sometimes cited as an example of what can happen: as Kuhlmann travelled up in a lift to the conference hall at which she was due to speak, the chefs on an intermediate floor spontaneously fell to the ground.[38] The Toronto Blessing has similarly, it is claimed, arrived spontaneously at a number of churches (D. Roberts 1994: 32, 39, 146).

Some phenomena associated with the Blessing have been interpreted

---

34. The structure of this section of the paper partly derives from Spickard's (1993) categorization of sociological approaches to religious experience.

35. See Glock and Stark 1965: 63.

36. Once we begin to talk of 'religious experiences' the notion of 'raw experience' becomes less meaningful: 'to be religious is at least partly to have a framework within which to interpret experience, and the interpretation will be part of the experience' (Spilka 1985: 164).

37. This is not to preclude the possibility that the Holy Spirit may also be operating.

38. This is recounted in *The Anointing*, by Benny Hinn, one of the seminal figures (D. Roberts 1994: 15) behind the Toronto Blessing. It was cited by the pastor at the late-Sunday-evening meeting at Queen's Road Church, 13 November 1994. John Wimber cites an instance of 'falling' associated with a non-pentecostal church 'with (no prior) experience or understanding of the sort of things that began to happen' (Wimber 1985: 24-27). See also MacNutt 1994: 164.

differently by non-participating churches, or even historically within Charismatic Renewal. Roaring like a lion has been interpreted by some as a prophetic symbol referring to Jesus as the 'Lion of Judah', in one case breaking the power of the Dragon over the Chinese people,[39] in another case 'literally chasing out the power of sin and declaring His righteous anger at the remaining captivity of (the recipient's) soul' (Chevreau 1994: 187, 188). Others, referring instead to C.S. Lewis's *The Lion, The Witch, and The Wardrobe*, have interpreted the roaring as a sign that 'Aslan is coming' (*HTB in Focus*, 14 August 1994: 7). Still others have seen it as a sign that God is 'putting some backbone back into our men' (*HTB in Focus*, 14 August 1994: 4)! Clifford Hill has criticized the phenomenon, noting that the prophet Jeremiah associates roaring like a lion with 'the occult spirit of Babylon' (*Dunamis*, Autumn 1994, no. 89: 11).[40] The phenomenon of 'falling' has been labelled in different ways. The traditional description of falling within Pentecostalism is 'being slain in the Spirit'. Where falling occurs as part of the Blessing its proponents prefer terms such as 'resting in the Spirit', because the older term does not do justice to the sense of peace and the divine enlivening and empowerment that is said to be received (MacNutt 1994: 24, 27; Chevreau 1994: 15).

Some phenomena have not found widespread acceptance within participating churches. John Wimber, for instance, has been concerned about the occurrence of barnyard animal and other zoological noises, and is reported as saying: 'I [do not] see it as something that ought to be endorsed, embraced, affirmed or accepted by the Church. I think we ought to ignore it' (*Church Times*, 30 September 1994: 8). The Elim Churches magazine *Direction* similarly had hesitations about animal noises on the grounds that God only 'humbles but never humiliates those who truly seek Him' (October 1994: 6). Even those who initially welcomed animal noises as part of the Blessing may, with hindsight, discount these phenomena.[41] Gerald Coates has questioned whether convulsions are a valid part of the Blessing, on the grounds that most, if not

39. Eleanor Mumford interpreted the roaring of Gideon, a young Chinese pastor, in these terms (HTB, 29 May 1994).

40. MacNutt also attributes roaring and growling like animals to demonic sources (1994: 64).

41. A *retrospective interpretation* may here be correcting a previous spontaneously offered *reflexive interpretation* (Spilka 1985: 181).

all, Scripture references to convulsions attribute them to a demonic source (*Renewal*, November 1994: 25).[42]

Getting the Idea

Normally a person will experience the Blessing only after accepting that the experience exists and what it means, or, at least, after weighing up carefully the idea of the experience. This experimental 'Beroean' (Acts 17.10-11) attitude to the idea of the Blessing is actively reinforced by the leadership who urge those interested to sit and 'look on and weigh up things'.[43] One twenty-three year old free-lance journalist told how she had said to God: 'Lord, I don't understand what's happening. If it's from you help me to understand it'.[44] Where significant others—co-religionists, respected 'level-headed' church leaders, friends or family—have already accepted the Blessing as a desirable and beneficial phenomenon a positive outcome to the weighing-up process may be predicted; in particular 'the leaders are the gatekeepers and what they will allow'[45] the people feel confident to allow (Vineyard Toronto leaflet, 20 April 1994). As Mary Jo Neitz concluded in her work on Roman Catholic Charismatics: 'what one finds is an interplay between "what is believed to be possible" and "what is", through which a general belief

42. Evangelical leaders have publicly admitted that they hold a diversity of attitudes to the Toronto Blessing: 'some have grave reservations about the value and significance of recent events…others speak of 1994 as a year of remarkable spiritual blessing' (Statement signed by fifty evangelical leaders, reported in *The Tablet*, 21 January 1995, p. 91).

43. Norman Moss: Queen's Road Church, 13 November 1994.

44. Personal interview. The 'experimental' approach is a well-attested feature of religious conversion processes in contemporary society (see, for instance, J. Lofland and N. Skonovd [1981] 'Conversion Motifs', *Journal for the Scientific Study of Religion*, 20.4: 373-85, 378-79); not surprisingly, believers will also adopt this approach when weighing up the merits of new religious phenomena (see, for example, Chevreau 1994: 176).

45. The leader generally exerts considerable control over the appearance of the phenomena associated with the Blessing. Where a leader fears that a meeting is getting out of control he will, for instance, announce the singing of a well-known traditional hymn such as 'Praise, my soul, the King of heaven' (see also D. Roberts 1994: 157). Where, on the other hand, a leader is happy to inspire relative spiritual anarchy he may suggest beforehand that God is moving in very novel ways and that we must 'keep up with the pace of the Spirit', even, as at York Vineyard Church, apparently inspiring people to sit on the floor pretending to be racing cars! Cf. MacNutt 1994: 150.

becomes meaningful for an individual in a particular situation' (Neitz 1987: 99).[46]

Perhaps the most important ways by which people are introduced to the idea of the Blessing are by means of introductory talks by the leadership and personal testimonies by recipients of the experience, within services and meetings.[47] Sometimes roving microphones are taken to people already 'on the carpet' and an informal interview is broadcast over the PA system; this practice amplifies the phenomenon in more ways than one![48] Interpretations of the Blessing vary, but include references to a sense of the awesome Presence of God contrasted with human sinfulness, his sovereign authority, his[49] joy, his peace, his nearness, his pleasure, his power, his brilliant glory. The Blessing is said to be accompanied by such features as a deeper love for and intimacy with God, a new love for Jesus, a greater sense of expectancy, forgiveness, emotional healing, the healing of relationships, physical healings, a new passion to read Scripture which itself 'comes to life', a desire and courage to witness, an increased desire to pray, commitment to evangelism, boldness to challenge unrighteousness, injustice and corruption in society, and, occasionally, deliverance from demonic influence. Sometimes the physical phenomena are interpreted as prophetic symbolic action on the part of God who is, for instance, believed to be (literally) 'shaking' the recipient out of their complacency and self-sufficiency[50] or demonstrating 'human weakness' to induce

46. Neitz describes how one woman received her first vision: 'with a new definition of visions she suddenly began to have them' (Neitz 1987: 104). Poloma and Pendleton in their recent study of the Assemblies of God concluded that 'belief in the availability and desirability of Pentecostal experiences seemed to pave the way for them' (1989: 428).

47. Some of these testimonies have been reproduced in popular paperback treatments of the Blessing (for instance, Chevreau 1994: 145-204). Teaching about, and practical experience of, the Holy Spirit is also an important component of the 'Alpha' course designed to introduce people to Christian faith, pioneered at HTB and now in use at over 500 churches.

48. At the Rodney Howard-Browne 'Signs and Wonders' meeting at Wembley Conference Centre, 12-15 December 1994, closed-circuit television pictures of those undergoing the Blessing were projected on to a huge screen behind the stage.

49. Sometimes reference is made to Jesus, sometimes to God: the term 'Lord' is ambiguous. Sexually-inclusive language is not used of the Godhead.

50. The case of St Paul is cited in comparison: he was literally 'knocked off his high horse' by God (Chevreau 1994: 68).

humility (*HTB in Focus*, 14 August 1994: 9; MacNutt 1994: 30, 173). It is generally described as being primarily for the already converted and a 'time of refreshment'. Sometimes people are warned that it might be, rarely, a bad experience, if they have not previously repented.

There is inevitably a high degree of informal social pressure on people to follow the lead of co-religionists who have already experienced the Blessing, reflected sociologically in frequent references by the leadership to the presence of the 'power of God' in the worship setting.[51] This is accentuated at some churches by the practice of removing chairs during 'ministry time' whilst many are standing to receive the Blessing or have already fallen; those still seated easily begin to feel 'the odd one out'.

Learning to Have the Blessing
Although favourable ideas about the Blessing are usually an important precondition for receiving and sharing the experience, any religious experience is also shaped by less conceptual means. Techniques and practical tips are passed on as part of a process of practical personal guidance for the individual who is trying to receive the experience,[52] much as a driving instructor helps the learner translate theory into practice on the road. Some of the practical advice comes from reading religious magazine articles (Poloma and Pendleton 1989: 428) and popular paperbacks about the Blessing. Many of the services and meetings within which it occurs are orchestrated[53] in such a way that early on there are practical demonstrations of individuals being prayed for and falling, often after they have publicly testified about the experience (D. Roberts 1994: 78). Practical guidance is later more personally mediated when members of the (lay) 'ministry team' pray in pairs with those wishing to receive the blessing. They may or may not make physical contact with the individual, but one of them will usually place or agitate his or her hand near the person's forehead, whilst another will be ready to act as 'catcher'. The ministry team will normally have been through an 'apprenticeship' period (D. Roberts 1994: 69) and have been

51. The Toronto worship setting is more fully described by D. Roberts 1994: 77-78.

52. For the would-be meditator in a rather different religious tradition this may take the form of suggestions such as taking up an alternative bodily posture or the provision of a mantra (Spickard 1993: 4).

53. The 'stage-management' metaphor is used of the Renewal Movement, both by the (sympathetic) sociologist Margaret Poloma (1982: 164) and by Peter Lawrence, a proponent of the movement (1992: 235).

trained according to certain accepted guidelines within that specific church, often borrowed from other churches. Vineyard Church Toronto's 'Suggested Ministry Tips' (20 April 1994), augmented by HTB's 'Ministry Values' (15 June 1994), have been widely circulated. These include the following 'Tips for Praying for People':

1. If the person is one of the 'hard ones' you might help them (by calming) their fears over loss of control by helping them know what to expect. For example, let them know that they will have a clear mind, that they can usually stop the process at any point if they want to, and that the Spirit comes in waves.

2. Some people have 'fear of falling' issues. Help them to sit down or to fall carefully, especially if they have back problems, pregnancy or fear of falling.

Members of ministry teams will encourage those they are praying with to face their fears—'the fear of deception; the fear of being hurt again or not receiving at all; the fear of losing control'.[54] They will urge them to 'focus on the Lord, not on falling' and to 'give the Holy Spirit permission to do with you what He wants to do' (Vineyard Toronto, 20 April 1994). Often those ministering will repeat short phrases such as: 'Receive His power', 'The Lord is with you', 'More of your Spirit, God' or 'Breathe in the Spirit', which are designed to increase receptivity. Perhaps the most important part of the technique is the advice to stop analysing and 'just relax and ask him to come' (Lawrence 1992: 131; D. Roberts 1994: 141).

5. *Tired Leaders, Tired Churches—Why Have Churches Invested in the Toronto Blessing?*

Investment in the Blessing has been costly in terms of time, energy and, not least, money: transatlantic air trips to Toronto do not exactly come cheaply![55] This level of investment suggests that the Blessing is expected to have tangible benefits for the individuals and particularly churches involved. These are not confined to spiritual benefits. Indeed the

54. There are at least two main types of fear to be dealt with: (1) the fear that God will come and hence an implicit rejection of God's sovereignty and (2) the fear that he will not come, reflecting a sense of personal unworthiness to receive the Blessing; see Lawrence 1992: 129, 130.

55. £3500 was raised by Sunderland Christian Centre for this purpose in a single offering (D. Roberts 1994: 54).

Blessing may have come at a strategically useful time in the life-cycle of the churches concerned and the careers of their leaders. In addition, it may be what the 'charismatic market'[56] demands. The advent of the Blessing at this time makes sense when it is viewed alongside two major problems affecting charismatic churches: the precariousness of their market and the precariousness of charisma.[57]

A Precarious Market
One plausible reason for churches investing in the Blessing is as a means of safeguarding their share of a relatively static market. Evangelical charismatics have for some years begun to perceive each other less as competitors and more as salesmen/women of a similar product, simply 'marginally differentiated'[58] between almost identical brands. They have also tried to forge links with non-charismatic evangelicals.[59] This has probably partly been a response to the precariousness of their market. In spite of intensive investment in evangelism and church-planting the charismatic customer-base has not grown as much as anticipated in recent years. One explanation for this might be that the market has been fully-exploited: the market for charismatic Christianity may be more limited than they imagine. The JIM Mission in July 1994 spearheaded by Elim and the Assemblies of God aimed to mobilize 250,000 Christians to reach 250,000 souls for Christ. In the event only between twenty and thirty thousand responded with some sort of faith-response (*Alpha*, July 1994: 12, 13). At the same time, charismatic churches are suffering the perennial problem that faces every new movement: boredom and apathy on the part of the second generation. Churches risk losing their teen-agers who have grown up accustomed to charismatic phenomena.[60]

---

56. Contemporary consumerist society has extended the idea of *consumption* into the world of the sacred, although some churches have opposed this model (Davie 1994: 39, 40, 20, 21).

57. See Wallis 1984: 86-118.

58. Berger applied a similar model to the ecumenical movement (Berger 1969: 140-49).

59. The Toronto Blessing has been presented as a manifestation of *revival*, in order to emphasize common ground with evangelicals.

60. Even the exceptional intensity of the Toronto Blessing may not be enough to retain their commitment: at Airport Vineyard Toronto Roberts reports that the eleven-to-fourteen-year-olds 'don't think what's happening is "cool"' (D. Roberts 1994: 80). Some British church-teenagers are hesitant about the Blessing because it appears too 'New-Ageish' or even cult-like.

Many charismatic churches seem to have seized on the Blessing as a means of retaining their customers. They have had to become more 'sensitive to their market'. Significantly, the Blessing is perceived as predominantly a 'time of refreshing' for the already-converted. One response to market stagnation is to give the customer 'more of the same'[61] or more of what attracted them in the first place, rekindling the original fire. The Blessing has been described as 'the spiritual equivalant (*sic*) of a seven-course dinner at a fancy restaurant' (*Alpha*, September 1994: 4). Charismatic customers demand something more than they could get in virtually any other church. The initial attractions of the charismatic renewal included the sense of novelty and excitement that it gave, the direct, unmediated and unpredictable encounter with God that it offered, and the heady experience of the power of a God who was anything but dead. In many respects this represented a reaction against key characteristics of modern society.[62] Ironically, as we shall see below, charismatic churches have been themselves increasingly infiltrated by the modernity which is so inimical to charisma. The Blessing has come at a time when, as leading Baptist minister Rob Warner put it, 'the fresh sparkle of novelty (had) been increasingly replaced by familiarity': the Spirit had been domesticated and tamed (*Renewal*, November 1994: 10). Sandy Millar, vicar of HTB, spoke for many when he said: '(renewal) was looking very tired...these manifestations are restoring to us the intimacy with God for which we cried out when we first became Christians' (*Church Times*, 23 September 1994: 7). Many have spoken of 'returning to their first love' or of 'falling in love with Jesus all over again' (Chevreau 1994: 182).

Another response to market stagnation is to adjust to shifts in consumer preferences. Where people are under increasing stress and risk 'burnout'[63] in their working lives, it is not surprising that the religious

61. An alternative description for this process as it affects the religious market might be 'the further transcendentalizing of one's product' (Wallis 1984: 101).

62. Walker 1987: 203, 204; although the comparison would horrify many charismatics, in this respect they are similar to Counter-Cultural, Human Potential or New Age movements, equally often anti-modern in orientation. See York 1994; Neitz 1987: 228, 238, 239.

63. A recent report by Professor Cary Cooper for the Health and Safety Executive lists the following most stressful jobs: teachers, doctors, dentists, nurses, social workers, uniformed services, middle managers, blue collar workers, public utility workers and workers in the media (*The Guardian*, 17 November 1994: 3); see also Handy 1994: 9, 28, 179. Significantly, this coincides strongly with the

consumer may prefer not to be constantly under pressure from their church to be hyperactive for the Lord, but, instead, to be attracted by a phenomenon that gives them the opportunity to 'rest in the Spirit'.[64] Eleanor Mumford spoke of 'many very weary pastors' and their 'even more weary wives' flocking to Toronto (HTB, 29 May 1994; see also Chevreau 1994: 19; D. Roberts 1994: 163).

Precarious Charisma

One reason why the leadership of charismatic churches has been so interested in promoting the Blessing may be their hope that it will renew the charismatic appeal of their leadership and reverse tendencies to become just like any other organization. In the world of sociology the term 'charismatic' has a slightly different meaning to the one we have presupposed so far.[65] When the term is used of a leader it usually denotes an extraordinary individual considered to have exceptional, even superhuman, powers or qualities. The successful charismatic leader generates a personal following, based on his/her perceived ability to resolve certain problems or crises for the followers. Charisma dynamically transcends both the ordinary routine of everyday life and traditional religious apparatus. However, charisma is intrinsically volatile and ephemeral. It typically evaporates or becomes 'routinized' over the course of time, especially when the leaders age and die, as is starting to happen within charismatic renewal.[66] One of the special features of 'charismatic churches' is the way in which the property of charisma, in the sociological sense, is perceived to be shared by the membership and to permeate the whole group (Poloma 1982: 34).

If you had been asked to classify the leaders of charismatic 'new

occupational profile of the Queen's Road Church, Wimbledon membership.

64. The more laid-back, less strident, approach of pastors and evangelists may also reflect changing preferences on the part of the religious consumer (Roberts 1994: 90). Although there is much talk of new models of ministry, involving greater lay involvement (Chevreau 1994: 62, 153; D. Roberts 1994: 120) and the pastor acting more as a 'coach' or 'facilitator', this may simply be a different way of the present leadership exercising power.

65. See the sociology of Max Weber (1864–1920) and his followers, for instance: Wallis 1984: 103-18; Poloma 1982: 170, 230-33, 239, 241.

66. Rob Warner has noted that 'First-generation renewal has been around for more than a generation. Several early leaders have died, others are drawing near to retirement, and so need to begin to hand over the reins' (*Renewal*, November 1994: 10).

churches' in terms of the type of authority they exercised, then, in the early days, you might have placed them towards the 'charismatic authority' end of the spectrum. Although one has to reckon with some retrospective mythologizing it appears that their followers were frequently on first-name terms with them and organization was relatively free and unstructured (Walker 1989: 53, 58, 61, 283).[67] Nowadays many of the leaders, at national and local levels, have begun to wake up to the fact that their leadership style has drifted along the spectrum and become less charismatic and more bureaucratic, akin to that exercised by captains of industry. Baptist minister and author of a popular paperback on the Blessing, Guy Chevreau, confessed that in recent years he had immersed himself in books about 'leadership, innovation, infrastructure, time management, goal setting and strategic planning' (Chevreau 1994: 12; cf. 184). Chevreau suggests that countless church leaders have, with the best of intentions, 'run aground, if not exhausted themselves and the churches they serve' thanks to the influence of 'growth and business management strategies' (Chevreau 1994: 206).

Inevitably, for charisma to survive, albeit in attenuated form, it must be institutionalized in more 'efficient' and 'rational' ways such as this. Nevertheless this still leaves a series of problems for charismatic churches. If the charismatic movement has been partly a reaction against modernity, the increasing adoption of distinctly modern management styles by the leadership is bound to stimulate nostalgia for a more charismatic leadership style. Leaders, often close to burnout because of the new leadership styles, have an extra incentive to turn back the clock. For some, the Toronto Blessing has given the opportunity for having a kind of religious 'mid-life crisis' in which they have radically reevaluated the direction of their ministries. Ken Costa, HTB churchwarden, confessed that 'we've tried might and power and organisation of the church—and we've seen nothing but the decline of every form of our expression of love towards God' (*HTB in FOCUS*, 14 August 1994: 9). Fort Wayne Vineyard pastor Ron Allen's description of his departure for Toronto is highly symbolic: 'I left my computer (and) took my Bible' (Chevreau 1994: 150). With the help of the transfusion of the Blessing leaders have begun to renew their charismatic appeal.[68] Hot-foot from

---

67. More rational structures of leadership began to be established in the early 1970s, Bryn Jones, in particular, pioneering 'successful and rational financial structures' (Walker 1989: 73, 70).

68. See also Poloma's treatment of routinization of charisma amongst Catholic

Toronto, they offer a dynamic new phenomenon that they hope will turn their churches, and indeed the world, 'upside down' in the spirit of Acts 17.6.

Paradoxically, the Toronto Blessing is itself very much part and parcel of the modern world. Its rapid spread owes a lot to the latest communications technology and the availability of mass transatlantic air travel. At a more profound level, its proponents speak of it in pragmatic terms that reflect the functional rationality that dominates western societies. 'If it works, trust it!' seems to be the message.[69] 'It is not means, but the end that is of consequence' (Chevreau 1994: 143-44).

6. Why Has the Blessing Taken This Form?

The Blessing could have taken other forms. For instance, religious consumer interest could have been revived by means of snake-handling or walking on red-hot coals, phenomena already extant within fringe evangelical groups in the USA. Instead, the Blessing is characterized by such features as bodily disinhibition, a strong sense of God being 'in control', and, at times, a mystical sense that the experience of God cannot be expressed in human language. I want to suggest that each of these three features could have been predicted in the light of socio-economic and cultural changes affecting the churches concerned.

a. *From Fasting to Pogoing—Changing Attitudes to Bodily Disinhibition*
Until recently, evangelical attitudes to the body have been very strait-laced and restrained. Evangelicals have been expected to be always in control of their bodies and their emotions which are 'for the Lord' (Synnott 1992: 91). If evangelicals of previous generations were to witness the (spiritual) drunkenness sometimes associated with the Blessing they might well turn in their graves.[70] HTB has had to reassure taxi drivers that their fares are '"not drunk as you suppose" and safe to

Charismatics (1982: 170, 230-33, 238-39, 241) and the Assemblies of God (1989: 419).
    69. See further, Hervieu-Léger 1993: 145; as with other forms of fundamentalism the Blessing is both antimodern and distinctively modern (Robertson 1992: 170).
    70. The sight of the (sober, but bodily-expressive) former topless model and now born-again Christian, Samantha Fox, singing at the summer 1994 *Greenbelt* Christian arts festival might have further disoriented them!

have in the taxi' (D. Roberts 1994: 33-34). Although the mind is clear, the body is overtaken by spiritual drunkenness, and behaves as if inebriated by alcohol (Fearon 1994: 27).[71] Old-style evangelicals might also be unhappy that the practice of totally abstaining from alcohol has gone out of fashion in many evangelical churches (Hunter 1987: 58-59), especially those that are charismatic (Walker 1983: 96; Walker 1989: 97). Alcohol-induced drunkenness is not approved of, but drinking that leads to lesser degrees of bodily disinhibition is no longer necessarily castigated. The body has begun to be experienced as something that can be enjoyed, rather than, as before, feared and watched at all times lest it get out of control. Evangelical charismatics have increasingly adopted a positive and holistic view of the human person, in contrast to earlier, dualistic and Cartesian, views that devalued the body and treated it like a (dangerous) machine.[72] This is reflected in the holistic orientation of charismatic healing ministry (Neitz 1987: 237-38)[73] and in modern evangelical attitudes to sex which no longer believe that 'Sex is dirty... Sex is disgusting... Sex is degrading... Save it for your wife!' (Chalke in *Alpha*, December 1994: 39).

During the second half of the twentieth century, in particular, attitudes to bodily disinhibition have undergone a sea-change throughout society. Historically, capitalism had demanded self-discipline, restraint, the sub-ordination of animal passions, frugality and regularity (including the bowels!) from its workforce and this had been reflected in the inner-worldly asceticism of the 'Protestant Ethic', which remained influential long after its Puritan roots were forgotten (Turner 1984: 64-65, 218; Turner 1992: 196-97). The Protestant Ethic was eventually undermined by the 'new capitalism' dating from the early decades of the twentieth century, which needed 'to stimulate a demand for pleasure and play in the area of consumption' (Bell 1976: 75; Turner 1984: 25, 172). Consumers, with the help of easy-credit, came to expect instant, rather than deferred, gratification. The 1960s counter culture replaced 'good-ness morality' with the 'fun morality' of a more permissive society

71. See, for instance, Chevreau 1994: 13.

72. Neitz 1987: 238; at the same time sociologists of religion have begun to take a greater interest in the human body (McGuire 1990)!

73. It has been said of the Blessing that 'it's almost as if the medical and spiritual are coming together as one!' (Chevreau 1994: 181). Proponents of the Blessing acknowledge that other secular or pagan forms of therapy have a similar holistic orientation: for instance, the 'laughter therapy' of New Age (D. Roberts 1994: 144).

(Bell 1976: 71). The result is that the late capitalist consumer is expected to be permanently unsatiated and 'seething with desire for new things and experiences' (Simpson 1993: 156).[74]

The relatively new evangelical attitudes to relaxation of bodily restraints reflect these wider socio-economic changes, which, given the strength of traditional evangelical attitudes, have taken some time to percolate through, although they had already been previewed in the demonstrative 'happy clappy' worship of charismatic churches.[75] 'All my life I've longed to be naughty', Eleanor Mumford confessed to HTB. It was the Blessing that finally permitted her to 'roll about on the floor like a drunk woman'![76] Frugality and fasting seem to have gone out of fashion, instead it is as if the worshipper is invited to a high-spirited party.[77] 'God is (no longer) a god of moderation in all things'.[78]

Not surprisingly, the Toronto Blessing reflects and reinforces some of the features of consumerist society. Pastors teach that recipients should not be satisfied with just one experience of the Blessing: 'don't be afraid to come for more and more and more'.[79] Like the material abundance of consumer society the Blessing is not in short supply! The consumer goals of happiness, health and personal fulfilment painlessly accompany the Blessing. Indeed, secular therapists have been impressed by the way in which the Blessing short-cuts many of their methods.[80] The theological background to the Blessing downplays more mainstream traditional Christian teaching that speaks in terms of self-giving, self-sacrifice and self-denial. John Wimber has been criticized for neglecting the cross and suffering in his own teaching[81] and both Rodney Howard-Browne and

74. See also Featherstone 1991.

75. As one might expect, older-style evangelical churches which still publicly disapprove of drinking are less likely to be enthusiastic about the Toronto Blessing.

76. HTB, 29 May 1994.

77. Mumford, HTB talk. Chevreau cites a story from the desert fathers: a young monk asks an older, wiser monk what else he should do—'I (already) practise a little fasting…'—'Become FIRE!!!' the older monk advises (Chevreau 1994: 205). Interestingly, discipline and self-denial would seem to make an individual less susceptible to falling (MacNutt 1994: 137).

78. Rob Warner, 'Times of Refreshing' Conference, Queen's Road Church, Wimbledon, 29 November 1994.

79. Queen's Road Church, 23 October 1994. See also Chevreau 1994: 200.

80. *Renewal*, November 1994: 15, 27.

81. 'Making Room for a Visit from God', *Church Times*, 30 September 1994; see also Church of England 1991: 106.

Benny Hinn, long-time friend of Airport Vineyard pastor John Arnott, have been associated with the 'health and wealth' 'prosperity gospel' of the 'Word of Faith' movement (D. Roberts 1994: 62, 96-99; Fearon 1994: 105-107). In such ways the bodily disinhibition associated with the Blessing appears to fit and reflect the consumerist society of modern Britain. One of the acknowledged dangers for the Blessing is that within this context of 'commodity culture' it will be treated merely as 'a trip for its own sake' and eventually discarded for the next 'latest thing' (Fearon 1994: 190).

Simultaneously, the bodily disinhibition of the Blessing might also be interpreted as a form of resistance to increasing societal, or even, in some cases, church, control over the body. The human body can sometimes become a 'source of playful energies' and a 'site of resistance' to societal over-regulation of the body.[82] This may help to explain one of the functions of the Blessing. In spite of signs of economic recovery, British consumers in 1994 still felt constrained to spend modestly and carefully.[83] After the credit-financed 'spend...spend' 1980s, consumers, often now with 'negative equity' mortgages, preferred to hold on to their savings. This was still perceived to be a time of economic self-restraint. Some workers, who found themselves having to begin to work on Sundays, experienced the invasion of their erstwhile leisure time.[84] The experience of the Blessing represents one way in which consumers and workers were able to, temporarily at least, escape, through 'ludic religion' (R. Roberts 1994: 8), some of these economic constraints.

The Blessing, in some cases, represents a response to over-heavy regulation of the body by churches. The 'shepherding' or 'covering' practised by some new churches has sometimes extended to control by the leadership of a person's love life or place of residence (Walker 1987: 201-202; Walker 1989: 285-93, 177-88; Enroth 1992).[85] MacNutt

82. See McGuire 1990: 293; Turner 1992: 10; 'the body, as simultaneously constraint and resistance...is the dominant means by which the tensions and crises of society are thematized' (Turner 1992: 12).

83. 'Barclaycard says shoppers intend to emulate Scrooge', *The Guardian*, 22 November 1994; see also Handy 1994: 37.

84. Richter 1994.

85. The words of prophecy sometimes uttered by recipients of the Blessing might also function as a form of resistance to heavy direction by the leadership. Revelational experience of this kind is always potentially subversive of existing religious hierarchy (Glock and Stark 1965: 56-57). Even those churches that encourage or tolerate revelational experiences may treat them with caution: the Evangelical Alliance has

describes how a woman found release, through being overcome by the Spirit, after experiencing the strictest form of shepherding for a period of eight years (MacNutt 1994: 69).

b. *God is Not a Gentleman!—Changing Attitudes to Divine Gender Roles?*

The God of the Toronto Blessing is strongly characterized as a macho male. This is a God who is dynamic and forceful and very much in control. Proponents of the Blessing have repeatedly stated that the old idea that 'God is a gentleman' (both polite and English!) is out of date and inaccurate. It is repeatedly claimed that there is no biblical basis for the belief that 'the Holy Spirit is a gentleman, and does nothing without our consent' (Chevreau 1994: 101) nor anything 'to embarrass you' (D. Roberts 1994: 159). 'God is not a wimpish fop, but a red-blooded male' seems to be the message. Equally, the church leadership needs to have some male 'backbone' put back into it by the Blessing.[86]

The Toronto Blessing appears to be, consciously or unconsciously, part of a move to re-masculinize the church. The reader who is used to thinking of the institutional churches as bastions of patriarchy and resistance to women's ministry may be surprised to find the argument framed in these terms. Nevertheless, feminization has affected most churches, particularly since the nineteenth century. As the process of secularization has increasingly deprived religion of social power and restricted its influence to the private sphere of home and family so God and Jesus have been depicted in gentler terms.[87] The activity of God has been seen less in terms of control and domination and more as characterized by caring and nurturing.[88] 'Gentle Jesus, meek and mild' has been the order of the day (Fearon 1994: 139).

Receiving the Blessing involves a willingness to surrender control to a God 'who is in control and sovereign'.[89] 'God is not a gentleman, God

recently expressed concern about 'false memories' of child sexual abuse elicited by 'words of knowledge' (*The Independent*, 17 December 1994).

86. Mary Pytches (*HTB in FOCUS*, 14 August 1994: 4). Although there are also moves in the direction of the 'new man' who is able, for instance, to cry in public as part of the Blessing (*Direction* No 65, October 1994: 3).

87. See Roberts 1984: 356-57.

88. Carl W. Roberts (1989) notes that women have a greater tendency than men to characterize God as nurturing; men, by contrast, tend to speak of a God of 'power, planning and control' (Davie 1994: 119-20).

89. 'Renewal Manifestations', Foothills Christian Fellowship, El Cajon, CA.

is God' (*Alpha*, September 1994: 3). The secret is to 'give God the reins and let him reign'. One recipient reported that 'the Lord came...and overpowered me in such a way that I know His ability to give is greater than my unwitting ability to resist' (Chevreau 1994: 158). Rodney Howard-Browne warned his 'Signs and Wonders' audience at the Wembley Conference Centre: 'some of you are going to get hit tonight [just] because you're sitting in the wrong seat!' (13 December 1994). Being 'overcome by the Spirit' is interpreted as 'an extraordinary demonstration of God's omnipotence' (MacNutt 1994: 46). Here we have a God made in *man's* image, the 'deification of unilateral power', reflecting masculinist notions of the nature of power (Clack 1994).[90]

Whilst the Blessing helps to re-masculinize God and the (male) church leadership,[91] obversely it places the ordinary recipient of the Blessing into a fairly passive, traditionally-feminine role, which, particularly as far as women are concerned, is likely to be disempowering. The relationship between Jesus and the worshipper is analogous to that between husband and wife. The church is identified as the Bride of Christ, for whom Jesus is coming.[92] Quasi-sexual imagery is sometimes used to describe the Blessing experience. One (female) recipient reported: 'I'm actually just enjoying Jesus, and have the sense He's enjoying me' (Chevreau 1994: 161).[93] In some cases recipients describe their experience in terms of the labour of child-birth (Chevreau 1994: 159). Ironically, the more passive the worshipper is, the more impersonal is the divine-human relationship, such that the Holy Spirit eventually becomes more an 'it' than a 'he', as we shall see below. The experience does not demand complete passivity from the recipient, since this would make it an impersonal affair, instead of a genuine *relationship* with the Holy Spirit.

---

90. The Toronto Blessing may also offer a person who usually carries heavy responsibilities, at work or church, the refreshing chance to be not always in control. Equally, for those used to being at the beck and call of others the Blessing may offer the chance to be controlled by a beneficent, rather than merely bureaucratic, power.

91. Although the Toronto Blessing (literally) knocks the leaders off their feet and makes them look silly (D. Roberts 1994: 41) paradoxically it also reinvigorates their authority. As in the Roman Saturnalia rites or the Feast of Fools, the temporary suspension of a leader's authority, with the incipient fear of chaos that brings, may make the reassertion of that authority even more welcome. The temporary humiliation of the leader may also reflect sectarian egalitarianism.

92. Eleanor Mumford, HTB, 29 May 1994.

93. Note the asymmetry of the relationship symbolized in the upper case used for the divine personal pronoun.

c. *Charismatic Mysticism—Changing Communication Patterns*
The Toronto Blessing is essentially a non-verbal form of religious experience. It is true that it can be accompanied by words of various kinds of prophecy and recipients are encouraged to verbalize and write down what they have experienced, but at its heart the Blessing is non-verbal in form. In fact it is sometimes described in mystical terms (Fearon 1994: 199). It has sometimes been compared to the experience of Christian mystics such as Teresa of Avila (MacNutt 1994: 18, 35, 88). Interestingly, Jonathan Edwards, eighteenth-century evangelist and one of the historical heroes of the Toronto Blessing movement, has himself been described as an 'evangelical mystic'.[94] Mysticism is a mode of religious experience typically involving such features as a sense of oneness with all things, a sense of timelessness and spacelessness, a sense of deep and profound peace, the dissolution of sense of self,[95] and a sense of ineffability—the mystical experience is beyond human language and in some cases the mind may simply be conscious of 'the void' (Spilka 1985: 176-78; Hay 1987: 91-92).[96] Rudolf Otto characterized mysticism as in essence 'the overstressing of the non-rational or supra-rational elements in religion' (Otto 1923: 22). Evangelicals are, however, keen to distance themselves from what they term 'Eastern mysticism' and its 'disengagement of the mind' (*Alpha*, October 1994: 6).[97]

Charismatics claim that they have been taught by the Blessing that they had become 'too matey with God'. They have rediscovered that God will not fit human 'boxes' and bursts out of human thought categories: God is 'supra-rational'. They distance themselves from the 'rational evangelical god of the intellect' (Poloma 1989: 418; Roberts 1994: 183). Recipients of the Blessing sometimes describe their experience, in impersonal terms, as 'being surrounded by the light of God', as

94. Chevreau 1994: 71; Sarah Edwards, his wife, reports that 'the glory of God seemed to be all, and in all, and to swallow up every wish and desire of my heart' and that her 'soul has been as it were overwhelmed, and swallowed up with light and love, a sweet solace altogether unspeakable...' (cited in Chevreau 1994: 79, 80, 85).

95. Interestingly, Neitz has also noted that the 'line between self and God is ambiguous' amongst Catholic charismatics (1987: 236).

96. The *extrovertive* mysticism of the Judaeo-Christian tradition tends to draw back from speaking of oneness between God and creation and of the loss of personal identity in a moment of ecstatic union (Spilka 1985: 177, 181; Hay 1987: 91-92).

97. Ironically, the 'Word of Faith' movement, with which some of the Blessing's progenitors have been associated, has been criticized for the 'strong strands of Eastern mysticism' and 'monism' within its teachings (Fearon 1994: 108).

being 'transparent with light', as 'resting under the cloak of glory', as a 'state of blissful abandonment' or like 'electric current'. The Sea of Faith returns in waves of power! Sometimes recipients report 'out-of-body' experiences: Belma Vardy reported seeing herself 'walking in a lush green pasture, hand in hand with Jesus' (Chevreau 1994: 179-80). One man reported that, whilst overcome by the Spirit, 'he experienced a sensation as if he were melting into the chairs' (White 1989: 15-16).

Guy Chevreau of Airport Vineyard Toronto suggests that the phenomena of the Blessing are, as it were, 'an unfamiliar, non-verbal language (which) is being used to describe and declare what the Spirit of God is doing in people's lives' (1994: 28). Indeed the cognoscenti can recognize 'an extensive repertoire of kinetic language that seems to symbolize the Spirit's desires and actions' (Chevreau 1994: 193). Chevreau recognizes that some religious experiences are beyond the power of words to describe. Interestingly, he cites Aquinas, who while saying Mass in December 1273 was so moved that he never wrote or dictated another word in his life (Chevreau 1994: 42)! Normally verbose and articulate pastors have similarly been virtually reduced to temporary silence by their experience of the Blessing. Some recipients of the Blessing 'struggle for words that adequately describe what they have experienced', others resort to poetic language (Chevreau 1994: 212).

Although charismatic evangelicals are careful not to downplay the centrality of the Bible, the written Word of God in their religion, and search for biblical precedents for the Blessing, they recognize that, as Gerald Coates put it, 'when God comes in power, non-biblical things (can) take place!' (*Alpha*, July 1994: 46). It is claimed that 'a touch of God himself must surely be more important than the "Word of God" being read' (Pytches, in MacNutt 1994: 7). 'Rigid biblical literalism is not conducive to the Spirit of revival' (Chevreau 1994: 53). God does not limit himself to working in ways that can be unambiguously 'proof-texted' from the Scriptures. In this sense charismatic evangelicals are not consistent biblical fundamentalists. In fact biblical fundamentalism has proved difficult to sustain amongst evangelicals generally. Rob Warner has complained that 'a growing number of evangelical Christians today are biblically illiterate' (*Renewal*, November 1994: 11). The eclectic and trite nature (Fearon 1994: 87) of some of the words of prophecy given by people experiencing the Blessing reinforces this conclusion. The influence of the 'power evangelicalism' associated with John Wimber has further helped to marginalize and de-emphasize Scripture (McGrath 1993: 160).

It is not without significance that evangelicals have, in the Blessing, enthusiastically embraced a non-verbal form of religious experience and expression. They live in a post-modern world, in which there are no privileged vantage points and relativism denies the validity of trans-cultural 'truth'. Religious beliefs have been reduced to the status of mere opinions and 'one person's opinion is as good as another's'. Although evangelicals sincerely believe that they have 'absolute truth' on their side, post-modern society cannot admit this possibility. One response, already predicted by the sociologist Ernest Gellner, is that religious expression may dissolve in this way into 'speaking in tongues or (logically) silence' (Gellner 1992: 36). Paradoxically, charismatic evangelical churches may be reflecting two quite different responses to post-modernity: fundamentalism (Walker 1989: 130) and either meta-language or non-language.

It is also plausible that this essentially non-verbal Blessing reflects the increasing difficulty evangelicals have in making their gospel intelligible to modern society.[98] As Steve Chalke remarked: (as evangelicals) 'too often we've preached "The Word", but when we've not been understood, our response has simply been to shout louder' (*Alpha*, October 1994: 35).[99] Another response, I would suggest, has been to stop shouting and settle for the Toronto Blessing's essentially non-verbal approach.

Intellectual middle class evangelicals may, however, face a further tension, which the Blessing may help to mediate. It is not simply that *other* people find the gospel unintelligible, evangelicals themselves may be finding traditional religious language implausible when they themselves are 'full participants in cultural modernity'—because, for instance, of their everyday work milieux (Hervieu-Léger 1993: 146). The world of 'information superhighways' seems a million miles from the world of faith. If intellectual middle class evangelicals are finding that the gospel does not seem to be 'speaking the same language' any more, one solution is to adopt the inarticulate meta-language of glossolalia, another is to embrace the non-verbal Toronto Blessing. Both solutions avoid head-on

---

98.   It is not only evangelicals who experience difficulties in communicating their religion, particularly with those born since 1960—see Davie 1994: 124.

99.   Tim McClure compares evangelicals to 'the English abroad, shouting incomprehensible orders to their contemporaries who, like generations of foreign waiters, shrug their shoulders and walk away' (*Trust*, October 1994: 4).

engagement with the language of modernity. In this way the Blessing can be seen as helping to mediate the acute contradiction between their religious 'cultural capital' and the day to day realities of living and working in the 1990s (Hervieu-Léger 1993: 146).

Not every church in Britain, as we have seen, has warmed to the Toronto Blessing. But, for those that have, it has been a timely arrival. As we have seen, for sociological reasons, if no other, the Toronto Blessing, from Airport Vineyard, touched down at just the right time!

BIBLIOGRAPHY

Bell, D.
    1976   *The Cultural Contradictions of Capitalism* (London: Heinemann).
Berger, P.
    1969   *The Social Reality of Religion* (London: Faber and Faber).
Chevreau, G.
    1994   *Catch the Fire: The Toronto Blessing, An Experience of Renewal and Revival* (London: Marshall Pickering).
Church of England: The Doctrine Commission of the Church of England
    1991   *We Believe in the Holy Spirit* (London: Church House Publishing).
Clack, B.
    1994   'Omnipotence, Masculinity and God', paper given at the Philosophy of Religion Seminar, King's College London, 8 December.
Davie, G.
    1994   *Religion in Britain since 1945: Believing without Belonging* (Oxford: Basil Blackwell).
Enroth, R.
    1992   *Churches that Abuse* (Grand Rapids: Zondervan).
Fearon, M.
    1994   *A Breath of Fresh Air* (Guildford: Eagle).
Featherstone, M., M. Hepworth, and B.S. Turner (eds.)
    1991   *The Body: Social Process and Cultural Theory* (London: Sage).
Gellner, E.
    1992   *Postmodernism, Reason and Religion* (London: Routledge).
Goldingay, J. (ed.)
    1989   *Signs, Wonders and Healings* (Leicester: Inter-Varsity Press).
Glock, C.Y., and R. Stark
    1965   *Religion and Society in Tension* (Chicago: Rand McNally).
Handy, C.
    1994   *The Empty Raincoat: Making Sense of the Future* (London: Hutchinson).
Hay, D.
    1987   *Exploring Inner Space: Is God still Possible in the Twentieth Century?* (London: Mowbray).

Hervieu-Léger, D.
1993   'Present-Day Emotional Renewals: The End of Secularization or the
         End of Religion?', in W.H. Swatos, Jr (ed.), *A Future for Religion?:*
         New Paradigms for Social Analysis (London: Sage): 129-48.
Hunter, J.D.
1987   *Evangelicalism: The Coming Generation* (Chicago: University of
         Chicago Press).
Lawrence, P.H.
1992   *Doing What Comes Supernaturally* (Eastbourne: Kingsway).
MacNutt, F.
1990   *Overcome by the Spirit* (Guildford: Eagle, new prologue, 1994).
McGrath, A.
1993   *Evangelicalism and the Future of Christianity* (London: Hodder &
         Stoughton).
McGuire, M.B.
1987   *Religion: The Social Context* (Belmont: Wadsworth).
1990   'Religion and the Body: Rematerializing the Human Body in the
         Social Sciences of Religion', *Journal for the Scientific Study of*
         Religion 29.3: 283-96.
Neitz, M.J.
1987   *Charisma and Community: A Study of Religious Commitment within*
         the Charismatic Renewal (Oxford: Transaction Books).
Otto, R.
1923   *The Idea of the Holy* (London: Oxford University Press).
Poloma, M.M.
1982   *The Charismatic Movement: Is there a New Pentecost?* (Boston, MA:
         Twayne).
Poloma, M.M., and B.F. Pendleton
1989   'Religious Experiences, Evangelism, and Institutional Growth within
         the Assemblies of God', *Journal for the Scientific Study of Religion*
         28.4: 415-31.
Porter, S.E., and P.J. Richter (eds.)
1995   *The Toronto Blessing—Or is It?* (London: Darton, Longman & Todd).
Richter, P.J.
1994   'Seven Days' Trading Make One Weak? The Sunday Trading Issue as
         an Index of Secularization', *British Journal of Sociology* 45.3: 333-
         48.
Roberts, C.W.
1989   'Imagining God: Who is Created in Whose Image?', *Review of*
         Religious Research 30.4: 375-86.
Roberts, D.
1994   *The 'Toronto Blessing'* (Eastbourne: Kingsway).
Roberts, K.A.
1984   *Religion in Sociological Perspective* (Chicago: Dorsey).
Roberts, R.H.
1994   'Power and Empowerment: New Age Managers and the Dialectics of
         Modernity/Postmodernity', *Religion Today* 3: 3-13.

Robertson, R.
1992   *Globalization: Social Theory and Global Culture* (London: Sage).
Samarin, W.J.
1959   'Glossolalia as Learned Behaviour', *Canadian Journal of Theology* 15.1: 60-64.
Sargant, W.
1959   *Battle for the Mind: A Physiology of Conversion and Brain-Washing* (London: Pan Books, revised edn).
Simpson, J.H.
1993   'Religion and the Body: Sociological Themes and Prospects', in W.H. Swatos, Jr (ed.), *A Future for Religion? New Paradigms for Social Analysis* (London: Sage): 149-64.
Spickard, J.V.
1993   'For a Sociology of Religious Experience', in W.H. Swatos, Jr (ed.), *A Future for Religion? New Paradigms for Social Analysis* (London: Sage): 109-28.
Spilka, B., R.W. Hood, Jr, and R.L. Gorsuch
1985   *The Psychology of Religion: An Empirical Approach* (Englewood Cliffs, NJ: Prentice-Hall).
Springer, K. (ed.)
1987   *Riding the Third Wave* (Basingstoke: Marshall Pickering).
Synnott, A.
1992   'Tomb, Temple, Machine and Self: The Social Construction of the Body', *British Journal of Sociology* 43.1: 79-110.
Swatos, W.H., Jr
1993   *A Future for Religion? New Paradigms for Social Analysis* (London: Sage).
Turner, B.S.
1984   *The Body and Society: Explorations in Social Theory* (Oxford: Basil Blackwell).
1992   *Regulating Bodies: Essays in Medical Sociology* (London: Routledge).
Walker, A.
1983   'Pentecostal Power: The "Charismatic Renewal Movement" and the Politics of Pentecostal Experience', in E. Barker, *Of Gods and Men* (Macon, GA: Mercer University Press): 89-108.
1987   'Fundamentalism and Modernity: The Restoration Movement in Britain', in L. Caplan (ed.), *Studies in Religious Fundamentalism* (Albany, NY: State University of New York Press): 195-210.
1989   *Restoring the Kingdom: The Radical Christianity of the House Church Movement* (London: Hodder & Stoughton).
Wallis, R.
1984   *The Elementary Forms of the New Religious Life* (London: Routledge & Kegan Paul).
White, J.
1989   *When the Spirit Comes with Power* (London: Hodder & Stoughton).

Wimber, J.
1985   *Power Evangelism* (London: Hodder & Stoughton).
York, M.
1994   'New Age in Britain: An Overview', *Religion Today* 3: 14-22.

POSTMODERNISM, A/THEOLOGY, AND THE POSSIBILITY OF LANGUAGE AS UNIVERSAL EUCHARIST

J. Stephen Fountain

Charles Winquist has observed the similarities between the theological movement from transcendence to radical immanence in Thomas Altizer's thought and the play of *différance* in Derrida's philosophical deconstructions, noting that in both, 'the origin of identity is the substitution of a signifier, a name, for the transcendental signifier and a displacement into a network of signifiers' (1928: 338). For Altizer, whose theology and interpretation of history are written under the 'grand trope of the death of God' (Winquist 1982: 339), God is understood as the signified 'God' whose name entails the death and radical kenosis of the transcendental signifier, 'God'. The history of theology becomes then for Altizer a history of historically evolving reinterpretation of that signifier, a reinterpretation which is, for Altizer, the presence of the absence of the transcendental. Altizer's theological programme, then, relies fundamentally upon his activity as reader, as reinterpreter and re-writer of the Word of God which negates the transcendental, objective, inactual reality of the immobile God of Christendom. Altizer's re-reading of God himself draws not only upon a critique of the interpretative activities of the institutional Christian tradition, but also upon a reinterpretation of marginal 'theologians' such as Milton, Blake, Joyce, Hegel and Nietzsche, who were, rather than reinforcing the property of the eternal return of the God of Christendom, writing Scripture themselves and effecting the historical evolution of the faith, an evolution that scholasticism has sought to avoid, and indeed, to reverse. Such reinterpretation is for Altizer a re-enactment of an original Christianity, but the emphasis here is not on a return to an original authoritative text, but upon the apocalyptic manner in which that text is presented, grounded in a historically evolving faith. For Altizer, as Winquist observes, 'theology cannot take possession of an original text because in the beginning there is silence' (1982: 339); the 'original text', for Altizer, is a text which is always already effaced and written under erasure. The God of Altizer's theology is a God who has written Godself as other than God, and a God the theology of whom is written as other-than-theology, by those who have acknowledged, as Altizer, the 'textuality of the divine' (Raschke 1988: 138; Jasper 1995: 15). Acknowledgment of the 'textuality of the divine' implies a shift from the objective notion of the logocentric (or at least a shift within that system if logocentrism is a tradition from which we cannot escape), the hermeneutic and theological, toward the poetic, a fall 'from the book to writing and theological thinking' (Jasper 1995: 20). This is a fall which, like the fall which Altizer equates with the death and genesis of God, is a *felix culpa*, enacting the very embodiment of that movement which is simultaneously death and resurrection, an embodiment that grants actuality to history and enacts within that history a total grace. That movement is for Altizer the epic movement of Spirit which is the redemptive and sacrificial negation of God, a historical movement reflected in literary epic movements and in the epic of the individual and universal consciousness. This movement is most essentially a movement of the negation of eternal return.

In his essay, 'The Beginning and Ending of Revelation', Altizer chronicles the ending of the cycle of eternal return by the self-naming of I AM, a beginning in which 'world itself become(s) the arena and the horizon of ultimate praxis, a praxis releasing the ultimacy of primordial and sacred acts into the actuality of life and world itself' (1990a: 79). Now while the effect of the self-revelation of I AM is for Altizer historically developing, the revelation of I AM irreversibly establishes its own beginning and the 'beginning of the ending of eternal return' (1990a: 79). History itself, says Altizer, is a 'realization of that revelation', a realization that has evolved an ever more deeply negative consciousness of transcendence, developing through multiple movements and identities over the course of centuries (1990a: 80). That consciousness has, however, in the twentieth century, reached a 'global embodiment' (1990a: 80), in a total presence of the absence of the transcendent, a total presence which is a universal grace, a result of the apocalyptic movement of a historically evolving faith (1990a: 88-89). That grace is known in the absolute silence of the self-negating God, a silence which is the fulfilment of the speech of the self-revelation of I AM, the consummation in which ' "God said" has wholly and finally passed into silence'; 'if grace is everywhere, and is everywhere here and now, it is everywhere as death and nothingness, and finally as the death and nothingness of I AM' (1990a: 108). The finally present totality of death and ending is, for Altizer, the apocalyptic ending which is the apocalypse (ending and revelation) of God, an apocalypse in which 'the death of the Crucified God is now universally realized as a final and total event', and 'actuality' which is the 'total realization of the Crucified God' (1990a: 108).

Thus for Altizer God is God in God's self-embodiment and negation in the world itself, so that the reality of God lies not in the transcendent to which the realization of God refers, but in the realization itself, an embodiment of the negation of the transcendental signified. This act of negation is most fully realized in the crucifixion, 'the sacrifice of that God who is fully God in kenosis and self-emptying', and the negation of that God who is only the God of Glory, a negation which is the final realization and actualization of that God of ultimate sacrifice (1990b: 78). The full realization and enactment of that negation is symbolized by Altizer by a universal liturgy and eucharistic anamnesis, a totalizing, now at the end of history, of the sacrifice of God and negation of the God of glory which is 'represented or renewed in the liturgical action of the eucharist or mass', and the sacrifice which is 'proclaimed in authentic Christian preaching' (1990b: 76-77).

The negation of the God of Glory in the God of Sacrifice, especially as embodied in the liturgical movement of the eucharist, is a theological understanding shared with Altizer by Robert Scharlemann, whose explications of the kenotic God tend toward the more systematic than do Altizer's. In Scharlemann's meditations upon the being of God in the Eucharist, to say that 'God is in the Eucharist' is to say that 'the sacrament of the eucharist symbolizes or makes perceptible the one activity of being within the many activities of the final agent, God' (Klemm 1982: 308). The event of the sacrament discloses the self-revelatory activity of God which is always happening everywhere (Klemm 1982: 308), and the eucharist functions as a 'revelatory language event', in which language, 'the process of speaking and hearing, is the self-embodying of God' (Klemm 1982: 308). In language, God 'embodies deity as other than himself'; 'God is manifest as other than God in the event of language', and eucharist, as a re-enactment of the primary symbol of God's self-negation, reveals the depth of that manifestation (Klemm 1982: 308). The 'presence' of God in Scharlemann's theology, as in Altizer's, requires a critique of traditional ontology in which the being of God is the presence of God's absence, or, in which the way that God 'is' coincides with the way that God 'is not', or is as God is 'other than God', as Scharlemann explains in his intricately paradoxical essays, 'The Being of God When God is Not Being God', and 'Being "As Not"' (1989: 30-65). The same theme of ontological theological critique is undertaken by Jean-Luc Marion, in his *God Without Being* (1991), which also turns toward the eucharist for its focus.

Marion presents the case for an understanding of God without Being, that is, for a theology which is from the beginning conscious of its own tendency toward idolatry, even in assigning to God its highest designation, that of Being. A theology in which God is understood solely as bound to, or participating in, the realm of Being remains, according to Marion, anthropocentric and idolatrous in its attempt at mastery of God through reason. Reason is not completely discounted by Marion, however, but it cannot be maintained as the basis for a knowledge or worship of God.

In admitting no less of G̶o̶d̶ (whose name is consistently crossed out in the work) than absolute otherness, Marion understands theology's task as one of worship and thanksgiving, metaphorically presented through the activity of the eucharist. True theology, for Marion, founded upon the kerygmatic revelation of the historical death and resurrection of Jesus Christ, carries out the task of a 'eucharistic hermeneutic', which relies upon a thoroughgoing emphasis upon the revelation of the crucified G̶o̶d̶ in the present. Not only does the eucharist signify the gift of 'union with Christ' in the corporal ecclesial body, but as presence is understood as gift in a eucharistic context, time itself may be understood as gift for the sake of partaking within it in the gift of the eucharistic present:

> The eucharistic presence comes to us, at each instant, as the gift of that very instant, and, in it, of the body of the Christ in whom one must be incorporated. The temporal present during which the eucharistic present endures resembles it: as a glory haloes an iconic apparition, time is made a present gift to let us receive in it the eucharistically given present (Marion 1991: 175).

Thus in the mystery of the 'properly Christian' understanding of temporality, the 'ultimate paradigm of every present', according to Marion, is given the gift of the eucharistic present.

While Marion's understanding of the 'eucharistically given present' closely resembles Altizer's 'total presence' (which is understood as a universal eucharist), Altizer's understanding of history and temporality is founded upon the idea of the embodiment of the death of God. For

Marion the death of God does not serve as such a temporal metaphor; Marion views the philosophical concept of the death of God as the death of an idolatrous confining of God to human terms, specifically to the distinction between being and nothing, presence and absence. Like Altizer, Marion places God beyond being and nothing (Scharlemann 1990: 116), but the death of God for Marion is the death of an idolatrous concept which stopped short, as all concepts do, of an understanding of the God who reveals himself, but who remains absolutely other.

Marion's understanding of the crossing of God, in Altizer's opinion, contains a contradiction in its granting of a Pseudo-Dionysian mystical transcendental absolute unity to God, an eternal return which negates the very self-negation of the Christian God, alongside a Hegelian notion of the kenotic 'gift' of the Crucified God. 'Surely Marion is radical in calling for the "Crossing" of Being', says Altizer, but while Marion employs the language of Hegelian *Aufhebung* to explicate the 'giving' of the Crucified God (employing '*relève*', Derrida's translation of the Hegelian term), he 'immediately calls upon the Pseudo-Dionysius, that thinker who is most infinitely distant from Hegel...rejoicing in a deeply mystical call that we become messengers announcing the divine silence', messengers who have abandoned 'everything whatsoever both in this "world of nothingness" and in the "world of being"', because of the deep discontinuity between 'the false light of our world and the absolute darkness of the Godhead' (Altizer 1993a: 6). Yet, Altizer notes, Marion's emphasis upon the Crucified God is in complete opposition to the language of Pseudo-Dionysius, language from which images of kenosis are lacking. Perhaps then, Marion's Dionysianism is a modern Catholic Dionysianism, Altizer suggests, a Dionysianism which knows Godhead as absolute darkness, but which can know an openness to 'non-being' which 'is itself an arena of the gift of the crucified God' (1993a: 11). Such a Catholicism can know the world itself as the gift of the Crucified God, 'a God which appears only in its disappearance, and which "is" only in the sense that it has wholly and totally given itself': God without being (Altizer 1993a: 12). Altizer suggests that such an understanding would present a fully and uniquely Catholic notion of world which 'is nature and grace at once', a history, a world, an existence which is 'a sacramental world', not in the Pseudo-Dionysian sense of a reflection of 'Heavenly and Ecclesiastical Hierarchies', but as the gift and the giving of the kenotic God, a 'universal eucharistic presence of the Lamb of God' (1993a: 12).

A universal eucharistic presence in which existence is itself understood as the body of the kenotic God is a restatement of Altizer's understanding of 'total presence', a coincidence of the opposites of the divine and the corporeal which Altizer finds developing within what he calls the Christian epic tradition, a tradition epitomized by the historical evolution of the 'theological' discourses of Milton, Blake and Joyce. That is a tradition which shares with Marion an understanding of the absolute darkness of Godhead and the negativity of the kenotic movement of the transcendent, known in images of absence and personified in the character of Satan.

It is in their knowledge of Satan, says Altizer, that the works of Milton and Blake find their continuity, the Satans that they present being Satans which are historical and actual embodiments of their respective worlds, the seventeenth and nineteenth centuries (Altizer 1990b: 170). The twentieth century has witnessed a comprehensive nihilistic epiphany of Satan, says Altizer, factually in its unique historical horrors and also literarily in its 'twin epics', Joyce's *Ulysses* and *Finnegans Wake* (Altizer 1993b: 141). The historicization of the radical dichotomous character of the self-negating God is consummated in these twin epics, and that consummation realizes and embodies a historical negation of the 'primordial movement of eternal return' in a universal apocalypse (Altizer 1993b: 116).

Joyce's *Ulysses*, in Altizer's reading, presents a continuation of the Miltonic and Blakean understanding of the self-kenotic negation of God, making manifest a 'Christ who is Satan, a Christ who is "God becomes man becomes fish", and who is now a nameless or anonymous Christ' identical with Lucifer, whose fall is a *felix culpa* (Altizer 1990b: 170-71). Celebrating a 'God-Satan who *is* Christ', Joyce's *Ulysses* presents, Altizer points out, a renewed heretical Sabellian Son of God, 'the Father who was Himself His Own Son', a Father whose fatherhood disappears in a liturgically embodied mystery of incarnation and crucifixion, a Father known as a 'Hangman God' and revealed as only a 'noise or voice in the street' (Altizer 1985: 219; Altizer 1993b: 106). This 'noise or voice in the street', however, is the 'all in all' of the self-sacrificing Creator, a kenotically revealed totality which makes possible the apocalyptic prayer to 'Our Father who art not in heaven', a prayer heralding the arrival not of Elijah, but of the Joycean New Jerusalem, the 'New Bloomusalem', and its Christ-like figure, the extraordinarily ordinary Leopold Bloom (Altizer 1992: 19; Altizer 1985: 219; Altizer 1993b: 106).

Altizer offers the reading of Leopold Bloom as a reversal of the docetism that becomes apparent in all previous Christology, ushering into historical consciousness a Christ-figure who is an actual human being (1985: 225). That is an understanding which Altizer claims has developed through the epic tradition, from Dante's inability to portray Christ as in any way human, to Milton's refusal to 'enact or envision him as eternal and divine Word', and Blake's inability to cast Christ's fullness into a 'singular or individual form' (1985: 225). Altizer parallels this new Christological understanding with a new understanding of the Eucharist, insomuch as the fully human Christ who is now revealed is priest and victim, present in a eucharistic presence 'in our time and flesh' (1985: 225). Herein a new epic language is present, for within *Ulysses* Altizer finds Bloom's epic heroism expressed in antiheroic 'everyday words and acts', which are, and this is Bloom's priestly function, 'indistinguishable from those of their audience or reader' (Altizer 1985: 226). Therefore Bloom is Christ-like by virtue of his 'reversal of every mythical identity of Christ', in a totally historical identity and world; it is impossible to 'imagine Bloom as Christ', says Altizer, but this is because Bloom's identity so reverses the traditional glorified image of Christ, but does so in such a way that Bloom's textual presence 'affects us even as does a ritual enactment', making present the actuality of 'life itself' in the reversal of the negativity of a purely majestic Christ (1985: 227).

In *Finnegans Wake*, Altizer submits, Bloom is transformed into H.C. Earwicker, H.C.E. ('*Hoc est corpus meum*: take read, this is my body, broken for you', as Mark C. Taylor reads it [1990: 64]), Here Comes Everybody, a Blakean 'The Eternal Great Humanity Divine', who is consumed in the cosmic *missa jubilea*, enacted in Joyce's transformation of liturgical language into the language of the everyday, 'a wholly fallen language' (Altizer 1985: 233, 244). The language of Joyce, and most of all the language of *Finnegans Wake*, says Altizer, is a language embodying the fall, the 'divine death' which is re-enacted throughout its (non)narrative, and a language which calls upon its reader to 'enact that which is read', in a eucharistic re-enactment in which the body of Christ becomes the realization of death and chaos in history, a conjunction of Christ and Satan in which the transcendent Creator is known as Satan and the 'Satanic' reality of history, and realized in Joyce in a transformed liturgical language which is divine and human at once (Altizer 1990b: 172; Altizer 1985: 234-37):

> ...the language of the *Wake* is not only human and divine at once, it is totally guilty and totally gracious at once, for our final epic language is a cosmic and historical Eucharist, a Eucharist centered in an apocalyptic and cosmic sacrifice of God. Now a primordial chaos and abyss is indistinguishable from Godhead, just as an original chaos has passed into the center of speech. But now this ultimate chaos is fully and finally present, and present in and as this apocalyptic and liturgical text (Altizer 1985: 234).

Altizer points out that the central action of the *Wake* is a re-enactment of 'primordial sacrifice', or fall, the language of which is the 'night language' which is the language of the death of God, the language of the 'fall, condemnation and crucifixion of H.C.E.', who is not only the Father, but is also, Altizer observes, Yggdrasil, the 'cosmic Tree, which in the Eddas symbolizes the universe, a universe which goes on trial as the "Festy King"' in the *Wake* (Altizer 1992: 20; Altizer 1985: 239; Altizer 1993b: 107). Within the Eddas Yggdrasil is also derived from 'Yggr', meaning 'deep thinker', or God, and 'drasil', meaning 'horse or carrier'; therein Yggdrasil 'becomes at times "bearer of God"' connoting at once the cross and the Virgin, as well as the tree which was the source of original sin (Himler 1977: 55). Altizer links 'original sin' and 'original sun' within the centre of the Joycean negative Godhead which negates itself in the very language of the *Wake*, a negation 'consummated in the resurrection of Anna Livia Plurabelle, a resurrection which absorbs the power of Godhead'; that resurrection culminates in a universal eucharist which is cosmic crucifixion and resurrection, a final 'Yes', which also evokes the imagery of the tree, in the 'cosmic dispersal of (A.L.P)'s body or leaves' (Altizer 1990b: 171; Altizer 1993b: 107, 131-32).

The eucharistic language of the *Wake* re-enacts the self-sacrifice of the eternal God, a self-sacrifice grounded in an act of original sin by which the Father knows and is conjoined with his creation, the apocalyptic moment evoked by the images of the tree of knowledge, the God-bearing trees of incarnation and crucifixion, and the apocalyptic tree located at the centre of the universe, Yggdrasil (Altizer 1992: 23-24). It should be remembered that the apocalyptic falling of Yggdrasil, which Altizer here identifies with the death of the eternal Father represented by H.C.E., entails the freedom of the two humans therein, the parents of a new civilization, who will live under a new sun, more brilliant than the previous one, even perhaps symbolizing a Joycean re-enactment of the granting of full humanity by the Edenic tree, and also by the tree of incarnation and crucifixion. All of these would be understood by Altizer to be re-enacted in the eucharistic language of the *Wake*, a language which historically enacts a universal eucharistic presence, not leastly in its epic quality, by which its reader enacts the language therein.

In the night language of the *Wake*, a language written in the absence of the Sun, 'writing or scripture finally ends', making way, Altizer proclaims, for that 'primal and immediate speech...which is on the infinitely other side of that writing which is Scripture or sacred text' (1985: 237). However, Altizer's understanding of Joyce and of Scripture is all too dialectical to end there. 'Scripture is more universally present in *Finnegans Wake* than it is in any other text', its sacrality passing into 'ribaldry, banality and blasphemy', releasing the grace of a transcendent Heaven into 'what Scripture can only name as Satan and Hell' (1985: 238). This the text of the *Wake* is not commentary upon Scripture, but is, in a transformed embodiment, Scripture itself (a notion directly related to Altizer's Christology). The New Testament, says Altizer, appears in the *Wake* in an inverted form, in which the four evangelists are 'false witnesses', participating in a chaos which is the 'apocalyptic epiphany of total grace' (1985: 238). Within the universally eucharistic language of the *Wake*, Scripture is both present and absent in a writing which is the ending of the written, a presence which is the absence of the transcendental and the originary; the presence/absence of Scripture is a eucharistic and apocalyptic presence, a total presence which is present only in its passing away:

> Now writing itself becomes indistinguishable from the original act of creation, and therein it becomes far more violent and chaotic than it has ever been before, and so much so that even if *Finnegans Wake* is for the most part written in English, it is written in an English that can be read only by learning to read anew. Every new epic calls for and demands a new art and act of reading... Thereby ritual fully passes into writing, and so writing ends as a writing which is only writing, and a writing is born which is inseparable and indistinguishable from that chaos and abyss which appeared to come to an end with the advent of writing and art (Altizer 1985: 238-39).

Altizer's reading of Joyce is a radical critique of the traditional notion of Scripture, yet it is an interpretation which takes its departure from the connection between Scripture and eucharist, writing and ritual, which Carl Raschke presents succinctly in relation to deconstruction's critique of the metaphysics of presence. The 'classical meaning of *scriptura*', says Raschke, 'refers to the densification of word and text into a public

de-*scription*, the metamorphosis of mere writing into the document'
(1988: 134). The written 'document' is understood as the site of the representation of presence, standing separate from 'the act of writing
which gave it body' (1988: 134). The written, as opposed to 'writing', is
therefore 'charged with the sense of the *aliter*', which accounts for the
gilding and illumination of Scripture (1988: 134). Illuminating the understanding of the 'book', the end of which post-structuralist thought has
heralded, Raschke points out that 'Scripture is the "book", and is not
simply the material ensemble of inscriptions; it is a veritable theophany'
(1988: 134). The theophany of the book takes place of course in the
reading, a reading which therefore becomes a presence-evoking ritual;
such an understanding is woven into the very fabric of the term:

> 'Book' is etymologically connected to 'beech', an 'edible tree' (cf. the
> Greek root *phago-*). Thus the book is the tree, the symbol of life, that is
> ingested as a sacrament. Reading in the classical context is akin to the cel-
> ebration of the 'mass', the assimilation of meanings, the consumption of
> the god, the transfer of presence (Raschke 1988: 134).

Certainly Altizer's understanding of the eucharistic function of language
is derived from such a tradition, but rather than effecting a mere
'transfer of presence' which is a representation of an originary presence
(of an eternal God, the Father, a Platonic nous or 'sun' which instills in
profane matter its Spirit), Altizer's understanding of the eucharistic
activity is founded upon his understanding of a 'total presence', which is
an apocalyptic presence, present in its passing away, a presence of the
absence of God. Altizer's dialectical enactment of the presence/absence
of Scripture, while certainly bearing similarities to the deconstructionist
notion of 'the end of the book', which Raschke notes as being 'founded
upon the Hebraic passion for iconoclasm, for de-situating holiness and
making it a temporal disclosure' (1988: 134), moves beyond Derrida's
notion of '*écriture*', in an action Raschke foresees, toward a notion of
Scripture as 'oeuvre' or 'poiesis' (1988: 134). 'Poiesis' entails, Raschke
points out, a Heideggerian/Ricoeurian 'coming to presence through
language' rather than 'the installation of presence in the book', a manifestation of 'the "fullness" within the flux of the historical' (1988: 134).
Raschke's notion of 'poiesis' opens up the possibility of a notion of text
which 'parlays into a set of paradoxical references' which 'establish the
language of text as scripture', a notion compatible with Altizer's understanding of the dialectical historical development of the negative presence of the transcendental (Raschke 1988: 135). In Altizer's terms that

historical development entails the enacting of the Word or Kingdom of God in the negating of the eternal Author, the Father, and focuses on the 'total presence' of the apocalyptic revelation, in which the death of God is equally understood as the genesis of God; Raschke, too, critiquing the tendencies of the a/theological deconstructive trend in theology, calls for an overcoming of the 'sentimentality of absence' present in an overemphasis upon the 'vanished author of the text', toward a 'theological thinking' in which the 'Kingdom of God...is present among the grief of absence' (Raschke 1988: 138).

Such a presence of the Kingdom of God, like Altizer's transformed Scripture and ritual, entails, as Raschke points out, an understanding of religion as a 'pre-metaphysical return of the repressed' (Raschke 1988: 137), which finds expression in images of birth as well as death, for as Altizer has observed, it is the Mother of God whose presence is known in the absence of God; that presence coincides, of course, with the birth of a new writing, as Altizer points out, in the language of Joyce:

> Thereby ritual fully passes into writing, and so writing ends as a writing which is only writing, and a writing is born which is inseparable and indistinguishable from that chaos and abyss which appeared to come to an end with the advent of writing and art (Altizer 1985: 238-39).

In the absence of the Father, the Author(ity), the reading of such writing enacts the presence of the (M)other; the improper relations embodied in the liturgical and profane 'night language', a 'dream language', which follows in the *Wake* of the death of God may well have resulted in the birth of a new writing, and a new reading—between speech and writing, between the transcendent and the immanent, between heaven and earth, between the Sun and the Virgin soil. In that decentred centre grows the tree which bears the revelation of 'the return of the repressed'.

'Our epic destiny', says Altizer, 'was first interiorly enacted in Eve's temptation and fall', a fall effected by the irresistible temptation of 'that ecstatic delight induced by a purely negative and thus purely forbidden consciousness, a delight consummated in that ecstasy which she knew in tasting the forbidden fruit' (1993b: 97); that is a fall which is re-enacted in the eucharistic 'presence' manifest in writing the death of God. The reader before the book (the 'edible tree', as Raschke observes) re-enacts the situation of Eve before the tree of Life, a situation re-enacted by the Virgin before the cross and offered by the Prayfulness, the playful prayful-ness of the language of the *Wake* (Joyce 1992: 601), which marks the sacrifice of Authority for the sake of the reader, whose eucharistic enactment negates and preserves the opposition between the two, participating in the ceaseless interpretation, the eternal dissemination of the text, the body of the Author(ity). In Joyce, authorial authority is sacrificed in a language which consciously requires the interplay of the act of reading. Thus the authority of the reader is established, but that is an authority that is incessantly de-centred by the text itself, in a wrestling toward an apocalypse which is always present and is always not-yet.

Such an apocalyptic deferral may also be observed within Mark C. Taylor's *Erring*, a groundbreaking, though now somewhat dated, work which has been called 'apocalyptic theology with a vengeance', and in which, according to Altizer, 'Taylor seeks a genuinely Christian theology, centered in Incarnation and Crucifixion' ('The Triumph of the Theology of the Word', in Wyschogrod *et al.* 1986: 528, 525). However, Altizer goes further (admitting more of the work than Taylor himself would), and claims that *Erring* is also 'in quest of a purely Biblical or Scriptural writing', seeking 'a pure revelation of Word which can only be a total erasure of word' (Wyschogrod *et al.* 1986: 525). Further, while condoning Taylor's subversive method, Altizer criticizes Taylor's tendency to ignore the actuality of texts in favor of a 'pure or disembodied thinking', the 'trace' which dissolves all actual presence (Wyschogrod *et al.* 1986: 525). However, Altizer does point out that, following Scharlemann, Taylor understands 'the crucified God' as 'eternally and kenotically embodied in *word*', so that 'God is what word means, and word is what God means' (Wyschogrod *et al.* 1986: 527). Thus Taylor understands 'the divine itself as writing' and writing as enacting the death of God, 'inscribing the disappearance of the transcendental signified' (Wyschogrod *et al.* 1986: 527).

Surely this is not so far away from Altizer's distinction between the unmoving, self-sufficient God of Christendom and the God who is incarnate in the Word and the Kingdom. The important distinction here, however, as Taylor points out in his response to Altizer, is that for Altizer the death of God implies the 'total presence' of the parousia, the Kingdom, or the Word, while for Taylor the death of God entails its deferral and total absence (Taylor, 'Masking: Domino Effect', in Wyschogrod *et al.* 1986: 551). However, if the apocalyptic moment is the deferral of apocalypse, or if, in Altizer's terms, total presence is known apocalyptically, in its passing, in its absence, there is finally no disagreement between Altizer's 'total presence' and Taylor's deferral of presence, or at least there is a dynamic oscillation found in both. Denying the dissolution of dichotomy, Taylor's theology, like Altizer's, 'errs' in that space between presence and absence. 'The time and space of erring', says Taylor, are opened by a fourfold 'domino effect' comprised of 'Hegel's acknowledgement of the death of God', 'Kierkegaard's claim that Christendom is at its end', 'Nietzsche's announcement of Dionysus (whose other name is the Anti-Christ or Bacchus)', and 'Derrida's recognition of the closure of the book' (Wyschogrod *et al.* 1986: 555). 'In erring', Taylor asserts, 'I am doing nothing other than struggling to think the domino effect of masking by thinking the unthinkable oscillation of alterity and the impossible alterity of oscillation' (Wyschogrod *et al.* 1986: 555). Such oscillation is not dissolution, as Altizer seems to think, as we shall see; oscillation, marks Taylor, 'derives from the Latin word *oscillum*, which means a swing and originally referred to a mask of Bacchus that hung from a tree in a vineyard to sway in the wind' (Wyschogrod *et al.* 1986: 555). Taylor's *Erring* is indeed a series of unmaskings: unmasking the self to find God, unmasking God to find presence, and on and on, even as Altizer's iconoclastic writings unmask the God of Christendom; but the process of unmasking is unending, as mask upon mask is revealed.

Such unmasking is initiated for Taylor by the advent of the post-modern consciousness (an almost meaningless catch-phrase now, but in Taylor's *Erring* it is enough to identify it with the 'radical implications of the death of God' [1984: 7]) which simultaneously alters the whole of the network of concepts with which Taylor illustrates the classical Western onto-theo-logical *Weltanschauung*. This network, which Taylor exemplifies with the use of the related concepts of God, self, history and book, rests, according to Taylor, upon a hierarchically oppressive and repressive system of unequal bipolar opposition, from which emancipation may be gained not simply by a reversal of the hierarchy, but through the effecting of a 'dialectical inversion that does not leave contrasting opposites unmarked, but dissolves their original identities' (1984: 7-10). Of course, the question is whether the 'dissolution of their original identities' is an actual possibility, or whether such an aim is fundamentally a reactionary escapism. That is, dialectical inversion, when applied to bipolar opposites such as origin and *telos*, should result in a dynamic of affirmation and critique; however, 'dissolution of original identities' would necessarily bring that dynamic to a halt, in an attempt to step outside the very system the subversion of which may be effected only from within. Taylor does indeed stress the 'parasitic' character of such an inversion, exhibited by the preclusion of the deconstructive critique's separation from the system it subverts, so perhaps 'dissolution of original identities' is just an unfortunate choice of words. At any rate, it must be affirmed that Taylor's critiques are representative of an irreversible alteration in the climate of the theological environment. Taylor's a/theology represents a definite theological paradigm shift in which, under the influence of post-structuralist thought, God becomes 'writing', self becomes 'trace', history becomes 'erring', and book becomes 'text' (1984: 13). The alteration of these terms marks a change in theological focus and method from an obsession with presence and domination toward a notion informed by subversion and *kenosis*, a change which epitomizes, for Taylor, the difference between modernism and postmodernism (1984: 13).

While Taylor's portrayal of the underlying dichotomies of western metaphysics allows for the equation of theology with modernism, Altizer, in the preface to his *Genesis and Apocalypse*, suggests that the possibility of recovering theology in a 'postmodern' world is offered by the very fact that it was the theological enterprise as a 'science' which was the first discipline to fall victim to modernity, or at least to have been forced into a kind of unnoticed dormancy, in which a kind of transformation may have been taking place (Altizer 1990b: 13). In order to effect a metamorphosis from within the all-engulfing postmodern silence, Altizer states that theology must be reborn into a 'profoundly atheistic if not nihilistic world', a world which owes its very existence to the 'uniquely modern realization of the death of God' (1990b: 13). Regarding 'postmodernism' as a nostalgic reaction against modernism, Altizer heralds the birth of a fully 'modern' theology, a theology which remains to be written, but a theology which, like Taylor's a/theology, is driven by a kenotic understanding of the dialectic of polar dichotomies (Altizer 1993b: 1-4). For Altizer, however, the notion of *kenosis* and the possibility of subversion are unavailable to a postmodernism which, seeking a *dissolution* of identities, cannot know beginning itself. The possibility of *kenosis* requires, in Altizer's estimation, a genesis which is an ending of an originary transcendence; in fact, that is its very definition. To seek a dissolution of dichotomous identities is to seek an ahistorical pure presence, a presence of which history itself, in Altizer's reckoning, requires the negation. An ahistorical system is, of course, one without a future, without newness.

It is newness with which Altizer is concerned in so much of his work, a radical novelty which distinguishes Christianity's kenotic understanding of God from a cycle of eternal return. This is Altizer's concern regarding 'postmodernism' and the apparent contradiction between its reliance upon bipolar opposition for its critique's impetus and the alleged (by Altizer at least) aim of its critique to dissolve the bipolar identities; just as no actuality at all is possible in a cycle of the same, or in a system which posits an eternal transcendence, no critique is possible in a quest for the dissolution of distinctions. A dialectic which hopes to dissolve distinctions is most fundamentally a cycle of the same, and if a postmodernist theological agenda draws from such a philosophical paradigm, then it is, according to Altizer, nothing new at all, but a reactionary 'renewed medieval, or patristic, or pagan theology' (1993b: 2). The generalization of individual theological or critical efforts under a rubric such as 'postmodern', however, runs a serious risk of misunderstanding those efforts. Further, the debate over whether or not 'postmodernity' is, or can be, anything more than late modernity continues among thinkers such as Rorty, Dupré, Habermas and Lyotard (Dupré 1993: 277-95), and such paradigmatic historical dichotomization must remain dynamic and subversive, as both Altizer and 'postmoderns' would agree, if it is to serve as a useful method of elucidation.

Despite the differences within current a/theologies, their commonality lies in their efforts to present the inevitability of the breaching of unitary homeostasis, the metaphorical process which is that breaching, and the continual masking/unmasking which, acknowledged or not, constitutes its continual and simultaneous confirmation and negation. That breach is known in the negation of eternal return found within Altizer's concentration upon the self-emptying God known in the incarnational movements of Creation, Fall and Crucifixion. It is exercised in the developing knowledge of the negative movement of the transcendent, a movement known in Marion's eucharistic language, a language which marks the sacrifice of the (A) (a)uthor-ity of which Taylor writes and which signals the rise of the voice of the repressed.

Such a breach marks the birth—the breach birth?—of the one of whom Irigaray writes: 'To interpret Him (the Crucified) therefore means "go beyond" if possible without return. Not be satisfied with such a love. Leave it to the men of *ressentiment*, and try to create another world' (*Marine Lover of Friedrich Nietzsche*, in Oppel 1993: 106). That is a world the history of which is consistently masked, hidden, discovered and re-written, a story without end, requiring a 'historically evolving faith', which acknowledges the inevitability of metaphoric continuation. The movement away from the eternally returning unity, represented by the One, the Good, the patriarchal Sun, the eternal, unmoving God of Christendom, requires an understanding in which God is no longer an objective subject of theology, but the abject Word which is written from within the poetic discourse, not the origin of metaphor, but the trace of absence which marks the course of metaphorical anamnesis. An understanding of the self-kenotic God, the God who is other-than-God, requires theology which is other-than-theology, a writing which is the total presence of apocalypse, the embodiment of the God who is Word, a universal eucharist.

Our epic destiny, as Altizer calls it, is a destiny of interpretative activity, a destiny which is terminated by an interpretative paradigm which reasserts textual and transcendent authority. The dynamic unity of reader and writer/text is an incessantly oscillating relationship, exemplified by the fact that Altizer's granting authority to the texts of writers such as Milton, Blake and Joyce depends upon the subversion of that authority in the re-writing, in the interpretation of those texts. The sacrifice of authority which negates the metaphysics of the proper, the sterile system of eternal return, is enacted by a reading/writing which is, in Altizer's terms, a universal eucharist, the total presence of apocalypse. To be sure, that is a reading which is the result of a conscious effort on the part of the reader, an openness to the voice of the repressed, but it also calls for a writing which is itself interpretative activity, sacrificing its own authority for the sake of the reader, and for the sake of the interpretative activity. In such writing, reader may become author, writing may become liturgy in which priest (author) and congregation (reader[s]) are united, not in re-presentation, but in the deferral of meaning which is itself the 'goal' of the interpretative activity, the 'total presence' of meaning, and apocalypse which is always present and always not-yet.

BIBLIOGRAPHY

Altizer, T.J.J.
    1985   *History as Apocalypse* (Albany: State University of New York Press).
    1990a   'The Beginning and Ending of Revelation', in *Theology at the End of the Century* (ed. R. Scharlemann; Charlottesville: University of Virginia Press): 76-109.
    1990b   *Genesis and Apocalypse* (Louisville, KY: Westminster/John Knox).

1990c   'Is the Negation of Christianity the Way to its Renewal?', *Religious Humanism* 24: 10-16.

1992   'The Satanic Transgression of Crucifixion', unpublished essay.

1993a   'Dionysian Theology as a Catholic Nihilism', Lecture in 'Special Session on *God Without Being*, Jean-Luc Marion', AAR Annual Meeting, November.

1993b   *The Genesis of God* (Louisville, KY: Westminster/John Knox).

Dupré, L.

1993   'Postmodernity or Late Modernity?', *The Review of Metaphysics* 47.2: 277-95.

Himler, A.

1977   'The World-Tree Yggdrasil', *Parabola* 2.3: 54-55.

Jasper, D.

1995   'From Theology to Theological Thinking: The Development of Critical Thought and its Consequences for Theology', *Literature and Theology* 9.3.

Joyce, J.

1992   *Finnegans Wake* (London: Penguin).

Klemm, D.

1982   ' "This is My Body": Hermeneutics and Eucharistic Language', *ATR* 64.3: 293-310.

Marion, J.-L.

1991   *God Without Being* (trans. T. Carlson; Chicago: University of Chicago Press).

Oppel, F.

1993   ' "Speaking of Immemorial Waters": Irigaray with Nietzsche', in *Nietzsche, Feminism and Political Theory* (ed. P. Patton; London: Routledge).

Raschke, C.

1988   *Theological Thinking: An In-quiry* (Atlanta: Scholars Press).

Scharlemann, R.

1989   *Inscriptions and Reflections: Essays in Philosophical Theology* (Charlottesville: University of Virginia Press).

1990   'A Response', in *Theology at the End of the Century* (ed. R. Scharlemann; Charlottesville: University of Virginia Press).

Taylor, M.C.

1984   *Erring* (Chicago: University of Chicago Press).

1990   *Tears* (Albany: State University of New York Press).

Winquist, C.

1982   'Thomas J.J. Altizer: In Retrospect', *Religious Studies Review* 8.4: 337-42.

Wyschogrod, E., T. Altizer, A. Lingis, J. Prabhu, and M.C. Taylor

1986   'On Deconstructing Theology: A Symposium on *Erring: A Postmodern A/theology*', *JAAR* 54.3: 523-57.

GOD AND LANGUAGE: A FEMINIST PERSPECTIVE ON THE MEANING OF 'GOD'

Beverley Clack

Introduction

When God is spoken of within academic theology, there is a tendency to assume that any participant in the discourse of the subject will know what is meant by that word 'God'. Philosophers of religion, as participants in that part of the subject which aims to conceptualize God, have attempted to describe God in definitive terms. According to Richard Swinburne, God is 'something like a "person without a body (i.e. a spirit) who is eternal, free, able to do anything, knows everything, is perfectly good, is the proper object of human worship and obedience, the creator and sustainer of the universe"'.[1] As such, it is often assumed that the language used of God refers to a divine being.

Understanding theological language in this way can lead to debates concerning the propriety—or otherwise—of using male or female pronouns or imagery for God. If the word 'God' is understood as a name for a particular being, the question of whether we should refer to God as 'him' or 'her', 'he' or 'she' seems important. Feminists working in the area of religion have never been concerned with this issue, however, seeing it as a trivialization of the task facing feminist theologians. This paper, likewise, will not be concerned with whether God is a 'he' or a 'she'! Indeed, I intend to question the assumption that religious language refers to a divine being. If I am successful, the question of which gender may be properly ascribed to the word 'God' is irrelevant.

At the outset, I intend to explore the claim that language used of God, rather than referring to a divine being, in fact reflects human ideals and values. If such an idea is taken on board, the concept of God as

---

1. R. Swinburne, *The Coherence of Theism* (Oxford: Clarendon Press, 1977), p. 1.

formulated by philosophers of religion can be shown to reflect the values of those who have formed this concept. As such, the concept of God can be shown to reflect masculinist values and interests. Masculinism is the basic belief in male supremacy which underpins and supports patriarchy.[2] While feminists need to challenge the way in which perceived 'masculine' qualities are habitually ascribed to God, acceptance of the claim that language of God reflects human values need not be problematic. It need not be assumed that all theological language will reflect masculinist values. Once the dynamic between human ideals and the concept of God has been established, different values can be explored by employing different forms of theological language. Thus consideration will be given in this paper to feminist thealogy. Thealogy means literally 'the study of the Goddess', and is an area of feminist thinking which aims to help women explore what it means to be a woman by employing the image of the divine woman, or 'Goddess'. It is in this way that discussions concerning the gender of God may in fact be relevant; but, as shall be shown, the way in which thealogical language is employed suggests a different model of God from that which is traditionally advocated.

Human Values and the Concept of God

Any feminist approach to the concept of God recognizes that God-language tells us as much about ourselves as it does about God. When Mary Daly claimed that 'if God is male, then the male is God',[3] she was exposing this dynamic. What we say about God we in some sense say of ourselves. In order for God to be God, God must, at the very least, represent our highest hopes and deepest values.[4] If a series of values attributed to God is identified with maleness in a given society, then a hierarchy of male over female is perpetuated. God is understood as male, and the male, to all intents and purposes, is understood to represent the power and authority of God. 'God the Father' is an image which thus supports patriarchal claims to male supremacy. Even when

2.   Cf. A. Brittan, *Masculinity and Power* (Oxford: Basil Blackwell, 1989).
3.   M. Daly, *Beyond God the Father* (London: The Women's Press, 1986), p. 19.
4.   This idea could be taken further, as Feuerbach does, when he introduces the notion of projection. Under such an account, a process is ascribed to the human mind whereby God becomes the repository for projected human values.

such power is not explicitly assigned to the male, there remains the sense that to be male is to embody 'the norm'. This is most obviously expressed in the claim that using the male generic is appropriate when talking of humanity as a whole. An account of theological language which uses exclusively male language for God accepts and legitimates this claim. The assumption seems to be that it is 'more natural' to use male pronouns and images when one talks of God, just as it is 'more natural' to use male gender language when talking of 'humanity'.

When it has come to formulate its concept of God, philosophy of religion has not been exempt from this dynamic between the ideals of humanity and their representation in the divine. It is tempting to believe that a philosophical discipline can escape the limitations of its context. However, when the philosophical concept of God is examined, it becomes clear that this is far from the case. In a patriarchal society, the concept of God has been formulated—on the whole by men—in terms of perceived masculine strengths. God is created in the image of man. So, God is defined in terms of power, knowledge, detachment. God is described as impassible, unable to suffer—an attribute which, tellingly, has connotations of invulnerability. God is also described as immutable. To claim that God is immutable is to stress the importance of changelessness, immovability and fixedness. Academic arguments usually assume that such immutability is a laudable feature of a divine being. This quality is also seen as a laudable feature of academic argument itself. This parallel in expectations of God and expectations of a good argument is hardly surprising since the academic arguments themselves have been defined and set up within a society dominated by masculinist values. Yet the crucial point is this: if these attributes of God are taken as a whole, we are left with a telling picture of God made in 'man's' image. Replace the word 'God' with the word 'man' and one is left with the stereotypical picture of what constitutes masculinity in patriarchal society.

Feminists have responded to this connection between ideas of God and humanity in different ways. For some, notably Sallie McFague, the answer is to accept the ideas of the great medieval scholar Thomas Aquinas on the fundamental unknowability of God. According to Aquinas, we can know *that* God exists, but not *what* God is. Making this distinction has an effect upon the way in which religious language is understood. If God's true nature cannot be known, as Aquinas suggests, it is necessary to use a variety of images for God in order to escape the temptation of thinking that God's true reality can be known. Thus myriad ways of referring to God which include female and non-gendered language should be used alongside the traditional masculine images for God.[5] This approach suggests that a referential account of religious language is adequate if correctly applied and understood. Other feminists are more controversial. If the concept of God reflects masculinist ideals, the traditional Judaeo-Christian image at the heart of the western concept of God needs to be rejected. In its place they suggest a return to a female image for the divine, a return to the Goddess. Theology becomes thealogy. However, this need not involve accepting a referential account of the way in which religious language operates. God as a male supernatural being is not being replaced by an alternative supernatural being who is female. Instead, a non-referential and 'non-realist' account of religious language is advocated.

Thealogy and Religious Language

Whilst much feminist work in the area of religion has been concerned with offering a critique of patriarchal religion,[6] some feminists have begun to offer an alternative female-centred approach to the concept of deity. Instead of 'doing *thea*logy' they have turned their attention to *thea*logy. Theology, it is claimed by writers like Naomi Goldenberg,[7] studies an exclusively male God. Thealogy, by way of contrast, studies the Goddess, a deity defined in female terms. The insights of thealogy have a wider implication, however, than that comment suggests. Far from offering merely a reversal of patriarchal or male-dominated religion to matriarchal or female-dominated religion, thealogy provides an important model for understanding the way in which theological language is used.

The model of religious language adopted by feminist thealogians can be identified as non-realist. In this sense, the interpretation of language which thealogians offer can be linked to ideas which are currently being developed within what could be termed 'mainstream' theology. The

5. For examples of this approach, see S. McFague, *Metaphorical Theology* (London: SCM Press, 1982), ch. 5; J.A. Clanton, *In Whose Image?* (London: SCM Press, 1990), ch. 2.

6. See, for example, Daly, *Beyond God the Father*, ch. 1.

7. See N.R. Goldenberg, 'The Return of the Goddess', in A. Loades and D.L. Rue (eds.), *Contemporary Classics in the Philosophy of Religion* (Chicago: Open Court, 1991), pp. 437-38.

debate between 'realist' and 'non-realist' theologians raises similar issues to those addressed by feminists working with the idea of 'God'.[8] Realist theologians work with a referential account of theological language; in some sense, our theological language refers to an entity called 'God'. Non-realists suggest a different account of theological language which focuses on the symbolic, evocative and poetic uses to which language can be put.

Consideration of Don Cupitt's 'non-realist' discussion of God is helpful when considering the account of theological language which thealogians are developing. Cupitt's work has done much to popularize a concept of God which recognizes the connection between God and human values. While his ideas on the nature of God and theology are constantly evolving, it is fair to say that the concept of God defined in his book *Taking Leave of God* remains his lasting contribution to the contemporary discussion on the nature of God-language.[9] In this work, Cupitt moves away from the traditional idea of God as an external, objective, existent being, to an understanding of God as a symbol for the religious and spiritual life. As such, he develops a non-referential and non-realist account of religious language. A similar model of religious language, I shall argue, is being developed by feminist thealogians.

Cupitt's theology begins by challenging the claim that God is a reality external to human life and culture. He begins with the problem evil poses for belief in a God who is ontologically distinct from ourselves. Evil is not only problematic because God apparently fails to act in the world. It is also problematic if God *does* act in the world, for the limited nature of such action seems to suggest a morally ambiguous God.[10]

Yet if Cupitt intends to show why we *cannot* believe in an existent, objective God, he also wants to show why we *must not* believe in such a God. A God who is ontologically distinct from human beings would be

---

8.   For a summary of this debate, see P. Vardy, *The Puzzle of God* (London: Collins, 1990).

9.   (London: SCM Press, 1980). 'The Sea of Faith' movement within the Anglican Church is clearly indebted to his radical reinterpretation of the central tenets of the Christian faith. A. Freeman's *God in Us* (London: SCM Press, 1993) is to a large extent a simplified account of Cupitt's early theology.

10.   'The air-crash survivor thanks God for his deliverance, but what of those who died? A God who schedules some to survive and some to die in a forthcoming air-crash is clearly repugnant.' Cupitt, *Taking Leave of God*, p. 7.

'spiritually oppressive',[11] for such a God would be opposed to what Cupitt believes to be the purpose of the religious life. According to Cupitt, religion requires an inner transformation. While morality deals with external actions, religion, it could be claimed, deals with internal attitudes. In order for religion to be good religion—in other words, the kind of religion which affects one's inner disposition—it must dispense with reliance on a God who is *external* to human experience. Instead, God must be understood as 'indwelling the believer'.[12] Thus Cupitt develops an account of God which connects the divine to human spirituality.

Implicit in his rejection of an external deity is the rejection of a God who is understood as over and above humanity; and for feminists, this rejection affects the hierarchical structuring of human relationships. To claim that there is no God governing the cosmos in the guise of a king affects the way in which human relations are perceived. Historically, this account of divine-human relations has been mirrored by the notion that men represent God in this equation, while women represent humanity. With the death of the monarchical God, this model of male/female relations can no longer look to theology for its justification.

Having rejected the idea that 'God' is the name for a supernatural being, Cupitt defines God in the following way. God is, according to Cupitt, 'a unifying symbol that...personifies and represents to us everything that spirituality requires of us'.[13] In other words, God represents both the spiritual life itself which leads to the formation of a particular kind of person, and the goal of the spiritual life—which could be described as the fully integrated human existence.

Thus, God is not to be understood as some kind of supernatural being. God is not something distinguishable from human spirituality. Understanding God in this way has a profound effect upon the way in which the nature of religious language is to be understood. The word 'God' only has meaning within the religious life. In this sense, Cupitt's ideas are close to those of Wittgensteinians like D.Z. Phillips.[14] Language of God is not referential: there is no ontologically distinct being called 'God' to whom such language refers. When the word 'God' is used, it is

11. Cupitt, *Taking Leave of God*, p. 7.
12. Cupitt, *Taking Leave of God*, p. 5.
13. Cupitt, *Taking Leave of God*, p. 19.
14. Cf. 'Philosophy, Theology and the Reality of God', in D.Z. Phillips, *Wittgenstein and Religion* (Basingstoke: Macmillan, 1993), pp. 1-2.

used as a symbol for the reality and importance of a particular form of life, that is, the religious or the spiritual life.

Defining the meaning of 'God' in this way leads Cupitt to reconsider the meaning of the attributes traditionally and habitually ascribed to the divine—power, knowledge, simplicity, aseity, eternity. Cupitt relates these apparent descriptions of the divine nature to human ideals and the values one needs to foster if committed to living the spiritual life. So, for example, he describes God as 'wise and all-knowing, in the way in which the religious requirement is experienced by us searching our hearts, because its demand for spiritual integrity will not allow us to keep any drawers locked'.[15] In this way, Cupitt allows the divine attributes to have meaning and power, despite his denial of the objective existence of God. Indeed, the divine attributes only have meaning in so far as they can be paralleled with the characteristics necessary for the pursuit of the spiritual life.

Consideration of Cupitt's work is valuable, not least because he shows what happens when religious language is not viewed descriptively, but as a poetic or symbolic way of exploring certain human values. In this way, Cupitt denies the validity of a referential account of theological language. Language used of God should not be understood as describing a divine being. Rather, 'God' is that which symbolizes the spiritual life.

Feminist thealogy develops this idea of God. Indeed, one of the most important thealogical insights concerns the lack of interest in the Goddess as a being whose existence could be proved. It is precisely this approach to divinity that is rejected by most thealogians. Starhawk, a radical feminist writer from the United States, makes this rejection explicit:

> When I say Goddess I am not talking about a being somewhere outside of this world nor am I proposing a new belief system. I am talking about choosing an attitude: choosing to take this living world, the people and creatures in it, as the ultimate meaning and purpose of life, to see the world, the earth and our lives as sacred.[16]

Jane Caputi in her book *Gossips, Gorgons and Crones* makes a similar point when writing of the Goddess as 'O-Zona' or the 'Lady of Slaughter'. For Caputi, this image of the Goddess of destruction describes her own sense of outrage at the wanton destruction of the

---

15. Cupitt, *Taking Leave of God*, p. 103.
16. Starhawk, *Dreaming the Dark* (London: Unwin Hyman, 1990), p. 11.

environment. She is not describing a deity who could be discerned as an entity independent of human life. She writes:

> Now, I assure you, I am not proposing that there is a divine woman hanging out in the upper atmosphere. I am not suggesting that we worship O-Zona or try to establish a personal relationship with her. Nor do I intend us to become supporters of ozone depletion, seeing this phenomenon as a manifestation of divine will. Rather, I am suggesting that the diminishment of the ozone layer must be understood as a manifestation of female Powers, especially those raging, chaotic, creative, and destructive— essentially transmutational—Powers associated with the Crone.[17]

Belief in the Goddess is not belief in a divine being who is female. The Goddess is not understood as a being distinct from human individuals whose existence could be proved. Debates do not take place between those seeking to prove the existence of (the male) God or (the female) Goddess. Instead, feminists such as Starhawk and Caputi accept and develop the idea that concepts of God express human values. So, Starhawk writes of 'Goddess' as a way of responding to the things of this world, as a way of expressing the significance of human life and relationships. Caputi uses the image of the Goddess as the 'Lady of Slaughter' to express her outrage at the destruction of the planet, and the devaluation of female 'powers'. When a thealogian approaches the concept of divinity, she is using the language of the Goddess specifically as a way of exploring what it means to be a woman, and particularly what it means to be a woman at this time in human history.

A good example of how the use of Goddess-language operates is to be found in the work of Carol Christ, who sees the Goddess as a symbol which enables women to come to terms with their sexuality in a positive way. She writes of the Goddess as a 'symbol [which] aids the process of naming and reclaiming the female body and its cycles and processes'.[18] Christ points out that, like the Christian God, the Goddess is often described in triune terms. She is Virgin, Mother and Crone. Acceptance and appropriation of the different stages of a woman's life in this dramatic way enables women, Christ writes, 'to value youth, creativity and wisdom in themselves and other women'.[19] Thus the task of

---

17. J. Caputi, *Gossips, Gorgons and Crones* (Santa Fe, NM: Bear & Co., 1993), p. 237.

18. *Womanspirit Rising* (ed. C. Christ and J. Plaskow; London: Harper & Row, 1979), p. 281.

19. *Womanspirit Rising*, p. 281.

thealogy is intimately connected to issues of female self-awareness and self-acceptance.

Stephen Clark in his recent book *How to Think about the Earth* seems to miss this crucial point concerning the relationship between religious language and self-understanding. Clark's account of 'the return of the Goddess' criticizes writers like Starhawk on the grounds that they are *creating* ways of endowing the world with meaning, rather than seeking for inherent meaning in the world which could be evidentially established. The idea of the importance of evidence is one associated with a referential account of language. If religious language is understood as referring to God, evidence is first required for establishing the existence of that God. The requirement of evidence for belief in any concept of God is one reiterated throughout Clark's piece. For example, he writes:

> We need a new religion, maybe, but we also desperately need an eye for evidence.[20]

A comment like this stands in direct contrast to the point that thealogians are making. The importance of the Goddess cannot be established by providing evidence for the existence of such a celestial entity. In philosophy of religion there has been a time-consuming and, as I see it, ultimately fruitless search for a 'proof' for the existence of God. This search seems misguided. Belief in God cannot be based on an appeal to evidence of this sort. Language concerning the Goddess is not used referentially, but as a symbolic way of exploring the nature of womanhood. As such, the importance of an image of 'God' or 'Goddess' resides with the impact that any particular image of the divine has upon our understanding of the world and of ourselves.

God-language has a particular impact upon the way in which groups and individuals understand themselves. As a woman brought up in the Christian tradition, I have never heard God described in my image. I have often wondered what it would be like to hear God described habitually in female pronouns and imagery. The difference between male and female self-esteem and self-acceptance might in part arise in response to an androcentric understanding of God.

Sociological studies have suggested that there may be evidence for this purported connection between self-esteem and models of God.[21]

---

20. S. Clark, *How to Think about the Earth* (London: Mowbray, 1993), p. 24.
21. Cf. P. Benson and B. Spilka, 'God Image as a Function of Self-Esteem and

Feminist theologians have argued for a similar connection. Jann Aldredge Clanton has recorded the responses of women and men to the masculine language used of God. In a survey of women either who have been or who continue to view themselves as 'Christian', she discovered that many women church-goers felt 'excluded, unimportant, lonely, isolated, angry, cheated, very disappointed, and hurt'[22] by the maleness of the God worshipped in church. By way of contrast, some of the men interviewed by Clanton obviously benefitted from such imagery and language; so much so that any challenge to the 'masculine' concept of God was greeted with anger. Clanton records one man's angry response to her suggestion that female pronouns and imagery could legitimately be applied to God:

> I would feel angry—insulted—God is a male. Jesus said that if you have seen me you have seen the Father. Women should be flattered to be feminine. And I don't think that they would want to be God.[23]

A clear indication of the self-confidence (some might say arrogance) which comes about from internalizing a message which equates one's self with God! By employing the image of the Goddess, feminist thealogians are exploring the way in which this symbol might be used to empower women. Female experience, spirituality and sexuality are explored and affirmed.

The way in which thealogians consider the Goddess has implications for any attempt to talk about God or, to use a more inclusive term, God/ess.[24] At the heart of talk of the Goddess is the denial of the necessity for establishing the objective existence of such a being. God/ess-language need not be understood as referring to a divine entity, but as a medium for exploring human values and ideals. This insight raises an important question for what might be termed 'mainstream' theology. How necessary is the idea of an objective, existent God for Christian faith? The revisionary ideas of Cupitt and also Stewart Sutherland[25] likewise deny the centrality of an existent God to the Christian faith.

Locus of Control', *Journal for the Scientific Study of Religion* 12 (1973), pp. 297-310.

22. Clanton, *In Whose Image?*, p. 75.

23. Clanton, *In Whose Image?*, p. 82.

24. The term 'God/ess' is used to signify an inclusive approach to the concept of God, 'God' being a term which is, rightly or wrongly, associated with male gender language.

25. S. Sutherland, *God, Jesus and Belief* (Oxford: Basil Blackwell, 1990).

Like Cupitt, thealogians insist that the meaning of 'God' is to be found in its appropriation into the life of the individual. Exploring the notion of Goddess, and its attendant female imagery and pronouns, can bring women to a greater sense of self-esteem, and thus empowerment.

Conclusion

At the beginning of this paper I suggested that the debate concerning the gender of God was unimportant and a trivialization of the issues with which feminist theology is concerned. However, as this paper has suggested, there are other ways of considering the gender of God which do not necessitate belief in an existent reality to whom we give the name 'God'. Feminist thealogy works with a model of religious language which denies the validity of interpreting God-language referentially. Rather, language which is used of God expresses human values and ideals. Historically, the values which have been ascribed to God have reflected masculinist concerns and interests. Yet feminist thealogians are suggesting that by using the language of 'Goddess' women can explore their own ideals and values.

This might seem to suggest a divisive account of the religious life. Men will need to worship a male God and women a female Goddess in order for both sexes to realize the promise of religion—which, as Cupitt suggests, is the fully integrated life. Yet the model for religious language offered in this paper need not lead to separatism. The development of alternative images for God and the use of inclusive language offers hope to both women and men. Men, as well as women, have benefitted from the wide range of language and imagery developed by the 'Women-church' movement. The aim of this movement is to explore different ways of perceiving God. A good example of one such group of women and men who meet together to develop alternative liturgies is the St Hilda's Community.[26] Exploring images of God that challenge the stereotypical masculinist ideal of the all-powerful creator may help men to realize that there are different ways of being male. Movements such as this suggest that the day is coming when both women and men can affirm the opening words of one St Hilda's prayer, 'O God, our Father and our Mother', finding in such words a meaningful account of that word 'God'.

---

26. Cf. *Women Included* (London: SPCK, 1991), a book of alternative prayers and services developed by the St Hilda's Community.

INVISIBLE WOMEN: GENDER AND THE EXCLUSIVE LANGUAGE DEBATE

Linda Thomas

The purpose of this paper is to address the use of exclusive language within religious language. Since the area of 'religious language' is rather broad, a narrow view is taken here, narrowing 'religious' to 'Christian' and 'language' to English. Within Christianity, the paper focuses on the Anglican and Roman Catholic traditions in Britain. Within the area of exclusive language, the emphasis is on the use of the terms *he* and *man* to mean both male and female human beings, sometimes known as 'he-man' language. I also approach this topic from at least three perspectives: as a Christian, as a feminist and as a linguist. It is however the linguistic aspect of this debate which I wish primarily to focus on.

The exclusive language issue has been the subject of debate for some time but remains topical, not least in the wake of the publication last year of a new Roman Catholic catechism translation, from which all inclusive language was removed, in favour of exclusive he-man language. The General Synod of the Anglican church also debates the issue from time to time. There are strong views on both sides. It is argued that *he* and *man* cannot and do not include the female of the species and thus women are invisible within the language of the Church, which continues to use these terms. Inclusive language would replace *he* with *they* or *she or he*, and *man* with *human* or *people* for example. The opposite view holds that the terms *he* and *man* are historically and grammatically validated as inclusive terms, and that we all know that that is what they mean.

The importance attached to this issue stems from the belief that issues of language are far from trivial. Whilst those who condemn the inclusive language movement do so on the grounds that it is ideological pro-gramming, control by thought police, or the imposition of 'political correctness' (see Cameron 1994 for a discussion of the use of this term in this context), those who support it do so on the grounds that what is encoded in a language has important symbolic and conceptual implications which should not be ignored or taken implicitly for granted. Language is central to human existence in that it is the only medium at our disposal for expressing ideas, and for encoding concepts and values. Language both orders and represents our physical and social worlds. Language philosophers will tell us that our views of the world are at most constrained and at least influenced by the language we speak; that we view the world through linguistic spectacles. Languages encode culturally salient facts about the world in different ways; for example, different languages make different colour distinctions, or different kinship distinctions, or encode different perceptions of time. They also encode culturally salient values, from which it is possible to deduce the way in which a particular group may be perceived by that culture. Examples in English include the existence of a far larger store of insult terms for women than for men, or the derogation of meaning of most terms for women over time (such as *mistress* which far from being a female equivalent of *master* currently almost always signifies a man's extramarital lover, or *lady* which can be applied to any female from a member of the nobility to a cleaner whilst the same broad sweep does not apply to *lord*). The existence of such linguistic asymmetries suggests the existence of different values and perceptions. If language represents realities then the encoding of terms for human beings in he-man language excludes women and makes them invisible, represents the world as primarily male, and reinforces a perception which is both misleading and undesirable. He-man language helps maintain a 'male-as-norm' or androcentric world view, which is very pervasive, as we shall see.

In addition to the centrality of language to human society, Sara Maitland (1983) also points to the centrality of language to Christianity. It is a verbal religion and it is 'by words and by the Word that Christians claim to know God'. It is therefore essential that we should get the words right.

For the purposes of this discussion, the validity of the claim of inclusiveness for the terms *he* and *man* can be considered separately, beginning with the pronoun *he*. Pronoun systems are of interest to linguists both grammatically and in terms of their social significance. Japanese, for example, has several forms of personal reference for the second person signifying several levels of perceived relative status.

Examples from Crystal (1987) are: *anata*, standard polite form, not used to superiors; *anta*, informal; *sochira*, polite form, very formal; *kimi*, chiefly to men of equal or lower status; *omae*, informal, colloquial, somewhat pejorative. Standard English no longer has a status marked second person form of address, the loss of which may in some part be connected to social change. In the case of third person gender marking, English, which has no grammatical gender (unlike French for example where all nouns have gender which then dictates pronoun choice), selects an appropriate pronoun according to 'natural' (semantic) gender. Pronoun usage is related to meaning and meaning to the biological sex of the referent. Thus we learn as children to refer to females as *she* and males as *he*. Where sex is unknown or undifferentiated there is a language 'gap', since *it* is used either when there is no biological sex (for example, inanimate objects) or when it is irrelevant (for example, insects or animals), but is considered an inappropriate and dehumanizing term in relation to humans. (At least that is the case for human adults; babies are sometimes referred to as *it* which might be an indication of how the culture views infants.) So we are left with the problem of which pronoun to use when sex is unclear. For example:

> Anyone could do it if ?? wanted to
> A sensible person would agree, wouldn't ??

Gaps in languages are not unusual, nor are they insurmountable. Where a language lacks a specific term, other bits of the language can be called in to fill the breach. Historically, English has used *they* to fill the sex-indefinite reference gap, so:

> Anyone could do it if they wanted to
> A sensible person would agree, wouldn't they?

They, of course, in the plural has no sex-definite reference and *they* can refer to an all-female, all-male or mixed sex group. It does not seem unreasonable to press it into service for the 'gap' in the singular and Ann Bodine (1975) records that *they* was accepted and widespread in both spoken and written usage prior to the nineteenth century. It was the eighteenth century though that saw the beginnings of the attack on *they* as the standardization of English reached a peak of activity. Grammarians allegedly describing the grammar of English codified the language in grammar books and dictionaries. The forms that they selected for codification then became the prescriptive norms. It was during this period that *they* was proscribed and *he* prescribed as the sex-indefinite pronoun supposedly meaning either 'he' or 'she' in that context. Given that *they* was already in general usage, there was presumably a reason why it was considered inappropriate. The reason given was that *they*, whilst agreeing in person, does not agree in number with a singular antecedent or referent. (This is an argument that is still put forward, though the same attention to plurality is stigmatized when non-standard varieties plug the plural second person gap by providing *yous*.) So, of the two candidates for sex-indefinite pronoun, *they* and *he*, *they* agrees in terms of person and gender, but not in number; *he* agrees in terms of person and number, but not in terms of gender. Each candidate has two out of three of the necessary features and is therefore, in linguistic terms, equally suitable. As Bodine points out though, the fact that *he* does not agree with an antecedent or referent in terms of gender seems to have been considered less important than the fact that *they* does not agree in number, although the reasoning for this line of argument is unclear. Gender reference is at least as, if not more, socially significant than number reference; in addition, if the appeal to 'natural gender' is made, then *she* must be equally as viable as *he*. Since *they* remains the preferred spoken form, it must also be the case, as Bodine says, that the non-singular nature of *they* is only present in discussions of meaning, rather than in real meaning.

In conjunction with the proscription on *they* came the attack on *he or she* which Bodine states (1975) was claimed by the grammarians to be '"clumsy", "pedantic" or "unnecessary"'. Similar statements are still made. Bodine points out that corresponding constructions such as *one or more* or *person or persons* were not similarly attacked although, as she states, 'the plural logically includes the singular more than the masculine includes the feminine' (1975).

Although the eighteenth-century grammarians, on whose decisions we continue to rely, may have felt that they were making linguistically justified or logical choices, their argument, Bodine adequately demonstrates, cannot be supported on linguistic grounds. In which case, what was the motivation? Bodine points to the history of masculine 'superiority' in language prescription, quoting the following from Poole (1646):

> The Relative agrees with the Antecedent in gender, number, and person... The Relative shall agree in gender with the Antecedent of the more worthy gender: as, the King and Queen whom I honor. The Masculine gender is more worthy than the Feminine.

Although this judgment did not yet extend beyond relative pronouns, the idea of masculine 'worthiness' is one that existed in other areas of the debate on language use. By the time of Kirby (1746) we have 'comprehensiveness':

> The masculine Person answers to the general Name, which comprehends both Male and Female: as Any Person, who knows what he says.

And in the subsequent Act of Parliament of 1850, this comprehensiveness became statutory:

> An Act for shortening the language used in acts of Parliament...in all acts words importing the masculine gender shall be deemed and taken to include females, and the singular to include the plural, and the plural the singular, unless the contrary as to gender and number is expressly provided.

For indefinite number, either singular or plural will do; for indefinite gender only the masculine will do. Bodine suggests that the grammarians' choice of *he* was the result of an androcentric world view; that is that human beings were 'to be considered male unless proven otherwise'. The choice is a cultural and social one. In a world in which the masculine is worthier and more comprehensive, it is 'obvious' that the masculine pronoun should be chosen, especially when those doing the choosing are male. Language prescription is invariably tied up with social and political issues (see Bodine 1975; Crowley 1989). Linguistic change and social change are interlinked and language prescription can be seen as an attempt to conserve the status quo. Whilst sex-indefinite use of *they* is, as noted, still widely used in spoken language, the effects of language prescription continue and *he* is more likely to appear in written language with the appeal to 'correct grammar' to support its use. The roots of the grammar that prescribes such use and the basis of the choice are not questioned. The move to replace so-called sex-indefinite *he* is not a new 'assault' upon the language by irate and censoring women; it is a move to reinstate what a specific, and significantly male, group imposed as a change in the first place. As Cameron (1992: 96) says of *he*, 'since the form was originally prescribed for sexist reasons, feminists who find it sexist are hardly projecting some novel and bizarre interpretation on an innocent and neutral [grammatical] rule'. The choice of *he* is a revealing social choice.

The second half of the he-man duo is *man*. *Man*, it is claimed, is the generic term for the human species and includes female and male within its meaning. 'Everyone who speaks English knows this', according to Josephine Robinson (1993), Chair of the Association of Catholic Women, among many others. To prove her argument, she turns to discussion of the term 'inclusive', stating that there is no such thing as 'inclusive language', and, drawing a dubious distinction between language and the words that make up language, states that it is only words that are inclusive and exclusive, not language. Thus, she says, 'the word *flower* includes roses and daffodils and excludes potatoes and trees' and the word *man* meaning human being includes women and men (and presumably girls and boys) and excludes angels and animals. The area of linguistic analysis to which these inclusive and exclusive relationships belong is semantics, specifically the study of sense relations. A general word (lexical item) such as *flower* is a superordinate term, and a specific lexical item (a hyponym), such as *rose*, is included within it. It is a one-way relationship. *Rose* logically entails *flower*, but *flower* does not entail *rose*. Co-hyponyms, that is other words in the set, are mutually exclusive, so *rose* excludes *tulip* just as *tulip* excludes *rose*. We know partly that a tulip is a tulip simply because it isn't one of the other hyponyms. It gets its meaning from its place in the set, as much from what it isn't as from what it is. When looking at gender terms, the same kind of pattern emerges. So *deer* for example includes *doe* and *stag* which exclude each other; *sheep* includes *ewe* and *ram*. Again though, there are lexical gaps. *Dog* has only two, not three terms, giving *dog* for male and *bitch* for female. *Man* it could be argued comes into the same category, with *man* having the additional meaning 'male' and *woman* meaning 'female'. However, in the case of *dog* there is little difficulty with the lexical gap. To say 'my dog's just had puppies' is perfectly acceptable. 'My man's just had a baby' is definitely not. Even in use as a 'true' generic, referring to the species as a whole rather than to an individual member of it, the terminology doesn't work. Try:

Man is a mammal. Man gives birth to live young (which he breastfeeds).

If this statement strikes us as odd, it is because we don't understand *man* to mean 'human' but to mean 'male'. Notice that the strangeness of this example is compounded by the injunction to use *he* for generic reference. Biblical language also has a problem with this kind of reference leaving us with 'man that is born of woman' which unfortunately confuses the 'generic', making woman a separate category from man.

There is other evidence on how the term *man* is currently understood. Research suggests that meaning derived from *man* is not mainly that of 'human being' or 'people' but that of 'male human being'. When asked to compile artistic representations of 'Industrial Man', 'Political Man', 'Social Man' and so on, undergraduate students came up with representations that predominantly represented male man. This interpretation is not restricted to the informants of researchers. The psychologist and philosopher Erich Fromm, writing on the use of so-called generic *man*, states,

> The use of 'man' [as a term of reference for the species *homo sapiens*] without differentiation of sex, has a long tradition in humanist thinking, and I do not believe we can do without a word that denotes clearly the human species character...even in English the word 'man' is used in the same sex-undifferentiated way as the German *Mensch*, as meaning human being or the human race.

So far so good, but in another work he states,

> Man's vital interests are life, food, access to females.

The alleged generic has become confused in this thinker's mind with 'male of the species', and this is but one example. A recent instance comes from ITV's *News at Ten:*

> For decades pubs have been man's best friend. He could take his wife, his girlfriend, but not his children.

Clearly a male man; the 'generic' use here excludes women. Owen Hickey's (1989) not uncommon claim that those who misunderstand generic uses do so 'wilfully' does not seem to be borne out.

Women are not really represented by the so-called generic; they are excluded. And the confusion which exists in secular language also exists in religious language. Sara Maitland quotes from the Book of Common Prayer:

> It is evident to all men diligently reading Holy Scripture and the ancient authors, that from the apostles' time there have been these orders of Ministers in Christ's Church: Bishops, Priests and Deacons. Which offices were evermore had in such reverent estimation that no man might presume to execute any of them except he were first called, tried, examined and known to have such qualities as are requisite for the same.

Maitland points out that *men* in the first instance means presumably female and male men, but *man* in the second and its corresponding pronoun *he* clearly has only the latter interpretation. Except that that interpretation is also problematic, for, as she says, the second reference then refers to Bishops and Priests, who can only be male, but not to Deacons, who can be female. Maitland's comments were written prior to the ordination of women within the Church of England, but the point remains valid. *Men* and *man* in this context were used to refer to different things and extracting the meaning is problematic. Maitland suggests the confusion is compounded by the continuation:

> And the Bishop knowing…any Person to be a man of virtuous conversation and without crime.

What kind of man, she asks, does this refer to? The Church of England's Alternative Service Book also preserves 'generic' reference, so we confess that we have sinned against God and against our 'fellow men' and we acknowledge the incarnation of Christ for 'us men and for our salvation'. The *men* here are supposed to include me. When the curate at my church started a Saturday 'Prayer Group for Men', that did not include me. *Man* is not only difficult to interpret, it also fails to include 'female'. As Cameron (1992) also points out, use of 'generic' *man* symbolically confirms male supremacy and the male-as-norm view. Since much of religious language is symbolic, this is a function that should concern us.

The argument against the movement to remove exclusive language becomes more difficult to uphold when other sex specific terms are considered. The supporters of 'generic' *man* may make appeal to history for support, and those who insist on 'inclusive' *he* may appeal to grammar prescription. It's not clear, however, what argument there is for claiming that *son* includes *daughter* and that *brother* includes *sister*. We cannot invoke the same semantic system that was claimed to support use of generic *man* because *son* and *daughter* are co-hyponyms and mutually exclusive, as are *brother* and *sister*. Even in terms of usage there is no occasion on which, having one child of each sex, I could claim to have two sons, or that my children were brothers. As Maitland says, when a priest says 'pray brethren' or the words of a hymn read 'O brother man fold to thy heart thy brother', 'it is well nigh impossible to feel a sense of incorporation' (1983: 166).

Exclusive language confirms the androcentric view of the world as male, unless otherwise stated. In a male-as-norm world view, female is automatically different, deviant, unusual. And such androcentrism does not just belong to the domain of sex-specific terms. Confirmation of the culture as androcentric is evident from the male-as-norm meaning which creeps in to what should be neutral terms. Deborah Cameron (1992) quotes an extract about refugee camps from the *Sunday Times* magazine:

> The lack of vitality is aggravated by the fact that there are so few young adults about. They have all gone off to work or to look for work, leaving behind the old, the disabled, the women and the children.

Adult in this extract, Cameron points out, means 'adult male', since although the context may make it quite reasonable to exclude 'old', 'disabled' and 'children' from the term *young adults* there is no sense in which women can be excluded. Presumably they account for a proportion of such young adults. Examples like this are not difficult to find; they turn up regularly in newspapers, on TV, on the radio. Consider the exclusive use of the term *American* which should be neutral, from *The Daily Mail*:

> Top of the list of the aphrodisiac aromas which turn on Americans is pumpkin pie…Scientists studied 31 men…

Or from *The Guardian Weekend* in a humorous note on briefcases, addressed, I thought, to all of us who carry one:

> Some briefcases have concertina sections…Remember to clear this out when you come back from trips abroad, otherwise you'll open up for a key presentation and your wife's nightie will billow out on to the boardroom table.

It is interesting that there is very little comment about extracts such as these. It seems that in an androcentric world, they pass us by, but there can be little doubt that for these writers, Americans are men, as are the carriers of briefcases. Cameron quotes another extract from *The Guardian*, revealing similar exclusive reference:

> A coloured South African who was subjected to racial abuse by his neighbours went berserk with a machete and killed his next-door neighbour's wife, Birmingham Crown Court heard yesterday.

Cameron again points out that since presumably the victim also lived next door to the attacker, then she was also his neighbour. *Neighbour* in this context means 'male'. Biblical reference to *neighbour* in the commandments suffers a similar distortion. The commandment 'thou shalt not covet thy neighbour's wife' in the King James version undergoes various linguistic changes in various revisions, becoming 'you must not covet your neighbour's wife' in the 1989 Revised English Bible. *Neighbour* here also means 'male'. Additionally, the 1970 New Bible Commentary says: 'the singular form of address 'you' (AV 'thou') while standing collectively for Israel, more particularly refers to each Israelite', except of course in this context, the women.

Maitland suggests that it is difficult to persuade anyone not already convinced of the arguments that the issue of exclusive language is a serious one, and given our apparently ready acceptance of andro-centrism, she is right. Women are accused of anger, a wish to censor, a wish to interfere with the language or a morbid sensibility. When, how-ever, the boot is on the other foot, the picture changes. When men began to enter the profession of primary school teaching, they objected to the continuation of the use of the pronoun *she* to refer to the undiffer-entiated teacher on the grounds that it was insulting and demeaned the profession. It contrasted, they said, with the 'vital image' which teachers were attempting to portray (in a way which *he* presumably would not). Similar subjective comments are made about inclusive religious language in terms of 'lack of dignity', 'weakening of sense', 'diluting richness'.

After the publication of the new catechism last year, Archbishop D'Arcy justified his decision not to use inclusive language by suggesting that the first translation, which did use inclusive language, had departed from the original. In an interview in *The Tablet* (21 May 1994), using a medical metaphor, he was asked whether the 'major surgery' performed on inclusive language would be seen as an affront to women. His response:

> The surgery is not being done on the English... The patient to be operated on was the French... The first translation departs from the original and the patient has suffered and needs some healing.

I cannot agree that references to suffering and healing are appropriate when talking about languages. It is impossible to inflict pain and suffer-ing on a language. Languages cannot be abused, only their users. It is people who decide how to use the language at their disposal, how to control it, and what meanings to embody in it. In this way people can inflict pain and suffering on other people, but not on a language.

The exclusive language used to refer to human beings confirms women in second class status, both in society in general and conse-quently in the church. It is not, of course, only language that places them there, but where such undesirable cultural norms exist, any means that can reasonably be taken should be taken to counteract them. Linguistic reform is only one tool but the church would be better off for using it.

BIBLIOGRAPHY

Bodine, A.
1975 'Androcentrism in Prescriptive Grammar: Singular "They", Sex Indefinite "He", and "He or She"', *Language in Society* 4: 129-46.
Cameron, D.
1992 *Feminism and Linguistic Theory* (London: Macmillan, 2nd edn).
1994 ' "Words, Words, Words": The Power of Language', in S. Dunant (ed.), *The War of the Words* (London: Virago Press).
Crowley, T.
1989 *The Politics of Discourse* (London: Macmillan).
Crystal, D.
1987 *The Cambridge Encyclopedia of Language* (Cambridge: Cambridge University Press).
Hickey, O.
1989 *The Tablet*, 13 May 1989.
Maitland, S.
1983 *A Map of the New Country: Women and Christianity* (London: Routledge & Kegan Paul).
Robinson, J.
1993 *The Universe*, 14 February 1993.

FROM PERFORMATIVITY TO PEDAGOGY: JEAN LADRIERE AND THE
PRAGMATICS OF REFORMED WORSHIP DISCOURSE

David Hilborn

1. *Pragmatics, Discourse and Liturgy*

Dean Inge once likened liturgical study to stamp-collecting, and confessed that he could see little point in either. I take a more positive view,
but I do so recognizing that most liturgists remain preoccupied with the
work of textual and historical reconstruction, and have been slow to
embrace a more broadly 'semiotic' approach to sacral performance. In
what follows, I shall develop this more semiotic line of analysis in a way
which seems to me to be especially appropriate. Specifically, I shall focus
on the dynamics of language-use in Christian worship, and shall show
how study of these dynamics can be informed by insights from modern
linguistic pragmatics.

Pragmatics is concerned with how language functions in relation to
context, and with how it operates as an instrument of human interaction.[1] Recent anatomies of the subject trace its origins to the American
philosopher Charles W. Morris (Levinson 1983: 1; Mey 1993: 35). In
1938, Morris proposed the outline of a unifying 'semiotic' or 'science of
signs' (1938: 79-80). Claiming precedents in Aristotle, Ockham and
Locke, he presented the 'sign' as a basic phenomenon of communication or 'semiosis', describing it as 'the means by which something is
referred to by someone' (1938: 81, 123).[2] More particularly, Morris
drew his conception and terminology from the work of Charles Sanders
Peirce (1839–1914), whom he described as 'second to none in the

---

1.   For similar basic definitions, see Stalnaker 1972: 380; Haberland and Mey
1977: 1; McCarthur 1992: 800; Richards, Platt and Platt 1992: 284.

2.   Detailed studies of the origins of semiotics in the history of philosophy are
provided by Eco 1976, Hawkes 1977 and Aarsleff 1982. Lange-Seidl 1986 traces this
history with specific relation to the pragmatic dimensions of semiosis.

history of semiotic' (1938: 109).[3] From these foundations, Morris cast the discipline of semiotic into a trichotomy where *syntactics* would examine 'the relations of signs to one another', *semantics* 'the relations of signs to the objects to which [they] are applicable' and *pragmatics* 'the relation of signs to interpreters' (1938: 84; cf. Peirce 1960: 2.227-308).

Morris's original definition of pragmatics was meant to cover more than just language. Indeed, his grand ambition was to provide all human expression and experimentation with a coherent analytical framework. Hence his semiotic trichotomy was to be applied to 'art, testing devices, medical diagnoses, signalling instruments' and even 'smoke', as well as to 'human speech' and 'writing' (1938: 79, 115). Clearly, too, the significant 'sign systems' of liturgy can be many and varied; they might, for instance, include dress, posture, gesture and proxemics, as well as language itself. Indeed, though few in number, there have been some worthwhile attempts to place religious ritual within this more general pragmatics perspective (e.g. Lardner 1979; Enninger and Raith 1982; Lukken 1987). Nonetheless, there can be little doubt that as it has evolved in its own right into a 'mature' academic discipline (Horn 1988: 116), pragmatics has developed substantially as a branch of *linguistics* (Leech and Thomas 1990: 173-74). Furthermore, it is this specific development of 'linguistic pragmatics' which suggests itself most strongly as a tool of liturgical exposition, since it is in its liturgical context that religious language is definitively 'put to work'.

It is a key axiom of pragmatics that the 'meaning' of words is determined by their contingent function rather than by their etymology (Crystal 1971: 63). Pragmaticians study language *discoursally* rather than *philologically*. In the first place, 'discourses' are clearly linguistic phenomena, representing 'continuous stretches of language longer than a sentence'—stretches in which one phrase or utterance endogenously 'contextualizes' the phrases or utterances which follow it (Crystal 1991: 106; Auer 1992). More specific to pragmatics, however, is the analysis of discourse as an interactive enterprise in which many relevant features are *extralinguistic*, and where meaning is seen to emerge from 'a dynamic process in which language is used as an instrument of communication in a context by a speaker/writer to express meanings and

---

3. 'Semiotic' as a term has since largely been superseded by the plural 'semiotics'. For an account of the term's history see Sebeok, Hayes and Bateson 1964.

achieve intentions' (Brown and Yule 1983: 26). From this point of view, *liturgical* discourses must be understood to comprise more than the written service *texts* studied by traditional liturgists; rather, they should be regarded as the verbal instantiations of a wider realm of sacral *enactment*. Margaret Mary Kelleher bears out this emphasis when she suggests that a modern hermeneutics of liturgy would define it as 'a form of ecclesial performative meaning—a ritual in which an assembly performs...meanings and values which are constitutive of its identity' (1993: 306).

In view of these definitions, it is somewhat ironic to note that the very word 'liturgy' itself bears at least a trace of pragmatic significance. Most liturgists at some point stress its roots in a Greek compound (λειτουργία) derived from words for 'labour' (ἔργον) and 'people' (λαός) (Power 1984: 148; Beach 1986: 314; Fageberg 1992: 181ff.). Though the term related originally to service performed by an individual for the public at large, and though it is thus likely to have meant 'work *on behalf* of the people' rather than 'work *of* the people' (Wolterstorff 1992: 274), the resonance of its compounding 'activity' and 'community' has hardly been lost on liturgical scholarship. In his seminal work *The Shape of the Liturgy* (1945), Dom Gregory Dix called memorably for a re-emphasis on church worship as 'primarily something done' rather than something 'said', arguing that while eucharistic celebration since the Latin Middle Ages had been cast as 'saying' and 'hearing' Mass, 'the ancients on the contrary habitually spoke of "*doing* the eucharist" (*eucharistiam facere*), "*performing* the mysteries" (*mysteria telem*) and "*making* the synaxis" (*synaxin agein, collectam facere*)' (Dix 1945: 12-13). This emphasis has since proved very influential, but it warrants further scrutiny from the semiotic viewpoint which I have outlined, and in particular, from a linguistic-pragmatic approach to the church service. Elsewhere, I have presented a comprehensive and contemporary 'pragmatics of liturgical discourse' (Hilborn 1994). Here, I shall focus primarily on one of several strands of linguistic pragmatics—namely 'speech act theory'.

The best-read text in the history of pragmatics remains J.L. Austin's *How to Do Things with Words*. Posthumously edited from lectures delivered in the '50s, this book challenges the strictly referential and truth-conditional semantics of logical positivism (cf. Ayer 1936). Indeed, it is a challenge which becomes more radical as Austin's argument unfolds. Austin begins by making a crucial distinction between purely denotative or *constative* utterances, and utterances whose purpose is not to *describe* something so much as to *do* it (1962: 6). This second group of expressions Austin terms *performatives*, and it is significant for our purposes that he sees them occurring particularly within ritual settings— for example 'I baptize', 'I declare them to be husband and wife', 'I repent', 'I covenant' and so on (1962: 11, 64, 83, 157). As Austin's exposition proceeds, however, the original constative/performative duality begins to collapse, and is replaced by a conception which sees *all* expressions as 'speech acts' dependent for their meaning on the 'total speech situation' in which they arise (1962: 148). Rather than being assessed according to their respective 'truth' or 'falsity', these speech acts are represented as 'felicitous' or 'infelicitous' according to various 'conditions' which different circumstances impose on their effective use (1962: 12ff.). This thoroughgoing relation of linguistic meaning to function and context is schematized by Austin's identifying various 'illocutionary acts' with deeds done *in* saying certain things, over and above mere 'locutionary' acts *of* saying defined in purely lexical or phonetic terms. He also recognizes that speech action is 'perlocutionary'—that is, oriented towards some definable goal or outcome (1962: 109-32).

As developed by Austin's pupil John Searle (1969, 1979), and as refined by Bach and Harnish (1979), Recanati (1987) and others, speech act theory has considerable potential for the analysis of liturgy. Its stress on language as a means to action; its sensitivity to performance, ritual and local 'rules' as components of linguistic meaning; its acceptance on these premises of 'empirically unverifiable' statements—these commend it for the study of religious discourse in general and sacral discourse in particular. Despite this, it has been appropriated only sporadically by those working on such discourse, and even then, there has been very little dialogue between those concerned (cf. Evans 1963; Gill 1969; Jeffner 1972; Smith and McLendon 1972; Manansan 1974; Martinich 1975a, b; McLendon and Smith 1975; Vincent 1979; Ware 1981; Crystal 1990; Tilley 1991; Wolterstorff 1993). Here, I shall attempt a rather different approach. First, I shall compare theological understandings of liturgical language-use in two major Christian traditions, and seek to relate these to speech act and pragmatic theory. Then I shall offer examples drawn from actual church services, as well as from the service books and orders more normally studied by those theologians and linguists who have discussed the discourse of liturgy. The comparison will constitute a Reformed or 'Calvinistic' response to the Louvain Catholic philosopher Jean Ladrière's brief but highly suggestive article 'The Performativity of Liturgical Language' (1973). The 'field' examples come from a survey of language-use in 10 congregations of my own denomination—the United Reformed Church in the United Kingdom (URC). Each of these congregations submitted audio recordings of their morning service from Advent Sunday, 1 December 1991, along with a special questionnaire designed to recover relevant contextual information. The recordings were then transcribed using a 'poetic line' analysis advocated by the sociolinguists Wallace Chafe (1986) and Deborah Tannen (1989: 202-203). (For further details, see Hilborn 1994.)

2. *Ladrière and Liturgical Language 'Performativity'*

In keeping with speech act understanding, Ladrière makes it clear that liturgical language 'cannot be analysed in terms of information theory: it does not consist in the reporting of events, the description of objects, the formulation of theoretical hypotheses, the statement of experimental findings, or the handing on of data'. Rather, such language is to be 'characterized in that it is a certain form of action'. It thus 'puts something into practice; in short, it possesses an "operativity"'. It is not to be thought of as 'merely a verbal commentary on an action external to itself; in and of itself, it is action' (1973: 51). Given this starting-point, Ladrière rightly identifies his 'basic problem' as 'to discover how liturgical language *works*', and then to determine 'the *exact kind* of [operation] proper to liturgical language' (1973: 51, my emphases). Initially, he approaches this problem by invoking Austin's original distinction between 'constatives' and 'performatives'. Thus he proposes that 'in order...to express the operative (non-descriptive) nature of liturgical language, we may use the term "performativity"' (1973: 52). Ladrière soon acknowledges, however, that first Austin, and then Searle, collapsed this distinction into more nuanced models of illocutionary activity, and that the analysis of liturgical discourse should in fact be conducted within the wider sphere of 'pragmatics'—that is, within a realm where linguistic interpretation takes full account of 'users... speakers and those spoken to' (1973: 52-53). Perspicuously given the development of pragmatics since Austin, Ladrière maintains that the 'very complex' nature of liturgical language should no longer be understood in the sense of a 'general principle of operativity' (1973: 55). In effect, this means a thoroughly discoursal pragmatics along the lines I have suggested. But even within the bounds of classical speech act theory, Ladrière is justified in claiming that 'every effort must be made to conceive liturgical language as a whole, or in the general context in which [liturgical] sentences function' (1973: 55).

When thus considered, Ladrière suggests insightfully that liturgical discourse will be 'seen to possess a *threefold performativity*: that of an *existential induction*, that of an *institution*, and that of a *presentification*' (1973: 55). Inasmuch as participation in the liturgy means being 'inducted' existentially into a community and an institution, it means simultaneously entering a language-game constituted by 'very exact rules' (1973: 58-59). Indeed, one cannot in practice separate the church's corporate being from its corporate 'rite': each owes its identity crucially to the other. Thus 'language is not the expression of a community constituted before it and apart from it and is not the description of what such a community would be, but the location in which and the instrument by means of which the community is constituted' (1973: 59). As David Fageberg has remarked, this statement represents the ultimate corrective to more typically Protestant emphases on prior 'theological concepts' regulating subsequent 'liturgical actions'—that is, on a biblical or doctrinal *lex credendi* predetermining a sacral *lex orandi*. Ladrière's understanding of sacral discourse is indeed far more 'primary' than this: 'for [Ladrière], liturgical illocutionary and symbolic acts *create* the community and *create* attitudes which come into effect when the liturgical rite is transacted. *The liturgy creates the attitudes...it does not merely give expression to them*' (1992: 139-40, my emphasis).

Important as existential induction and institution are, it is Ladrière's third dynamic of *presentification* which reveals most about his view of liturgical language performativity. 'By all those acts which it effects', he contends, liturgical language 'makes present for the participants, not as a spectacle, but as a reality whose efficacy they take into their very own life, that about which it speaks and which it effects in diverse ways: the mystery of Christ, his life and death, and his resurrection: the revelation conveyed to us in him of the mystery of God: the accomplishment of the eternal plan by virtue of which we are called to become children of God, co-heirs of Christ in eternal life' (1973: 59-60). This vital 'making present' is achieved for Ladrière in three main ways. First, he proposes that it is accomplished by *repetition*. Repetition in the liturgical context means more than 'mere quotation'; it is, rather, 'the resumption into acts of today of words written or spoken at a given moment in the past' (1973: 60). In fact, Ladrière's original French term *reprise* in this sense better captures the thrust of his analysis, which envisages established canonical formulae being 'taken up' afresh by each contemporary assembly, and thus imbued with illocutionary force through the instantiation of liturgical discourse in particular ecclesial contexts.

The second way in which presentification occurs for Ladrière is through *proclamation*. Significantly from his Roman perspective, Ladrière sees this reaching its 'culmination' in the creed or 'confession of faith', rather than in the sermon. Like his fellow Catholic Mary John Mananzan (1974), Ladrière regards the enunciation of the creed in worship as providing a paradigmatic bridge between doctrinal and affective (that is, attestational, ratificational and commitmental) speech. In this sense, he characterizes it, almost paradoxically, as a set of 'propositional acts'—acts which 'bring into existence a form of discursive articulation in which the very content of the mystery [of salvation] becomes manifest' (1973: 60).

Ultimately, though, it is Ladrière's third dynamic of presentification— the dynamic of *sacramentality*—through which liturgical language is seen to have 'its most profoundly actualizing effect' (1973: 61). Sacramentality in this regard is a fundamentally eschatological phenomenon—one which links not only the diachronic and synchronic dimensions of sacral discourse, but which also points towards what has yet to be fulfilled (1973: 61). Indeed, he goes so far as to emphasize that it is the 'registration' of liturgical language in this eschatological perspective which 'allows it its characteristic performativity' (1973: 61). Again showing his Catholic orientation, Ladrière claims that 'in repeating the words of the Last Supper, the celebrant does more than commemorate it'. Rather, he 'repeats once again that which Christ did, in giving again to the words which Christ used that efficacy which Christ gave them, *in conferring upon them again the power to do what they mean*' (1973: 61). What is proposed here, then, is not just 'repetition' or even 'reappropriation', but a 'real presence' *re-enactment* of Gospel events. Admittedly, Ladrière begins by dubbing this re-enactment 'secondary' in terms of performativity, to the original 'institution' of sacred words and acts by Christ himself (1973: 61). Nevertheless, he *goes on* to propose that by 're-effectuating' such words and acts in 'the context of the prayer of the Canon', a modern-day congregation can in fact *'restore them to their primary performativity'* (1973: 61, my emphasis). Furthermore, while thus 'resuming' that 'which has already taken place', the same congregation also makes 'an announcement of that which is still awaited' (1973: 61).

Unfortunately, Ladrière does not support this grand 'liturgical discourse eschatology' with specific linguistic analysis—but he does commend such analysis to others (1973: 61). Indeed, he maintains that only *with* such evidence would it be possible to show 'in what way [liturgical language] really "makes present" that which it talks of' (1973: 61). It is this challenge that my own 'fieldwork' approach attempts to meet, but before examining specific examples, it is necessary to appreciate the way in which Ladrière addresses the problem of *how* liturgical 'performativity' and 'sacramentality' are brought about by, in and through the assembly itself—that is, of how sacral discourse is 'made present' to 'users...speakers and those spoken to' (1973: 52). Vitally, Ladrière resolves this question in terms of *faith*. 'Faith' for Ladrière is that which supremely 'impels' liturgical language and 'endows it with performativity' (1973: 61). He goes on to contend that this faith is not to be seen as some 'prior experience' generated in a context separate from and antecedent to the liturgy, which it is the function of liturgical language then to 'describe'. Rather, 'between liturgical language and faith there is a kind of dual assumption'. According to Ladrière,

> Faith takes up this language and gives it its own efficacy, inasmuch as faith is a resumption of the mystery of Christ, the acceptance of salvation and hope of benefits yet to come. Language is to faith a kind of structuring field which allows it to express itself in accordance with the reality to which it corresponds. The language is proclamation of the very content in which the faith is truly embodied, and is a sacramental accomplishment of the mystery which is thus announced and witnessed. Its threefold performativity enables faith to be expressed (1973: 61-62).

This on its own appears to imbue 'faith-driven' language with a quite extraordinary causality. Even so, Ladrière is quick to deny that this causality could be interpreted in a fideistic or even occultic sense—that is, as something generated by 'human believing' alone. On the contrary, 'faith' is itself to be understood as a product of divine grace—something, moreover, which is mediated specifically by God's eternal λόγος. Thus 'faith...is the hearing of the Word and the *effective action* of the Word in human life' (1973: 62). Even further still,

If faith is the reception of the Word and if liturgical language receives from faith its characteristic performativity, that language is itself an echo of the Word. In the celebration it is the Word to which faith allows access that becomes present and operative in our own words. The word became flesh and dwelt among us. Insofar as in and by faith we become participants in the mystery of the incarnation, our speech acts, in the liturgy, become the present mainstay of the manifestation of the Word (1973: 62).

Ladrière's argument turns, then, on a 'circle' of sacred language comprehension. Liturgical self-involvement comes by faith, which is defined primarily as the 'hearing of the Word'; liturgy is the archetypal medium through which this Word is 'made present', but is at the same time constituted *by* the Word. Hence not only the Word itself, but faith and worship too, have their past, present and future source in God, who alone is 'prior to' the discourse of praise.

3. *The Reformed Perspective*

Now at first glance, what has just been outlined might seem quite close to the basic tenets of *Reformed* theology. The superintendence of the Word in worship; the emphasis on 'faith alone' as the operative fuel of liturgy; the stress on 'hearing' as constitutive of 'believing' and 'participating' in the church community—all these are axiomatic in Reformed theologies of worship from John Calvin (1559) through Karl Barth (1936: 88-111) to Jean-Jaques von Allmen (1965) and Hughes Oliphant Old (1992). Nonetheless, as I have already hinted, the *detail* of Ladrière's argument is more readily *contrasted* with Reformed understanding, and it seems likely that it will be such differences of detail which will determine just how smoothly his 'performativity hypothesis' can be translated into a pragmatics of Protestant liturgical performance in general, and of Reformed liturgical performance in particular.

While Ladrière's relating of presentification to 'Word' and 'faith' suggests a strong connection with Reformed liturgical theology, closer inspection of his argument reveals traces of an 'essentialist', *de re* view of sacral language causation which would yet distinguish his liturgical pragmatics as 'Roman Catholic', from a more consciously 'Calvinistic' or 'Reformed' liturgical pragmatics. Certainly, Ladrière does on occasion write as if liturgical language were possessed *in and of itself* with a peculiar illocutionary force, rather than receiving this force from liturgical *usage* alone. To borrow Wolterstorff's description of Aquinas's liturgiology (1993), Ladrière manages—in spite of elsewhere deploying firm *de fide* and *de Verbo Dei* explanations of sacral discourse performativity—to imply a linguistic *sign-agency* even while emphasizing the *God-agency* of liturgical language. Within this sign-agency, sacral performativity appears to reside in the very form, structure and composition of the words themselves, rather than in their contextual appropriation. Hence liturgical language is seen by Ladrière to 'put something into practice' (1973: 51). It is not just taken up operatively by its worshipping *users*—it also has an operative 'nature' (1973: 52). It thus 'awakens' in the person deploying it an 'affective disposition' which 'opens up' their existence to a 'specific field of reality' (1973: 56). At a corporate level, this same liturgical language is not just an 'instrument' used by the Christian community to constitute itself as a community: it is also the very thing which inherently *establishes* and *realizes* that community. Similarly, it '*makes present...*that about which it *speaks* and which it *effects* in diverse ways' (1973: 59, my emphasis). It thus has a 'revelatory essence' and 'origin' (1973: 60). Given these definitions, it comes as little surprise when Ladrière concludes by saying that liturgical language constitutes a 'sacramental accomplishment' of the mysteries it 'announces' and 'witnesses to'. What is more, this 'sacramentality' applies not just to the immediate performatives of sacramental celebration like the Epiclesis, Absolution and Baptismal Pronouncement; it is, rather, intrinsic both to the whole 'canon' of eucharistic observance including the *Sursum corda*, *Sanctus*, *Benedictus*, Offertory, Petition, Intercession, *Anamnesis*, Narrative and Ascription of Praise (1973: 58)— and seems often to cover the very fullest range of church service expression, from Opening Sentences to Benediction.

Now it is true that Ladrière sees 'le langage liturgique' as a 'totality' of illocutionary forces rather than a diaspora of atomistic sentences (1973: 55). Nevertheless, he does still appear to 'sacramentalize' the actual *object* of liturgical language to an extent that would not be compatible with classical Reformed doctrine—and which must in any case be questioned as to how faithfully it reflects Austin and Searle's *own* models, which at least present themselves as models of how *people* do things *with* words, rather than of any 'operativity' possessed by words themselves. It is significant that a similarly agentive and causative 'linguistic essentialism' informs the more recent Roman Catholic liturgical theologies offered by David Power and Aidan Kavanagh. For Power (1984: 148), the entire canon must be thought of 'sacramentally', while in Kavanagh's view, liturgical discourse 'itself begins to *think* and *speak*

for the assembly and turns wholly into music, not in the sense of outward, audible sounds, but by virtue of the power of momentum of its
inward flow' (1984: 86, my emphasis).

It is at this point that one begins to detect echoes of what Calvin and
his successors so vigorously *opposed* in the Mass—namely, the notion
that any set verbal formula could *in and of itself* ensure a 'holy' (or
'felicitous') act of praise (Calvin 1559: III.20.29; cf. Wainwright 1980:
263-83). Just as the Anglican Evangelical Thiselton (1974) sees this as a
questionably 'magical' basis on which to expound biblical speech acts,
so Vincent pertinently comments that 'the Calvinian critique of the way
in which the Catholic Church manipulates the words of institution rests
on this overriding perception: that there is no need to attribute to God
any "occult" power. The fiction of such a power is the result of a
fictitious word, of a false word which wreaks betrayal even as it is whis-
pered' (1979: 153). Certainly, it does seem that Ladrière, Power and
Kavanagh's attachment to 'the canon' as a lexically fixed and relatively
monolithic 'entity' predisposes them to the sort of operative-linguistic
essentialism I have been highlighting. No doubt too, this predisposition
makes it easier for them then to promote 'theology' as something
wholly 'brought about' in and by the language of worship, rather than
as something which must be brought along to, and 'expressed by' such
language (cf. Auer 1992).

In contrast, Reformed liturgiology from Calvin onwards has always
been far more sceptical about the capacity of *any* set form of ritual
language to realize 'true worship' or 'true doctrine' as a function of its
own *composition*. Indeed, the concept of 'canon' which is so fundamental to Ladrière, Power and Kavanagh's 'pragmatic' was one of the very
first pillars of Roman liturgiology to be cast down by Calvinism—and
not least by Calvinism in England. As R.C.D. Jasper points out (1986:
139), its abolition was 'almost an article of faith for the Reformers
except for Cranmer. In nearly all Reformed rites it was normally
reduced to the narrative of the institution with the possible addition of a
prayer for worthy reception'.[4] Closely allied with this 'anti-ritualist'
trend was the pragmatically significant abolition and adaptation of fixed
dialogues. Where not dismissed altogether, these were transformed into
straight monological prose, to render them more semantically coherent
and thus 'explicable'. Oecolampadius, for instance, retained the *Kyrie* in

---

4.   For a detailed account of Reformed simplifications of the canon, see Spinks
1984: 17-36.

his *Manière et Fasson* (1525), but only as three sentences of monolithic Ministerial speech voiced in succession from an equally monolithic rendering of the penitential Ps. 130.1-8 (Oecolampadius 1525: 213). The result is prosaic in both senses of the word, not to say discoursally incongruous:

(1) ...O Israel hope in the Lord! For with the Lord there is steadfast love, and with him is plenteous redemption. And he will redeem Israel from all his iniquities.
Lord, have mercy. Christ, have mercy. Lord, have mercy on us for ever and ever.
Hear the Absolution...

Elsewhere, attempts were made to monologize previously dialogic portions through a more studied introduction of those lexical ties and clausal connectives which characteristically mark out semantically coherent 'text' from less explicitly and more pragmatically inferred interaction (cf. van Dijk 1977: 208-13). So, Farel's *Sursum corda* came to read as follows:

(2) Therefore lift up your hearts on high, seeking the heavenly things in heaven, where Jesus Christ is seated at the right hand of the Father; and do not fix your eyes on the visible signs which are corrupted through usage. In joy of heart, in brotherly union, come, everyone, to partake of our Lord's Table, giving thanks unto Him for the very great love which He has shown us (Farel 1524: 223).

As it underwent translation into an English language and context, Reformed liturgy subsumed once intrinsically dialogic discourses even further into the form of 'didactic monologue'. Traces of the *Gloria* in this extract from Richard Baxter's *Savoy Liturgy* are, for instance, very faint indeed:

(3) Worthy is the Lamb that was slain, to receive power, and honour, and glory: for he hath redeemed us by his blood, and hath made us kings and priests unto God. Where sin abounded, grace hath abounded much more. And hast thou, indeed, forgiven us so great a debt, by so precious a ransom? Wilt thou, indeed, give us to reign with Christ in glory, and see thy face and love thee, and be beloved of thee? (Baxter 1661: 403).

These examples demonstrate the roots of the Reformed church's move away from implicit, elliptical meanings defined by pragmatic association with the wider performative environment of worship, towards that more explicit and demonstrable form of expression which characterizes the discourse of pedagogy. This shift was but one manifestation of what both Louis Bouyer (1963: 58-59) and Nicholas Wolterstorff (1992) describe as the movement of Reformed churches towards an excessively propositionalistic 'dogma' of liturgico-linguistic meaning. Just as significant in this movement was the English Puritans' development of a 'pure scriptural' paradigm of Reformed worship. Specifically, this paradigm was reified in the replacement of set forms and service books by 'multi-choice' and extemporary prayer. Where Calvin himself had endorsed linguistic variation at some points but retained fixed texts at others, English Separatists like John Field (1545–88), Henry Barrow (1550–93) and Robert Browne (1550–63) disavowed set liturgy altogether. Seemingly oblivious to the liturgical provenance of much in Scripture itself, these men and their followers held that the revealed 'apostolic model' of prayer was archetypally 'spiritual'—that is, contingently and spontaneously expressed in response to 'present wants and occasions' (Barrow 1591–93: 366). Later, some even came to equate attachment to 'prayer books' with the sin of idolatry (Cotton 1642: 70; Smyth 1645: 29). From these standpoints, certain Puritan leaders went so far as to question regular recitation of the Lord's Prayer, lest it become too sacramentalized and 'talismanic'. Thus the *Barrowist Deposition* of 1587 contended that it was 'a form of prayer not to be used for the Apostles did not used to say it' (cit. Burrage 1912: i.56), while the *Brownist Confession* of 1596 argued more subtly that rather than being given by Christ as a set verbal formula, it suggested 'not that we should be tied to the use of these very words, but that we should according to that rule make all our requests and thanksgivings unto God, forasmuch as it is a perfect form and pattern conveying in its plain and sufficient directions of prayer for all occasions and necessities that have been, are, or shall be to the Church of God' (cit. Davies 1948: 98). The contrast with Ladrière's 'performative language' essentialism is clear.

Even among those Calvinists who remained within the Church of England, the drive for a less rigidly monolithic and 'textualized' worship than that offered by the Book of Common Prayer became considerable. Right-wing Presbyterians tendered an alternative liturgy to Parliament based on Knox's *Genevan Service Book* (Davies 1948: 111), while Independents like John Owen (1616–83) went much further in advocating a thoroughly extemporary approach (Davies 1948: 111-12). By the time of the Westminster Assembly, summoned by Parliament during the Civil War between 1643–48, both Presbyterian and Independent opposition to the BCP had hardened into support for a *Directory* of worship which pronounced it an 'offence' and a 'burden' to countenance 'the reading of all the Prayers' (*Westminster Directory* 1644: 8). Although this *Westminster Directory* did not wholly reject the use of set forms, its predominant approach is one in which, though biblically-based 'contents' and 'structures' are defined, ministers are allowed freedom to pray 'in their own words', as they are led by the Holy Spirit.

After the Restoration under Charles II and the Act of Uniformity in 1662, those subscribing to more extemporary techniques over against the BCP found themselves forcibly ejected from the Church of England. Ever since, 'nonconformist' or 'Dissenting' Reformed worship in England has been characterized by either 'directory' or extemporary models of sacral language-use, and thus, by a repertoire of discourses which are either 'free' or 'semi-free' in nature (cf. Ferguson 1985: 208-209). So, the editor of the latest URC *Service Book* insists that its use is purely discretionary and admits that even producing such a book at all might seem odd to some in his tradition (URC 1989: vi-xiii). Most importantly, however, Reformed approaches to worship have derived largely from a conviction that the written Word of God is not only the 'supreme liturgical criterion' (Davies 1948: 52), but also and more specifically, a repository of prior divine ordinances or 'propositions', which it is the purpose of worship then subserviently to expound and 'explain' (Bouyer 1963: 59). Certainly, a tendency to 'over-inform' seems to have been a feature of English Reformed worship since its inception. No doubt this can be put down to over-compensating for a perceived 'occultism' in the linguistic philosophy of the Mass, but even commitedly Reformed liturgists will admit that their tradition has gone too far in its converse attachment to doctrinal didacticism (Routley 1960: 108-12; Mayor 1972: 27; Spinks 1984: 82). In Wolterstorff's terms, this has led to no less than an 'overwhelming' of the 'worship dimension' of Reformed church services by the 'proclamation dimension' (1992: 297). Moreover, it would appear that the compulsion to 'footnote', 'editorialize' and teach through Reformed liturgy is as pervasive in my own field data as it was in early Reformed worship.

The opening few lines of *Calvin's Collect for Illumination*—an innovation from his 1542 Geneva rite—provide a good example of the didacticism I have been identifying. As much as petition, it provides a dense dogmatic disquisition on the providence and uniqueness of God, the doctrine of atonement, human sin, the means of grace, soteriology, pneumatology and Christology:

> (4)   We pray thee now, O most gracious and merciful Father, for all men everywhere. As it is thy will to be acknowledged the Saviour of the whole world, through the redemption wrought by thy Son Jesus Christ, grant that those who are still estranged from the knowledge of Him, being in the darkness and captivity of error and ignorance, may be brought by the illumination of thy Holy Spirit and the preaching of the Gospel to the straight way of salvation, which is to know thee, the only true God, and Jesus Christ whom thou hast sent (Calvin 1542/45: 200).

It is noticeable here that much of the sermonizing and exposition in question takes place through 'supplementary' subordinate clauses—and especially those of a relative type—e.g. 'As it is thy will to be acknowledged the Saviour...'; 'those *who* are still estranged from the knowledge of him...being in darkness...'; '*which* is to know thee...and Jesus Christ, *whom* thou hast sent', etc. Adverbial groups are also used to carry significant doctrinal information: '*through* the redemption wrought *by* thy Son'; '*by* the illumination of the Holy Spirit'; '*to* the straight way of salvation'. In addition, substantial 'pedagogic' modification and qualification of nouns loads further dogmatic weight onto the prayer: '*most gracious and merciful* Father; 'the Saviour *of the whole world*'; '*thy Son* Jesus Christ'; 'the *only true* God', etc. These phenomena are mirrored in the seminal *Middleburg Liturgy* of the English Puritans (1586), whose sometime post-sermon prayer is, if anything, even more replete with didactic deviation:

> (5)   Almighty God and Heavenly Father, since thou hast promised to grant our requests, which, we shall make unto thee in the Name of our Lord Jesus Christ thy wellbeloved Son, and that we are also taught by him and his Apostles, to assemble our selves in his Name promising that he will be among us, and make intercession for us unto thee, for the obtaining of all such things, as we shall agree upon here on Earth: we therefore (having first thy commandment to pray for such as thou hast appointed rulers and governers over us, and also for all things needfull, both for thy people, and for all sortes of men, forasmuch as our faith is grounded on thine Holy Word and promises, and that we are here gathered together before thy

face, and in the Name of thy Son our Lord Jesus), we, I say,
make our earnest supplication unto thee, our most merciful God
and bountiful Father...(Middleburg 1586: 325-26).

With particular relation to Baxter's *Savoy Liturgy* of 1661, but with
more general reference to English Puritan rites, Erik Routley has
observed a governing principle that 'nothing must be left to the imagination...' (1960: 108). With the Anglican contention that a brief and oft-
repeated prayer can inspire personal devotions arising from it 'the
Puritans would have nothing to do'. The result, he concludes, was an
excess of 'literalism' which virtually obliterated 'style', 'rhythm', and
'graceful turns of phrase' and which preferred 'that crudity which
comes from Scripture to that urbanity which smacks of "the church"'
(1960: 108-109). Indeed, Baxter went so far as to repeat the practice of
the earlier Middleburg and 'Waldegrave' liturgies by printing relevant
Bible references in the margin of his text! (Davies 1948: 126).

From a modern URC setting, my field corpus still throws up numerous examples of doctrinal assertion made in passages where more explicitly performative discourse might be thought appropriate. Now, as
before, sub-clauses generally and relative clauses especially, along with
adverbials, modifiers and qualifiers, are the most noticeable vehicles for
such 'sermonization':

(6)   MINISTER: Father as we come to you on this day we come
                 to praise and to worship,
                 to glorify your name,
                 for you are the one who has sent *Jesus*,
                 and will /save the earth/...
                 Thankyou: that he has come *once*...as a baby.
                 The one who was able to step into history to declare
                 your love,
                 to i*dent*ify with our human lives
                 in their frailty and sin...,
                 to come a*mongst* us
                 and to share *all* that you have in store for us.
                 To declare your kingdom...
                 and to bring...forgiveness,
                 and new life
                 through his death on the cross...

(AS 4: 35-58[5]—Prayer of praise and invocation
[extemporary])

Here, certainly, the *lex credendi* dominates the *lex orandi*: credal
dogma is so explicitly 'brought along' to the prayer that its stated purpose of 'praise' and 'glorification' is relatively much less apparent.
Theological exposition enters pervasively also into the following prayer
of thanksgiving from Blackford Bridge:

(7)   MINISTER: We give you *thanks*
                      for our *life* and sal*v*ation in Jesus,
                      who became one with us.
                      Who died,
                      and who *rose again*,
                      that we might have *life* in him.
                      Be made members of your church,
                      and heirs of your *king*dom.

        (AS 9: 152-59)

Intriguingly, none of the churches in my Advent Survey recite a creed
proper, and in this they actually diverge from the liturgical practice of
Calvin and Knox—if not from subsequent English Independent proce-
dure (Davies 1948: 135). Having said this, 'credal' speech acts are still
dispersed liberally throughout their services and as such, serve to
increase the 'informational' burden. Hence, rather than a terse 'General
Confession' from which worshippers can infer their own particular sins
(as in URC 1989: 5), the Minister at Warsash offers this very pointedly
sermonized act of penitence:

(8)   MINISTER: Father it would be easy to enter into *judg*ment,
                      and con*demn*,
                      *shop*keepers and *shop*pers alike,
                      for ig*nor*ing,
                      the Lord's Day.

5. 'AS' denotes material drawn form the Advent Sunday survey of United
Reformed Church worship presented in Hilborn 1994 (Appendices). The subsequent
number indicates which of the 10 participating United Reformed Churches' tran-
scripts is being quoted: 1. Herne Hill, London; 2. Emmanuel, West Wickham; 3.
Thatcham, Berkshire; 4. Derriford, Devon; 5. Warsash, Hampshire; 6. Wheatley,
Oxon.; 7. Weoley Castle, Birmingham; 8. Bulwell, Nottingham; 9. Blackford Bridge,
Greater Manchester; 10. St. George's, High Heaton. The subsequent figures refer to
line numbers from the original transcript.

> It would be easy to con*demn*,
> the houses of parliament,
> for…not putting their *foot* down,
> and for th- and to con*demn* the local auth*o*rities for
> not…en*for*cing the law.
> But Father we have to recog*nize* that it is your
> *church* that is under *judg*ment.
>
> It is *our fault*,
> that things have come to this pass.
> (AS 5: 335-46)

So too, at Derriford URC, communion is prefaced by the following exposition, which has roots in Calvin's own eucharistic Exhortation (1542/45: 219):

> (9) MINISTER: We *come* to the table to *share*,
>   as family together.
>   We come to:
>   bring our THANKFULNESS TO THE LORD,
>   we come to be part of the body of Christ
>   to ex*press*,
>   the fact,
>   that we are one *body*
>   in *Je*sus,
>   whose body was given for us.
>   (AS 4: 581-91)

At Blackford Bridge, the minister's introductory account of baptism elaborates markedly on the equivalent rubric in the URC *Service Book* (cf. 1989: 31):

> (10) This is not a *Christ*ening.
>   We do not believe that you can make anybody a *Christ*ian by
>   doing something *to* them.
>   It's not a naming ceremony,
>   we believe that God *knows* your *name* before you were ever
>   *born* or *thought* of.
>   When people *first* became *Christ*ians,
>   they were bap*tized*.
>   / / were dipped under *wat*er,
>   as a *sign* that they had *drowned*,
>   *died* to the old way of life,
>   and risen with *Jes*us to be born
>   into a *new* life.
>   *Filled* with the Holy Spirit.

They made *prom*ises that they would *foll*ow this life of
Jesus…to the end.
In the URC we *still use* this moment of *bap*tism,
for those who become *Christ*ians,
for Christian *par*ents / / their children to be called,
to *share* in this new *cov*enant,
this new a*gree*ment with God.
And so have *made* these *prom*ises,
on be*half* of their children.
In the *faith* and *hope*
that in the fulness of time,
they *too* will be led,
to *faith* in Jesus,
and seek the gift of the Holy *Spir*it
in confirmation.
In this faith,
and in this *hope*,
we meet today
to bap*tize*
Lucy…Emily…Routledge.
(AS 10: 62-92)

Now it is undoubtedly a key prerogative of Reformed liturgical
theology that sacramental action must be accompanied by an expository
'word': it is on this premise, indeed, that many Reformed churches have
insisted that baptism and communion can be administered only by
ordained 'preachers of the gospel', so as to provide a check against their
being attributed an 'inherent' power distinct from the power of the
λόγος itself (Calvin 1559: IV.4.14; Heppe 1950: 595-96, 605). Indeed,
Knox thus memorably talked of the sacraments being 'annexed to
God's Word' in full corporate worship rather than being 'used in private
corners, as charms or sorceries' (1556: 105). All the same, one wonders
whether such exposition might not be better confined to the sermon,
rather than being allowed to proliferate in the kind of supplementary
homilies exemplified above. What is more, even if it could be excused
for the *sacraments*, it is just as obtrusive at other points in the service.
Between the reading and the anthem, for example, the Minister at
Wheatley URC seems obliged to reiterate the 'theme' of worship, even
though it has already been made quite clear in a lengthy prelude to the
lection:

(11) MINISTER: Cyrus *com*ing from the *east*
to save Israel.
And in*deed*
later *on*
we: have the notion that the…wise men coming
from the *east*,
the *star* comes from the *east*,
and if you *think* about it
a lot of *churches…face east*
in order to…as it were sym*bol*ically
face the coming of *Christ*
who comes…from the *east*.
And the choir is going to *sing*,
'People from the *east*',
which is a / / song…carol.

(AS 6: 82-96)

Similarly, the Minister at Emmanuel, West Wickham is drawn to underline in advance the theological significance of a hymn whose own message is quite straightforward:

(12) MINISTER: Now we're going to sing the hymn…on the *sheet*,
'Lord Jesus *Christ*,
you have *come* to us,
you are *one with* us,
Mary's *son*',
and that's what our *prayer* was saying just now
and so we're
*say*ing it again now…in this *hymn*.

(AS 2: 356-62)

Interestingly, both (11) and (12) display 'anaphoric' as well as 'cataphoric' contextualization: they expound *previous* discoursal activity as well as discoursal activity which is yet to come. A similar strategy is in evidence at High Heaton, following the New Testament reading from Acts 20.17-32:

(13) MINISTER: Thank you Gill.
'I com*mend* you',
says *Paul*,
'to the *care* of God,
and to the *message* of *his grace*,
which is able to *build* you *up*,
and give you the blessings *God has* for
all of his people'.

Grace,
*bless*ings,
gifts,
things in our *next* hymn,
let's...before we turn to the...word *prop*erly,
sing together from Church *Hymn*ary,
'For thy *gift* of God the *Spirit*'.
(AS 10: 346-59)

Here, once more, we can see how the biblical Word of God is established as the 'supreme criterion' of sacral discourse. Although Scripture is self-evidently varied in its linguistic composition, it is often appropriated in Reformed liturgy as a self-actualizing legal code, implicitly orienting, validating and regulating the language of the service. Archetypally, this can be seen when it is quoted at the very beginning of worship, as if to sound a thematic keynote for what follows. But it is additionally a feature of medial service discourse—not only in traditional 'slots' like the Invitation to Communion, Narrative of Institution and Absolution, but also as a 'contextualizer' of intercessory and penitential prayer:

(14)   MINISTER: let's just bow our heads now and,
                   be still,
                   because we are *in*
                   the presence of *God.*
                   The Almighty One...
                   as we re*mem*ber,
                   in God's *Word,*
                   in St John's *Gos*pel,
                   'the Word became *flesh,*
                   and *dwelt among* us'.
                   (AS 10: 405-14)

(15)   MINISTER: So Jesus says to us...
                   'I have *come,*
                   that you may *all*
                   have life'.
                   Let us then bow our heads in prayer for a moment,
                   that we *seek* God's forgiveness,
                   for those *things* in our lives,
                   of which we may be a*shamed.*
                   Let us pray.
                   (AS 7: 476-84)

Sometimes, the Scriptural contextualization of a prayer can turn into the scriptural *sermonization* of a prayer, and here the Reformed penchant for didactic over-informing is particularly noticeable:

(16)   MINISTER: The story Jesus told re*minds* us,
                   that *our*…faithfulness
                   will be found in our,
                   im*par*tiality,
                   in our being *gracious*
                   as *you* are gracious.
                   We know we depend upon,
                   your grace,
                   …(6.0 seconds)…
                   help us put *aside* those things that we,
                   build up for our own sakes [...]
                   (AS 8: 274-83)

(17)   MINISTER: At *all times*
                   dear God,
                   your truth con*demns* us,
                   and we: are *accused* by,
                   your very *B*ible,
                   and by its history.
                   But your *love*,
                   pleads *with* us,
                   and it *challenges* us to stop wasting our *strength*.
                   And to *come*,
                   where…real…life…be*gins*.
                   And so Lord,
                   in penitence,
                   we come before you.
                   (AS 1: 60-73)

(18)   MINISTER: We thank you Lord,
                   that without your love and attention,
                   we could *all* be like /modern/ goats in your story.
                   We rejoice,
                   that *even goats*,
                   can be re-born as sheep.
                   (AS 7: 420-25 cf. Matthew 25)

Here indeed, are echoes of that Puritan scriptural 'footnoting' which Routley cast as so distinctive a feature of early English Reformed worship (1960: 108-109). Certainly, many of the cases we have been citing

prompt the judgment that even modern Reformed worship deploys contextualizing strategies in an excessively 'telegraphed' way. To borrow
another term from pragmatics, such passages are almost forcedly
metadiscoursal (Mey 1993: 269-85): they *refer to* and *comment on* the
'speech activity' of worship rather than themselves *instantiating* such
activity in a primary manner. Of course, to the extent that 'referring to'
and 'commenting on' are themselves actions (and see Austin 1962: 133-
47), they mediate a *kind* of performativity, but this performativity is
parasitic upon the definitive enactments of praise, proclamation and
sacramental expression.

Theodore Jennings (1985: 162-208) has defined God-talk as variously
'Kerygmatic', 'Oralogical' and 'Doxological'. *Kerygmatic* discourse is
that in which God's Word is perceived to come definitively to his
people—for example in lections, preaching and prophecy. *Oralogical*
discourse is that in which the faithful express some want or lack—e.g. in
confession, petition and intercession. *Doxological* discourse, by contrast,
is associated with the articulation of spiritual fulness—of 'in ecstasis'
address to God through adoration and exaltation. Anterior to these categories, however, Jennings also identifies forms of religious language
which are 'explicative' and 'meta-explicative'.

In the specific terms of Jennings' argument, explicative discourse relates
to the 'analogical' and 'apologetic' language of natural, political and
parabolic theology and meta-explicative discourse to root metaphysical
concepts in the philosophy of religion. More generally, however, Jennings
allows (1985: 155) that explicative religious language 'uses God-talk to
"explain" an event in terms of a structure or to "explain" a structure'.
This often means casting apparently profane phenomena in a sacred
light, but it can also reciprocally mean interpreting noumenal concepts in
quotidian language. In tending so diligently to 'explain' itself, Reformed
worship gives the impression that the doxological and kerygmatic
elements of liturgy either cannot or should not stand alone—that they
cannot be left to yield up their own 'explanation'.

The corollary of this is a presumption, yet again, that *lex credendi*
must precede and regulate *lex orandi*—that the experienced speech-
activity of worship is subject to the prior 'rules' of biblical and doctrinal
'thought' as defined in propositionalistic terms. As a result, contextualization can 'hold up' the enactment of worship even while *signalling*
that enactment. It is almost as if the 'route' through Reformed liturgy is

interrupted by a plethora of metadiscoursal 'signposts'—signposts which have been placed in the middle of the road rather than at its side, and which thereby become obstacles to performativity rather than facilitators of it.

The privileging of extemporary orality by the Puritans has, it seems, bequeathed a legacy of explicative language which extends not only to theological commentary, but also to more mundane 'stage directions'. Without a written rubric for reference, such directions are typically devolved to ministerial utterance, and thereby acquire a prominence which they rarely merit. Rather than keeping the congregation's attention on God, the minister has frequently to discuss the mechanical progression of the rite itself: structural metadiscourse thus punctuates the δόξα and κήρυγμα of worship:

(19)   MINISTER: OK,
                   right.
                   we will,
                   move on in our service a little bit then,
                   and hear
                   our first *read*ing
                   reading from the *Gos*pel,
                   from Matthew chapter... *twen*ty-five.

         (AS 8: 214-22)

(20)   MINISTER: In a moment we will sing our closing hymn,
                   and then share in the *grace* together.

         (AS 7: 682-83)

(21)   MINISTER: I wonder if you'd just turn for a *mo*ment to Songs
                   and *Hymns*,
                   and number one *hun*dred and forty-*sev*en,
                   and what I'm going to ask is that we should
                   er... just be *si*lent,
                   for a m- a moment or two,
                   and to ask God,
                   by his *Scrip*tures,
                   to help us to- to *grow*
                   and to dwell in *him*.
                   And then we're going to *sing*
                   (stay in your seats please do but we'll... we'll sing
                   through *very gently* and perhaps just *once*... if we may).

         (AS 10: 380-89)

4. *Conclusions*

I have been suggesting that Ladrière's appropriation of speech act theory diverges somewhat from the use which Reformed liturgiology might make of it, and of other developments in linguistic pragmatics. Most especially, I have underlined several points in Ladrière's argument at which he appears to accord liturgical language an intrinsic operativity or 'causality'. In particular, I have inferred this from his presentation of the canon as itself instituting the church community and itself re-effectuating the action of the Last Supper in the contemporary celebration of communion. For all the subtlety of Ladrière's overall argument, I have identified within it traces of what Calvin and his English Puritan followers had attacked polemically as 'occult' conceptions of the language of the Mass. Specifically, I have concluded that Ladrière has failed to grasp Austin's point that language has no inherent power apart from its users and contexts. I have also suggested that the persistence of such traces most probably derives from the fact that Roman Catholic liturgy is still strongly tied to set lexical and grammatical realizations, so that it is more tempting there to posit a stable instrumental link between linguistic form and pragmatic function. By contrast, I have underlined that Reformed liturgiologies have widely repudiated such fixed texts precisely on the grounds that the operativity of worship resides not in specific words or phrases but in the power of God to mediate his scriptural Word through the mouth of the preacher in language suited to each particular service of worship.

From another point of view, I have related the divergence between Ladrière's 'performative language doxology' and Reformed sacral doctrine to recent work by Catholic liturgical theologians like David Power, Aidan Kavanagh and David Fageberg. Developing the ancient nostrum *lex orandi, lex credendi*, I have shown how Power, Kavanagh and Fageberg suggest that the 'propositional' language of Christian doctrine should be seen to *arise from* the 'performative' language of Christian liturgy, rather than regulating it dogmatically in an *a priori* fashion. Positively, I have borne out Fageberg's claims by affirming from both diachronic analysis and synchronic scrutiny of my field corpus of United Reformed Church worship that an excessively propositionalistic view of doctrinal and scriptural truth has diverted English Reformed worship away from affective and participative discourse strategies and towards too exhaustively pedagogical and 'over-informative' an approach to church service communication. In particular, I have shown how this has been manifested in a shift from dialogical and unison speech towards what may be dubbed *didactic monologism* and *contextualizing metadiscourse*. In turn, I have argued that this shift has gone hand-in-hand with the Reformed preference for extemporization over written rites and symbolic actions, since the whole burden of 'exposition' and 'instruction' must then be borne by speech alone—something which often leads to prosaic commentaries swamping more 'eventful' kerygmatic and doxological discourses.

After all this criticism of my own tradition, I shall end by tipping the scales back more favourably on its side. If *lex orandi, lex credendi* is allowed too much to replace *sola scriptura* as the supreme criterion of worship, there will be a danger that the Word of God will be too easily undermined by the 'traditions of men'—a danger whose perception was, of course, one of the primary motives of the Protestant Reformation of liturgy. As Old has commented in this regard, 'liturgical tradition alone can hardly serve as its own norm. There are too many times when liturgical practice goes awry. There are too many times when we have to say, yes, we know what the current practice is, but we would like to know what it *should* be. It is at this point...that we turn to Scripture' (1992: 13-14).

Even here, of course, there is a paradox, since Scripture is itself often derived from liturgy (Daniélou 1956). Nonetheless, to maintain that a 'performative language' approach to worship can wholly vitiate the need to ask what Jeffner (1972) calls the crucial 'reference questions' of Christian theology is to court a crude religious relativism quite incompatible with either Reformed *or* Catholic faith. Sure enough, pragmatics enables us to move beyond both purely verificationist and purely confessional definitions of sacral meaning, but if it thereby leads us down a post-modern path of voluntaristic anti-metaphysicalism, it is likely that worship will drift into a pattern not dissimilar to that followed in the Salian rites of ancient Rome, where even the priests had lost touch with the semantic content of what they recited (Bayet 1957: 50, 86ff.). Explication and didacticism do seem to have stifled 'performativity' in Reformed worship, but it is equally clear that their abandonment would have even more serious consequences.

BIBLIOGRAPHY

Aarsleff, H.
1982　　*From Locke to Saussure: Essays on the Study of Language and Intellectual History* (London: Athlone).

Auer, P.
1992　　'Introduction: John Gumperz' Approach to Contextualization', in P. Auer and A. di Luzo (eds.), *The Contextualization of Language* (Amsterdam: John Benjamins): 1-37.

Austin, J.L.
1962　　*How to Do Things with Words* (ed. J.O. Urmson and M. Sbisà; Oxford: Oxford University Press, 2nd edn).

Ayer, A.J.
1936　　*Language, Truth and Logic* (repr. Harmondsworth: Penguin Books, 1971. Originally published by Victor Gollancz).

Bach, K., and R. Harnish
1979　　*Linguistic Communication and Speech Acts* (Cambridge, MA: MIT Press).

Barrow, H.
1591–93　　*The Writings of John Greenwood and Henry Barrow 1591–1593* (ed. L.H. Carlson; London: Allen & Unwin, 1970).

Barth, K.
1936　　*Church Dogmatics. I.1. The Doctrine of the Word of God* (ed. G.W. Bromiley and T.F. Torrance; trans. G.W. Bromiley; Edinburgh: T. & T. Clark, 1975. Originally published as *Die Kirchliche Dogmatik I: Die Lehre vom Wort Gottes*, I [Zollikon–Zürich: Evangelischer Verlag]).

Baxter, R.
1661　　'The Savoy Liturgy', in B. Thompson 1961: 373-405.

Bayet, J.
1957　　*Histoire politique et psychologique de la religion romaine* (Paris) (Cit. Bouyer 1963: 54).

Beach, B.B.
1986　　'Liturgies', entry in J.G. Davies 1986: 314-38.

Bouyer, L.
1963　　*Rite and Man* (London: Burns & Oates).

Brown, G., and G. Yule
1983　　*Discourse Analysis* (Cambridge: Cambridge University Press).

Burrage, C.
1912　　*The Early English Dissenters* (2 vols.; Cambridge: Cambridge University Press).

Calvin, J.
1542/45　　'The Form of Church Prayers: Strassburg, 1545, and Geneva, 1542', in B. Thompson 1961: 183-210.

1559　　*Institutes of the Christian Religion* (ed. J.T. McNeill; trans. F.L. Battles; Library of Christian Classics, 20, 21; Philadelphia: Westminster Press, 1960).

Chafe, W.
1986   'How we Know Things about Language: A Plea for Catholicism', in D. Tannen (ed.), *Languages and Linguistics: The Interdependence of Theory, Data and Application* (Washington, DC: Georgetown University Round Table on Languages and Linguistics): 214-25.

Cotton, J.
1642   *A Modest and Cleare Answer to Mr. Ball's Discourse of Set Formes of Prayer* (London: Henry Overton).

Crystal, D.
1971   *Linguistics* (Harmondsworth: Penguin Books).
1990   'Liturgical Language in a Sociolinguistic Perspective', in D. Jasper and R.C.D. Jasper (eds.), *Language and the Worship of the Church* (Basingstoke and London: Macmillan): 120-46.
1991   *A Dictionary of Linguistics and Phonetics* (Oxford: Basil Blackwell, 3rd edn).

Daniélou, J.
1956   *The Bible and the Liturgy* (Notre Dame, IN: University of Notre Dame Press).

Davies, H.
1948   *The Worship of the English Puritans* (Oxford: Dacre Press).
Davies, J.G. (ed.)
1986   *A New Dictionary of Liturgy and Worship* (London: SCM Press).
Dix, Dom G.
1945   *The Shape of the Liturgy* (London: A. & C. Black).
Eco, U.
1976   *A Theory of Semiotics* (Bloomington: Indiana University Press).
Enninger, W., and J. Raith
1982   *An Ethnography of Communication Approach to Ceremonial Situations: A Study on Communication in Institutionalised Social Contexts—The Old Order Amish Church Service* (Wiesbaden: Franz Steiner Verlag).

Evans, D.D.
1963   *The Logic of Self-Involvement* (London: SCM Press).
Fageberg, D.
1992   *What is Liturgical Theology?* (Collegeville, MN: Pueblo).
Farel, G.
1524   'La Manière et Fasson, 1524', in B. Thompson 1961: 216-24
Ferguson, C.
1985   'The Study of Religious Discourse', in *Georgetown University Round Table on Language and Linguistics, 1985* (Washington, DC: Georgetown University Press): 205-13.
Gill, J.H.
1969   'J.L. Austin and the Religious Use of Language', *Sophia* 8: 29-37.
Haberland, H., and J.L. Mey
1977   'Editorial: Linguistics and Pragmatics', *Journal of Pragmatics* 1: 1-12.
Hawkes, T.
1977   *Structuralism and Semiotics* (London: Methuen).

Heppe, H.
1950 *Reformed Dogmatics* (trans. G.T. Thomson; London: Allen & Unwin).
Hilborn, D.
1994 'The Pragmatics of Liturgical Discourse' (unpublished PhD thesis, University of Nottingham).
Horn, L.R.
1988 'Pragmatic Theory', in F.J. Newmeyer (ed.), *Linguistics: The Cambridge Survey, Vol. I: Linguistic Theory: Foundations* (Cambridge: Cambridge University Press): 113-45.
Jasper, R.C.D.
1986 'Canon', entry in J.G. Davies 1986: 139-40.
Jeffner, A.
1972 *The Study of Religious Language* (London: SCM Press).
Jennings, T.
1985 *Beyond Theism* (New York: Oxford University Press).
Kelleher, M.M.
1993 'Hermeneutics in the Study of Liturgical Performance', *Worship* 67.4: 292-318.
Knox, J.
1556 *The Liturgical Portions of the Genevan Service Book* (ed. W.D. Maxwell; Westminster: Faith Press 1965).
Ladrière, J.
1973 'The Performativity of Liturgical Language', *Concilium* 9: 50-62.
Lange-Seidl, A.
1986 'The Pragmatic Dimension of Semiotics', *Journal of Pragmatics* 10: 109-22.
Lardner, G.V.
1979 'Liturgy as Communication: A Pragmatics Perspective' (unpublished PhD dissertation, Temple University) (reprinted by UMI).
Leech, G.N., and J. Thomas
1990 'Language, Meaning and Context: Pragmatics', in N.E. Collinge, *An Encyclopedia of Language* (London: Routledge): 173-206.
Levinson, S.C.
1983 *Pragmatics* (Cambridge: Cambridge University Press).
Lukken, G.
1987 'Semiotics and the Study of Liturgy', *Studia Liturgica* 17: 108-17.
Mananzan, M.-J.
1974 *The 'Language-Game' of Confessing One's Belief* (Tübingen: Max Niemeyer).
Martinich, A.P.
1975a 'Sacraments and Speech Acts I', *Heythrop Journal* 16.1: 289-303.
1975b 'Sacraments and Speech Acts II', *Heythrop Journal* 16.2: 405-17.
Mayor, S.
1972 *The Lord's Supper in Early English Dissent* (London: Epworth Press).
McCarthur, T. (ed.)
1992 *The Oxford Companion to the English Language* (Oxford: Oxford University Press).

McClendon, J.W., Jr, and J.M. Smith
1975   *Understanding Religious Convictions* (Notre Dame: University of Notre Dame Press).

Mey, J.L.
1993   *Pragmatics: An Introduction* (Oxford: Basil Blackwell).

Middleburg
1586   'The Middleburg Liturgy of the English Puritans', in B. Thompson 1961: 309-41.

Morris, C.W.
1938   'Foundations of the Theory of Signs', in O. Neurath, R. Carnap and C.W. Morris (eds.), *International Encyclopedia of Unified Science*, I (Chicago: University of Chicago Press): 77-138.

Oecolampadius, J.
1525   'Form and Manner of the Lord's Supper, Infant Baptism and Visitation of the Sick, as They are Used and Observed in Basel', in B. Thompson 1961: 211-15.

Old, H.O.
1992   *Themes and Variations for a Christian Doxology: Some Thoughts on the Theology of Worship* (Grand Rapids: Eerdmans).

Peirce, C.S.
1960   *Collected Papers of Charles Sanders Peirce II: Elements of Logic (Second Printing)* (ed. C. Hartshorne and P. Weiss; Cambridge, MA: Belknap Press of the Harvard University Press).

Power, D.N.
1984   *Unsearchable Riches: The Symbolic Nature of Liturgy* (Collegeville, MN: Pueblo).

Recanati, F.
1987   *Meaning and Force: The Pragmatics of Performative Utterances* (Cambridge: Cambridge University Press).

Richards, J.C., J. Platt and H. Platt
1992   *Longman Dictionary of Language Teaching and Applied Linguistics* (Harlow: Longman).

Routley, E.
1960   *English Religious Dissent* (Cambridge: Cambridge University Press).

Searle, J.R.
1969   *Speech Acts: An Essay in the Philosophy of Language* (Cambridge: Cambridge University Press).
1979   *Expression and Meaning: Studies in the Theory of Speech Acts* (Cambridge: Cambridge University Press).

Sebeok, T.A., A.S. Hayes and M.C. Bateson (eds.)
1964   *Approaches to Semiotics* (The Hague: Mouton).

Smith, J.M., and J.W. McClendon, Jr
1972   'Religious Language after J.L. Austin', *Religious Studies* 8: 55-63.

Smyth, J.
1645   *The Differences of the Churches of the Separation* (Cit. Davies 1948): 95 n. 2.

Spinks, B.D.

1984   *From the Lord and 'the Best Reformed Churches': A Study of the Eucharistic Liturgy in the English Puritan and Separatist Traditions, 1550–1633* (Rome: CLV).

Stalnaker, R.

1972   'Pragmatics', in D. Davidson and G. Harman (eds.), *Semantics of Natural Language* (Cambridge: Cambridge University Press): 380-97.

Tannen, D.

1989   *Talking Voices* (Cambridge: Cambridge University Press).

Thiselton, A.C.

1974   'The Supposed Power of Words in the Biblical Writings', *JTS* 25: 283-99.

Thompson, B.

1961   *Liturgies of the Western Church* (repr. Philadelphia: Fortress Press, 1980).

Tilley, T.W.

1991   *The Evils of Theodicy* (Washington, DC: Georgetown University Press).

URC (United Reformed Church)

1989   *Service Book* (Oxford: Oxford University Press).

Van Dijk, T.A.

1977   *Text and Context: Explorations in the Semantics and Pragmatics of Discourse* (London: Longman).

Vincent, G.

1979   'La théologie calvinienne du sacrement à la lumière de la linguistique', in W.H. Neusner (ed.), *Calvinus Ecclesiae Doctor* (Kampen: Kok).

Von Allmen, J.-J.

1965   *Worship: Its Theology and Practice* (trans. H. Knight and W.F. Fleet; London: Lutterworth Press).

Wainwright, G.

1980   *Doxology: The Praise of God in Worship, Doctrine and Life* (London: Epworth Press).

Ware, J.H.

1981   *Not with Words of Wisdom: Performative Language and Liturgy* (Washington, DC: University Press of America).

Westminster Directory

1644   *The Westminster Directory* (ed. I. Breward; Grove Liturgical Study No. 21; Bramcote: Grove Books, 1980).

Wolterstorff, N.

1992   'The Reformed Liturgy', in D.K. McKim (ed.), *Major Themes in the Reformed Tradition* (Grand Rapids: Eerdmans): 273-304.

1993   'Philosophical Reflections on Calvin's Doctrine of the Sacraments: An Approach through the Philosophy of Language', Lecture delivered at Nottingham University, 11 November 1993. Notes made by the author.

ANALOGY: AQUINAS AND PANNENBERG

Michael Nevin

Analogy is a word which expresses, in its theological sense, a correspondence between God and humanity and therefore the possibility of using language expressive of God if humans can become aware of this correspondence. Thus it might be said that both God and humanity *are* and that therefore we can use the word *be* of God. Such a statement would imply that we can know that *we* exist, that we can know that *God* exists and that in this two-fold knowledge can be found the notion of analogy. (I would add here that to know that God exists from a knowledge of creation is a mediated but direct apprehension of God.) There are however two other possibilities which would eliminate analogical thinking.

It might be that God and humanity *are* in the same way—that we therefore use the word *be* univocally. It might be that God and humanity *are* in irreconcilably different ways—that therefore we use the word *be* equivocally.

Thomist tradition holds that we can know God as the cause of the universe by strictly creative causation: that a creator must be uncaused and therefore self-subsistent and therefore unable to be conceived as merely possible and therefore a being whose essence it is to exist and therefore as infinite since a finite essence is always conceivable as merely possible. He is therefore transcendent to his universe and immanent in his universe since he is respectively independent of it and present to it. Thus God *is* not in the same way that the universe *is*. Indeed he wholly transcends the being of the universe. And yet to know *that* he is, as it is claimed that we do, means that we do know something that we can say about God that is true. Hence the idea of analogical language as language that is attributed to God in a way that is *at the same time* both like and unlike. Thus God is like us in that we both exist, but unlike us in that his existence transcends ours.

It should be noted that analogical language here presupposes analogical being. But it might be argued that the analogicity of being is nothing more than a product of negative knowledge of God on our part. Existence might mean nothing more than God is not nothing, is over against nothing. The positive idea of God's being may be a complete blank to us. And perhaps apophatic language means no more than this since, for example, John Damascene states that God does not belong to the class of existing things but adds 'not that he has no existence' (Migne, *PG*, XCIV, p. 800 BA). And goes on to say *he is above existence itself* without, however, eliminating the verb is.

Yet it might be enquired that if the knowledge we have of God is negative how does Aquinas obtain the various ideas such as uncaused, self-subsistent, whose-essence-it-is-to-exist, infinite. If God is for us incomprehensible, the problem of arriving at such notions arises. In response to this it should first be remembered that God's incomprehensibility arises not from a lack of meaning but from a meaning that is too deep for the human mind, viz. the idea of a self-subsistent being. And it is because he is a self-subsistent being that God is incomprehensible. To say that God's essence is not finite, that he has so to speak, no delimiting shape, is to say that he cannot be conceived intramentally. (One should remember that from Revelation we learn that even the Father does not conceive himself intramentally, as it were, but that his conception, or logos, is a personal reality other than the Father.) Thus it is that the various attributes that Saint Thomas derives from the notion of God as creator (cf. *Summa Theologiae*, 1A, pp. 3-11) arise as indications of a being that is incomprehensible *quoad nos* but incomprehensible because in himself he is the utter positivity of being.

Thus far we have been speaking about God as he can be known by the human intellect without special revelation, that is, from creation alone. But the problem of analogy arises also in the very sphere of revelation itself. Thus it seems to me that if God were absolutely transcendent, not only could he not create (since he would not be able to be present to his creation) but neither could he reveal nor become incarnate (since both demand the closest intimacy).

I shall presuppose that equivocity and univocity do not meet our case, since the former means that in speaking about God we do not know what we are talking about and that on the level of reality, as opposed to language, we have seen the impossibility of an absolutely transcendent God. While the latter means either that God is not transcendent (and therefore not God) or that being-Creator (with all its attributes) actually only comes into being, as a creature therefore, with his creation, and thus possesses a univocity of being with other creatures. God in himself however would be totally indeterminate, a being about whom we cannot even use the word being, or, on the level of revelation, the word Trinity.[1]

We are now in a position to consider some noteworthy critics of analogy from whom I shall separate two, Karl Barth (another and different view of Barth is, however, possible) and Wolfhart Pannenberg.[2] The first because he is the classical representative of the extreme swing away from analogicity and the latter because he attempts and partially succeeds in correcting the oscillation.

For Barth the only way in which humanity is related to God is as sinner to redeemer and thus humanity's only response is in faith to revelation in Scripture. A person's objective power of knowing God, described by Paul in Romans, is doomed to frustration unless that person is recreated in Christ. The object of natural theology is an idol. The analogy of being is 'the invention of anti-Christ'. Once revelation is accepted Barth can speak of an analogy of faith which, however, always respects the transcendence of revelation. Of this position a Catholic might comment that it is still the human mind that knows even in faith and to be illuminated even by revelation still means a radical capacity to know God on the part of humanity.

Pannenberg argues that since the divine disclosure is indirect all *speech* about God is analogical. God is disclosed in the world or in humanity since the character of humanity's being is infinitely directed towards something beyond itself, to humanity's ultimate concern, or, to speak with Luther, to the goal of the human's (ultimate) trust. Humanity itself is to be understood in no other way than as the question about the unknown, about the counterpart that lies beyond the given world horizon and which we call God. His notion of interpretation of history argues that there can be no meaning in history unless an ultimate meaning is understood to exist and one day will appear, as humanity's ultimate horizon, in history. Now not only does this seem to me to be an

---

1.   This is the position of a brilliant univocist, R. Neville, *God the Creator: On the Transcendence and Presence of God* (Chicago: University of Chicago Press, 1968); and see his 'Creation and the Trinity', *TS* 30 (1969).

2.   W. Pannenberg, *Basic Questions in Theology: Collected Essays* (trans. G. Kehm; 2 vols.; Philadelphia: Fortress Press, 1971); see also J. Moltmann, *Hope and Planning* (trans. M. Clarkson; New York: Harper & Row, 1971).

attempt to 'prove' the existence of God by natural reason but it also proves too much since it also proves by natural reason the notion of a *parousia*. No doubt Pannenberg would argue that the notion of *parousia* arises from the resurrection of Christ and that that event gives meaning to history. But it is difficult to see how he could deny *all* meaning to history without revelation. Indeed the strong Protestant position *would* implicitly deny meaning to all being without revelation, but Pannenberg's argument in 'Hermeneutics and Universal History' and Moltmann's argument in 'The End of History'[3] seem to me to be statable as reasoning without the superstructure of revelation. How then does Pannenberg regard Saint Thomas's 'proof' of the existence of God from the finitude of being as we experience it in the world? He writes that for Aquinas 'the world of creaturely reality is analogous to God, whereas the reversal of this relationship, which occurs in our speaking about God insofar as this is accomplished by making him analogous to our experience already shows up the inadequacy of our knowledge of God': he goes on to add that if this solution were thought of as 'paronymy' rather than as 'analogy' one might find a 'fruitful point of departure in the direction of the state of the matter expounded' by Pannenberg himself.[4] Such a notion of analogy, as that of Aquinas, means that 'the world falls short of its divine archetype, so that the reverse transference back to God of what is read off of the world is no longer able to attain to the purity of the divine archetypes'. So far so good: no Catholic would find area for disagreement here. But now he goes on to say somewhat oddly that this conception originated in the Neoplatonic idea of emanation since in this view both being and knowledge are transmitted from above to below and that an idea of analogy, 'which grounds analogy both ontologically and poetically from God's side...has led Karl Barth to suspend his criticism of the analogy of being (*analogia entia*) (CD, II/1, pp. 81-82). In fact, the roots of his own doctrine of analogy, which are expressed with particular clarity in his anthropology (CD, III/2, pp. 205, 220-21, 320), are to be found here.'[5] Now this seems to me to be odd because a doctrine of emanation means that God depends on the lower emanations in order to be God since

3. W. Pannenberg, 'Hermeneutics and Universal History', in *History and Hermeneutic* (trans. P.J. Achtemeier; ed. R.W. Funk and G. Ebeling; New York: Harper & Row, 1967); J. Moltmann, 'The End of History', in *Hope and Planning*.
4. Pannenberg, *Basic Questions in Theology*, I, p. 213.
5. Pannenberg, *Basic Questions in Theology*, I, p. 214.

without them he would not be what he is by nature, an emanating God. But if God's being is dependent then we do not have an analogy of being but a univocity of being and it is interesting to note that it is the Platonic tradition in Catholic theology, for example Scotus, that throws up the notion of univocity. The only answer to this criticism seems to me the argument that God freely creates (thus he is not the Emanator) but that his freedom does not require alternative courses of action even the alternative of being able not to create, that therefore he is independent of his creation, and that he is not to be included in the category of being at all.[6] The notion of univocity of being between humanity and God always ends up it seems by excluding God from the category of being altogether.

That Pannenberg is as uncomfortable as I am about this notion of grounding analogy both ontologically and noetically from God's side, since if there is a noetic and an ontological analogy there must be a radical capacity on the part of humankind to know God and if humanity is to use words about God at all, even revealed words, these words will arise from creation and the reflections of human reason, as evidenced by this subsequent statement that 'the Thomistic doctrine of analogy is nevertheless probably right in holding that, in fact, all analogizing proceeds from below to above, and begins with some experience of the world. We have already emphasized that according to Thomas it is precisely this point that is the root of the inadequacy of all human knowledge of God.'[7] He goes on however to point out that Thomas had to place a positive significance in analogical knowledge, as opposed to Neoplatonism, since mystical union with the Origin which is found in that system affords a certainty prior to all rational knowledge. But here another difficulty arises. To know the Origin in a way that is communicable even to the mystic, for without some expressive communication there would be the strange paradox of an experience without content, requires the use of conceptual or imagistic language which if it is to have any validity even for the mystic means that it will imply an analogicity between what it expresses on the human level and what it expresses on the divine level. Hence the use of imagery from sexual love, words denoting moral excellence, even phrases like 'beyond being' or 'infinite incomprehensibility'. To have the experience is not enough since the

---

6. I.W.K. Trethowan, *Absolute Value: A Study in Christian Theism* (London: Allen & Unwin, 1970), p. 110.

7. Pannenberg, *Basic Questions in Theology*, I, p. 215.

experience has to be known or possessed and this includes the notion of judgment or expression.

Pannenberg returns to the notion of analogy again but after what he has said about Thomas providing a point of departure for a synthesis of their two views he again strangely misunderstands what Thomas was trying to express by 'analogy'. He notes that 'by the end of the thirteenth century, Duns Scotus and, later, William of Ockham recognized that analogy itself presupposes a univocal element'.[8] He quotes with approval Erich Przywara, who, by insisting on the Fourth Lateran Council's formula (that between creator and creature no similarity can be found so great but that the dissimilarity is greater),[9] arrives at the notion of dynamic transcendence or God's ever-beyondness (*Je-Über-Hinaus*), transcending 'everything that exists or can be thought of apart from God himself'.[10] He goes on to link this approach with the apophatic theology of the Eastern Church and then once again states that this is what Thomas was also concerned to defend, *but did not succeed in doing* by his notion of analogy since it implied not only an analogical use of language but also an analogical relationship of being since God is understood primarily as cause of the world. And it is not proved that we can know anything of a cause by its effect, especially where we are dealing with a *sui generis* cause such as a Creator.

Now I am not at all sure what it could mean to say that there is a valid use of analogical language which is not based upon an analogical relationship of being for either the language has some meaning in which case there is an analogicity of being or the language is meaningless and therefore not language (which is defined as a meaningful expression, in some way, of the reality which it expresses). Further to this, I do not see how one can argue that a cause remains completely unknown in its effect. At least we know that the cause is not nothing and in the case of a creator we must also hold that it is an uncaused cause and *therefore* incomprehensible *quoad nos*. That is, we must return to what I have said already that God's incomprehensibility is not an incomprehensibility only, but it is an incomprehensibility that arises out of known facts and

8.   Pannenberg, *Basic Questions in Theology*, I, p. 225.

9.   H.J.D. Denzinger and A. Schönmetzer, *Enchiridian Symbolorum, Definitionum et Declarationum de Rebus Fidei et Morum, Editio XXXIII* (London: Herder, 1967), p. 262.

10.   E. Przywara, *In und Gegen: Stellungnahme zur Zeit* (Nürnberg: n.p., 1955), p. 278.

known facts that allow this whole question of God's 'super-being' or dynamic transcendence or ever-beyondness to arise. If it were just incomprehensibility and *nothing more* one might wonder what the whole fuss is all about. We could not even begin to talk about it and to say, for example, that God is the answer to the at-present unanswerable question that the existence of humanity posits to the human mind. God has therefore a positive incomprehensibility and not a merely negative one. Further, because God is a *sui generis* cause analogy is a *sui generis* process of understanding and criticism of it as a mixture of univocity and equivocity depending upon a separable common *logos* present in both the known and the unknown term—'The cognitive power of analogy depends upon this presupposition of an identical [!] logos'[11]— depends upon an analysis of analogy in terms other than the unique relationship between creature and creator. The whole point of Catholic analogy is that there can never be a separation between what is like and what is unlike in the two terms of this unique analogy since there is no composition in God, and the divine being, which is infinite, cannot be equated with either one of the two parts into which one might conceivably split one of his creatures.

This now brings us to the positive part of Pannenberg's exposition. He wants to argue for what he calls 'paronymy' in contrast with analogy. Paronymy occurs on the linguistic level and might be defined as the relationship which pertains between different words having the same root. Thus *just, justice, justly* are paronymous. Difference of meaning arises from difference of function. Thus we find that the word *good*, for example, may be used in different ways of different realities though there is a common root meaning that may be attached to the various modes of expression, even though, in the case of God and humanity, there is nothing in common between the realities concerned. The root meaning is the common factor not the beings about whom the word is used. At first sight this seems to be a most bizarre construction of thought. For if we use the word *good* of humanity and use it validly we must presume that it relates to something real in humanity or it is a waste of breath. And likewise of God. But if this is true then the two realities about which *good* is used validly would be either univocal or analogical, a conclusion which Pannenberg would find awkward.

However he escapes this dilemma with a subtlety that one cannot but

---

11. Pannenberg, *Basic Questions in Theology*, I, p. 224.

admire. He introduces the notion of *doxological adoration*. Words which are used doxologically *to* God, like holy, are based upon an experience of God, as adorable, on the basis of his works. Only if one remembers that such statements are rooted in adoration can the doctrine of God be protected against false conclusions. In adoration the devotee sacrifices his 'I' and at the same time and by the same token his conceptual univocity of speech. Before God he is, as it were, annihilated and therefore his speech is annihilated also. But the question arises here of the basic experience which enables the devotee to recognize the presence of a divine intervention in human life. In my view this would imply a notion of analogy in Thomas's sense in that an experience of God in history implies, inasmuch as it is recognized as such, some prior notion of what God might be, a notion which is not eliminated by the presence of a divine faith-illumination. However, putting that on one side, let us see Pannenberg's description of the event. He claims that the word designating God (e.g. omnipotent) which derives from our contingent experience of power and which is transferred to God does not stem from or have anything really to do with the description of the events at, for example, the Red Sea.[12] The event is related to the divine power which determines its total horizon. It has a reference to the totality of reality and to its divine ground. And it is recognized as such by the very improbability of the event: the sea opening. The actual event itself does not add up to a *person* acting on the Israelites' behalf but does so only, presumably, by an inference on the part of the person who experiences the event. Now I do not see this distinction all that clearly. If I see a miraculous or improbable happening and infer the presence of an omnipotent and personal ground of being, it does not seem to me that it is correct to say that the event has nothing really to do with the revelation of the person manifested in it. And further that if the event enables one to recognize the presence of the meaning ascribable to the whole of reality, past, present and future, and therefore the use of a word about him (omnipotent), then surely we are back in the realm of scholastic analogy. Otherwise why should we use the word omnipotent and not some other word, such as fragile or illusory? Pannenberg takes note of this objection and replies by saying that we use the word concerned by a deliberate equivocation, that is, presumably, we choose a word which won't really do for God realizing that it won't really do.

---

12. Pannenberg, *Basic Questions in Theology*, I, p. 251.

But this is no answer to the problem since we choose one word rather than another presumably because it is more fitting to do so. To reply again that we choose words which express what we consider to be more worthy within our human experience, thus to be good in this world is more worthy than to be bad and therefore we call God good, is again no answer since there seems to be no reason why *our* criterion of worthiness should be applicable to God. However Pannenberg still is left with the defence that we learn about the criterion of judging what God is from historical and improbable events in history so that by a series of divine and interventional events the Israelites and ourselves are able to build up 'a characterological picture' of God which we know to be God because such a being gives a total meaning to our existence. This, he would argue, means that we never need to leave this world and this world's words in order to express God. I have no desire to criticize the notion that we can know God through faith in his revelation of himself through historical events nor do I think it is ultimately contradictory to say that we arrive, in our notion of God, only at seeing contingent puzzles solved, that is, God from his effects, so to speak, but then I do not think that Thomas would either and that is what analogy is all about. It may be that we must always philosophize within faith but that does not imply that the philosophy has no validity in its own right. It may be that faith gives us the notion of a creator-God to think about which we then subsequently understand by rational reflection upon the contingency of the world but the fact that we have been put on the right track by faith does not mean that reason cannot walk along it.

At this point it would be relevant to recall that Pannenberg will allow only an analogy of *language* in our language about God. And the analogy is between the normal use of language and the theological one. Thus *potent* may be used of a person and also used of God. They are analogous uses of the word, but they do not imply analogous realities. What then does he say of the validity of applying the word 'potent' in our adoration of God as we stand before the *fascinans et tremendum mysterium* since it cannot have the function of being applicable to God. His reply is that God takes the word: it is released from the manipulation of our conceptual thought and we 'must learn ever anew from the reality of God what the word...properly means'.[13] Adoration and true meditation do not succeed in attaining a true concept of God since to

13. Pannenberg, *Basic Questions in Theology*, I, p. 216.

conceive God would be to return from 'the self-sacrifice of the ego which is thinking the thoughts of God' to an act of conceptualization by which the finite ego is once again self-possessed and presiding over the reality of God.[14] Now it is here that I think we can find more common ground than at first appears.

It is not a notion of God that we worship but the living God who is unconceptualizable except in the process of the living generation of the eternal Logos by the Father in the dynamic love of the Spirit. But the concept that God is unconceptualizable is derived from the study of the notion of God as self-subsistent. What I have called the positive incomprehensibility of God is a concept which indicates something obscure and dim about God but nevertheless remains a valid indication. If this were not accepted then where does the validity of describing God apophatically arise? Moreover the direct experience of God in adoration or mysticism, precisely because God is not comprehensible or conceptualizable by an adequate concept, is not apparent to the devotee unless he can put his experience into language which, however provisional its character, can develop towards greater and greater adequacy only because some sort of validity in the original usage already exists. We cannot develop greater meaning from inanity. Something is only provisional insofar as it really does stop a gap. Even to speak of the revelation of God in Jesus is to speak of a revelation which remains provisional until the universal end of history or *parousia* when we shall wholly possess and be possessed by the Father who is the alpha and the omega, the origin and the end of all. And even this possession is never to be completed as we learn more and more what it means to be God. (Cf. Aquinas, *In 4. Sent.*, d.49, q.2, a.3.)

In sum, it seems that there are three possible godward activities:

1. To love God as an *experience* of a person who wills God and this activity remains the concern of those who like Pannenberg concentrate upon adoration in incomprehensibility.
2. To know God as an *intellective* activity of a person reflecting on the meaning of history, which is both natural and supernatural. Thus creation, since the historical act of creation is the act of God whereby a temporal-spatial being (human) comes to be, who is called to God, is a form of revelation.

---

14. Pannenberg, *Basic Questions in Theology*, I, p. 220.

3. To possess God, inchoately or finally, as a relationship of *presence*, which is in turn a function of memory. And it is in a wise reflection upon the memory from which hope springs and passes into possession, where the past is recalled and the future anticipated, that the possible development of theological unity between the two approaches I have discussed lies, that memory which is the analogue of the origin and the end of all reality that we call the Father. (Cf. Anselm, *Homologion*, c. 50: 'In memoria summi spiritus intelligitur Pater'.)

Part II

LITERATURE

LIVING POWERS: SACRED AND SECULAR LANGUAGE IN EUROPEAN ROMANTICISM

David Jasper

> If words are not THINGS, they are LIVING POWERS, by which the things of most importance to mankind are actuated, combined and humanized.
>
> S.T. Coleridge, *Aids to Reflection* (1825)

In 1816, Coleridge published the first of a series of pamphlets which he called 'Lay Sermons', in the face of the social unrest following the long war with France. It was entitled *The Statesman's Manual, or the Bible the Best Guide to Political Skill and Foresight*. Greeted with derision on its first appearance, *The Statesman's Manual* contains one of Coleridge's most brilliant passages on the Bible and its language, describing its narrative and images as

> ...the living *educts* of the imagination; of that reconciling and mediatory power, which incorporating the Reason in Images of the Sense, and organizing (as it were) the flux of the Senses by the permanence and self-circling energies of the Reason, gives birth to a system of symbols, harmonious in themselves, and consubstantial with the truths, of which they are the *conductors*. These are the Wheels which Ezekiel beheld, when the hand of the Lord was upon him, and he saw visions of God as he sate among the captives by the river of Chebar. *Whithersoever the Spirit was to go, the wheels went, and thither was their spirit to go: for the spirit of the living creature was in the wheels also.* The truths and symbols that represent them move in conjunction and from the living chariot that bears up (for *us*) the throne of the Divine Humanity. Hence, by a derivative, indeed, but not a divided, influence, and though in a secondary yet in more than a metaphorical sense, the Sacred Book is worthily intitled *the* WORD OF GOD.[1]

1. S.T. Coleridge, *Lay Sermons*, in R.J. White (ed.), *The Collected Works*, VI (Princeton: Princeton University Press, 1972), p. 29.

With its typically dense language, this passage demands a paper in itself. Here I concentrate upon one element only—the wheels of the chariot described in Ezek. 1.15–20. The symbols of Scripture—its language—as a driving force and agent of progression actually carry 'the throne of the Divine Humanity', the truths represented by these symbols—nothing dead and abstracted, but the language of the Bible *consubstantial* with their truths—that is, words as 'living powers' in a huge, harmonious system.

In his jottings on Eichhorn's studies of scriptural literature, Coleridge affirms that 'The Bible *is* that which it is capable of reflecting'.[2] Hugely effective, scriptural language cannot be glossed or substituted. It *is* what it *says*, and indeed, of poetic language in general, Coleridge is profoundly conscious of its power. Writing to William Mudford in 1822, he asserts: 'Words are not *Things*; but they are *Spirits* and *living Agents* that are seldom misused without avenging themselves'.[3] Coleridge was intensely aware of the Bible as poetry, and of the closeness of the genius of great poetry to Scripture, frequently comparing Shakespeare with the Bible, and specifically his capacity to realize the individuality of character within a universal vision—as Coleridge puts it in *The Friend*: '...that just proportion, that union and interpenetration of the universal and the particular, which must ever pervade all works of decided genius and true science'.[4]

Through his life-long obsession with the 'living powers' of words, Coleridge moved through the practice of poetry, criticism, philosophy and theology towards his great, unfinished project (to be crowned by a detailed commentary on the Fourth Gospel) of reconciling the 'I am' and the 'it is', the final realization of the primary Imagination, and the achievement of the 'one mighty alphabet' which confirms the universal (it is) in the particular (I am), the finite in the infinite, the subject in the object. It was, for him, a deeply theological task, based not upon the Berkeleian doctrine of 'a universal language of nature' by which God manifests himself to human perception, but an organic sense of words

---

2. S.T. Coleridge, *Marginalia*, II, in G. Whalley (ed.), *The Collected Works*, XII (Princeton: Princeton University Press, 1980–), p. 423.

3. S.T. Coleridge, *Collected Letters*, V (ed. E.L. Griggs; Oxford: Clarendon Press, 1971), p. 228.

4. S.T. Coleridge, *The Friend*, I, in B.E. Rooke (ed.), *The Collected Works*, IV (Princeton: Princeton University Press, 1969), p. 457. See further, *The Statesman's Manual* (1816), *Confessions of an Inquiring Spirit* (1840).

flowing from and into one another; language not from God, but conducting us *to*, and at the same time supporting, 'the throne of the Divine Humanity'. This, it will be appreciated, is potentially a radical moment for theology.

It is on this point that Coleridge continually takes exception to Johann Gottfried Eichhorn in his historical criticism of the Bible; that is, to Eichhorn's failure to understand the language of poetic imagination. For example, Eichhorn, in his *Introduction to the Old Testament* (1780–83), dismisses Ezekiel's vision as 'mere drapery, mere poetic fiction' (*blosse Einkleidung, blosse poetische Dichtungen*), exchangeable for others in the mind of another poet. To this Coleridge retorts:

> It perplexes me to understand, how a Man of Eichhorn's Sense, Learning, and Acquaintance with Psychology could form, or attach belief to, so cold-blooded an hypothesis. That in Ezechiel's Visions Ideas or Spiritual Entities are presented in visual Symbols, I never doubted; but as little can I doubt, that such Symbols did present themselves to Ezechiel in Visions— and by a Law closely connected with, if not contained in, that by which sensations are organized into Images and mental sounds in our ordinary sleep.[5]

Coleridge repeatedly accuses Eichhorn of allegorizing poetry too fully in a historical sense, or else dismissing the poetry of Scripture as 'mere poetic garnish'. What Eichhorn fails to appreciate is the universal poetic imagination, present pre-eminently in the Bible but also in all great poetic genius, above all Shakespeare. In particular, Eichhorn wholly misunderstands the imaginative power of the Apocalypse, which Coleridge cannily reads in the manner of his own 'Kubla Khan'. As Elinor Shaffer succinctly puts it:

> The references are interchangeable, they flow in and out of each other. Geographical mobility is uncannily combined with exact location, timelessness with precise and known history. The superimposition and blending of meaning is perfect.[6]

In his reading of Eichhorn, Coleridge repeatedly returns to the themes of the poet as profoundly religious, and poetic language as irreducible, organic, and emerging from the imagination as the vehicle—recall the

---

5.   *Marginalia*, II, p. 410.
6.   E.S. Shaffer, *'Kubla Khan' and The Fall of Jerusalem* (Cambridge: Cambridge University Press, 1975), p. 101.

wheels of Ezekiel's chariot—which carries (for us) the divine truths with which it is consubstantial.

This sense of the role of the poet and poetic language is, of course, widespread in Romantic literature. Novalis remarks more categorically than Coleridge would ever have done: '...the true poet has always remained a priest, just as the true priest has always remained a poet' (*Blütenstaub* No. 71). Friedrich Schlegel: 'Only he who has a religion of his own, an original view of the infinite, can be an artist' (*Ideen* No. 13). Shelley: 'A poet participates in the eternal, the infinite, and the one' (*A Defence of Poetry*).[7] But the key to Coleridge's particular understanding is his celebrated definition of the primary Imagination in Book I of *Biographia Literaria* (1817):

> The primary IMAGINATION I hold to be the living Power and prime Agent of all human Perception, and as a repetition in the finite mind of the eternal act of creation in the infinite I AM.

Words, we recall, Coleridge also described as 'living powers'. Here the imagination becomes the place of meeting of finite and infinite, situated in the human mind. Only in and through the imagination can Coleridge's reconciliation of the 'I am' and the 'it is' (the 'infinite I AM') be effected. The I AM looks back not only to the divine reply to Moses in Exodus 3, but to the *Ich bin* which Coleridge would have encountered everywhere in German transcendentalism, in Kant, Fichte and Schelling, as the first principle, self-consciousness or spirit.

In other words, deeply sensible as Coleridge was of the profoundly religious nature of the poetic vocation and the language of poetry, his deeper sense of its origins is in the human mind. The Bible, after all, is only worthily entitled the Word of God in a *secondary* (yet in more than a metaphorical) sense. In one sense he would have agreed with Shelley that 'poetry is connate with the origin of man' (*A Defence of Poetry*). Coleridge, however, remained—indeed became more than ever in old age—a deeply religious even a God-fearing man, 'groaning', as he put it, 'under a deep sense of infirmity and manifold imperfection' (*Confessions of an Inquiring Spirit*)—the words of the poet only 'made beautiful by grace'. His vision of language completely focused the finite and the infinite, the temporal and the eternal, the human and the divine. But—and this is my central point in this paper—this nervous and

7.   All these passages are quoted in L.R. Furst, *European Romanticism: Self-Definition* (London and New York: Methuen, 1980).

infinitely complex vision inspiring both his reading of the Bible and other poetry could not hold for those who came after Coleridge, and bequeathed an anxious rift between the language of the sacred and the language of the profane of which we are the heirs, still, as Matthew Arnold (one of its most sensitive victims, as we shall see) tragically put it in 'Stanzas from the Grande Chartreuse':

> Wandering between two worlds, one dead,
> The other powerless to be born—

anticipating Nietzsche's proclamation of the 'death of God'.

But we return first to a greater poet than Arnold, though one far less exercised by a religious spirit than Coleridge. In 1812, William Wordsworth, Coleridge's collaborator in *Lyrical Ballads*, told Crabb Robinson that 'perhaps' he felt 'no need of a Redeemer'. What we find throughout Wordsworth's poetry is an appropriation of the language of Christian devotion, as J.R. Watson has put it, 'for his own intelligent understanding of the external world. He is asserting the right of the individual to fashion his deepest beliefs from his own experience and not from some doctrinal formula.'[8] Such daring self-sufficiency and claim for the right of the individual in poetic exploration is unthinkable for Coleridge with his delicate sense of epistemological balance and his feeling for the symbol in language as an experience of Incarnation, partaking 'of the Reality which it renders intelligible; and while it enunciates the whole, abides itself as a living part in that Unity, of which it is the representative' (*Lay Sermons*, p. 30).

Beside this Wordsworth's language is, one might say, deeply 'profane'. Indeed, in his most extended discussion of the relationship between religion and poetry in the '*Essay, Supplementary to the Preface to Lyrical Ballads*' (1815), Wordsworth's very anxiety to establish the affinity between them serves only to make the distinction more plain. To read carefully again 'Tintern Abbey', shifting delicately as it does between the external world of nature and the internal mind of the poet, is to re-enter the poet's preoccupation, his own 'blessed mood' through the language of the Bible and devotion:

8.   J.R. Watson, 'Wordsworth and the Credo', in D. Jasper (ed.), *The Interpretation of Belief: Coleridge, Schleiermacher and Romanticism* (London: Macmillan, 1986), p. 161.

> —that serene and blessed mood,
> In which the affections gently lead us on—
> Until, the breath of this corporeal frame
> And even the motion of our human blood
> Almost suspended, we are laid asleep
> In body, and become a living soul;
> ...
>
>   If this
> Be but a vain belief, yet, oh! how oft—
> In darkness and amid the many shapes
> Of joyless daylight; when the fretful stir
> Unprofitable, and the fever of the world,
> Have hung upon the beatings of my heart—
> How oft, in spirit, have I turned to thee,
> O sylvan Wye! thou wanderer thro' the woods,
> How often has my spirit turned to thee!
> ...
>
> Nor greetings where no kindness is, nor all
> The dreamy intercourse of daily life,
> Shall e'er prevail against us, or disturb
> Our cheerful faith, that all which we behold
> Is full of blessings.

In these three, brief extracts from 'Tintern Abbey' one gets a sense not only of the particular language which Wordsworth uses to propel his meditation—'soul', 'belief', 'spirit', 'blessings'; but also of the religiously familiar turn of phrase and image—'the fever of the world', 'shall e'er prevail against us'. Even more significant are the biblical parallels with the Pauline letters, when the body laid aside in sleep becomes the 'living soul', or the River Wye is turned to by the 'spirit' as the agent of salvation from the darkness, business and fever of the world.

Wordsworth is using the familiar language and imagery of Christianity to explore his experience in Nature and with his sister Dorothy in their 'cheerful faith', and its very familiarity and power serves only to emphasize the distance Wordsworth has here travelled from its traditional religious use and reference.

Five years after Coleridge wrote *The Statesman's Manual*, Goethe published his last novel, the desultory *Wilhelm Meisters Wanderjahre* (1821), quickly translated into English by Thomas Carlyle as *Wilhelm Meister's Travels* (1827). In the discussion of biblical literature in chapter 11 Goethe abandons the delicate balance maintained by Coleridge and the theological foundations of living language in his drive towards the cultivation of 'reverence' (*Ehrfurcht*), which is, in its highest form, 'self-reverence' (*Ehrfurcht vor sich selbst*). Like Wordsworth's 'egotistical sublime', Goethe's 'self-reverence' shifts the basis of traditional religious language, and in particular the language of the Bible, towards a preoccupation with the self and human experience in the world—that is, towards a profound secularization of religious language against which Coleridge struggled, particularly in his later years, and the consequences of which remain with us today. As Stephen Prickett succinctly puts it, 'In Germany what Hermann Usener was later in the century to call a "glacial-moraine" (*gletscherwall*) was created between biblical studies and the study of other literatures, both classical and modern, which...has left a massive and seemingly natural barrier dividing the cultural landscape'.[9]

Coleridge affirms at the beginning of his late, posthumously published, study of biblical literature, *Confessions of an Inquiring Spirit*, that his thoughts were inspired by the reading of Carlyle's translation of *Wilhelm Meister*. But if, for Coleridge, to read the Bible like any other book is to discover its uniqueness, Goethe treats it as a great poetic celebration of the human spirit. The great 'I am' is here finally divorced from its origin in the divine conversation of Exodus 3.

Still, like Coleridge, Goethe acknowledges the 'unity in diversity' of scriptural language, affirming of the canonical books of the Old Testament:

> These stand so happily combined together, that even out of the most diverse elements, the feeling of a whole still rises before us. They are complete enough to satisfy; fragmentary enough to excite; barbarous enough to rouse; tender enough to appease: and for how many other contradicting merits might not these Books, might not this one Book, be praised![10]

Notice the words used to express the effect of scriptural literature: 'satisfy', 'excite', 'rouse', 'appease'—words expressive of human feelings and emotions. If Wordsworth in 'Tintern Abbey' uses the language of religious devotion to explore his own inner life, Goethe here adopts a

---

9. S. Prickett, *Words and 'The Word'* (Cambridge: Cambridge University Press, 1986), p. 1.

10. J.W. von Goethe, *Wilhelm Meister's Travels and Apprenticeship* (trans. T. Carlyle; 1827; repr. London: Chapman and Hall, n.d.), p. 211.

wholly secular, emotive language in his reading of the Old Testament. Furthermore, since the Israelite religion does not embody God in any form, it leaves us 'at liberty to represent him in a worthy human shape'.

Thus, moving to the New Testament Goethe refers to Christ as 'that divine Man' with none of the tones of incarnational theology of Coleridge's 'throne of the Divine Humanity'. Goethe's Christ is purely individual, living 'a private life' without connection with 'the general history of the world'. The language and teaching of the New Testament, therefore, is, for Goethe, entirely private, intimate and interior, the deep life, and language, in other words, of Romanticism. What is therefore absent from the biblical gallery around which Wilhelm is conducted is any reference to resurrection or the risen Christ. The life of 'the divine Man' is simply a 'pattern and example', never more so than in the Passion, which is, above all else, private. For:

> We hold it a damnable audacity to bring forth that torturing Cross, and the Holy One who suffers on it, or to expose them to the light of the sun, which hid its face when a reckless world forced such a sight on it; to take these mysterious secrets, in which the divine depth of Sorrow lies hid, and play with them, fondle them, trick them out, and rest not till the most reverend of all solemnities appears vulgar and paltry... (p. 214)

Thus, as in Wordsworth, the Christian tradition is interiorized in human feeling and experience, a religion, we might say, of humanity.

We might compare Goethe's language in *Wilhelm Meister* with perhaps the most familiar image in German Romantic art, Caspar David Friedrich's *Cross on the Mountains*, painted in 1808. Conceived as an altarpiece, the painting notoriously uses a landscape painting for a devotional purpose. It was this (along with a host of technical faults) which most deeply offended its most celebrated contemporary critic, Freiherr von Ramdohr.

Why so? The point is that Friedrich, no more than Goethe, is not concerned with the Passion or Crucifixion as such. The painting portrays a landscape with a wayside crucifixion common throughout the mountains of central Europe. In criticizing its failure to work as Christian allegory, Ramdohr was—rightly, as it happens—criticizing Friedrich's work as religious art, at least in the Christian sense. But the *Cross on the Mountain* is intended to be no more theological, or Christian, than 'Tintern Abbey', and, more importantly, what really offended Ramdohr was its *Romanticism*—in the critic's own words: 'that mysticism that is now insinuating itself everywhere, and that comes wafting towards us from art and science, from philosophy and religion, like a narcotic vapour'.[11] What Ramdohr calls mysticism in the landscape of Friedrich is another form of Wordsworth's 'sense sublime' felt at Tintern Abbey by the river Wye, and Goethe's 'divine depth of Sorrow' seen in the life of the divine Man—a 'natural meaning', as Goethe puts it, making 'the common extraordinary...the extraordinary common'.

It was, not insignificantly, Ramdohr who was himself singled out for criticism in a work hugely influential in German Romanticism, Wilhelm Wackenroder's bizarrely entitled *Heartfelt Effusions of an Art-Loving Monk* (1797), to which Tieck also contributed. Responding to paintings seen in Dresden in 1796, Wackenroder affirms that art

> by the meaningful combination of coloured earth and a little moisture recreates the human shape in ideal form within a narrow, limited space (a kind of creative act that has been granted to mortals)—art opens up to us the treasures in the human breast, turns our gaze inwards, and shows us the invisible, I mean all that is noble, sublime and divine, in human form (*in menschlicher Gestalt*).[12]

We are a long way here from Coleridge struggling to hold together in his poetic language a 'systematic reconciliation of the "I am" and the "it is"'.[13] Immensely influential though he was in the nineteenth century, Coleridge formed no school of followers and remained outside the great and powerful institutions of the academy and church. For most he remained a failed poet, author of a few extraordinary poems like 'Kubla Khan' and 'The Ancient Mariner', and is only now beginning to be recognized as a major figure in European ideas and religious thought through the systematic publication of his writings and notebooks (a task still unfinished).

Fully to understand Coleridge's re-vision of Kant and German transcendentalism, particularly his readings of Fichte and Schelling, may be one the great theological tasks waiting to be done in our age of postmodern anxiety over language and religion. J.S. Mill's comment made in 1840 may now be more true than ever:

11. Quoted in W. Vaughan, *German Romantic Painting* (New Haven: Yale University Press, 2nd edn, 1980), p. 8.

12. Quoted in Furst, *European Romanticism*, p. 56.

13. See T. McFarland, *Coleridge and the Pantheist Tradition* (Oxford: Clarendon Press, 1969), p. 191.

> The name of Coleridge is one of the few English names of our time which
> are likely to be oftener pronounced, and to become symbolical of more
> important things, in proportion as the inward workings of the age manifest
> themselves more and more in outward facts.[14]

It has not been so. Meanwhile in Germany in 1827 (two years after
Coleridge's *Aids to Reflection*) Goethe coins the term *Weltliteratur*
('world-literature'), embracing for him, the nineteen languages in which
he worked and the seventy-three years across which he wrote. Behind
the word lies *Weltpoesie*, an expression rooted in the conceptions of
language and literature explored by Herder and Humboldt—the same
Baron Wilhelm von Humboldt who was given the task of creating the
new University of Berlin in which he formally and institutionally separated theology from the study of the humanities and went far to erect
that *gletscherwall* which freezes and hopelessly divides us in our
universities and colleges to this day.[15] *Weltpoesie* is that impulse towards
verbal invention which is universal, ubiquitously dramatizing for us the
'raw material of experience'. This universalism is politically seductive (as
George Steiner acknowledges in his recent Inaugural Lecture at
Oxford),[16] but ultimately, I suggest, deeply isolating. Matthew Arnold,
one of its most articulate victims in the nineteenth century, frequently
refers to Goethe, significantly quoting from him in his 1863 essay on
Heine:

> Through me [Goethe] the German poets have become aware that, as man
> must live from within towards outwards, so the artist must work from
> within outwards, seeing that, make what contradictions he will, he can only
> bring to light his own individuality. I can clearly mark where this influence
> of mine has made itself felt; there arises out of it a kind of poetry of nature,
> and only in this way it is possible to be original.[17]

Again, as in Wackenroder, the language of inwardness. But how far can
the individual bear this responsibility, this weight of the egotistical sublime? Language now emerges solely from deep within the human spirit
which, in its self-sufficiency, feels 'no need of a Redeemer'. Coleridge,

14. J.S. Mill, 'Coleridge' (1840), in J.B. Schneewind (ed.), *Essays on Literature
and Society* (New York and London: Collier-Macmillan, 1965), p. 290.

15. See G. Steiner, 'What is Comparative Literature?' (Inaugural Lecture at
Oxford University; Oxford: Clarendon Press, 1995), pp. 4-5, and Prickett, *Words
and 'The Word'*, p. 1.

16. Steiner, 'What is Comparative Literature?', pp. 4-6.

17. M. Arnold, *Essays in Criticism* (Everyman; London: Dent, 1964), p. 113.

on the other hand, so painfully aware of his own inadequacies, continues, as he readily admits, to feel 'the want, the necessity, of religious support'.

But Arnold, the late Romantic poet, is left with the dilemma well described by Isobel Armstrong:

> If the poem appears to conjure objects merely as 'phantoms', if the language fails to construct the external world as anything but a fleeting, disappearing entity, if the poet fails to construct a 'sun', as it were, which acts on him as he reciprocally acts on it, he is left with a poetry which is without a content, or which can only take mind as its content.[18]

It was so for Arnold, Tennyson, Browning. The failure of reciprocity, in other terms, is the failure of Coleridge's great project of religious reconciliation through language. Arnold, in *his* poetry, simply cannot bear the epistemological weight of his Romantic inheritance—the responsibility of yielding all from self.

Thus in the suicide of Empedocles we find poetry both offering and questioning a relationship—and finally its impossibility. In Arnold's dramatic poem *Empedocles on Etna*, Empedocles refers to the 'Living Clouds' round Etna echoed by 'the fainter sea below'. One is reminded how in Wordsworth's *Prelude* the mist round Snowdon echoes 'the real sea' below. (The same image appears also in Shelley's *Prometheus Unbound*.) But Arnold reverses Wordsworth's priorities—in the *Prelude* the sea is 'real': in *Empedocles* it is 'fainter' than the 'living clouds', which are themselves the stronger 'sea'.[19] (Notice the parallel between these living clouds and Coleridge's image of words as 'living powers'.) Where then lies reality—as a real or a fainter sea? In the airy, insubstantial clouds? The metaphor is fractured, and the sea—that hugely important image in the imperialist nineteenth century—becomes the medium of our dissociation from self, of the finite from the infinite, and finally our failure to articulate and communicate in words for which we can no longer bear the responsibility. The Saussurean linguistic crisis was inevitable from this moment, and we live with it still, without a language for theology or a theology bold enough to be imagined.

For Arnold the sea of faith has retreated with its 'melancholy, long, withdrawing roar' ('Dover Beach'). The sea no longer substantial, as the

---

18. I. Armstrong, *Language as Living Form in Nineteenth Century Poetry* (Brighton: Harvester, 1982), p. 47.

19. Armstrong, *Language as Living Form*, p. 48.

medium of faith, simply withdraws in the ebbing tide. But as the medium in which we live, as 'reality', the 'sea of life', in another of Arnold's poems, dooms us to isolation, to the self-sufficiency which finally renders us unable to speak at all, either in the language of prayer or the language of personal communication:

> Yes: in the sea of life enisl'd
> With echoing straights between us thrown
> Dotting the shoreless watery wild,
> We mortal millions live *alone*.

> ...A God, a God, their severance rul'd;
> And bade betwixt their shores to be
> The unplumb'd, salt, estranging sea.
> ('Isolation')

In our age of mass communication, this crisis of language, fuelled by our century of war and violence, is now more acute than ever, and, as Coleridge knew full well, it is at base a religious, if not a theological, crisis: that is, of language which has become deeply secularized and estranged from its living and fertile roots.

IN THE BELLY OF THE WHALE: THE RISE AND FALL OF
RELIGIOUS LANGUAGE IN THE EARLY MODERN PERIOD

Gerald Hammond

My focus is on official religious language, much of it biblically derived,
the kind which the Leviathan of the State encourages and prescribes in
its schools and in its Church, and the relation of this language to our
more private religious languages, the spiritual idiolects which any of us
may develop and possess. My theme, eventually, is to trace the decline
of a Reformation ideal. When the Church became a State Church there
was the possibility of a revolution in the English language, by which the
Word might inspire all of the words which we utter; but by the second
half of the seventeenth century this ideal had decayed to the point that,
for many people, what was left of it was only a language of guilt, fear,
and false comfort.

I ought to begin, however, by stressing that there was a real, private,
personal, but communicable religious English, which survived into the
twentieth century, but it belonged only to the poets—and not, as you
might imagine I mean, the 'official' religious poets like T.S. Eliot, but
the generally unacknowledged ones. Robert Frost, for instance, wrote a
sonnet which is as spiritual and religious as anything I know. Richard
Poirier quotes it at the very beginning of his study of Frost's poetry.[1] I
quote it now because, in its precision, in its movement between the
earthbound and the infinite, and most of all in its refusal to be self concerned it may stand as a contrast to much of the more obviously
religious language which I shall be quoting later:[2]

1.   R. Poirier, *Robert Frost: The Work of Knowing* (New York: Oxford
University Press, 1977), p. xiv.

2.   *The Poetry of Robert Frost* (ed. E. Connery Latham; New York: Henry Holt,
1979), pp. 331-32.

The Silken Tent

She is as in a field a silken tent
At midday when a sunny summer breeze
Has dried the dew and all its ropes relent,
So that in guys it gently sways at ease,
And its supporting central cedar pole,
That is its pinnacle to heavenward
And signifies the sureness of the soul,
Seems to owe naught to any single cord,
But strictly held by none, is loosely bound
By countless silken ties of love and thought
To everything on earth the compass round.
And only by one's going slightly taut
In the capriciousness of summer air
Is of the slightest bondage made aware.

The sonnet is relevant in all kinds of ways, not the least being its prevailing image of the tent bound by so many cords. *Religion*, so the best etymologies conjecture, means 'binding'.[3] Religion binds us to others, in community, and to our past, in Frost's line, 'By countless silken ties of love and thought'. Poirier, in his analysis of the poem, points out its religious frame of reference:

> The characteristics of litany which can be heard in the first line…suggest that if the tent belongs in 'a field' it also belongs in 'The Song of Songs', where the bride says that she is as comely 'as the tents of Kedar, as the curtains of Solomon'. The field itself eventually encompasses 'everything on earth'; it is the 'field' of the Lord or the 'courts of our God' in Psalm 92, where the righteous 'shall grow like a cedar in Lebanon'.[4]

Psalms, as I hope to show, are vital elements, for good and bad, in the development of communal and private religious languages.

Now for a more self-concerned religious statement. I found it in the letter page of *The Independent* the day I began to write this paper, looking for a clue to unwind. From Mr G. Brown, this letter took issue with an article concerned with the teaching of religion in school:[5]

3. The *OED* says that *religion* is 'of doubtful etymology', usually derived either from *relegere*, 'to read over again', or from *religare*, 'to bind', adding that 'the latter view has usually been favoured'.
4. Poirier, *Robert Frost*, p. xv.
5. *The Independent*, 23 December 1994.

> Sir: With regard to your leading article 'Ritual, the common thread of religion'...my first lesson at junior school was on the Bible and the subject was the 23rd Psalm. I believed in it from then, and have never questioned it since.
>
> For me, daily prayers and hymns make the start of the school day enjoyable and I would not want this experience to be denied to anyone. My parents never went to church; it was the school that gave me the faith I still have at 75.
>
> Yours faithfully,...

Mr Brown's letter is a moving little piece: in its way, spare and neatly written, conveying the certainty of faith. It is not quite as spare or as certain as a bumper sticker which I once saw in Texas: 'God said it. I believe it. That settles it.' One of my arguments is that like all language, religious language depends for its interpretation upon its context. On the bumper of one of those red-neck pick-up trucks, complete with rifle rack, that sticker became as frightening as it was funny. Mr Brown's declaration of a lifetime's untroubled faith is similar: 'I believed in it from then, and have never questioned it since' is framed by some very interesting items of autobiography. 'It' is the twenty-third psalm, which formed his first ever school lesson, and his parents never went to church. Interpretation is tempting. Mr Brown, now in his seventies, and lamenting the irreligious nature of today's schooling, is clearly a lover of words. The elegance of his letter, with its careful, uncluttered, balanced sentences, implies a fine, trained ear—and it was hearing the twenty-third psalm, doubtless in the AV translation, which opened the doors of perception to him. School offered him immediately a language of belief and beauty which his parents did not have and could not give; and some seventy years later he remembers the moment, and its language, which set him on his path through life. It is hard to imagine one of today's lessons on personal development having quite the same effect. Then again, it is hard for me to believe that such untroubled faith through life is a desirable quality. Mr Brown and the pick-up driver are fellow travellers.

Let me try another statement of absolute faith on you. It is from the Bible, and I quote it in William Tyndale's translation. One of the great proclamations of monotheism it is delivered to a body of troubled men, each of whom worships his own minor deity:

> I am an Hebrew: and the Lord God of Heaven which made both sea and dry land, I fear.

The context is everything. The same man says, further on in his story, again according to Tyndale's translation:

> I knew well enough that thou wast a merciful God, full of compassion, long ere thou be angry and of great mercy and repentest when thou art come to take punishment.[6]

The man is Jonah, and I quote him because he is probably the most successful speaker in the whole Bible. Prophecy is founded on utterance, a powerful example of speech act, and Jonah's words are efficient beyond the dreams of other prophets like Isaiah and Jeremiah. He says just one sentence—five words in the Hebrew—'there shall not pass forty days but Nineveh shall be overthrown', and the whole city repents, puts on sackcloth and ashes, fasts, and cries unto God. And this, remember, is a city so big that it takes three days to pass through it, and with a population so large that it has within it 100,000 children.

The author of Jonah was a truly crafty narrator, and one who had thought about the nature of religious language. Through his protagonist he mocks, or satirizes, or parodies—none of these words seems quite right—perhaps, better, he obliquely represents the absolute truth claims of this language.[7] Deriving directly from revelation and, if we are to believe the opening of John's Gospel, part of the godhead itself, the religious word is the doorway to truth. There is one God only and he made everything, the land and the sea, and I fear him: so says Jonah on a boat in a storm at sea. He had, of course, fled there to escape God's call to prophesy to Nineveh, so his affirmation of faith is completely ironic. If he 'fears' God and if he knows that God made the sea, why is he where he is, heading in the opposite direction from the great city? Likewise, God's mercy, compassion, slowness to anger and speed to forgive: great affirmations of faith and a true insight into God's nature, but delivered by a man who resents it all. Jonah would much rather that Nineveh were destroyed and were not the object of God's benevolence. Like all of the prophets, forced to utter God's words, Jonah is bound into an enterprise which will destroy his own life; but unlike the others

---

6. *Tyndale's Old Testament* (ed. D. Daniell; New Haven: Yale University Press, 1992), pp. 641 and 643.

7. See J.S. Ackerman's account of Jonah in *The Literary Guide to the Bible* (ed. R. Alter and F. Kermode; Cambridge, MA: Harvard University Press, 1987), pp. 234-43, where he argues that 'satire is a more appropriate designation of genre' for the book (p. 242).

his fate is exquisitely bitter, to be the saviour of the nation which will eventually exile and enslave his own people. It is no wonder, then, that his last words in the book named after him are heroically antagonistic. Tyndale renders them beautifully:

> And God said unto Jonas, art thou so angry for thy wild vine? And he said, I am angry a-good, even unto the death.

As with Mr Brown's story, so at the heart of Jonah's is a psalm. Thrown overboard in the storm and swallowed up by the big fish, Jonah sings in its belly a psalm of deliverance. The psalm gave Tyndale some pause as he translated it. In the prologue to the book he took care to instruct his readers in the narrative problems which it presented:

> When Jonas had been in the fish's belly a space and the rage of his conscience was somewhat quieted and suaged and he come to himself again and had received a little hope, the qualms and pangs of desperation which went over his heart, half overcome, he prayed, as he maketh mention in the text saying Jonas prayed unto the Lord his God in the belly of the fish. But the words of that prayer are not here set. The prayer that here standeth in the text, is the prayer of praise and thanksgiving which he prayed and wrote when he was escaped and past all jeopardy.[8]

This is an odd thing to write, that where the text says that Jonah prayed to the Lord out of the belly of the fish, and the prayer is then given, that we should not understand this prayer to be the prayer which Jonah then uttered, but one which he composed later, when back on dry land, the original prayer no longer surviving. As soon as you look at Jonah's prayer you can see the problem which Tyndale is trying to wish away. The prayer is a psalm, identical in tone and in many of its images, its vocabulary and verse structure to many of the psalms in the book of Psalms. It begins:

> in mine tribulation I called unto the Lord, and he answered me: out of the belly of hell I cried, and thou heardest my voice. For thou hadst cast me down deep in the midst of the sea: and the flood compassed me about: all thy waves and rolls of water went over me: and I thought that I had been cast away out of thy sight.

And in typical psalm structure it moves from this sense of loss and desolation to a thanksgiving for salvation and relief, closing like this:

---

8.   *Tyndale's Old Testament*, p. 635.

And yet thou Lord my God broughtest up my life again out of corruption.
When my soul fainted in me, I thought on the Lord: and my prayer came
in unto thee, even into thy holy temple. They that observe vain vanities,
have forsaken him that was merciful unto them. But I will sacrifice unto
thee with the voice of thanksgiving, and will pay that I have vowed, that
saving cometh of the Lord.

For Tyndale the problem is to reconcile this song of deliverance with
Jonah's predicament. Far from being saved, or even listened to, he is in
about the worst place it is possible to be, inside a whale in the depths of
the sea. Without taking Tyndale's way out and refusing to read what the
text says as a continuous narrative, accepting instead that this is Jonah's
song within the whale, how do we explain the incongruity? One way, of
course, is to make the typical manoeuvre of Bible critics and assume that
what we have here is a piece of botched-up editing, the psalm coming
from somewhere else and having been spliced clumsily into the Jonah
narrative.[9]

Such an explanation misses the point. The author of Jonah, most
crafty of narrators, is exploring the nature of religious language. Psalms
sung in the temple services are full of images of despair—being cast
away in mighty seas, waves breaking over one's head, being plunged
down to the depths, in the belly of hell—and then images of salvation—
having one's life brought up out of corruption.[10] In Jonah the psalm is
demetaphorized. These are real waves, real depths, real corruption, a real
belly. As with everything he says, Jonah's language here is stoutly
orthodox. Only the context turns it inside out. This man sings a song of
deliverance to celebrate his escape from God. For him, to be in the
whale in the depths of the sea is to be in the best place on earth, the
furthest and remotest point from Nineveh. Here he may legitimately be
himself and not the mouthpiece of God. Free from the tyranny of the
Word he uses religious language to validate his survival on his own
terms. The whale, however, is not taken in. A fine literary critic, his

9.   'Predictably, there are scholars who reject arguments for Jonah's composite
nature and defend the unity of Jonah. While a majority of contemporary commentators belong to this category, they do differ among themselves on whether the
"original" narrative included the psalm of chapter 2 (Landes, Magonet, Stuart,
Lacoque, Alter) or not (Trible, Wolff)'. J.M. Sasson, *Jonah* (AB; New York:
Doubleday, 1990), p. 17.

10.   E.g. Pss. 18.15-16; 48.7; 69.13-15.

response is absolute. As the psalm finishes, 'it vomited out Jonah upon the dry land'.[11]

Jonah, it turns out, is a powerful meditation upon the varieties of religious language. Prophecy, the word of God transmitted through a human being, is here uniquely potent: set against the multitude of prophetic visions and articulations in Isaiah, Jeremiah, and Ezekiel, Jonah's five words transform the world. The direct affirmation of personal faith becomes, in Jonah's mouth, a contradiction of his own experience and of conventional religious teaching. Rather than the fear of God being the beginning of wisdom, Jonah's fearing of the God who made the sea and the land is a prologue to folly. His assurance that God is ever merciful and compassionate is a torment rather than a comfort. And the psalm, the lyric impulse to praise God, here celebrates the death wish. Denial and rejection are the sources of Jonah's praise rather than, as the words would have it in any other context, acceptance and salvation. Whoever wrote Jonah was intent upon making his readers (or hearers) examine the nature of the religious language which came to them so easily and naturally. Psalms, sung in the temple rituals, had, for this writer, become composed of sterile formulae. By literalizing the language, and by the whale's reaction to it, the psalm's claim to convey revealed truth is ironized. In this book of the Bible, at least, the distance between the word and the man who utters the word is immense—and it remains so from beginning to end: 'Art thou so angry?' 'I am angry a-good, even unto the death'.

To read the book of Jonah as I have just done is perhaps unacceptable for many people even today. At the time of the Reformation it would have been near impossible, for it strikes against the absolute, monolithic quality which religious language, insofar as it is biblical language, is supposed to have. Indeed, to read Tyndale's reading of Jonah contained in the preface (which is nearly six times as long as the book itself) is to encounter a determined, sometimes contradictory effort to deny what the text actually says, not only in the curious recontextualizing of the psalm, which I have already cited, but from the beginning of Jonah's narrative to its end. Much of this, it is true, is standard Christian (and Jewish) exegesis of the story, but this only goes to show how religion must, to maintain itself, preserve monolithic, unambiguous meanings premised on the decontextualizing or recontextualizing of language.

---

11. This is the AV translation, superior to Tyndale's 'and it cast out' because it more graphically renders the Hebrew *wayyke*, from a root meaning 'spew'.

Tyndale's formula for this process, interestingly enough, is that we should learn to read Jonah 'fruitfully, and not as a poet's fable'.[12] Accordingly, Jonah's initial reluctance to go to Nineveh is based, Tyndale claims, upon his desire not to 'shame' God by preaching to Israel's enemies. The whole purpose of the exercise was 'to teach Jonas and to show him his own heart and to make him perfect and instruct us also by his example'. Jonah sleeps on the ship in the storm because of his bad conscience. And in Nineveh it seems that Jonah spoke not just five words, but whole sermons—he 'went fair and easily preaching here a sermon, and there another and rebuked the sin of the people, for which they must perish'. Finally, Jonah's anger at the story's end derives from the sense of prophetic glory which he has lost, 'in that his prophecy came not to pass'—a bizarre contradiction, when you stop to think about it, of the claim that he had been preaching all over Nineveh, for the prophetic purpose of such sermons could only be to urge the people to repent. In effect, reading Tyndale's account of the book is a curiously depressing experience, to see so responsive a translator, one so adept at finding a language of nuance and complexity, turn out to be so flat and dull an interpreter. A prisoner of his age, Tyndale cannot ironize the Bible. Revealed truth is contained in a word which must always be transparent.

Such a notion of a simple, single-sensed language began to collapse in the middle of the next century. Hobbes's *Leviathan* put the sword to its neck and, as Christopher Hill has recently argued in his book on the Bible in the English revolution, by the third quarter of the seventeenth century the inadequacy of religious language to convey anything meaningful to address the complexity of experience, social or political, had become embarrassingly apparent.[13] Earlier in the century the poets had become well aware of this embarrassment. To take two examples, from temperamentally different poets, I refer to George Herbert's poem 'Time' and Andrew Marvell's poem 'Bermudas'. Both poems adopt the strategy of Jonah, using religious language to destroy itself.[14] In Herbert's 'Time', the poet opens his door to find Time waiting there,

---

12. *Tyndale's Old Testament*, p. 631.

13. C. Hill, *The English Bible and the Seventeenth-Century Revolution* (London: Allen Lane, 1993); see especially section 5, 'The End of the Revolutionary Bible'.

14. More detailed accounts of these poems can be found in my *Fleeting Things: English Poets and Poems 1616–1660* (Cambridge, MA: Harvard University Press, 1990), pp. 171-75 and 267-71.

scythe in hand, ready to take him away. Many of us in his position might be tempted to slam the door shut but Herbert, the good Christian, knows that his duty is to welcome death, not recoil from it. He greets his caller by first of all chiding him gently for having taken so long to visit—'Thy scythe is dull, whet it for shame'. Time apologizes for his delay and then listens patiently while Herbert tells him why he is so welcome:

> Perhaps some such of old did pass,
> Who above all things loved this life;
> To whom thy scythe a hatchet was,
> Which now is but a pruning-knife,
>> Christ's coming hath made man thy debter,
>> Since by thy cutting he grows better.
>
> And in his blessing thou art blest:
> For where thou only wert before
> An executioner at best;
> Thou art a gard'ner now, and more,
>> An usher to convey our souls
>> Beyond the utmost stars and poles.
>
> And this is that makes life so long,
> While it detains us from our God,
> Ev'n pleasures here increase the wrong,
> And length of days lengthen the rod.
>> Who wants the place, where God doth dwell,
>> Partakes already half of hell.
>
> Of what strange length must that needs be,
> Which ev'n eternity excludes!

At this point Time interrupts him:

> Thus far Time heard me patiently:
> Then chafing said, 'This man deludes:
>> What do I here before his door?
>> He doth not crave less time, but more.'[15]

The point is clear enough. Like Jonah in his whale, Herbert, in the face of death, to the face of death, utters a stream of religious orthodoxies. To have said nothing at all was the only genuine response. As so often, religious language here is a blanket for self-concern, and for all of the

---

15. *The English Poems of George Herbert* (ed. C.A. Patrides; London: Dent, 1974), pp. 134-35.

rightness of what he says, he deserves and gets only scorn.

Andrew Marvell's 'Bermudas' is, if anything, more subtle—so much so, that most readers still do not understand the poem. Written in the 1640s, but set in time a generation earlier, the poem studies the first Puritan settlers in the New World. In the main it takes the form of a metrical psalm, in which the settlers, rowing to shore, praise God for his providence in guiding them safely to this paradise:

> He gave us this eternal spring,
> Which here enamels everything,
> And sends the fowls to us in care,
> On daily visits through the air.
> He hangs in shades the orange bright,
> Like golden lamps in a green night,
> And does in the pom'granates close
> Jewels more rich than Ormus shows.
> He makes the figs our mouths to meet,
> And throws the melons at our feet,
> But apples plants of such a price,
> No tree could ever bear them twice.[16]

These apples are pineapples literally, but figuratively Eden's apples. The settlers, doing what they do best, the strenuous labour of rowing, with the psalm as their working song, are importing into paradise the work ethic. Their psalm of praise is really the hissing of the serpent, for their arrival in Eden will destroy it; as Marvell quietly observes in his final adjective:

> And all the way, to guide their chime,
> With falling oars they kept the time.

Marvell, analyzing the mind set of the men who now, in the 1640s, rule England, finds their sublime certainty embodied in their language of praise. He knows, although they do not, that they are the ones who will destroy this paradise, and they will do so under the cover of a language which professes to glory in God's natural bounty.

After the Restoration religious language lingers on but only with increasing embarrassment, either as a vehicle for lower class ignorance, its final decline charted devastatingly in George Eliot's *Silas Marner*; or, among the better sort, as a means of self-delusion. Here, for instance, is a

---

16. *Andrew Marvell: The Complete Poems* (ed. E.S. Donno; Harmondsworth: Penguin Books, 1972), pp. 116-17.

Restoration man using religious language to avoid facing up to the realities of what he has done:

> *September 24, 1663.* In the afternoon, telling my wife that I go to Deptford, I went by water to Westminster Hall; and there finding Mrs Lane, took her over to Lambeth where we were lately, and there did what I would with her but only the main thing, which she would not consent to, for which God be praised; and yet I came so near, that I was provoked to spend. But trust in the Lord I shall never do so again while I live...so to my office writing letters, till 12 at night almost; and then home to supper and bed and there find my poor wife hard at work which grieved my heart to see that I should abuse so good a wretch, and that is just with God to make her bad to me for my wronging of her; but I resolve never to do the like again. So to bed.[17]

The Reformation, and the successive reformations which followed it through the sixteenth and seventeenth centuries, to adopt Christopher Haigh's historiography, first redefined the nature of religious language and then marginalized it to the point that it sticks out like a sore thumb in Pepys's diary, as a moment when, to avoid analyzing the desire and guilt which motivate him, he uses it to articulate resolutions which he has no real intention of keeping. In a way, this was a full circle, for religious language, on the eve of the Reformation, had virtually lost all meaning. I am not, of course, referring here to its use by intellectuals. A man like Thomas More used religious language to achieve a profound degree of self-analysis but, as events proved, More was well out of step with the world around him. One of the things that the Reformers wanted to reform in this wider world was language itself. Primarily by giving the people the Bible in English, but also through a growing stream of writings and sermons, the aim was to make the nation at all levels relearn how to speak.

How the nation spoke just before the Reformation we might gather from the poetry of John Skelton. Over sixty years old in the 1520s, when he wrote his best poetry, Skelton reproduces better than anyone else I know, how the last generation of English Catholics expressed themselves. *The Tunning of Elinor Rumming*, a poem centred on the variety of women who drink themselves into oblivion in a pub, shows how instinctively Elinor's clientele use religious language, and how devoid of any real meaning it is:

---

17. *The Diary of Samuel Pepys* (ed. R. Latham and W. Matthews; London: G. Bell & Sons, 1971), IV, p. 317.

> Then cometh another guest:
> She sweareth by the rood of rest
> Her lips are so dry
> Without drink she must die
> Therefore fill it by and by,
> And have here a peck of rye.
>
> . . .
>
> Another brought a spick
> Of a bacon-flick;
> Her tongue was very quick,
> But she spake somewhat thick.
> Her fellow did stammer and stut,
> But she was a foul slut,
> For her mouth foamed
> And her belly groaned:
> Joan said she had eaten a fyest.
> 'By Christ', said she, 'thou liest;
> I have as sweet a breath
> As thou, with shameful death!'
>
> . . .
>
> There came an old ribibe:
> She haled of a kibe,
> And had broken her shin
> At the threshold coming in,
> And fell so wide open
> That one might see her token—
> The devil thereon be wroken!
> What need all this be spoken?
> She yelled like a calf.
> 'Rise up, on God's half!'
> Said Elinor Rumming,
> 'I beshrew thee for thy coming!'[18]

Set against that lower class life the world of the court which Skelton describes in *The Bouge of Court*, here are the courtiers, politicians and churchmen, manoeuvring for position with, always, at the root of nearly every utterance, a veneer of religion to cover their viciousness:

18. From 'The Tunning of Elinor Rumming', lines 270-76, 335-46, 492-503; in *John Skelton: Selected Poems* (ed. G. Hammond; Manchester: Carcanet, 1980), pp. 73-90.

Ye remember the gentleman right now
That communed with you, methought a pretty space?
Beware of him, for, I make God avow,
He will beguile you and speak fair to your face.
Ye never dwelt in such another place,
For here is none that dare well other trust—
But I would tell you a thing, and I durst.

The sovereignest thing that any man may have
Is little to say, and much to hear and see;
For, but I trusted you, so God me save,
I would nothing so plain be:
To you only, methink I durst shrive me,
For now am I plenarly disposed
To show you things that may not be disclosed.
...
Lo what is to you a pleasure great
To have that cunning and ways that ye have!
By God's soul, I wonder how ye gat
So great pleasure, or who to you it gave.
Sir, pardon me, I am an homely knave,
To be with you thus pert and thus bold;
But ye be welcome to our household.

And, I dare say, there is no man herein
But would be glad of your company.
I wist never man that so soon could win
The favour that ye have with my lady.
I pray to God that it may never die.
It is your fortune for to have that grace—
As I be saved, it is a wonder case![19]

All of this is pre-biblical language, the degeneration of the great mysteries of the Catholic church over hundreds of years, its theological complexities reduced to oaths and pious platitudes. With the Scriptures locked up in Latin, and the clergy itself largely incapable of translating that Latin into the vernacular, the people at all levels merely used scraps and odds and ends of saints' lives and garbled Gospel tags to steer their way through life. Thomas More articulates the Church's dilemma very clearly when he opposes Tyndale's translation of the Greek *agapē* as 'love'. *Agapē* is so profound a concept, so complexly explored by generations of commentators, that to translate it with a word which carries

---

19. From 'The Bouge of Court', lines 197-210, 260-73; in *John Skelton: Selected Poems*, pp. 27-39.

as much contamination as does 'love' is to reduce its mysteries to a kind of lowest common denominator.[20] For the Reformers, however, this was exactly the point, not to reduce biblical language to the everyday but to elevate the everyday to the biblical; and to read the writings of English men and women in the first wave of the Reformation is to feel them responding with great excitement to new possibilities of language. At court, Sir Thomas Wyatt translates the penitential psalms, interweaving them with a narrative of David's repentance for his adulterous liaison with Bathsheba. Here is real self-analysis leading to a real explanation of desire and guilt. The sixth of the seven psalms ends, in Wyatt's translation, with the lines

> Plenteous ransom shall come with him, I say,
> And shall redeem all our iniquity

followed, immediately, by David's exploration of what he has just sung:

> This word 'redeem' that in his mouth did sound
> Did put David, it seemeth unto me,
> As in a trance to stare upon the ground
> And with his thought the height of heaven to see,
> Where he beholds the Word that should confound
> The sword of death, by humble ear to be
> In mortal maid, in mortal habit made,
> Eternal life in mortal veil to shade.

> He seeth that Word, when full ripe time should come,
> Do way that veil by fervent affection,
> Torn off with death (for death should have her doom),
> And leapeth lighter from such corruption
> Than glint of light that in the air doth lome.[21]

The king thinks about the word he has uttered and through it reaches a vision stretching beyond his own narrow predicament to encompass the whole of history. Through the absolutely human—'mortal' is repeated three times—Wyatt sees the light of redemption enter the world, one

20. 'Like wisdom was there in the change of this word charity into love. For though charity be always love, yet is not ye wote well love always charity.' Sir Thomas More, *A Dialogue Concerning Heresies*, 3.8; in *The Yale Edition of the Complete Works of St Thomas More* (ed. T.M.C. Lawler, C. Marc'hadour and R.C. Marius; New Haven: Yale University Press, 1981), VI, pp. 286-87; modernized spelling.

21. *Sir Thomas Wyatt: The Complete Poems* (ed. R.A. Rebholz; Harmondsworth: Penguin Books, 1978), p. 214.

lesson being the ironic one that Henry VIII's adulteries had introduced into England the Reformation which would redeem the nation.

Lower in the social order are the Plumpton family of Plumpton near Knaresborough, in Yorkshire. Robert Plumpton, a student at the Inner Temple, writes home to his mother c. 1536:

> ...I desire you, most dear mother, that ye will take heed to the teaching of the Gospel, for it is the thing that all we must live by; for Christ left it that we should altogether rule our living thereby, or else we cannot be in favour with God. Wherefore, I would desire you for the love of God, that you would read the New Testament, which is the true Gospel of God, spoken by the Holy Ghost. Wherefore, doubt not of it, dearly beloved mother in the Lord, I write not this to bring you into any heresies, but to teach you the clear light of God's doctrine. Wherefore, I will never write nothing to you, nor say nothing to you, concerning the Scriptures, but will die in the quarrel. Mother, you have much to thank God that it would please him to give you licence to live until this time, for the gospel of Christ was never so truly preached as it is now. Wherefore, I pray to God that he will give you grace to have knowledge of his Scriptures.[22]

It is significant that this is a son writing to his mother. A number of stories from around this period demonstrate a generational conflict, the older generation falling back on its pater nosters, oaths, and commonplace tags, the younger generation responding to a new English language of religious truth.[23] As his letter continues, Robert Plumpton picks on the word 'love' to emphasize to his mother how revolutionary are the words which she will read if she does as he asks and takes up Tyndale's New Testament:

> Ye shall perceive what the profession of our Baptism is, which profession we must have written in our hearts. Which profession standeth in two things; the one is the knowledge of the law of God, understanding it spiritually as Christ expoundeth it, Math. v.vi and vii chapters; so that the root and life of all laws is this, Love the Lorde God with all thy heart, all thy soul, all thy might and all thy power, and thy neighbour as thy self for Christ's sake. And love only is the fulfilling of the law, as saith S. Paule,

---

22. Text in A.G. Dickens, *Lollards and Protestants in the Diocese of York 1509–1558* (London: Hambledon Press, 2nd edn, 1982), p. 134. I have modernized the spelling.

23. As in the account of his father's persecution of him by William Maldon of Newington, reported by Foxe; see A.W. Pollard, *Records of the English Bible* (Folkestone: Wm Dawson & Sons, 1974), pp. 268-71.

and that whatsoever we do and not of that love, that same fulfilleth not the law in the sight of God.[24]

How far such a language penetrated the discourse of the multitude of the people is demonstrable, I think, from the sermons preached by men like Hugh Latimer and Thomas Lever. Latimer, particularly in the sermons which he preached before Edward VI, reiterated the ideal of an organic society, bound together by ties of justice and mutual obligation, through all classes, by the preaching of the word of God. In his own style, the easiness with which he moves from the highest to the lowest registers, Latimer exemplifies the fluidity of the new religious language:

We can not be saved without faith, and faith cometh by hearing of the word. *Fides ex auditu.* And how shall they hear without a preacher? I tell you it is the footsteps of the ladder of heaven, of our salvation. There must be preachers if we look to be saved. I told you of this gradation before in the tenth to the Romans. Consider it well. I had rather ye should come of a naughty mind, to hear the word of God, for novelty, or for curiosity to hear some pastime, than to be away. I had rather ye should come as the tale is by the Gentlewoman of London one of her neighbours met her in the street, and said mistress whither go ye, Marry said she, I am going to S. Thomas of Acres to the sermon, I could not sleep all this last night, and I am going now thither, I never failed of a good nap there, and so I had rather ye should a napping to the sermons, than not to go at all. For with what mind so ever ye come, though ye come for an ill purpose, yet peradventure ye may chance to be caught ere ye go, the preacher may chance to catch you on his hook. Rather than ye should not come at all, I would have you come of curiosity, as Saint Augustine came to hear Saint Ambrose. When Saint Augustine came to Milan, (he tells the story himself in the end of his book of confessions) he was very desirous to hear S Ambrose, not for any love he had to the doctrine that he taught, but to hear his eloquence, whether it was so great, as the speech was, and as the bruit went. Well, before he departed Saint Ambrose caught him on his hook and converted him so, that he became of a Manichee, and of a platonist a good christian, a defender of Christ's religion, and of the faith afterward. So I would have you come to the sermons. It is declared in many more places of scripture, how necessary preaching is, as this. *Evangelium est potentia dei, ad salutem omni credenti.* The preaching of the Gospel, is the power of God to every man, that doth believe. He means God's word opened, It is the instrument, and the thing whereby we are saved. Beware ye diminish not this office, for if ye do, ye decay God's power to all that do believe.[25]

24. Dickens, *Lollards and Protestants*, p. 134.

25. From Latimer's sixth sermon before Edward VI; see H. Latimer, *Seven*

This is the proclamation of the Reformation ideal of a transformation of language, reaching down from the monarch to the poorest in the land, all experiencing together the preached word. It was an ideal which, in some quarters, survived well into the next century. A provincial town like Halifax, for example, saw in the late sixteenth century monthly preaching festivals, where much of the population gathered to hear the word of God preached and its meaning debated.[26] In London, an intellectual like John Manningham, whose diaries survive, their value lying in Manningham's contemporary accounts of the performances of Renaissance plays, transcribes in them extensive summaries of sermons which he evidently took as much pleasure in attending and hearing as he did, say, *Twelfth Night*.[27] And, most notably, of course, there is the emphasis on the power of the preached word among the Puritan sects of the 1640s and 50s.

And yet, the signs are that very soon after Latimer's time the ideal was decaying. With Thomas Lever's sermons, delivered in the 1550s, we sense the beginnings of the failure of religious language to cope with the complexities of the emergence of a modern state. Lever's great theme, preached repeatedly from Paul's Cross, is to praise God's benevolence in giving his English people the Scriptures in English, so that they, before the whole world, may experience the fullness of revelation. But, as experience already shows Lever, one generation into the Reformation, the people fail to respond properly to the experience, but misrepresent and misappropriate the Word, turning religious truth into personal and political expediency:

> So that the free heart, and liberal gift of the rich, must make all that he may spare, common to relieve the need of the poor: yea if there be great necessity, he must sell both lands and goods, to maintain charity: And thus to have all things common, doth derogate or take away nothing from the authority of rulers. But to will to have all things common, in such sort that idle lubbers…might take and waste the gains of labourers without restraint of authority, or to have like quantity of every thing to be given to every man, is under a pretence to mend all, purposely to mar all. For those same men pretending to hate covetousness, would be as rich as the richest: and

Sermons before Edward VI (ed. E. Arber; London, 1865), pp. 166-67. I have modernized the spelling.

26. See H. Holroyde, 'Protestantism and Dissent in the Parish of Halifax', in *Transactions of the Halifax Antiquarian Society*, 1988, p. 30.

27. J. Manningham's *Diary* is located in the British Museum, Harleian MS. 5353.

saying that they hate pride, would be as highly taken as the best, and seeming to abhor envy, can not be content to see any other richer or better than they themselves be. Now I hear some say that this error is the fruit of the scripture in English. No, neither this, nor no other error cometh because the scripture is set forth in the English tongue, but because the rude people lacking the counsel of learned men to teach them the true meaning when they read it, or hear it, must needs follow their own Imagination in taking of it...

As for example of rich men, look at the merchants of London, and ye shall see, when as by their honest vocation, and trade of merchandise God hath endowed them with great abundance of riches, then can they not be content with the prosperous wealth of that vocation to satisfy themselves, and to help others, but their riches must abroad in the country to buy farms out of the hands of worshipful gentlemen, honest yeomen, and poor labouring husbands.[28]

Lever sees the ties of true community coming apart and although he vehemently denies the charge, is aware that the new freedom of religious language is being used to legitimize the various forms of self-interest.

My final resting place is one generation further on, by when the inadequacy of religious language to reflect experience becomes increasingly apparent. My spokesman is Thomas Whythorne, whose manuscript autobiography, written around 1576, is the closest we get to hearing an Elizabethan think and talk.[29] Whythorne, an itinerant music teacher to the gentry, and himself a minor composer, was a man deeply interested in language. One sign of this is the very experimental orthography with which he writes his autobiography. Another sign is Whythorne's own ruminations on language. Take those London merchants whom Lever attacked for their self-interestedness. When Whythorne gets among them, it is their way of talking which fascinates him:

Then when I accompanied the merchants, there was talk of gain and loss, and of such merchandise as was best for them to transport into this country and into that country for gain, and likewise of the commodities of other countries to be brought hither wherein gain was to be gotten. And then for the exchange of money how that went from time to time as well

28. From 'A Fruitful Sermon made in Paul's Church'; see T. Lever, *Sermons* (ed. E. Arber; London, 1870), pp. 27-28. I have modernized the spelling.

29. *The Autobiography of Thomas Whythorne* (ed. J.M. Osborn; Oxford: Clarendon Press, 1961). Whythorne's manuscript is transcribed in this edition in his own experimental orthography. I have modernized it in the quotations which follow.

beyond the seas as here in England. There was no other talk among all
these aforesaid but of gain and riches. At the first conversing among these
aforesaid, their talk was somewhat strange unto me because I had not been
used so much unto it a great while before (for when I was in Cambridge
there was no other talk but of learning and learned men, and how by
learning and the virtues of the mind men were exalted to promotion). Then
should I hear sometimes of one who had been in his office but a small
time, and when he came to it he was little or nothing worth and every man
paid, and yet now he was known to be both a purchaser, a builder, and also
a great monied man.[30]

Whythorne does not stop here, but goes on to analyze the extent to
which their language blinds them to the spiritual truths which they
should observe:

A great number in these days do measure honesty by wealth. As if they
praise a rich man they will say he is an honest man, I warrant him he is
worth so much (and then they will name a sum). Likewise if they despise
or dispraise a poor man, they will say that he is a beggarly knave, and not
worth a groat…[but] there is not the poorest nor most afflicted man that
goeth upon the ground or earth, but he may be as honest as the greatest
monarch that liveth and reigneth upon the earth, and his soul is as precious
in the sight of the redeemer, as is the soul of the greatest prince living.[31]

Remember that this is an Elizabethan in more or less private meditation.
His comments here are promising. He, at least, seems to be one member
of the 1570s society who has true religious values, expresses them
simply, and is not taken in by worldly lures. However, the rest of the
autobiography does not bear this out. For much of it Whythorne himself
is a bounty hunter, the bounty usually being possessed by the rich
widows whom he frequently comes across, often by being music tutor in
their households. Potentially the first modern autobiographer, he takes
us into his thoughts as well as his actions and experiences, and these
thoughts are often couched in religious language, as in his envy for the
rich merchants and his sense that he may be one of the despised poor.
Clearly a man of limited, almost non-existent sexual drive, and some
timidity, but physically attractive, he constantly finds himself tempted
to go to bed with the ladies, but fearing to make the wrong move
which might lose him his place in the household or the chance of an
advantageous marriage. One wooing, for instance, sees him trying to

30. *Autobiography*, pp. 138-39.
31. *Autobiography*, p. 140.

hook a widow, 'who is come of worshipful parents, and hath twenty
pounds a year dowry...who hath no child'. In spite of fairly obvious
hints on her part that he should play the man, Whythorne holds back so
long that he loses her. This is part of his self-analysis as he tries to
account for his failure:

> Now I do perceive some great likelihood that these proverbs and old
> sayings be true which have been devised upon this sort of wooings, the
> one of the which is thus. Blessed be the wooing that is not long a doing.
> And if I had followed this proverb then my wooing had been at an end by
> this time. Also an other saith that he who doth woo a maid shall not be
> worse welcome though he come but now and then to her, as in three or
> four days, but he that wooeth a widow must ply her daily. Also an other
> saith that he that wooeth a maid must go trick and trim, and in fine apparel,
> but he that wooeth a widow must go stiff before. I promise you so was I
> stiff, but yet considering that the time was not like to be long to the
> wedding day, and also that the market was like to last all the year long, and
> I loving her, meant not to attempt any dishonesty unto her, for a sinful fact
> it had been, till we had been married, and we should have provoked God's
> heavy displeasure and wrath to have lighted upon us for our wickedness,
> and if those be the causes of her revolt, then I do account her as good lost
> as found.[32]

Religious language in Whythorne's account is already being used in the
Pepysian manner, not as a means to explore himself but for him to avoid
self-exploration, to justify under pious affirmation his failure to act—
rather like Jonah in the belly of the whale.

Whythorne's crisis, as it was for many sixteenth-century Londoners,
was the plague:

> I had occasion to abide and continue still, in and nigh about London. The
> which city was now the plague of pestilence as I doubted to tarry there any
> longer for being swallowed up among those who were devoured with the
> same.

> So that now the fear of death did greatly trouble me, and I being at that
> present much unquieted with so many crosses at once, began to enter into
> the judgment of mine own conscience, and considered with my self that
> plagues and punishments are many times sent unto us from God for our
> sins, for in scriptures it is said, that if we do say we have no sins, we are
> deceived, and there is no truth in us. Also it is said, that the righteous man
> offendeth seven times a day. Then in the ten commandments God saith
> that he will punish the sins of the fathers upon their children unto the third

32. *Autobiography*, pp. 191-92.

and fourth generation of them that hate him, and if he will for our sins punish our posterity, how should we think otherwise but that our sins shall be more heinous in God's sight.[33]

As the plague gets worse, so Whythorne is thrown back on the Bible to find texts which counter his depression. Whole pages of the auto-biography are now taken up with them, culminating in Jas 5.13, *If any of you be vexed, let him pray, and if any be merry let him sing psalms.* Taking this hint, Whythorne rewrites one of his own poems. Given in full early in his autobiography, the poem had begun like this:

> Since I embrace
> My lady's grace
> In sort as I desire
>
> I will rejoice
> With pleasant voice
> Since quenched is this fire.

Now it begins:

> Since I embrace
> The heavenly grace
> In sort as I would have
>
> Rejoice I must
> Till I for dust
> Do yield my corpse to grave.[34]

In the belly of his whale, plague-ridden London, Whythorne rewrites the whole poem to turn it, like Jonah's, into a psalm of deliverance:

> But then God's grace
> Appeared in place
> Putting back that foul fiend
>
> And said to me
> Of comfort be
> For heaven is thine at end
>
> Wherefore rejoice
> Both sound and voice
> Let no tune mourning be

33. *Autobiography*, p. 145.
34. *Autobiography*, p. 42.

> But with delight
> With all your might
> Rejoice ye all with me.[35]

This I take to be one definition of religious language which the author of Jonah favoured: however idealistic its roots, it ends as a form of parody whose sole purpose is self-comfort. If the essential idea of 'religion' is binding together, in one word 'community', then religious language one or two generations after the Reformation perversely encouraged the drive towards English individualism. Whythorne sits in his room as the plague closes in to the point where it enters the very house in which he lodges. His response is not to flee London, nor to take any other kind of action, such as helping others, but to read the Bible to look for texts which may guarantee his own survival. And when Whythorne runs out of texts, he composes his own:

> After I had gathered and written all these foresaid comfortable sayings thus together, which are most worthy and needful to cure a distressed and wounded mind and soul, I being still minded and willing to occupy my mind sometime in this kind of exercise...I made this song...upon the 134 Psalm in the which the sinner giveth thanks to God for his graces bestowed upon him, and sheweth of God's goodness to such as be repentant:
>
> > I will give thanks to thee
> > O Lord in Trinity
> > Because thou hast heard me
> > My prayer all
> >
> > And in my tormentry
> > My hope in thee shall be
> > To turn mine enemy
> > When I thee call
> >
> > Even before each wight
> > I will sing day and night
> > By praise which art my light
> > And my whole trust
> >
> > Toward thy temple right
> > I worship will thy might
> > Praising thy name in sight
> > Of th'ill and just...[36]

35. *Autobiography*, p. 158.
36. *Autobiography*, p. 160. Whythorne actually means the 138th Psalm, not the 134th.

At this point, with Whythorne Englishing the Hebrew call to look 'toward thy temple' we are squarely back to Jonah who, in the whale, praised God for letting his 'prayer come in unto thee, even into thy holy temple'.

Whythorne's modern editor has little sympathy for all of this. Tracing the outline of the autobiography, he says of these passages:

> The autobiography suffers from this intensified zeal, for the pages are now burdened with discussions of sin and salvation, and cant phrases echoed from a hundred Tudor sermons.[37]

This is fair comment. One great aim of the Reformers was to reform language, to make, most famously, the singing of psalms natural to the ploughboy as he worked, and to give the people, from the monarch downwards, an instinctive appetite for revealed truth by the preaching of God's word. For perhaps a generation it worked, but by the 1570s it had decayed into cant and solipsism. Like the language of merchants, it became a form of jargon which took three or four more generations to work its way out of the national bloodstream. In that time great poets like Donne, Herbert and Vaughan tried hard to reform it, but by the 1670s it had lost all but the most marginal of places in the cultural consciousness.

37. *Autobiography*, p. xli.

CONCEITS OF MIND, CONCEITS OF BODY:
DIONYS FITZHERBERT AND THE DISCOURSES OF RELIGION
AND MADNESS

Katharine Hodgkin

To raise the question of the nature of religious language is by definition
to take that nature as to be interrogated, rather than as self-explanatory.
What identifies, defines, authorizes religious language? What factors
govern the inclusion or exclusion of a given text within the discourse of
religion, and whose are the voices that determine the issue? These questions are central to the text I am discussing, whose claim to inclusion
within the category of the religious (and thus crucially that of its author)
is problematic and contested. This text is an early seventeenth-century
manuscript by a woman called Dionys Fitzherbert, in her late twenties at
the time of writing, unmarried, and from a secular gentry family. It
recounts an episode of mental crisis, a period of what those around her
interpreted as an attack of insanity; its primary aim is to refute that diagnosis, locating her suffering instead within the spiritual framework of
despair and rebirth. As such, it very directly poses questions about its
own status on the threatening boundary between religion and madness.
On the side of religion, so to speak, there is the writer herself, who must
establish her sanity both argumentatively and demonstratively—both in
the validity of her propositions and in the form of the writing itself,
whose lucidity and coherence will enact the same qualities in her; with
her may be ranged the sympathetic clergyman who writes a preface to
her account (of whom more later), and the anonymous W.R. who adds a
brief poem praising her wit. On the side of madness, the text is less
specific; it is clear that she was diagnosed and treated as insane, and that
those around her at the time were in no doubt about it; nor probably
was the doctor in whose care she was placed for a while, or her large
and bewildered family. Uncertainly positioned, finally, there is the narrative's reader, seventeenth-century or modern, challenged to take up a

position as sceptic or believer: to say, this is not inspiration but madness; or to join her in attributing her sufferings to a battle between God and Satan.

The manuscript, at first sight, presents itself as straightforwardly spiritual. The first copy of it I encountered, in the Bodleian Library, was written in a hard-back book in a tidy and regular secretarial hand, dated mainly to 1607, and with the title, 'An Anatomie for the Poore in Spirrit, Or, the Case of an Afflicted Conscience layed open by Example'.[1] This title places it as an early example of a genre which was to become immensely popular over the following century—a spiritual work written to encourage the downhearted and doubtful, offering up as an example a particular case, which rightly read and interpreted will be uplifting and purifying.[2] Such exemplary cases could be written by various people— friends, ministers, widowers and widows. In the form of first-person narratives, they became especially popular amongst women, offering a genre which neither required nor laid immodest claim to any form of learning beyond literacy (and in general a close acquaintance with the Bible), and which by virtue of its religious subject-matter could compensate for both the impropriety of writing for the public eye at all, and the potential vanity of writing about oneself.[3]

Religious writing was often held to be the form of writing in which a

---

1.   This manuscript, Ms. Bod. 154, is for the most part a faithful copy of the original, though the spelling and punctuation has been tidied up, along with some more substantial alterations discussed below. It includes one extra preface and omits one. Quotations have generally been taken from the original manuscript (see n. 8), except in the case of this preface, which I quote from fairly extensively, as it is her most direct engagement with the diagnosis of melancholy. References henceforward are given in the text, abbreviated to 154.

2.   On exemplary lives in the early modern period in relation to the development of autobiographical writing, see M. Spufford, *Small Books and Pleasant Histories: Popular Fiction and its Readership in Seventeenth-Century England* (Oxford: Oxford University Press, 1981); P. Delany, *British Autobiography in the Seventeenth Century* (London: Routledge, 1969); O. Watkins, *The Puritan Experience: Studies in Spiritual Autobiography* (London: Routledge, 1972); J. Stachniewski, *The Persecutory Imagination: English Puritanism and the Literature of Religious Despair* (Oxford: Clarendon Press, 1991).

3.   On women's use of first-person narratives in this period, see E. Hobby, *Virtue of Necessity: English Women's Writing 1649–1688* (London: Virago Press, 1988); E. Graham, H. Hinds, E. Hobby and H. Wilcox (eds.), *Her Own Life: Autobiographical Writings by Seventeenth-Century Englishwomen* (London: Routledge, 1989). See also general works on women's writing, n. 4.

woman could most readily escape the taint of immorality or arrogance (laying claim to authority in one's own person) which hung about secular works such as romance or poetry; and for many women in the sixteenth and seventeenth centuries it offered the possibility of negotiating and to some extent challenging the restrictions which required virtuous women to remain invisible, inaudible and confined to the private sphere.[4] The directions in which she might properly engage herself were of course still subject to suspicious supervision, as Richard Brathwait makes clear in *The English Gentlewoman* (1631); just as his readers should not discuss politics, he observes severely,

> nor to dispute of high poynts of Divinity, will it sort well with women of your quality. These *Shee-Clarkes* many times broach strange opinions, which, as they understand them not themselves, so they labour to entangle others of equall understanding to themselves... *Women,* as they are to be no *Speakers* in the Church, so neither are they to be disputers of controversies in the Church.[5]

Women's place in religious discourse was thus narrowly delimited: prayers and meditations on daily life were acceptable, translations would pass, theological disputation was out. Such restrictions were to be dramatically breached in the Civil War years, when both women and men from all classes swept into print, writing pamphlets of all kinds, and most of them disputatious. This period also saw the rise of autobiographical narratives to a high point of popularity, in line with the radical Protestant theology which placed experience as the touchstone of truth.[6] But at the time Dionys Fitzherbert was writing, early in the seventeenth century,

---

4. A great deal of work has been done over the last ten years or so on women and writing in the sixteenth and seventeenth centuries. Bibliographical studies include P. Crawford, 'Women's Published Writings 1600–1700', in M. Prior (ed.), *Women in English Society 1500–1800* (London: Methuen, 1985); Hobby, *Virtue of Necessity.* See also P. Labalme (ed.), *Beyond their Sex: Learned Women of the European Past* (New York: New York University Press, 1980); M.B. Rose (ed.), *Women in the Middle Ages and the Renaissance* (Syracuse: Syracuse University Press, 1986); E. Beilin, *Silent but for the Word: Tudor Women as Patrons, Translators and Writers of Religious Works* (Ohio: Kent State University Press, 1985); S.P. Cerasano and M. Wynne-Davies (eds.), *Gloriana's Face: Women, Public and Private, in the English Renaissance* (London: Routledge, 1992).

5. R. Brathwait, *The English Gentlewoman* (London, 1631; English Experience facsimile reprint no. 215, Amsterdam, 1970), p. 90.

6. On the category of 'experience' in Puritan thought and practice, see Watkins, *The Puritan Experience*; Stachniewski, *The Persecutory Imagination.*

these new forms were still in their infancy, which makes her own enterprise all the more surprising. Not only is it autobiographical, but it is firmly and unashamedly argumentative, both on medical and theological grounds. To assert her experience as a spiritual trial rather than an episode of insanity requires her to take on both medical and clerical opinion, since in both she might be condemned, whether as damned or as mad.

The text, however, as I say, gives no immediate clue to this intention; it sets out to be assimilable into a known, though still relatively new, sphere. It is prefaced by a supportive letter from a friendly clergyman, and by a series of introductions addressed to a community of souls—'To all true mourners in Sion', one begins; 'Christian Reader', another. The proposed framework was a familiar one: spiritual birth, backsliding, punishment, despair, revivification. From this starting point, however, on first reading, I found it puzzling, enigmatic in its preoccupations compared to others of its genre. There were clues being thrown around which appeared to presuppose some knowledge on the part of the reader which I did not have, clues which only made sense at the point when I realized that the writer was writing about, and defending herself against the imputation of, insanity.[7] What presented itself as a straightforward exemplary narrative was thus at the same time an act of concealment; alongside it ran a narrative of another kind, a hidden story which the presentation and the title were concerned to mask. And this sense of the text as doubled, as having an inner story only extricable by following the paths of the labyrinthine narrative, was itself duplicated by the emergence of a second manuscript which was Fitzherbert's original account, subsequently put into fair copy for circulation, with a certain amount of purification and tidying up.[8]

---

7.   For example, in one of her prefaces, she writes, 'I desier you to conceder atentively the nature and maner of the tryalls & tentations I was tosed & aflicked withal...the first...the unsuportable bourdon of sine and the ferfull aprehention of god eternall wrath...the other are such as may in some sort seme rediculus but no tong can expres ther fors & violent working in a mased senc' (Ms. E.mus. 169, pp. 2v.-3r.); if the first of these is familiar, the second without further detail is mystifying.

8.   This second manuscript, also in the Bodleian Library, is numbered Ms. E.mus. 169, hereafter abbreviated in the text as 169. It is a smaller volume than the other, soft-bound, and written in a clear italic hand, with relatively few amendments, though some additions.

Multiple possible truths, it seemed, were put into play by this multiplying narrative; many questions might be asked about the nature of her experience and the writing of it, and the relation between the two. The dress into which the narrative was trying to put itself did not really fit; there were too many points of stress, too many gaps left unfilled. It was a narrative at once situated entirely within the discourse of religion, and also curiously oblique to it; one which must simultaneously take up a position in relation to madness, even if the only position was that of denial. In this essay, then, I attempt an exploration of some of these stress points and obliquities, of the ways in which religion is represented in this narrative in relation to the particular crisis that Fitzherbert faces— that of needing to make sense of an experience of unreason. Before turning to consider the directly religious aspects of the narrative, however, I make a brief detour to look at some aspects of the connections between religion, melancholy and madness in the early modern period, and at Fitzherbert's rejection of the imputed link.

The relation between religious despair and melancholic madness, it was clear to many of Fitzherbert's contemporaries, could be uneasily close.[9] Sixteenth- and seventeenth-century texts set out in a spirit of gay confidence to elucidate the distinction, and fall back in confusion. William Perkins, in his *Treatise of Conscience*, poses the question, 'whether there be any difference betweene the trouble of Conscience, and Melancholy? for many hold, that they are all one', and answers with great decision, 'They are not all one, but differ much. Affliction of Conscience is one thing, trouble by Melancholy is another'; but his brief and sketchy exposition of the difference makes little progress beyond that assertion.[10] Timothy Bright devotes several substantial chapters of

---

9. For discussions of madness, melancholy and religion in the early modern period, see L. Babb, *The Elizabethan Malady: A Study of Melancholia in English Literature from 1580 to 1640* (East Lansing: University of Michigan Press, 1951); M. MacDonald, *Mystical Bedlam: Madness, Anxiety and Healing in Seventeenth-Century England* (Cambridge: Cambridge University Press, 1985); R. Porter, *Mind-forg'd Manacles: A History of Madness in England from the Restoration to the Regency* (London: Athlone Press, 1987). More specifically on religious melancholy, see S. Snyder, 'The Left Hand of God: Despair in Medieval and Renaissance Tradition', *Studies in the Renaissance* 12 (1965); M. MacDonald, 'Religion, Social Change and Psychological Healing in England 1600–1800', in W. Sheils (ed.), *The Church and Healing* (Oxford: Basil Blackwell, 1982). See also Stachniewski, *The Persecutory Imagination*.

10. W. Perkins, *Whole Treatise of Conscience* (London, 1601), Book I, p. 194.

his *Treatise on Melancholy* to the specific characteristics of affliction of conscience for sin, concluding, 'if they be diligently compared...in whatsoever respect these unreverent and prophane persons list to match them, they shall be of diverse nature, never to be coupled in one fellowship'; yet he himself reassures the friend to whom the treatise is ostensibly addressed that his affliction should be considered 'as mixed of the melancholick humour and that terror of God', precisely coupling the two categories he wishes to maintain distinct.[11]

The language of the soul in spiritual torment comes dangerously close to that of insanity, and its sufferings in both cases can be paralleled: the foremost common element is despair. Many seventeenth-century autobiographers emphasize the urgency and terror of their conviction that they were damned beyond measure, guilty of the sin against the Holy Ghost, the worst sinners alive; the requirement that one should have felt the full force of despair as a necessary prelude to belief in salvation through God's grace could be perilous.[12] William Willymat, in his *Physicke to Cure the Most Dangerous Disease of Desperation*, distinguishes between 'a wicked kind of Desperation of Gods promises, power, goodness & mercie towards sinners', and 'an holy desperation of a mans owne defectes, infirmities, and corruptions'; experientially, though, it could be hard to tell which one you were suffering from.[13] Moreover, despair itself, Burton suggests in *The Anatomy of Melancholy*, may be the result of a predisposition to melancholy, which leaves the sufferer vulnerable to devilish attacks—'such men are most apt by reason of their ill-disposed temper, to distrust, fear, grieve, mistake and amplify whatsoever they preposterously conceive, or falsely apprehend'.[14] And once in the grip of spiritual despair, conversely, melancholy—again understood as a specific medical and humoural condition—may be the

---

11. T. Bright, *A Treatise of Melancholie* (London, 1586; English Experience facsimile reprint no. 212, Amsterdam, 1969), pp. 190, 191.

12. J. Bunyan, *Grace Abounding to the Chief of Sinners*, first published in 1666, is the most celebrated example; see also H. Allen, *Satan his Methods and Malice Baffled* (London, 1683). On despair in general in Protestant theology, see works cited in n. 9.

13. Quoted in Wymer, *Suicide and Despair in Jacobean Drama*, p. 6.

14. R. Burton, *The Anatomy of Melancholy* (3 vols.; London: G. Bell & Sons, 1926–27), III, p. 453.

result, the symptom of the disordered conscience. The two are at once separate, and inextricably connected in a circle of cause and effect.

It is thus in relation to this nexus of ideas—a convergence between sorrow over sin, despair at one's own sinfulness, the melancholy humour, and full-blown madness—that Fitzherbert must construct her case for her own sanity, against those who explain her sufferings in terms of 'melancholly or I know not what turning of the braine' (10r. 154). But if one of my first questions in this essay concerned the factors governing the assignment of a given text to the realm of the religious or the insane, a preliminary answer, it must be said, is that in her case it is hardly surprising if those who saw her were inclined to resort to this explanation, given the range of symptoms she seems to have been exhibiting. At her lowest points, she claims, she knew nobody, ate coal, and smiled senselessly at everything. The initial phase of her disorder involved raving delirium, in which she did not recognize her relatives, and was tied down; after this most acute period had passed, she remained for several months deeply dejected, weeping continuously, and subject to a variety of anxious and fearful convictions, most concerning death—that her father would have her put to death, that she would never die, that there was no such thing as death, that she had committed the sin against the Holy Ghost, that she was destined to be burned forever, and so forth—all readily identifiable to the seventeenth-century physician as melancholic delusion. The very ease of the identification becomes for her an exacerbation of her suffering, in the sheer weight and obviousness of the case for insanity. Her problem is precisely to give a meaning that contradicts the obvious, that recuperates these extreme and frightful experiences into a religious framework.[15]

15. The question of why she is so anxious not to be labelled mad is one I won't go into in any detail here. I would suggest that part of the reason may be a resistance to the particular construction of melancholy in relation to femininity, which emphasizes the flesh and sexuality; see my discussion, 'Dionys Fitzherbert and the Anatomy of Madness', in K. Chedgzoy, M. Hansen and S. Trill (eds.), *Voicing Women: Gender and Sexuality in Early Modern Writing* (Keele: Keele University Press, forthcoming). I would also suggest that it has to do with the fear that the episode might not be wholly finished. By placing an incomprehensible catastrophe within the narrative of punishment for sin, she assigns a cause to it, and also a logical ending; once the punishment is completed, she is free. As part of a spiritual drama, it can be complete on its own terms; if on the other hand it were madness, then it would be her body that undermined her, imbalanced humours which might at any moment throw her again into confusion—which relates also to the argument about gender.

One of her most pressing problems in this respect is that she has no name to give to her affliction except negatively—those who are not mad although they appear to be so; and she refers constantly to those 'in this case' and similar circumlocutions. Her explanation places her significantly as part of a community of sufferers, rather than a solitary exemplum of an extraordinary form of divine punishment—she is among that portion of God's elect selected for a trial of particular horror and strangeness, but a trial which can still be seen as essentially the same in character as say Job's; the form it takes, she implies, is contingent. She will not call it madness or melancholy, although she must acknowledge that in appearance it is dreadfully similar—she attributes this to 'the malice of the divell in joining and mixing theis things soe together to make them thereby the more undescernable in the eye of the world' (10v. 154). But she also claims that to 'well-seeing eyes' the difference is nonetheless apparent, and devotes a good deal of attention to explaining the symptomatic differences, as well as insisting on the contrasting causes of the two types of affliction (10v. 154).[16]

The primary distinction she wishes to establish is between the organic and the spiritual. Her own sufferings, originating in the heart and spirit, throw her body out of order: 'uppon theis violent and strong passions of the mynd', she argues, 'the whole body is much disordered'; but 'melancholly or any other distemperature of the body', she insists, are 'not the first Cause thereof' (11r. 154). But this distinction, clear at moments, at others is subject to an oscillation at the level of language: even for Fitzherbert the distinction between mind and body is never as clear as she would like it to be. This problem can be illustrated in the curious and interesting word 'conceit', which crosses the boundary between mind and body which it supposedly helps to establish, destabilizing the distinction by its own physiological ambiguity, both cause and effect.[17] A conceit is in the first place a delusion, a perceptive error located in the mind, the product of a disordered brain—sufferers 'fall into Conceits' in

16. Problems of perception and the nature of the 'well-seeing eye' are also discussed more extensively in my 'Dionys Fitzherbert and the Anatomy of Madness' (see previous note).

17. For 'conceit', see *Oxford English Dictionary*. A participant unknown to me at the conference informed me that in Young's Concordance a 'conceit' is identified as something *beside* or *outside* the self, an intriguing suggestion which I have not so far been able to follow up, but which seems to highlight again the problematic relation between the internal and the external cause.

which they believe they cannot eat, for instance, but she is eager to demonstrate that this is only a delusion, and if they can be persuaded of their error then they will indeed be quite capable of eating (11r. 154). But at the same time a conceit can be the physiological cause of error, breeding humours which are themselves the source of deception, as if delusion itself were generative; thus she refers to 'those pestiferys humers which came of so many deadly concaits' (8v. 169). Like its modern relative 'conception', it can refer both to process and result, to the activity of conceiving and to what is conceived. The circle of conceit leads only back to itself: instead of cause and effect as sequence, they become indistinguishably concurrent.

The problem is not of course specific to Fitzherbert: one might say that the categorical oppositions she wishes to establish between organic and spiritual are somehow untenable in medical and theological discourses of the time. Thus the sympathetic prefacing letter written by Dr Chetwynd, Dean of Bristol, supposedly in support of her position, in a curious way threatens to undermine it by its indifference to the rigid distinctions she wishes to establish. When he tells her that God on first afflicting her saw her 'grown cold and careless through prosperitie... pufed upp with vanity; In a word...too full of blood', he is addressing her simultaneously in metaphor and in literal description, and the two combine to provide the metaphorical terms in which to continue:

> his resolution was to lett yow be lett bloud in the veine to make yow sound; and hereto Satan offered his service to hope to make yow bleed unto death, when God that could stopp the veine when he saw good, meant no such matter...[18]

The idea of blood connotes both worldly desires—to say she is 'too full of blood' implies metaphorically a commitment to the flesh and fleshly vanity—and physiological imbalance—an excess of blood, literally understood, specifies an excess of passion and heat. The divine blood-letting which he uses as a metaphor for her crisis would thus resolve both spiritual and organic conditions simultaneously. And the consolation he offers for the atheistic words she spoke in the period of her raving similarly blends medicine and theology. Her wild words, he tells her, 'were noe more I think to be accounted yours then the speeches of

---

18. Dr Chetwynd's letter in loose copy is attached to Ms. E.mus. 169, without page numbers.

those that in burning fever & other such diseases speake ydely they know not what...they were not indeed from yow but from Satan, and most of them ymediately from the humour that was soe distempered in yow'.[19] Invoking Satan and humours in a breath, he demonstrates a lack of interest in which of the two should be held ultimately responsible, which is in complete contrast to Fitzherbert's own account. But despite her commitment to the distinction, like Chetwynd she is undermined by the language she must resort to.

So long as she remains within the discourse of medicine, she is trapped by an imprecise and ambiguous terminology which will not allow her to establish the desired separation of mental and physical disorder; and here is another reason, perhaps, for insisting all the more on the language of the spirit: Chetwynd's version of the religious narrative may be unsatisfactory in certain respects, but nonetheless the language of religion is a far more promising frame for her narrative. Religious language accordingly structures Fitzherbert's text, both on the literal level and as the organizing principle of the narrative. But as I said earlier, the structure it gives does not entirely contain the story being told; contradictions and ambiguities cannot altogether be repressed. If in the argument she presents she locates her experience for her readers within a reasonable spiritual framework of backsliding, despair, torment and eventual recovery, in the course of the narrative it is clear that this framework does not succeed in accounting for all the experience she wishes to make sense of; the detail of what she is describing pulls her back towards the insanity she is so anxious to repudiate, even while her comments on and interpretation of her affliction insist on its internal spiritual coherence. So her calm recommendations that those in her case be encouraged to pray and read the Bible, for instance, or her recommendation that cures may be brought about through an appeal to the evidence of the senses, is in outright conflict with her own description of herself at a time when she refused ever to look at the Bible, and the world of the senses offered only confirmation of delusion. If, as I suggested earlier, her ability to tell a lucid and logical history of her crisis and recovery enacts and demonstrates that recovery, it appears that she can tell this history only by being ruthlessly selective about what can and cannot be included in the narrative.

This adds to the enigmatic effect of the text; for she must constantly

---

19. Dr Chetwynd's letter, attached to Ms. E.mus. 169.

refer to what she resists giving a name to. Thus she repeatedly implies blasphemous and atheistical thoughts and speech, but what was actually said and how far she went is left unspecified. 'I fell into strang & fantasticall Imagnations such as I think are not mete to be repeted for I confes they were both wiked & prosumtious' (3v. 169), she admits, for instance. A preacher caused her great distress by answering the question 'if on of gods elict might not be in my case' with the opinion 'that god would keep his from such blasphemys' (6r. 169). She refers to 'the words of athisme that I had spoken' (10r. 169), but what composed the imaginations, the blasphemies, the atheistic words is too bad to be mentioned except at a remove and in denial. Characteristically she confesses bad thoughts only if she can immediately recuperate them by identifying a saving moment of God's grace in connection with them. This is particularly true in relation to Catholicism, which seems to have been a recurrent temptation, but one which can be named only in the insistence that the temptation never really gripped her. When the devil tempts her with the reflection that since 'god hath sufired me to fall and that so dangursly that it is imposible for me to rise againe therfor ther is no such thing as I did believe or els the religion that I profest was not true but the contrary rather', she immediately, reassuringly, continues, 'then whould be sete before my eies what an ennimy I had always bene to it & how I would aferm the pope to be Antychrist'; underminingly, 'and now had confest my self to be [so *deleted*] as bad and that therfor ther religion was the likeler to be the truth'; but never surrendering, 'but so many douts came into my mind about it that I never could resoulf upon it' (10v.-11r. 169). The inescapable sense that she is in fact an unreliable narrator, that things may in fact have been worse than she will allow, thus destabilizes the status of the narrative as the true and exact history it claims to be; marginal hints in the prefaces and the appended letters disrupt the fluency of the account she offers as complete.

This is also interestingly apparent in amendments made between the original and the fair copy: certain things are too frightful for even madness to speak them with impunity. Thus she herself seems to have deleted her own conviction that she was Antichrist, substituting (as in the passage just quoted) 'as bad' or something similar: the word occurs several times in her original manuscript, but each time is vigorously scratched out. She or an editor, it is impossible to say which, also tidied up a variety of small points in the interests of orthodoxy and sanity. References to the binding of her hands are removed—this seems more plausibly accounted for by the wish to remove herself from the associations of Bedlam than by the wish not to embarrass those who had bound her. References to her own conviction during the time of her disorder that she had committed treason are also deleted. Suggestions that she may have been specially chosen or inspired by God are toned down: suggestions that to God belongs the credit for her recovery, conversely, are emphasized. In a sense, she must make her narrative more religious by making it less so. Remarks about the quasi-magical significance her name had for her, for instance, as denoting one specially chosen by God, are omitted from the fair copy; and one of her prefaces stresses that although her first calling was an independent one, nonetheless it was subsequently ratified by ministers, and not to be discounted as odd or vainglorious.[20] The aim throughout seems to be to produce her as a woman of solid piety and orthodoxy, who has no dealings with demons, whether Antichrist or traitors, who was never insane, merely troubled, and who is now entirely in control and suffers from no residual eccentricity. The narrative itself, however, strains against this construction, in its very religiousness: the multiple resonances of biblical models insist on the ambiguity of the stories she tells.

For Fitzherbert as for other spiritual writers of the early modern period, as I said earlier, the Bible provides both the organizing principles and the vocabulary which give meaning to her experience. Her own language, of course, is saturated with biblical imagery and with direct quotation. Meditating on the causes of her downfall, she reflects in a characteristic blend, 'I was growne to secure and pufide up I had passed so many tryalls I thought with David I shall never be moved but thou o lord hidest thy face and I was sore trobled I had forgoten to be wachfull and unmindfull that the roring lion goes about seking whom he may devore therfor hee toke me unawares' (7r. 169)—a sentence which in a mixture of direct reference and verbal echo combines references to half a dozen verses of the Psalms, to 1 Corinthians, and to 1 Peter, and which describes in terms so much part of the structure of her thought that she probably barely perceives them as metaphorical, an experience which has no direct connection with lions.

More self-consciously, but also according to a practice commonplace amongst Puritans, she takes biblical chapters and parables as exact

20. For a detailed account of the alterations made between the two MSS, see my thesis, 'Dionys Fitzherbert and the Writing of Madness' (Sussex University D.Phil. thesis, 1994).

models through which to narrate her own experience. Once again this seems to suggest the presence of anxieties and desires that cannot explicitly be spoken: biblical identification allows at least the partial emergence of the psychically or ideologically unacceptable, sometimes by way of adopted personae in themselves slightly baffling. At the end of her main narrative, she identifies recovery itself with the recovery of the capacity to write, and specifically to write once again in the spiritual language she had lost:

> the next sabaoith as sone as I was up came into my mind a swete medetation of the resurection to my incredable comfort being of a long tym debart from such comfortable cogitations the same day I made the prayer and confession of sines fowing: and the next day I went to Bristow meaning >by gods aide< to take the cors I have now done (17v.-18r. 169).

The prayer and confession of sins she mentions enacts a popular identification with the Prodigal Son (Luke 15); it is thus both a declaration of past errors, and a passionate invocation of the father who has been offended, and in this respect peculiarly appropriate to Fitzherbert, who suffered from considerable fear and anxiety in relation to a father with whom she evidently had a history of conflict, but whom she was determined to represent as loving. Despite this aptness, however, her positioning of herself in the invocation strikes an odd note:

> o father I have sined against heaven and befor thee and am no more worthy to be called the sonne make me as one of thy hired servants. yea make me a slave to thy servants so I may be thine…(20r. 169).

To her father—on heaven or on earth—she figures herself not as a daughter but as a son. Since the passage is mainly direct quotation (typically she takes abjection a stage further and demands to be a slave to the servants rather than just a servant), the male identification can of course be read as no more than the formal adoption of a position in implied quotation marks. Yet in this instance it also seems to hint at a discomfort with direct address to the father, as if she can only do it by quotation, even if this involves becoming a son.[21] To invoke the Father

---

21. Cross-gender identifications in religion of course have a long history, both in Catholic and Protestant spirituality. See for instance C.W. Bynum, *Jesus as Mother: Studies in the Spirituality of the High Middle Ages* (Berkeley and Los Angeles: University of California Press, 1982); P. Mack, 'Gender and Spirituality in Early English Quakerism', in E.P. Brown and S.M. Stuard (eds.), *Witnesses for Change: Quaker Women over Three Centuries* (New Brunswick, NJ: Rutgers University

at all, God or human, is never easy for her; her preference is always for 'Lord' as a form of address. In representing and giving thanks for her return to normality, she chooses a tale of family reconciliation; and yet by taking this particular tale, she is able to address it *outside* the family, to the God who is her 'true' father; a double orientation which enacts the ambivalent desire for both identity and separation which governs much of her narrative.

The ways in which identifications with biblical stories enable her to express feelings of ambivalence and difficulty in relation to her family are seen still more clearly in another example. In one of the prefaces to her narrative, Fitzherbert refers to the narrative of the sufferings and sins of Jerusalem in Ezekiel 16, and comments, quoting v. 3, 'evry christin may in some mesure aply it unto him self' (2r. 169). Now this is not immediately obvious: the verse in question, as she quotes it, runs as follows:

> thus saith the lord god unto Jerusalem. thine habitation & thy kindred is of the land of Canaan. thy father was an Amorite and thy mother an Hittite.[22]

'I porposed', she continues, 'to have made aplycation of it to the sevrile acurinces of my whole life'; but this is an identification she instantly withdraws, adducing the familiar Renaissance woman's reason of 'many defictes & inabilyty ther unto for want of lerning' (2r. 169). Want of learning, however, does not as a rule deter her; this seems to be the only occasion on which she invokes ignorance as a defence. The tale which she avoids telling through this plea is one which can be read as simultaneously uncannily apposite and unacceptably threatening; a history of familial and spiritual conflict, of the daughter alienated from ungodly parents and sisters, it would transgress the unspoken injunction that families be represented only as good and loving; and yet by hinting at it she reminds us of that possibility.

Her summary of the chapter, detailing a special covenant, a fall into worldliness, punishment, and recovery, is in itself a comprehensible frame for her own experiences as she narrates them, as well as one

Press, 1989). However, Fitzherbert does not on the whole seem to belong in the kind of ecstatic tradition that would encourage such fluidity, and the identification in her case is I think working more actively against the grain.

22. Fitzherbert quotes from the Geneva Bible of 1560, the version generally in use before the publication of the Authorized Version of 1611. Quotations are taken from the facsimile edition, ed. Lloyd E. Berry (Wisconsin: Wisconsin University Press, 1969).

which might seem more generally applicable to any Christian. But the particular verse she cites also draws attention to a story of rejection, conflict and betrayal within the family, and to the way in which Jerusalem's kin—with potentially corrupting effect—are represented throughout the chapter as pagan and sinful, in contrast to Jerusalem, the chosen one. The relentless biblical repetitions insist on the sinfulness of mother, father and sisters; born to heathen parents, polluted from infancy, Jerusalem/Fitzherbert is rescued from pollution only by divine favour:

> thy navel was not cut: thou wast not washed in water to soften thee: thou wast not salted with salt, nor swadeled in clouts.
>
> ...
>
> And when I passed by thee, I sawe thee polluted in thine owne blood, and I said unto thee, when thou wast in thy blood, Thou shalt live... (Ezek. 16.4, 6).

And her punishment is to be re-identified with mother and sisters (Samaria and Sodom), in a verse which represents the breakdown of all civil and natural relations:

> Thou art thy mothers daughter, that hath cast of her housband & her children, and thou art the sister of thy sisters, which forsoke their husbands and their children: your mother is an Hittite, and your father an Amorite (Ezek. 16.45).

To tell one's life history as myth or parable, then, at its simplest can be to find a space in which to speak the forbidden. Her own narrative, marked by the tension between worldly and spiritual pleasures, between her wish to belong to her family and her wish to escape from it, can tell such stories only in a muted way. Among the symptoms of her disorder is her inability to recognize members of her family, a persuasion that her brothers are her enemies, that she is sister to another gentlewoman, that her family will kill her as a punishment for her claim to be kin to them. If in times of crisis the sense of alienation and rejection finds expression in such extreme forms, in times of more control the recognition of the self in narratives such as that of Jerusalem may provide a way of containing and yet permitting that sense to find other and less destructive forms.

Religious categories and terminology, then, on the one hand can provide a way of recuperating and reinterpreting an experience which threatens the sense of self too drastically; they also, however, provide the language of that experience itself. Her account of the time of her mental disorder is as I have said patchy, both for the reasons suggested earlier and also because in writing distraction she writes across a void, looking back to a time in which she does not recognize herself; but the fragments she gives unsurprisingly suggest a close connection between the preoccupations of sanity and insanity. The language of terror and delusion is the language of faith in distortion; the pillars on which she has built herself crumble into incomprehensible shapes, but the materials remain the same. Meanings and values are inverted to allow forbidden temptations to speak: she herself is Antichrist, she has committed the sin against the Holy Ghost, she will become a Catholic and live by the strictest order she can find. In madness faith itself becomes the mark of idiocy. Offered the Scriptures to comfort her, she rejects them with scorn; Satan causes her to say, 'thos books weer made but to deceve such foles as I was...take me said I and nail me up so as that booke saith hee was and see when I shall die thinging in very ded I could never die' (23r.-v. 169). Books, which she declares she had always loved, become objects of scorn and loathing; her intellectual faculties, in which retrospectively she fears she may too much have prided herself, are overthrown; faith which was her support becomes her downfall. This eventual specifying of her blasphemies comes in a letter appended to the main text; both an identification of the self with Christ (harking back to the unspecified presumptuous imaginings) and implicitly a denial of Christ's divinity, in the suggesting that he was no more than she was; she too is immortal. Once again too it is immediately followed by denial—'I apele to all that have knowen me if I were like to geve such a reson if I had bene in my right sences no shurely I hop I shuld inded rather have plocked my own eies and tong' (23v. 169), and followed with a complicated argument about how Satan seeing her impervious to atheism tried unsuccessfully to destabilize her belief in her faith, but even in her greatest distraction she preserved some notion of the truth. The question is to what extent words spoken become real, and how far her words are, as Dr Chetwynd put it, to be regarded as her own. Words with an acknowledged religious source can be permitted and accounted for; but the words she attributes to Satan remain doubtful, open to interpretation.

This instance thus highlights the paradox she faced in wishing both to deny madness and to record the course of her malady. Much of the time, as I have said, she simply avoids stating precisely what the most shocking words she spoke were. This still leaves a great deal that is hard to account for. And if some of the time she tries to account for it by drawing attention to elements of true faith still present even at moments of greatest confusion—so that her terror of burning, for instance, and her conviction that she would never die, is interpreted as a fear of the eternal flames of hell—at other moments, as in that just cited, she must accept some elements of the character of a distracted woman, out of her wits, because otherwise what she has said is a blasphemy so fearful that if her will assented to it in any form she will surely be damned. She thus not only *behaves* or *appears* like a madwoman—raving, laughing and crying, in the grip of wild and unreasonable persuasions—but she must be *like* a madwoman in some more fundamental sense, in the sense of having lost control over and knowledge of herself and her speech.

It is thus striking that of all the varied early modern vocabulary for describing the forms of madness, the only one she willingly applies to herself is 'distracted'. Michael MacDonald identifies this as denoting one of the more extreme forms of insanity—one of three words used by the physician Richard Napier to describe the 'patently insane', along with 'mad' and 'lunatic', and her preference for distraction over melancholy may thus seem perverse.[23] But the particular characteristic of distraction, significantly, was linguistic wildness: 'their distinctive action was idle talk—raving, seemingly incomprehensible speech'.[24] To accept distraction, then, while refusing madness, would be a way of discounting the *content* of her speech, without necessarily conceding the notion that her mind was seriously out—as if insanity could be confined to the level of language, to the surface of the body, rather than—to return to my starting point—being an organic and physical affliction. Or in Foucault's terms, distinguishing between passion and delirium in the classical period, in which one figures as an extravagance of body and the other of mind, she could be said to be attempting to move herself from the realm of passion to that of delirium, to locate her malady again in language rather than in the body.[25]

23. MacDonald, *Mystical Bedlam*. See pp. 116-20 especially for a discussion of the vocabulary used in relation to mental disorder.

24. MacDonald, *Mystical Bedlam*, pp. 142ff.

25. M. Foucault, *Madness and Civilization: A History of Insanity in the Age of Reason* (trans. R. Howard; Cambridge: Tavistock Press, 1987), ch. 4. Foucault proposes a distinction between two therapeutic approaches to madness in the classical period: one 'which addresses madness as essentially *passion*—that is, a certain compound (movement-quality) belonging to both body and soul', the other 'which

For Fitzherbert, then, the languages of religion and madness are not readily separable. In a (perhaps excessively) functionalist sense, one could say that religion provides a context in which to make sense of a traumatic and frightening collapse; but clearly it is more than that. Religion is itself a constitutive principle of speech, and thus of the speaking subject, both in the structure of the narratives of the self and in the very texture of those narratives; and in so far as madness is also identified as a disorder of speech, then religion is inevitably implicated in the forms of insanity. Moreover, if in one sense it can serve to rescue her from madness, in another it plunges her deeper in, becoming a destructive language as well as a recuperative and constitutive one. The terrors of her faith, and her ambivalence or hostility to the rigidity of the regime it imposes on her, are evident in her account alongside its reassurances.

The manuscript clearly had more than a solipsistic purpose, although she does seem to have used the writing of it as catharsis or therapy. It is impossible to know how far it succeeded in its designated effect, of persuading those who had witnessed her disorder that she was suffering in the spirit not in the brain. On the other hand, that she found friends and supporters within the ranks of the religious professions at least is clear not only from the endorsement of the Dean of Bristol, but also from the very fact of the manuscript's survival, left by her to the keeper of the Bodleian library, who must have seen something worth preserving in it. To such well-seeing eyes, at least, she presumably represented what she wanted to represent, an emblem of the battle for her soul, experiencing the dire effects of the conflict in her own person in a strange but not unprecedented way. She does not appear, however, to have figured as a visionary, which might have been another possible outcome. Among the papers attached to the narrative is an account from some twenty years later of a strange allegorical vision seen in the night sky in Berkshire; it is tempting to suppose that had she lived forty years later, she might have found a context in which her extraordinary experiences would have been given quite a different meaning, that she might have become a prophet among the radical dissenting groups of the revolutionary period.[26] But among the secular gentry of Jacobean

---

addresses madness as error, as double inanity of word and image, as *delirium*', see p. 184.

26. For women visionaries and prophets of the seventeenth century, see Hobby, *Virtue of Necessity*; P. Mack, 'Women as Prophets during the Civil War', *Feminist Studies* 13 (1982); S. Wiseman, 'Unsilent Instruments and the Devil's Cushions:

England, the closer model would probably be Lady Eleanor Davies, generally reputed to be mad for her prophetic activities and demonstrations;[27] and Fitzherbert significantly never attempts to claim any form of higher truth for her raving speech, or suggest that it could in any way represent another voice than Satan's. The more urgent need for her is to distance herself from the appearance of madness, and the attempt to claim prophetic value for her words would take her in an entirely different direction.

I started with the question of who authorizes religious language, and how; in a sense it is not a question directly addressed by this text, which is less revealing about how Fitzherbert may be positioned by others than about how she may position herself, what interpretations are available to her. I started too with the point that the reader is required in some way to take sides on the issue, that her narrative interpellates the reader as authorizer, so to speak; I finish, inevitably, by declining that position, in so far as it requires a pronouncement on whether she was 'really' mad or sane. I have emphasized the sense in which the religious frame in which she locates her history does not succeed in containing it; but it would be equally true to say that the discourse of madness is no more successful as a means of explicating the narrative; the imputed frame of insanity does not 'fit' any better than the one she wishes herself to claim. The raw event of 'insanity' can never be separated from the cultural and linguistic paradigms in which it is experienced and interpreted: if it is true to say that she was mad, it is equally true to say that she was in the grip of a spiritual crisis. To conclude with an illustration of this

Studies 13 (1982); S. Wiseman, 'Unsilent Instruments and the Devil's Cushions: Authority in Seventeenth-Century Women's Prophetic Discourse', in I. Armstrong (ed.), *New Feminist Discourses: Critical Essays on Theories and Texts* (London: Routledge, 1992).

27. Lady Eleanor Davies or Douglas, who saw visions, published pamphlets and was led by the Lord into various forms of eccentric behaviour, was at the beginning of her career (in the 1620s) generally regarded as mad, rather than as seditious or inspired. This changed once she started predicting the King's death (she was imprisoned), and by the time of her own death in 1652 she was one among many women prophets, rather than unique and bizarre; but the dismissive and patronizing responses she met with initially indicate the bewilderment with which divine manifestations were likely to be greeted in early seventeenth-century aristocratic circles. See T. Spencer, 'The History of an Unfortunate Lady', *Harvard Studies and Notes in Philology and Literature* 20 (1938); Hobby, *Virtue of Necessity.*

point: I have twice asked students to read this text in a class on auto-biography, and the question of the writer's sanity has inevitably been raised. Students in the first group regarded her quite unproblematically as crazy, and were on the whole uncomfortable with the idea that she might be anything else; there was no seriously dissenting voice. In the second group, an evangelical Christian said firmly that he thought she was suffering from conviction for sin, and carried the class with him. Madness and religion, now as then, perhaps, speak at least the elements of a common language.

'SPEAKING TO GOD IN HIS PHRASE AND WORD': WOMEN'S USE OF THE PSALMS IN EARLY MODERN ENGLAND

Suzanne Trill

According to Monica Furlong, '[a]fter the question of ordination itself nothing, except perhaps homosexuality, is liable to get General Synod...so incensed and unhappy as a discussion of "inclusive language"'.[1] This description of the contemporary debate about the language used in Church of England services highlights a crucial issue at stake when examining the 'nature' of 'religious language'; that is, the question of the gendering of that language. Those who oppose change appear to believe that such alterations threaten God's 'masculine' identity and, often inadvertently, reveal 'their rejection...of actual women'.[2] Whether implicitly or explicitly, those who reject inclusive language are maintaining an exclusive discourse, which denies women a place in the Church. According to one recent critic, the inherent patriarchalism of the Bible is so entrenched that it is not even possible for women to be 'resisting readers'.[3] The foregrounding of the gender bias of Christian discourses draws attention to contemporary socio-cultural influences upon the articulation of religious beliefs, and begs the question of what is considered to be an appropriate language in which to address God. This

1. M. Furlong, *A Dangerous Delight: Women and Power in the Church* (London: SPCK, 2nd edn, 1992), p. 71.
2. Furlong, *Dangerous Delight*, p. 86. For the other side of this argument, see W. Oddie, *What Will Happen to God?* (London: SPCK, 1984), and G. Leonard, I. MacKenzie and P. Toon, *Let God be God* (Essex: Longman, 1989).
3. E. Schüssler Fiorenza, in *Bread Not Stone: The Challenge of Feminist Biblical Interpretation* (Boston: Beacon Press, 1984), calls for a 'hermeneutics of suspicion' because 'certain texts of the Bible can be used against women's struggles for liberation not only because they are patriarchally misinterpreted but because they are patriarchal texts' (p. xii). Cited by M.O. Thickstun, *Fictions of the Feminine: Puritan Doctrine and the Representation of Women* (Ithaca: Cornell University Press, 1988), p. 4.

was an important issue of debate in sixteenth- and seventeenth-century England; as John Donne put it, those who sought new ways of addressing God only succeeded in squaring the circle and thrusting 'into strait corners of poore wit / Thee, who art cornerlesse and infinite'.[4] While, during this period, women were very definitely positioned as secondary to 'man', the question of their position within church institutions was also a matter of debate, perhaps most obviously during the period of the civil wars. Prior to this, the controversy about the nature of womankind provoked male and female writers to utilize biblical tales, particularly the creation myth, in order to defend or attack 'Woman's' character.[5] The significance of such stories was hotly contested and women were involved in attempting to redefine the way in which biblical texts applied to their lives; one female poet, Emilia Lanyer, actively challenged misogynist readings by rewriting Christ's passion and placing women firmly at the centre of the story.[6] While there was no call for 'inclusive' language, many early modern women were acutely aware that contemporary readings of the Bible excluded them.

Notwithstanding this debate, Christian discourses provided one way of legitimizing women's subordinate status and were used to uphold the definition of the ideal 'Woman' as 'chaste, silent and obedient'.[7] Although instructed to be silent, women were encouraged to read the Bible and frame their speech with biblical expressions. The fact that women were permitted to use such discourses is confirmed by the number of texts they produced and patronized in the genres of prayer and meditation. Many modern critics see this as illustrating early modern women's internalization of negative attitudes toward their sex, and as an indication that their sense of self was determined by their use of an 'alien', male discourse. Consequently, those who wrote in these genres

---

4.   John Donne, 'Vpon the translation of the Psalms by Sir Philip Sydney, and the Countesse of Pembroke his Sister', in *Donne: Poetical Works* (ed. H.J.C. Grierson; Oxford: Oxford University Press, 1985), pp. 318-19, ll. 2-4.

5.   See K.U. Henderson and B.F. McManus (eds.), *Half-Humankind: Contexts and Texts of the Controversy about Women in England, 1540–1640* (Urbana: University of Illinois Press, 1985).

6.   E. Lanyer, *Salve Deus Rex Judaeorum* (1611), in *The Poems of Shakespeare's Dark Lady: Salve Deus Rex Judaeorum by Emilia Lanyer* (ed. A.L. Rowse; London: Cape, 1978).

7.   See S. Hull, *Chaste, Silent and Obedient: English Books for Women, 1475–1640* (San Marino: Huntingdon Library, 1985).

are defined as the least 'oppositional' women writers of their age.[8] However, such a deterministic approach to the theory of language is inadequate to explain women's application of biblical discourses to their own experience. The issue here is that of the capacity of language to shape our understanding of 'reality', to position us in the world, and to order our subjectivity; it is to address the question of who 'owns' language and how that ownership can be challenged, appropriated and re-worked to serve another purpose or an Other's ends. In order to explore these questions, I intend to focus upon early modern women's use of one particular religious discourse, that of the Psalms. And, ultimately, to examine how one female autobiographer, Lady Anne Clifford, used that discourse to construct her life. Although attributed to a male author, the first person narration of these poems invites an identification between the text and the reader, which *theoretically* transcends sexual difference and which, perhaps somewhat paradoxically, appears to offer women a space for self-expression.

While the use of the Psalms is not unique to Protestantism, a marked increase in their significance is apparent in the 'Reformed' church. *The Book of Common Prayer* informs us that the whole book of the Psalms is to be read monthly, and includes a table for the daily reading of this book of the Bible. The Psalms were frequently represented as the epitome of the 'Scriptures'; Calvin, for example, declared that they represented ' "[a]n Anatomy of all Parts of the Soul"; for there is not an emotion of which anyone can be conscious that is not here represented as in a mirror'.[9] It is this capacity to reflect, and arguably produce, the soul which makes the Psalms so important to Protestantism; indeed, as Calvin indicates above, the Psalms could be said to define the limits of Protestant consciousness.[10] Whereas in George Herbert's poems on

8.   *Silent but for the Word: Tudor Women as Patrons, Translators, and Writers of Religious Works* (ed. M.P. Hannay; Kent, OH; Kent State University Press, 1985) discusses the way in which early women writers internalized the word of God; B.K. Lewalski, *Writing Women in Jacobean England* (Cambridge, MA: Harvard University Press, 1993), illustrates the desire to reclaim 'oppositional' women writers.

9.   *Commentary on the Book of Psalms by John Calvin* (ed. J. Anderson; Grand Rapids: Eerdmans, 1948), I, p. xxxviii; see also T. Becon, *Davids harpe ful of moost delectable armony* (1542), sig. A7v, cited in R. Zim, *English Metrical Psalms: Poetry as Praise and Prayer, 1555–1601* (Cambridge: Cambridge University Press, 1987), p. 30.

10.   The importance of the Psalms in the production of Protestant subjectivity is

'The Holy Scriptures' it is the Bible as a whole that is 'the glass that mends the looker's eyes', here it is specifically the Psalms that fulfil this function. It is the words of the psalmist that 'find [the readers] out' by means of 'parallels' which 'make [them] understood'.[11] But the Psalms do not just reflect the believers' experience; significantly, they were perceived to be unique in their capacity to enable them to *articulate* their experience. As one sixteenth-century commentator explained, 'whereas all other scriptures do teach us what God saith unto us,...[the psalms] do teach us, *what we shall saie unto God*'.[12]

Thus the Psalms present an acceptable manner of communicating one's experiences with God. Arguably, in this they represent a 'pre-existent symbolic order', which is able to constitute or produce individual subjectivity. However, although believers might seem to be articulating themselves in the same language, ritually repeating the text from biblical sources, the meaning of those words varied according to the context in which the psalm was applied or which particular part of it was used. The application of a particular psalm to an event in an individual's life brings the apparent stability of 'God's Word' into question. Contemporary devotional texts, for example, create composite psalms; they forge new prayers for particular occasions from a number of different psalm quotations. This strategy illustrates that an individual speaker or writer can manipulate a stable or 'pre-existent Symbolic order'; by choosing a verse or a number of verses from a single psalm and combining them with others, the individual can create a new and coherent request to God.[13]

While the Psalms were central to the constitution of a Protestant subjectivity, it is my contention that the Psalms were peculiarly significant

discussed by Alan Sinfield in *Faultlines: Cultural Materialism and the Politics of Dissident Reading* (Oxford: Oxford University Press, 1992), p. 166.

11. George Herbert, 'The Holy Scriptures. I', 1. 9, 'The Holy Scriptures. II', ll. 11-12 in *George Herbert and Henry Vaughan* (ed. L.L. Martz; Oxford: Oxford University Press, 1986), p. 50.

12. A. Gilby, *The Psalmes of David* (1581), sig. A3v, cited in Zim, *English Metrical Psalms*, p. 28.

13. The tradition of producing composite psalms stretches from at least St Augustine's *Psalter* for his mother. There are numerous examples of texts in this tradition published during the Renaissance, including D. Featly, *Ancilla Pietatis: Or, the Hand-maid to Private Devotion* (1628); T. Sorocold, *The Supplications of Saints: A Book of Prayers Divided into Three Parts* (1612); and W. Hunnis, *Seven Sobs of a Sorrowfull Soule for Sinne* (1583).

for Protestant women. The Psalms provided the foundation of children's education; they learned their alphabet from this discourse and, subsequently, how to read and write. Although this was the case for children of both sexes, the limitations upon women's educational expectations meant that the Psalms remained a crucial text for them. Contemporary conduct literature and educational treatises are sometimes vague about what women should learn, but they all agree upon the pivotal significance of devotional practices, which emphasized the use of the Psalms. Exemplary biographies and funeral sermons during this period also stressed women's use of this discourse as a sign of their 'ideal' femininity.[14] This would appear to indicate that women's continued use of the Psalms is a sign of their restricted role; moreover, as the majority of devotional texts were written by men, it would appear to confirm the idea that women had to internalize a 'male' discourse that determined their sense of 'self'.

However, when male authors try to produce texts that deal with specifically female experiences or relate to particular women, they frequently respond by substituting gendered pronouns. In this, they tacitly recognize a need to take their audience into account when rewriting the text and, albeit unconsciously, reveal the gender specificity of the supposedly 'universal' male pronoun. The practice of regendering the Psalms is most clearly demonstrated in Thomas Bentley's *The Monument of Matrones* (1582). This text serves three functions: it provides guidelines for women's conduct; prayers and meditations for their devotional activities; and, as it includes texts by Catherine Parr, Elizabeth Tyrwhitt and Frances Abergavenny, it is an early example of an anthology of women's writing. Modelled on the New Testament tale of the wise virgins, Bentley's text is divided into seven 'lamps'; the fourth of which is primarily composed of psalms and prayers for the use of mothers and daughters. These psalms are politically orientated and pertain to Elizabeth I's government and other issues affecting the 'realme'.[15] By this method, although they were excluded from political

---

14. See, for example, the life of Mrs Jane Ratcliffe in S. Clarke, *A Collection of the Lives of Ten Eminent Divines* (1662). In 'Medieval Women Book Owners: Arbiters of Lay Piety and Ambassadors of Culture', *Signs* 7 (1982), pp. 742-68, S.G. Bell highlights the significance of alphabet Psalters in the instruction of children, particularly daughters.

15. See, for example, the psalm entitled 'On the Seventeenth daie of November,

office or active, military defence of the realm, women were encouraged
to play their part in the reformation of the nation by exerting their will
upon events through the force of prayer. These prayers preface a translation of Psalm 72, the main function of which, according to early
modern commentators, was to delineate the responsibilities of the ruler.
This particular version narrows the focus of the psalm so that it is specifically concerned with contemporary debate about women's authority to
rule.[16] In addition to the rudimentary alteration of pronouns, this version
incorporates additions that draw attention to Elizabeth's sex:

> Defend, O God, with thine owne hand, this woorthie woman and sacred
> Queene, whose endeavour thou hast used to restore peace to thy Church,
> and religion to thy people. O save this woorthie Princesse Elizabeth, I saie,
> whome for this purpose thou hast indued with most rare and singular
> wisedome, power, constancie, and roiall gifts of grace. And grant that all
> men may dutifullie honour and obeie hir, as a prince of peace; a mother of
> Israel; a nurse of thy Church, woorthilie for hir vertues set over us by thee,
> O God, to reigne.[17]

In the light of the debate about female rulership, this translation constitutes a powerful commendation of the sanctity of Elizabeth's position,
and represents her rule as a blessing from God. This extract underlines
the symbolic interaction between Elizabeth's masculine and feminine
qualities, in relation to both her 'body natural' and her 'body politic'.
The 'masculine' roles of 'prince' and 'chiefe shepherd' are combined
with the 'feminine' roles of 'mother' and 'nurse', and the legitimacy of
her rule is founded upon her 'vertues'. Together, these roles identify her
as 'an example of all pietie and felicitie unto all kingdoms & nations of
the world, which shall accept hir blessed among women'.[18] By recalling
the magnificat, this translation situates Elizabeth as the Protestant

commonlie called the Queenes Daie', in T. Bentley, *The Monument of Matrones*
(1582), II, pp. 683-729.

　16.　A. Gilby's translation of Theodore de Beze's *The Psalmes of David* (1581)
includes a table of the Psalms which defines Psalm 72 as one that expresses 'the sum
of godly governement'. The most famous texts debating the efficacy of women's
rulership at this time were John Knox, *The First Blast of the Trumpet against the
Monstrous Regiment of Women* (1558), and J. Aylmer, *An Harborowe for Faithfull
and True subjectes, agaynst the late blowne Blaste, concerninge the Government of
Wemen* (1559).

　17.　Bentley, *Monument*, II, pp. 713-14.

　18.　Bentley, *Monument*, II, p. 714.

equivalent of the Virgin Mary.[19] As ruler of the nation and governor of the church, Elizabeth is positioned as a nurturing mother; although physically a virgin, she bears her heavenly spouse children by promoting God's word.[20]

Another area in which the Psalms are explicitly regendered is in relation to childbirth; this connection has its roots in the purification ceremony, and thus again could be seen as an indication of a male desire to control or define female experience.[21] Broadly speaking, these psalms instruct the woman to lament her sinfulness, to identify herself with Eve (acknowledging her as the cause of her pain), and to pray to God for her own and her child's protection before, during and after the birth.[22] The version of Psalm 22 in Bentley's anthology includes references to foremothers, and alters pronouns and other personal references to identify the woman with Christ on the cross during her 'travaile'. However, while these translations quite specifically regender the text in relation to female experience, the acknowledgment of difference here does not actually challenge the status quo. In highlighting the specifically female character of this experience, the use of apparently 'inclusive' language works to *exclude* men. This strategy emphasizes women's 'difference' as by isolating their experience it identifies them as Other to the male 'norm'. Feminizing the psalms in this explicit manner, therefore, actually accentuates women's exclusion from religious language in general.

While these psalms were mostly produced by male authors, a later poem by Mary Carey demonstrates how this discourse could provide her with comfort in an experience which male writers overlook; that is, miscarriage.[23] In 'Upon ye Sight of my abortive Birth' Carey echoes the

19 Magnificat, Luke 1, see especially v. 42. For a detailed discussion of the complex identification of Elizabeth I with the Virgin Mary, see H. Hackett, *Virgin Mother, Maiden Queen: Elizabeth I and the Cult of the Virgin Mary* (Basingstoke: Macmillan, 1995).

20. See Theodore de Beze's Psalms for Elizabeth I, entitled 'The Kings Heast, or Gods familiar speech to the Queene' and 'The Queenes Vow, or selfe-talke with God', in Bentley, *Monument*, I, pp. 306-62.

21. Bentley, *Monument*, III, p. 119.

22. A curious exception to this are the two prayers by Lady Frances Abergavenny; these do not make any reference to Eve; instead, they lay the blame for pain in childbirth on the sins of Adam; see Bentley, *Monument*, II, p. 106.

23. M. Carey, 'Upon ye Sight of my abortive Birth ye 31th. of December 1657', in *Kissing the Rod: An Anthology of Seventeenth-Century Women's Verse*

prescriptions in the prayers for childbirth, and in this she appears to be internalizing male definitions. However, although Carey represents the loss of her child as a just punishment for her former sins, the miscarriage also becomes a metaphor for her own spiritual development. Rather than emphasizing the penitential psalms, which were most widely associated with childbirth, Carey stresses Psalm 119. This psalm deals most directly with the ordering of the self in relation to God's word; thus, although Carey is aware of her need for penitence, her primary concern is to construct her own identity as God's daughter. It is primarily through this discourse that Carey is able to reconstitute her experience and gain an understanding of herself and God: she glosses her argument with biblical references that authorize her experience, and incorporates direct quotations from the Psalms into her poem, presenting these words as her 'own'. Although her subject matter refers to a specifically female experience, as she writes in the first person Carey does not need to alter the pronouns. Instead, she appropriates this discourse by reinterpreting and rewriting it in order to articulate her own experience.

Similar strategies are employed by female autobiographers in this period: Margaret Hoby, Alice Thornton and Anne Clifford's texts record their daily use of the Psalms, both in private meditation and public use (in church and in the household). Yet, although they use the 'same' discourse, they apply it to their lives in diverse ways. Hoby's references are the most oblique; in order to understand their significance, the reader needs to be aware of the patterns of daily psalm readings set forth in *The Book of Common Prayer*.[24] In *A Book of Remembrances*, Alice Thornton self-consciously constructs her text as a record of God's 'remarkable deliverances of myself, husband and children'. She seeks to vindicate God through her testimony of his 'deliverances' of her and her family, and frames her entries with the quotation: 'Bless thou the Lord, O my soul, and forget not all his benefits'.[25] Thornton seems to have learned her habit of psalm reading from her mother, whose exemplary use of that discourse is maintained even until her death. Even when

(ed. G. Greer, S. Hastings, J. Medoff and M. Sansone; London: Virago, 1988), pp. 156-61.

24. See *The Diary of Lady Hoby, 1599–1605* (ed. D.M. Meads; London: Routledge, 1930).

25. A. Thornton, *A Book of Remembrances* (c. 1657), in *Her Own Life: Autobiographical Writings by Seventeenth-Century Englishwomen* (ed. E. Graham, H. Hinds, E. Hobby and H. Wilcox; London: Routledge, 1989), p. 152; Ps. 103.1, 2.

describing her mother's behaviour upon her death-bed, Alice Thornton draws attention to her mother's 'continual praying of psalms', through which she speaks 'to God in his phrase and word', and informs her family 'that we could not speak to him from ourselves in such an acceptable manner, as that by which was dictated by his own most holy spirit'.[26] The only appropriate way of communicating with God, according to Thornton's mother, is to use 'his word and phrase'; one's 'own' language is unacceptable. This was certainly a lesson that her daughter learned thoroughly; not only does Alice Thornton record her daily reading of the Psalms, but this discourse also permeates many of the entries in her autobiography.[27] By identifying her experiences with the psalmist's, Thornton constructs a coherent narrative of her own trials and tribulations in which her life, like her mother's, becomes a pattern of patience, piety and faith.

Whereas Hoby and Thornton focus upon their personal devotions, Anne Clifford's *Diaries* demonstrate how this discourse sustained her in a very public confrontation with her husband and the King.[28] Her use of the Psalms enables her to stand firm in opposition to contemporary expectations of 'proper' feminine behaviour; by privately 'speaking to God in his phrase and word', Clifford is able to use that word to authorize her public actions. Like Alice Thornton, Clifford records God's benefits to her family, especially to herself and her mother: she too seems to have learnt the practice of daily psalm reading from her mother. However, the quotation that recurs throughout Clifford's text is '[t]he lines are fallen unto me in pleasant places; yea, I have a goodly heritage' (Ps. 16.6). Clifford references the majority of her scriptual quotations and it is, I believe, highly significant that she rarely mentions reading the New Testament. By way of contrast, she frequently records her reading of the Old Testament; the majority of her references are from the Psalms, but she also includes quotations from the Proverbs, Job and Ecclesiastes. This reflects the fact that Clifford, at least in her *Diaries*, does not appear to be centrally concerned with her own individual salvation; rather, her main preoccupation is to demonstrate God's vindication of her rightful inheritance of Westmoreland. By aligning her

---

26. Graham *et al.* (eds.), *Her Own Life*, p. 155.

27. See, for example, Thornton's record of her response to Ps. 147.4 (Graham *et al.* [eds.], *Her Own Life*, p. 150).

28. *The Diaries of Lady Anne Clifford* (ed. D.J.H. Clifford: Gloucestershire: Alan Sutton, 1990), cited within the text.

own genealogy and experience with that of the Israelites, Clifford is able to assert the legitimacy of her claim. In order to authorize her position, Clifford appropriates the discourse of the Psalms so that it 'truly applied unto [her self]'.

It is Clifford's faith and her strong attachment to her mother that provide her with the strength to stand firm in her desire to retain these lands in opposition to her husband and the King, throughout what she terms 'this Business'. Finding herself isolated and constantly encouraged to give in to 'her Lord's' demands and to submit herself to the King's judgment, Clifford relies upon God. Her assurance of God's presence accounts for her ability to confront the King and her capacity to express her determination to retain her lands. She receives comfort from the experiences of the psalmist throughout 'this Business' and assimilates quotations from the Psalms into her 'own' expression: 'my Lord wrote to me a Letter by which I perceived my Lord was clean out with me, & how much my enemies have wrought against me' (p. 48). When reminded of others' condemnation of her, Clifford knelt down and prayed to God 'to send a good end to these troublesome Businesses, my Trust being wholly in Him that always helped me' (p. 48, Ps. 71.1, 5). Later she requests that God would 'send me some End of my Troubles, that my Enemies might not still have the upper hand of me' (p. 49, Ps. 25.2). In a moment of transitory doubt, she writes 'by these proceedings I may see how much my Lord is offended with me, & that mine enemies have the upper hand of me', yet she declares that 'I am resolved to take all patiently, casting all my care upon God' (p. 56, Ps. 55.22).

In another entry Clifford describes her position through a series of oppositions:

> All this time my Lord was in London where he had all and infinite great resort coming to him. He went much abroad to Cocking, to Bowling Alleys, to Plays and Horse Races, & [was] commended by all the World. I stayed in the Countrey having many times a sorrowful & heavy Heart & being condemned by most folks because I would not consent to the Agreement, so as I may truly say, I am like an Owl in the Desert (p. 33).

In drawing this distinction between the representation of herself and her husband, Clifford evokes the oppositions between the court and country. This portrayal heightens the contrast between her husband's support and her own isolation, exposing the 'worldly' values upon which his support is based. By contrast, Clifford is rejected and in this, and in the description of her 'sorrowful & heavy Heart', she is aligned with the psalmist. In this entry, although she does not reference it as such, the description of herself as 'like an Owl in the Desert' is derived from Ps. 102.6. This psalm is particularly apposite for Clifford's situation at this point. It commences with an invocation to God to 'hear my prayer' and to 'hide not thy face from me; in the day when I am in trouble' for 'mine enemies reproach me all the day'. And it ends with a confirmation of God's protection of his people; the speaker's enemies will perish, but 'the children of thy servants shall continue, and their seed shall be established before thee'.

The significance of this quotation is made clear in 'The Kendal Diary', by which time Clifford has regained her lands. There she extols the virtues of the 'Retyred life' with reference to texts that emphasize God's controlling goodness and providence in the world of nature.[29] Here, she introduces a theme that is central to this diary, that is, 'the lines are fallen unto me in pleasant places; yea, I have a goodly heritage'. Within this context Clifford relates the story of her first grandchild's visit to her at Skipton: 'this was the first tyme that I saw him or anie of my Grand-children at Skipton, or in anie part of the Landes of myne Inheritance' (Ps. 45.16). In the Authorised Version this reads, '[i]nstead of thy fathers shall be thy children, whom thou mayest make princes in all the earth'. In Clifford's case this appears to refer both to the displacement of her father through her own acquisition of the lands, and to her assurance that her children will in turn inherit them.

Having established the legitimacy of her own inheritance through her genealogy, Clifford expresses the hope that her children will also inherit her love of the lands and make their lives there. Yet she recognizes that:

> this must be left to a Succeeding Providence, for none can know what shall come after them. Eccles. 3.22. But to invite them to itt that saying in the 16th Psalme, vv 5, 6, 7, and 8, may bee fittingly applyed: 'The Lott is fallen unto mee in a pleasant place. I have a fair Heritage.' And I may truly say that here:

> From many Nobel Progenitors I hold
> Transmitted Lands, Castles and Honours, which sway'd of old.

---

29. Clifford, *Diaries*, p. 106; references 'Eccles. 7.13; Pss. 104.13, 24; 16.6'.

> All which Benefits have been bestowen upon mee for the heavenly good-
> ness of my Deare Mother, whose fervent prayers were offered upp with
> greater zeale to Almighty God for mee and mine, and had such return of
> Blessings followed them, as that though I mett with some bitter and
> Wicked Enemies and many greate oppositions in this world, yet were my
> Deliverance so greate, as would not befall to any who were not visibly
> susteyned by a Divine favour from above. Psalm 41. And in this Country
> Life of mine I find also that saying of the Psalmist true: 'The Earth is full
> of the Goodnesse of the Lord'. Pss. 33.5; 104.24; 119.64 (pp. 112-113).

By prefacing her quotations with the assertion that they 'may be
fittingly applyed', or that in this experience she finds 'that saying of the
Psalmist true', Clifford draws attention to the fact that she is constructing her sense of self within another's discourse. However, her selection
of an individual psalm and specific verses testifies to her active participation in the construction of that text's meaning: the text is 'true' insofar
as her life proves it to be so. In the above example, Clifford demonstrates the complex reading practices hinted at by Herbert:

> This verse marks that, and both do make a motion
> Unto a third, that ten leaves off doth lie:
> Then as dispersed herbs do watch a potion,
> These three make up some Christian's destiny[.][30]

The specific verses she references stress God's love and protection for
the 'righteous', for whom he will provide their just reward. Additionally,
her reference to Psalm 41, defined by Theodore de Beze as a psalm of
praise and a source of comfort for those beset by traitors, not only
serves to justify her position and praise God for her deliverance, but also
reveals how the discourse of the Psalms was assimilated into her 'own'
expression: 'though I mett with some bitter and Wicked Enemies and
many greate oppositions in this world, yet were my Deliverance so
greate, as would not befall to any who were not visibly susteyned by a
Divine favour from above'. Her explicit referencing of God's word
apparently promotes a distinction between her 'own' words and
'God's' word. However, the assimilation of 'God's' word into her own
expression demonstrates that this distinction is not clear cut; rather, the
relationship between the speaker and 'the Word' is a dynamic one.

In the records of the months preceding her death, Clifford reveals
another method of appropriating the Psalms. At this point, the
connections between her family history and her religious beliefs come to

30. Herbert, 'The Holy Scriptures. II', ll. 5-8.

the fore. Clifford is more explicit about her religious practices than in her earlier entries, although the way in which she describes them implies that they had always formed an important part of her life. Her referencing of scriptural quotations increases accordingly, as do her allusions to church services. As in her earlier *Diary*, the emphasis is upon Ecclesiastes, Proverbs and the Psalms. Now, however, the entries in 'The Last Months' depict a cyclical use of these texts.[31] Clifford does not, as one might expect, make any special use of the penitential psalms. Instead she obsessively repeats Psalms 1, 23 and 121 with individual references to Psalms 55 and 12. Thus it would appear that these psalms have a particular resonance for Clifford herself. The first of these emphasizes the distinctions between the godly and the ungodly: 'the Lord knoweth the way of the righteous: but the way of the ungodly shall perish' (Ps. 1.6). It then affirms God's protection of the godly 'man' who meditates in the word day and night (1.2). Psalm 23 is perhaps the most familiar and widely-known psalm, which is still used in many Protestant churches today during the funeral service ('The Lord's my shepherd, I shall not want'). Psalm 121 is a powerful testimony of faith in God's protection and preservation. It is with a reference to this psalm that Clifford's *Diaries* end; the last verse of this psalm may be fittingly applied to Clifford at this juncture: 'The Lord shall preserve thy going out and thy coming in from this time forth, and even for evermore'. The books which figure so prominently during these 'last months' are also those which frame Clifford's perspective upon her earlier life. As well as being a record of her own personal victory, her faith in God, and her family, Clifford's autobiography testifies to God's providence for the example of her readers, so 'that they may know that this is thy hand; that thou, Lord, hast done it' (p. 120, Ps. 109.27).

Clifford, then, uses not 'Scripture' in the general sense, but specific books of the Bible, which are particularly resonant for her experience and give her life authority. The Psalms predominate in her text, offering her the positive assurance of God's protection and enabling her to stand firm in her opposition to her husband and the King. Despite her use of a quintessentially patriarchal text, Clifford is far from the 'chaste, silent

---

31. It should, however, be noted that this apparent repetition could be skewed by the fact that the editor, rather frustratingly, states that as 'almost every entry is followed by copious quotations from the Old Testament, particularly the psalms, Ecclesiastes and Job...in the interests of brevity, most of them have been omitted' (Clifford, *Diaries*, p. 230).

and obedient' woman of the Renaissance ideal. Her practice of reading
the Psalms daily, inherited from her mother, provided her with an
authoritative context in which to situate her own family history in relation to the history of God's Chosen people. In writing her autobiography, Clifford demonstrates her capacity to take control of 'God's'
word, rather than allowing it, or male expectations, to control her. In this
her *Diaries* illustrate the reciprocity between the Scriptures and the
reader that Herbert outlines thus, 'Such are *thy* secrets, which *my life*
makes good, / And comments *on thee*'.[32] The Scriptures contain God's
secrets, but they are revealed in the believer's life, which in turn reflects
God's glory and manifests the promises hidden in his word. Clifford
draws attention to the way in which the psalms 'find [her] out, and
parallels bring' as her own experience is reflected in that of the psalmist's.
At the same time, however, *her* life proves God's 'goodnesse', which is
verified by her victory regarding her inheritance and the 'Country life'
that she is consequently able to live.

Paradoxically, then, it is the very discourse that would seek to subju-
gate Clifford, which she uses to authorize her resistance. Although, as
the examples of psalms specifically produced for women by male
authors indicate, using this discourse is on some level a sign of the limitations of women's experience, this is only half of the story. While the
Psalms were invoked to define the limits of female subjectivity and
helped to form their sense of self, they were shaped by them as they told
their own story: Hoby, Thornton and Clifford take control of that discourse insofar as they choose which parts of it apply to them. Curiously
perhaps, it is not women who explicitly regender the Psalms, nor do
they seem to feel that this discourse excludes them; on the contrary, the
first person narration of these poems enables them to assimilate it into
their own expression and utilize it to their own ends. The language they
use cannot be defined as 'female', except perhaps insofar as the
speakers themselves are female, but this does not prevent them from
using it to articulate their experiences. As Toril Moi has pointed out,
'[t]here is not, unfortunately, such a thing as an intrinsically feminist
text'; texts can be read, re-read, resisted and reinterpreted in numerous,
conflicting ways.[33] Moi also points out that rather than looking to the

---

32. Herbert, 'The Holy Scriptures. II', ll. 9-10 (my emphasis).
33. T. Moi, 'Feminist Literary Criticism', in A. Jefferson and D. Robey (eds.),
Modern Literary Theory: A Comparative Introduction (London: Batsford, 2nd edn,
1986), p. 220.

'origins' of an idea or a discourse, we need to examine its effects; that is, we need to examine 'whether its effects can be characterised as sexist or feminist in a given situation'.[34] The discourse of the Psalms in the early modern period could be used for sexist purposes, but it could also provide the basis of resistance. Thornton and Clifford meditated upon God's word day and night, they used it as a lamp to their feet, and it directed their paths, but although they were subject to it, they simultaneously used it *as* subjects in order to tell their own stories.

34. Moi, 'Feminist Literary Criticism', p. 205.

RELIGIOUS PERSUASION AND THE LANGUAGE OF POETRY

Pat Pinsent

If, as Dr Johnson said of the poetry of Abraham Cowley (1618–67),
'Language is the dress of thought', it surely follows that the language of
religious poems written by people who diverge strongly in their beliefs
will also differ very much. What better period to examine such a possible
divergence than the earlier seventeenth century, a period in which religious differences caused so much bloodshed? In this paper I propose to
examine the writings of a number of poets on a subject about which differences in religious belief were likely to be as forcefully expressed as
any: Holy Communion.

The research on which this paper is based was concerned with poetry
about Christ and as a consequence topics such as his birth, death or resurrection could just as easily have been selected for consideration here.
The problem with these topics is that they afford too great an abundance
of possible material for analysis. The advantage of restricting attention to
the subject of Holy Communion is that it is relatively clearly defined, as
well as being one where differences in belief are likely to be accentuated.
Interestingly, with some obvious exceptions, it is a topic comparatively
little treated by the poets whose names come first to the tongue when
considering the literature of this period. It is scarcely surprising that the
poetry of John Milton (1608–74) and Andrew Marvell (1621–78) omits
this subject, though perhaps it is of some interest that it does not figure
among the preoccupations of the religious poetry of John Donne, as evidenced either by subject matter or imagery. The fervent Catholic con-
vert Richard Crashaw (1612–49), like the Jesuit martyr Robert
Southwell (1561–95) before him, contented himself with a translation of
the Latin eucharistic hymns, the 'Adoro Te' and the 'Lauda Sion'.
Scarcely surprisingly, Holy Communion does not figure large in the
works of the mainly secular Cavalier poets. The chief exception among
major poets to this relative sparsity of poems relating to the Eucharist is

of course George Herbert (1593–1633), to whose work I will be making some allusions later, but on the whole it is inevitable that most attention should be given to minor writers.[1] This is perhaps fortunate, as major poetry can tend to distort the perspective, by seeming to demand a disproportionate degree of scrutiny. In addition, considering minor writers has also the advantage of bringing us nearer to the ordinary, less exceptional, person of the period, a period in which poetic expression was a much more common mode than it is today. The term 'poetry' may at times need some qualifying, but on the whole the very weakest, and the most tendentious, verse has been omitted from consideration here.

Labelling a poet's religious persuasion in such a complex period is no simple matter. Information as to the denominations of the poets has been taken from sources such as the *Dictionary of National Biography* and Gillow's *Bibliographical Dictionary of the English Catholics* but the boundaries of terms such as 'Catholic' and 'Puritan' in this period are far from clear-cut. There were many varieties of adherents to Catholicism, from those who were imprisoned or hanged, drawn and quartered for their religion, through those who paid fines and sent their children to be educated abroad, to those who did not openly display any signs of the old religion but still hankered after it in their devotional life (as revealed in their poetry, their prose devotions, and their possession of 'papist' objects such as statues or rosary beads). Such factors are also relevant to whether or not their poetry was published in England.[2] The term Puritan is also fraught with difficulty of definition. Because this period is before the Act of Uniformity (1662), it is not possible to refer to Nonconformists, and we are sometimes unable to distinguish between Anglican clergy with Puritan sympathies (who probably retained their livings during the Commonwealth period) and outright sectaries, more like those portrayed in such a negative way in the plays of Ben Jonson. Sometimes the only evidence may be internal.

If the amount of verse written on the Eucharist by minor poets is compared with that on other subjects of importance in the life of Christ, it is easy to see that the religious allegiance of the poet is significant.

1.   The titles of the primary texts consulted were drawn from the appropriate *Short Title Catalogues*. Bibliographical details of the primary texts by minor writers are to be found in my unpublished thesis, *The Theme of Christ in Minor Religious Verse of the Earlier Seventeenth Century*, University of London.

2.   More details about publication are supplied in my paper, 'Religious Verse of English Recusant Poets', *Recusant History* (October 1995), pp. 491-500.

There is also a good deal of variation in the ways in which poets with differing beliefs both treat their subject matter and make use of scriptural and other source material. Despite an inevitable element of subjectivity in deciding on some of the sources concerned, the trends are likely to be valid overall.

Religious Allegiance	A	B	C	D
Percentage of group (n = 207)*	11.0	62.0	11.4	15.6
Verses on the Nativity	15.0	70.0	10.0	5.0
" " Miracles/Preaching	7.9	64.5	15.8	11.9
" " Passion	13.0	55.2	15.4	16.6
" " Resurrection/Ascension	10.2	71.2	10.1	8.7
" " Holy Communion	18.2	56.8	11.4	13.6
" " General Morals	4.0	48.0	24.0	24.0
Stress on Physical Suffering	21.8	51.0	15.5	12.1
Use of Paradox	14.1	65.0	12.3	8.8
Echoes of Canticles	21.4	50.0	14.3	14.3
" " Prophets	2.8	47.2	22.2	27.8
" " Psalms	2.7	54.0	13.5	29.7
" " Epistles	1.9	25.0	23.1	50.0
" " Catholic Devotions**	10.4	69.1	12.1	8.6
" " Medieval	25.0	52.8	16.7	5.5

A: Roman Catholic; B: Anglican; C: Anglican with Puritan leanings; D: Puritan.

* The proportions here refer to the number of actual poets, not the volume of their output considered.

** Work attributed to the Fathers of the Church, notably St Augustine. Quite often this contained later devotional material by more specifically 'Catholic' writers such as St Bernard of Clairvaux and St Francis de Sales.

In view of the declining emphasis on the Eucharist in public worship within the Anglican communion of the eighteenth and nineteenth centuries before the Oxford Movement, and its relative lack of centrality within the non-conformist churches even subsequently, it is perhaps a little surprising to see how much stress on Holy Communion there was in religious poetry written by minor writers of all persuasions during this period. All writers mentioning it seem to place a high value on the sacrament, and while they may differ as to the nature of their understanding, some kind of belief in the presence of Christ, whether physical or spiritual, seems very general. Even a strongly anti-Catholic polemical poem by Thomas Tuke (d. after 1664) contains the lines:

> Both of vs affirme, and not deceiued
> That hee's giuen i th'Eucharist, and receiued,
> Giuen of God, and receiu'd of the godly
> Which come fitted for that sacred Myst'ry.

Biblical language such as 'Manna', 'Bread of Life' and 'Lamb of God' referring to Christ and the sacrament is common in writers of all beliefs, and emphasis on the power of God, the Kingship of Christ, and the need for grace is to be found universally.

If however relevant passages from writers of different religious allegiances are analyzed more closely, a tendency towards polarization can be detected. Catholics and the kind of Anglicans who might be described during the reign of Charles I as Laudian are much more likely to stress the physical presence of Christ in the sacrament, and less likely to talk of the Eucharist as spiritual food for the soul. Words such as 'Feast', 'Altar', 'Chalice' and 'sacred' are more frequent in their verse, while 'Table', 'Cup', 'Faith', 'Heal', 'Sinners' are more prevalent in those with Puritan tendencies. This kind of vocabulary is by no means exclusive, but these excerpts from the Catholic Sir John Beaumont (1583–1627) and the Puritan Minister, Faithfull Teate (fl. c. 1655) are fairly typical:

> The Altar never wanting sacred bread
> Foreshewes his flesh, who hath our hunger fedd;
> Hee gives him selfe, while hee our wants condoles
> And thirsts to satisfie our thirstie soules
> Deepe wisdome is opprest, he makes his bloud
> Our drinke, his bodie is our dayly food.
> (Beaumont, *The Crowne of Thornes*, n.d.)

This long poem, which unlike Beaumont's collection of shorter verse, *Bosworth Field* (1629), was not published during the period, shows the kind of fondness for paradox and contrast techniques which was particularly characteristic of writers within the Catholic tradition, perhaps because antecedents for it are to be found in many of the Church Fathers. In comparison, the language of Teate is much plainer:

> Come my Disciples, here's an health likewise
>   To you, not me:
>   Let it go round
> Salvation's cup's the cup you see:
>   Your health is in my bloody wound
> Think of my blood as oft as ye drink this.
> (*Ter Tria*, 1658)

While this relatively unadorned language is not entirely typical of the rest of Teate's work, it does represent the tendency towards explicit didacticism often found in writers of a Puritan leaning. It also reveals his anxiety that the reader should not believe in the physical presence of Christ in the sacrament ('Think of my blood...'). Thus he goes a step beyond the frequent Anglican stress on Christ being present as a result of the faith of the communicant, which is reflected in the work of Sir John Stradling (1563–1637):

> A jewell 'tis, not to be bought, not sold,
> Himselfe (in truth) it is no worser thing.
> He parting left (in sort) himselfe behinde
> True faith must search this mysterie to find.
> ...His precious Bodie was (indeed) the meate,
> Which with our faith not with our teeth, we gripe.
>
> (*Divine Poems*, 1625)

Stradling's language here is relatively plain and the image of the jewel is fairly conventional and secondary to the message. Even so, however, his verse is notably less explicitly didactic than that of the Puritan, Edward Buckler (1610–1706), who was chaplain to Cromwell:

> That blessed Supper which doth feed and heal
> And in and to a soul that is believing
> A full release of sinnes doth freely seal:
> Where that body and that bloud
> Is presented on the table.
> Which are infinitely able
> To do hungri'st sinners good.
>
> (*A Buckler against the Fear of Death*, 1640)

The stress on the deliverance of sinners is characteristic of much Puritan verse. Christopher Cloberry (fl. 1659) writes:

> [Christ] who gave his foes his blood, and flesh for food.
> O love incredible to flesh and blood!
> It can be credited by none, but those
> Whom that true Manna turns to friends from foes.
>
> (*Divine Glimpses of a Maiden Muse*, 1659)

The title is perhaps the most elaborate language here and reflects the adoption of literary conventions in relatively unexpected areas.

The use of serious wit and often elaborate imagery seems to be more common among writers with a belief in the physical presence of Christ in the sacrament. The Catholic writers Henry Hawkins (a Jesuit) (1571–1646) and Sir Edward Sherburne (1618–1702) are not untypical:

> The Nuptial Supper now I see…What meat?
> Except a Lamb I nothing find…
> As with a fleece, in species white
> He long on earth appear'd in sight
> As with a fleece, by grace gaue heat:
> But now behold the Lamb thy meat.
>
> > (*The Devout Hart*, 1634)

Hawkins's images are biblical, but it is apparent that he is employing a greater degree of visualization than some of his peers, a characteristic which may be linked with his engagement in another of his works, *Parthenia Sacra* (1635), with the currently popular emblem tradition. In this, little pictures generally accompanied short verses, though occasionally the poem itself might by its shape figure its meaning.[3]

Unlike Hawkins, both of whose books were published abroad, as were a good many other texts by Roman Catholic writers, Sherburne's work was published in London:

> Then Nourishment our Natural Food imparts,
> When that into our Flesh and Blood imparts,
> But at this heavenly banquet, I
> Then find of strength a spiritual supply,
> When (as by Faith the sacred Food I eat)
> My soul converts into the Meat.
>
> > (*Salmacis*, 1651)

The qualifying of the reception of Christ by the need for faith has been seen as a means of averting the possible scandal given to Protestant readers. The conceits in these poems are fairly standard, and scarcely calculated to shock, but this is hardly the case with a poem by the Anglican writer Edmund Elys (1635–1707):

> O Blessed Lamb of God! shall we be fed
> On thee, whom our Dire Sins have Butchered?
> And are we Pious Anthropophagi?
>
> > (*Dia Poemata*, 1655)

This does not go as far, however, as the much earlier lines concerning the sacrament from a long poem by the Catholic, John Abbot (1588–c. 1650):

---

3. See R. Freeman, *English Emblem Books* (London: Chatto & Windus, 1948) for fuller information.

> Heers Bread (which God the Holy Ghost did make,
> And in the wombe of Sacred Virgin bake,
> Heating the Ouen with Charities best fire,
> The fewell was many a chast desire:
> The loaues with name of Jesus marked be,
> Hauing his hand and feet nayld to a tree.)
>
> (*Jesus Praefigured*, 1623)

The concrete nature of the Catholic belief that the bread has been tran-substantiated to the body of Christ allows Abbot to play with the conceit and make the audacious comparisons of the Holy Ghost to a baker and the Virgin's womb to an oven, which it is difficult to imagine from a poet of any other religious persuasion.

Joseph Beaumont (1616–99), a prolific Anglican poet, produced *Psyche*, one of the longest poems in the English language and which he spent fifty years revising. A whole Canto of it is devoted to 'The Banquet' where he reveals his fairly literal belief in the real presence of Christ in the sacrament and his own regret (in 1648) at being unable to share in this mystery:

> Sweet Jesus! O how can thy World forget
> Their Royal Saviour and his Bounty: who
> Upon their Tables his own Self hath set:
> Who in their Holy Cups fails not to flow
> And in their Dishes lie. Did ever Freind
> So sure a Token of his Love commend?
>
> (*Psyche*, 2nd edn, 1702)

This belief presumably underpins his own tendency towards a serious wit. In a shorter poem ('Holy Sacrament') he writes:

> What He once had borrowed, Hee
> Ment to keep eternally
> Yet in debt He could not be
> Unto poore Humanitie.

The solution to the dilemma which he has posed is that Christ bears his human body hence, to heaven, but also leaves it below in the form of 'mystick Bread / And into a Chalice shed' ('Holy Sacrament').

Several other Anglican poets also indulge in elaborate language and conceits. Many of these seem to be strongly influenced by the publication of George Herbert's *The Temple* (1633). The title of Christopher Harvey's *The Synagogue* (1640, 1647) suggests his not altogether fulfilled desire to emulate Herbert, though it is from his book of

emblems, *Schola Cordis* (1647), a reworking, like *The Devout Hart* by
Henry Hawkins, of the work of Alciati, that a relevant passage about the
Eucharist is drawn:

> Thy bounteous Redeemer in his bloud
> Fills thee, not wine alone,
> But likewise gives his flesh to be thy food,
> Which thou maist make thine owne,
> And feede on him, who hath himself revealed
> The bread of Life, by God the Father sealed.
>
> (*Schola Cordis*, 1647)

These lines perhaps suggest a hint of the doctrine of consubstantiation
('not wine alone') but certainly indicate a belief in the presence of Christ
in the sacrament.

Another member of this group of poets whose work displays likely
verbal echoes of the poetry of Herbert is Sir William Vaughan (1577–
1641)[4] who was an Anglican. His lines:

> My ravisht Muse, behold the Heavenly Vine
> With purple Grapes for Mortals prest to Wine.
> This costly food, Soules Manna purging Vice,
> The figure of his Bodies Sacrifice.
>
> (*Soules Exercise*, 1641)

recall Herbert's 'The Agonie'. In this poem, a vivid picture of Christ
'wrung with pain' on Mount Olivet, sustains a complex image inter-
relating Christ's blood forced from his veins as the result of the tension
between human sin and divine love, with the wine of the Eucharist:

> Sinne is that presse and vice, which forceth pain
> To hunt his cruell food through ev'ry vein. (lines 11-12)
> …
> Love is that liquour sweet and most divine,
> Which my God feels as bloude; but I, as wine. (lines 17-18)
>
> (*The Temple*, 1633, 'The Agonie')[5]

The subject of Holy Communion is central to a good many of Herbert's
poems.[6] One of the lesser known examples is 'The H. Communion'

4.   There seems to be no evidence to link him with the more famous poet, Henry
Vaughan.

5.   See C.A. Patrides (ed.), *The English Poems of George Herbert* (London:
Dent, 1974).

6.   For instance 'The Holy Communion', 'The Invitation', 'The Banquet', 'The

from the Williams MS (not to be confused with the one of the same name in *The Temple*) where he attempts to confront the mode of Christ's presence. He dismisses the notion that Christ becomes the bread of the sacrament and concludes:

> This gift of all gifts is the best,
> Thy flesh the least that I request.
>   Thou took'st that pledg from mee:
> Give me not that I had before,
> Or give mee that, so I have more
>   My God, give mee all Thee. (lines 43-48)

The somewhat convoluted logic here shows that even a major poet may not be at his best while dealing with doctrine rather than with devotion.

To analyze all Herbert's more successful poems with a eucharistic theme or imagery is impossible. It is however of interest to look at his more indirect use of such material in 'The Collar'. The effect of the rebellion 'I struck the board, and cry'd, No more...' which dominates 34 of the 36 lines of the poem is undercut by the eucharistic allusions. These, together with the muted references to Christ's passion and the complex effect of the chains of linked images throughout the poem, subtly prepare the reader for the surrender of the final lines:

> Have I no harvest but a thorn
> To let me bloud, and not restore
> What I have lost with cordiall fruit?
>   Sure there was wine
> Before my sighs did drie it: there was corn
>   Before my tears did drown it...(lines 7-12)

> But as I rav'd and grew more fierce and wilde
>   At every word,
> Me thoughts I heard one calling, *Child*:
>   And I reply'd, *My Lord*. (lines 33-36)

The extent of Herbert's references to the sacrament cannot be matched in number and quality by any other major seventeenth-century poet, though another devout Anglican, Henry Vaughan (1622–95), whose admiration for Herbert can be deduced from the number of poems in his collections which bear similar titles, does have one entitled 'The Holy Communion'. Its opening, 'Welcome sweet, and sacred feast', scarcely

Bunch of Grapes', 'Prayer I', 'Love Unknown', 'Peace', 'The Collar' and most significantly the last and probably best known poem in *The Temple*, 'Love III'.

compares however with Vaughan's more exalted poems such as 'I saw Eternity the other night' ('The World') or 'They are all gone into the world of light'.[7]

Richard Crashaw (1612–49) also paid his homage to Herbert, naming his first collection in 1646 *Steps to the Temple*.[8] The resemblance seems to end there, for Baroque elements which can only occasionally be glimpsed in Herbert (e.g. 'Love Unknown') and can surely be seen in the lines of William Vaughan quoted above ('ravisht Muse', 'purple Grapes') are abundant throughout Crashaw's verse. As indicated earlier, his verse on the subject of the Eucharist is largely confined to translations of hymns, but these are very free and enable him to transmute St Thomas Aquinas ('Pie pellicane, Jesu Domine, / Me immundum munda tuo sanguine'—literally, 'Jesu, pious pelican, cleanse unclean me with thy blood'[9]) into seventeenth-century Baroque style:

> O soft self-wounding Pelican!
> Whose breast weeps Balm for wounded man.
> Ah this way bend thy benign flood
> To'a bleeding Heart that gasps for blood.
> ('The Hymn of St Thomas in Adoration of the Blessed Sacrament')

It has only been possible to exemplify here a small proportion of the material written in this period on the subject of Holy Communion. What has been omitted, however, does not alter the tentative conclusions to which the poetry quoted seems to lead. There are indeed a number of differences between poets from different religious persuasions: the Puritans are often the most explicitly didactic in their verse on this subject, the Catholics most likely to use devices like paradox. None sense the incongruity which a later age would feel in associating wit with a subject which inspires reverence. Despite some differences in their vocabulary, to the modern reader the abundance of scriptural language from all writers seems to show more in common between their beliefs than the differences which were so apparent to them at the time. Writers of many shades of belief about the nature of Christ's presence all stress

---

7.   See F. Fogle (ed.), *The Complete Poetry of Henry Vaughan* (New York: Doubleday, 1964).

8.   See R. Crashaw, *The Verse in English* (New York: Grove Press, 1949).

9.   The pelican was seen as an image of the Eucharist as it was thought that she fed her young on her own blood. It is interesting to compare the nineteenth-century Jesuit poet Gerard Manley Hopkins's version of these lines: 'Bring the tender tale true of the Pelican: / Bathe me, Jesu Lord, in what thy bosom ran—/Blood...'

the need for devotion and preparedness. There is more verse on the subject than the relative neglect by some denominations in later periods would lead us to expect. What strikes the modern reader is more likely to be similarity than difference as far as language is concerned, though we are of course aware of interesting variations in style. In approaching the 'Eucharistic feast', no doubt all would endorse Herbert's sentiment in probably his best known poem:

> Love bade me welcome: yet my soul drew back,
> Guiltie of dust and sinne...

and rejoice in his conclusion:

> So I did sit and eat. ('Love [III]')

Kevin McCarron

Any affirmation about God can be no more than a metaphor.[1]

Rudolf Otto writes in *The Idea of the Holy*:

'Holiness'—'the holy'—is a category of interpretation and valuation peculiar to the sphere of religion. It is, indeed, applied by transference to another sphere—that of ethics—but it is not itself derived from this... we have come to use the words 'holy', 'sacred' (*heilig*) in an entirely derivative sense, quite different from that which they originally bore. We generally take 'holy' as meaning 'completely good'; it is the absolute moral attribute, denoting the consummation of moral goodness... But this common usage of the term is inaccurate.[2]

The 'holy', Otto goes on to note, has in addition to its moral significance, a 'clear overplus of meaning'.[3] This 'overplus' he considers at length in his book, coining the word 'numinous' to describe it. If the holy is a 'category of interpretation', as opposed to that which has an essential nature which we might comfortably define, then so too is the unholy, or that which is commonly perceived as evil.

Theology is an explicatory discourse; literature is a dramatic one. The novelist has always been more attracted to evil than good—the latter is notoriously difficult to portray, while evil has a fundamentally dramatic potential which novelists are happy to exploit. Although the theologian may be considered quite properly employed evaluating the belief that, for example, evil has no nature, it is not a something and that therefore

---

1. J.B. Russell, *The Prince of Darkness*: *Radical Evil and the Power of Good in History* (London: Thames & Hudson, 1989), p. 123.
2. R. Otto, *The Idea of the Holy* (trans. J.W. Harvey; Oxford: Oxford University Press, 1970), p. 5.
3. *The Idea of the Holy*, p. 6.

evil is a nothing, the novelist is not permitted to speculate on an absence in any extensive or compelling way. Both Hegel and Augustine use the word 'evil' just as a novelist might. For both writers evil takes its meaning from the individual personality: no longer should we ask *quid est malum?* (what is evil?), rather we should ask *unde malum faciamus?* (when do we do evil?). Hegel argues that evil is rooted in particularity:

> My particularity and finitude are precisely the factors which constitute my lack of identity with God. This is the meaning of the doctrine that man is by nature evil, a far profounder truth than the modern shallow view that man is by nature good. For evil is simply particularity. I do evil when I persist in my particularity...[4]

Augustine's conception of evil is clearly anti-Manichean: '...Augustine came to believe that evil originates not from some substance, but from perverseness of will'.[5] Evil, for the novelist, is a presence, invariably, indeed inevitably, a baleful one, reeking of brimstone and singed by fire, and, above all, one which is *personified*. It is rarely a force, a substance; it is invariably a person. When we think of evil in the novel we think of characters: Harriet Beecher Stowe's Simon Legree, Graham Greene's Pinky, Orwell's O'Brien. Rudolf Otto himself was keenly appreciative of *Wuthering Heights*, in which he found a supreme example of 'the daemonic' in literature.

Parenthetically, poetry, particularly modern poetry, seems to me to be different. Philip Larkin's work, for example, seems to offer an extensive evaluation of spiritual absence, what is *not* present, and in his early poem 'Preludes' T.S. Eliot makes a virtue out of vagueness. Near the end of this poem Eliot writes:

> I am moved by fancies that are curled
> Around these images, and cling:
> The notion of some infinitely gentle
> Infinitely suffering thing.

The words within the stanza: 'fancies', 'curled', 'images', 'notion', along with the use of caesura and enjambement, stress the uncertain nature of the narrator's religious experience, while the final lines mock

---

4.　Cited in W.T. Stace, *The Philosophy of Hegel* (New York: St Martin's Press, 1955), pp. 512-13.

5.　B. Russell, *The History of Western Philosophy* (London: Allen & Unwin, 1961), p. 350.

the belief that there might be anything at all beyond a world 'assured of certain certainties':

> Wipe your hand across your mouth, and laugh;
> The worlds revolve like ancient women
> Gathering fuel in vacant lots.

The novel, however, as a bourgeois phenomenon, is more concerned with itemizing, cataloguing and representing presences, than in interrogating absences.

In one sense, all fictional renderings of the conflict between good and evil follow the dramatic example seemingly set by Milton in *Paradise Lost*, a poem which allows itself the length of a novel, where God and Satan stand on different sides of the stage, implacably opposed to one another and unequivocally *different from* one another. However, *Paradise Lost* itself can be viewed as the dramatization of a paradox, and not as a conflict between the separate and opposing forces of good and evil. Alan Macfarlane writes of it:

> The central theme of *Paradise Lost* is the battle between good and evil. Yet the struggle is not between two opposed sides, but within the same principle. The poem is an attempt to state the paradox that good and evil are entirely separate, yet also entirely the same.[6]

This suggestion that good and evil 'are entirely separate, yet also entirely the same' can be found in the work of a number of different writers, although rarely within the work of novelists. For example, within the notes he appends to Baudelaire's poem 'Les Litanies de Satan', C.F. MacIntyre quotes from Baudelaire's own work *Mon coeur mis à nu*: 'In every man, at the same time, there are two simultaneous postulations, the one toward God, the other toward Satan'.[7] In Jean-Paul Sartre's book on Baudelaire he states specifically of these 'simultaneous postulations' suggested by Baudelaire: 'It must be understood that in actual fact these two postulations are not independent, are not two autonomous and opposing forces which are applied simultaneously at the same point, but that one is a function of the other'.[8] Alan Watts,

---

6. A. Macfarlane, 'The Root of All Evil', in D. Parkin (ed.), *The Anthropology of Evil* (Oxford: Basil Blackwell, 1985), p. 70.

7. C. Baudelaire, *Les fleurs du mal* (trans. C.F. MacIntyre; Berkeley: University of California Press, 1947), p. 392.

8. J.-P. Sartre, *Baudelaire* (trans. M. Turnell; London: Hamish Hamilton, 1964), pp. 69-70.

writing on the role of Satan in Christianity, makes no clear distinction between good and evil but views Satan and Christ as one: 'Still more repugnant to the theologians is the perception of the divine in Lucifer, the realization that the two serpents are one—Lucifer in descent and Christ in ascent'.[9] This seems erroneous to me; a theologian is likely to be quite happy with a deconstruction of dualism—it is the novelist, generally speaking, who would find this interweaving 'distasteful'.

Dualism, for the novelist, is expressible, even attractive; the portrayal of a *synthesis* of good and evil is less so. One of the principal reasons for this 'inexpressibility' is, of course, the duplicitous nature of language itself, the subject matter of this book. Otto notes of what he calls the 'life within the spirit':

> It gives the peace that passes understanding, and of which the tongue can only stammer brokenly. Only from afar, by metaphors and analogies, do we come to apprehend what it is in itself, and even so our notion is but inadequate and confused.[10]

Of course, Otto is not describing any simple dualism between good and evil, which can be expressed with relative ease, but rather the *numinous*—that which is another word for the holy, and which, it can be argued, is a synthesis of the forces we conventionally call good and evil.

William Golding's novel *The Paper Men*, published in 1984, is unique, to my knowledge, among contemporary novels in that rather than personify Good and Evil, it approaches the relationship more speculatively; the novel could be said to dramatize Hegel's observation that opposites are, in reality, the same indivisible phenomenon. Hegel writes of opposing forces in general:

> These two forces exist as independent entities: but their existence lies in a movement each towards each, of such a kind that in order to be, each has in reality to get its position purely through the other; that is to say, their being has purely the significance of disappearance. These moments are thus not allotted to two independent extremes, offering each other only an opposite pole: rather their true nature consists simply in each being solely through the other, and in each ceasing *eo ipso* to be what it thus is through the other, since it is the other.[11]

9.   A. Watts, *Myth and Ritual in Christianity* (London: Thames and Hudson, 1953), p. 82.

10.   *The Idea of the Holy*, p. 34.

11.   G.W.F. Hegel, *The Phenomenology of Mind* (trans. J.B. Baillie; Oxford: Oxford University Press, 1967), pp. 188-89.

These are clearly the precise, cautious words of the professional philosopher, while Golding's eloquent dramatization of this concept in *The Paper Men* results in a remarkable theological allegory; one of the most sophisticated of the late twentieth century. His novel employs parodies of incidents within both Bonaventure's *Life of St Francis* and Thomas Traherne's *Centuries of Meditations* and it consistently stresses the indivisible nature of good and evil.

The plot of this novel is extremely straightforward, as indeed Golding's plots usually are. A dissolute author, Wilf Barclay, is pursued for most of the novel by an eager academic critic, Rick Tucker, who wishes to write his biography. Barclay eventually decides to write it himself, and so Tucker shoots and kills him. *The Paper Men* was the most poorly received of any of Golding's novels. Lloyd Grove, the *Washington Post*'s reviewer, said that it was 'The weakest of the lot, so weak indeed that had it appeared before last Fall's (Nobel) committee meeting, the vote might well have been different'.[12] This is also the way in which the novel is generally regarded by critics—as a rather bad-tempered grumble about academics by an author who has himself been turned, in his own phrase, into an academic 'light industry'.

However, *The Paper Men* is only superficially concerned with social reality, and is not particularly concerned with the conflict between author and critic. If an allegory can be conceived as a metaphor that is extended into a structured system then *The Paper Men* can be read as an allegory. Throughout the novel there is a persistent parallel between two levels of meaning, so that the lives of Barclay and Tucker correspond to their equivalents in a system of ideas external to the plot.

It is noticeable that none of the criticism that has been written on *The Paper Men* assesses the possibility that the very distinction which is believed to animate the novel—the one which exists between Barclay the novelist and Tucker the academic, between the creative and the critical—could be an artificial distinction, or at least, a deliberately misleading one. This alone suggests that even those few critics who insist in print that Barclay is not Golding, tacitly assume in their actual reading of *The Paper Men* that the novel's dynamic is indeed autobiographical; that it is, essentially, a sustained attack on literary critics and criticism.

However, *The Paper Men* only appears to be a savage assault on literary criticism, as Golding obliquely employs several of the fundamental assumptions of contemporary literary theory to present his reader with

12. *The Washington Post*, 12 December 1986, section R.

an allegorical work which is not principally interested in the literary at all, but in the spiritual. Throughout the novel the distinction between the critical and the creative is repudiated and Golding actually finds himself allied with post-structuralism. The literary critic Terry Eagleton, for example, notes: 'There is no clear division for post-structuralism between "criticism" and "creation": both modes are subsumed into "writing" as such'.[13] As with Literature, so with Religion. Two ostensibly opposed visions, as Barclay sees them, or perhaps two 'categories of interpretation' as Rudolf Otto might see them, are ultimately seen as one. Golding uses the conflict between Barclay and Tucker, not as an end in itself as is commonly supposed, but as a way of first anticipating, then paralleling, the denial of an ontological antithesis.

When Barclay, in his endless flight from Tucker, arrives on the Sicilian island of Lipari, he is approximately sixty-five years old and a cynical, womanizing, alcoholic, as well as a confirmed atheist. Because Barclay is fond of stained glass he begins to make his way to the cathedral at the top of the island. This chapter is suffused with intertextual allusions and allegorical implications, and ostensibly unambiguous comments are quickly seen to possess other levels of meaning: 'There was a big hill and I began to stalk it'.[14] While such a statement as this can be read as meaning exactly what it appears to mean and no more, it could also, given what follows, contain a reference to Donne's 'Satyre: Of Religion':

> On a huge hill,
> Cragged, and steep, Truth stands, and hee that will
> Reach her, about must, and about must goe...

There is a mythic quality pervading Barclay's carefully detailed account of his journey prior to entering the cathedral, and he describes the island itself in bleak and violent imagery which anticipates the spiritual violence to come: 'the island consisted of powdered pumice with knives of black glass sticking up through it like a feast of steeples' (p. 119). Barclay's brief encounter with a number of corpses can be seen as a metaphorical re-enactment of centuries old initiation rites, as described in works by Arnold van Gennep and Mircea Eliade, during which the initiate is forced to share an enclosed space with a decaying human corpse so that

---

13. T. Eagleton, *Literary Theory* (Oxford: Basil Blackwell, 1983), p. 139.
14. W. Golding, *The Paper Men* (London: Faber and Faber, 1984), p. 120. (All subsequent references are to this edition.)

he might contemplate the inevitable death of the body and dwell on eternal spiritual life.

Barclay's climb up the long flight of steps also lays claim to the centuries of spiritual symbolism such an image evokes. That Barclay's experience here is slowly being revealed as one that is fundamentally initiatory in character is further suggested in his decision to remove his sunglasses precisely where he does:

> That was when I realized I still had my outsize sunglasses on… It was odd, standing inside the kind of preliminary wooden box between the inner and outer door to consider that it also implied I hadn't washed for some time. So I took them off, pushed open the inner door and sidled in (p. 122).

On the one level of meaning, Barclay is standing between the inner and the outer door of the cathedral itself, but on quite another level of meaning he is standing between the two worlds of the sacred and the profane.

Barclay's peripheral comment here on his own uncleanliness, like the earlier reference to the corpses, can also refer the reader directly to Eliade and van Gennep, both of whom record instances of initiates abstaining from their ablutions prior to undergoing the participatory rites which reincorporate them into their society. For both the initiates described in text books of religious anthropology and for Barclay in *The Paper Men*, the state of physical uncleanliness is a symbolic representation of their profane spiritual state. This metaphorical use of Barclay's grime is complemented by the presence of his 'outsize' sunglasses, which imply an obstruction of vision. When he removes them immediately before entering the cathedral, the suggestion is being made that this is a necessary precondition for seeing that which has previously been hidden from him.

Once inside, Barclay realizes that the cathedral has a peculiar type of resonance:

> What is more, there was something about that cathedral, an atmosphere… You could call it a complete absence of gentle Jesus meek and mild. I didn't like it and was in half a mind to leave but knew that if I did I should only find myself in an endless stream of time with nothing to help me forget it. I went on (pp. 122-23).

Barclay's perseverance in so uncongenial an environment may seem uncharacteristic of him, but it is significant that the alternative which he envisages is 'an endless stream of time'. This phrase of Barclay's alludes both to the novel's consistent preoccupation with the antithesis between past and present, and to Barclay's vague apprehension that the religious experience abolishes profane time, which is the only time that the secular world experiences.

Within the north transept Barclay discovers a silver statue of Christ, but he uneasily notes that the silver resembles steel somehow and immediately he begins to wonder precisely who, or what, the statue really represents:

> Perhaps it was Christ. Perhaps they had inherited it in these parts and just changed the name and it was Pluto, the god of the Underworld, Hades, striding forward. I stood there with my mouth open and the flesh crawling over my body. I knew in one destroying instant that all my adult life I had believed in God and this knowledge was a vision of God. Fright entered the very marrow of my bones. Surrounded, swamped, confounded, all but destroyed, adrift in the universal intolerance, mouth open, screaming, bepissed and beshitten, I knew my maker and I fell down (p. 123).

Barclay's experience is depicted as an unequivocally religious one, with no alternative readings for the sceptic, and his screaming, incontinence and fainting are, once again, found to have parallels in accounts of initiatory ceremonies reported by Eliade[15] and van Gennep. Rudolf Otto may provide an even more specific viewpoint from which to regard Barclay's encounter in the cathedral. In *The Idea of the Holy*, Otto uses the phrase 'mysterium tremendum' to describe any powerful religious apprehension. He notes that while this can be manifested in feelings of serenity and tranquility, which Barclay will later experience in Rome, this 'mysterium tremendum' also has its darker side:

> It may burst in sudden eruption up from the depths of the soul with spasms and convulsions, or lead to the strangest excitements, to intoxicated frenzy, to transport, and to ecstasy. It has its wild and demonic forms and can sink to an almost grisly horror and shuddering.[16]

Barclay's collapse further assists in the novel's constant denial of antithesis, for although this incident represents death, it also symbolizes rebirth. This very perception of life and death, not as opposing poles of an antithesis, but as a seamless and indivisible process, is understood by Barclay himself near the conclusion of *The Paper Men* and the origins

---

15. See, in particular, M. Eliade, *Rites and Symbols of Initiation* (trans. W.R. Trask; New York: Harper, 1975), pp. 1-40.

16. Otto, *The Idea of the Holy*, pp. 12-13.

of his revelation are to be found in his experience with the 'steel Christ' in the cathedral.

By focusing the reader's attention in the first half of the novel on the artificiality of the creative and critical antithesis, the novel builds on the resultant awareness in the reader to parallel and integrate this secular denial into the destruction of the spiritual antithesis which is central to the second half of the novel. From this moment on, the dominant concerns of *The Paper Men* become the artificial nature of the conventionally understood antithesis between Good and Evil, the profoundly ambivalent nature of religious authority, and the writer's need to use metaphor in order to express a vision of reality which is fundamentally spiritual. The juxtaposition in the cathedral of Christ with Pluto, in an atmosphere that is frighteningly empty of familiar religious reassurance, clearly constitutes an experience that many readers would probably describe as 'unholy'. However, it is precisely this antithesis that is commonly believed to exist between the holy and the unholy, good and evil, which is itself being assessed in this incident.

The power in the cathedral that causes Barclay to faint is neither good *nor* evil. It can be seen as, in Nietzsche's famous phrase, *beyond* good and evil. The force that is revealed to Barclay in the cathedral is naked religious power, revealed in all its purity, stripped completely of its moral and ethical trappings. Eliade writes: 'in Yahweh, too, we find the benevolent creator combined with another, terrible, destructive, and jealous god, and that negative aspect of divinity makes it plain to us that God is *Everything*'.[17] Otto says of that Old Testament phenomenon, 'the wrath of God':

> In the first place, it is patent from many passages of the Old Testament that this 'wrath' has no concern whatever with moral qualities... Anyone who is accustomed to think of deity only by its rational attributes must see in this 'wrath' mere caprice and wilful passion. But such a view would have been emphatically rejected by the religious men of the Old Covenant, for to them the Wrath of God, so far from being a diminution of His Godhead, appears as a natural expression of it, an element of 'holiness' itself, and a quite indispensable one. And in this they are entirely right.[18]

Barclay, however, is thoroughly modern, as are the majority of his readers, in his belief that what he has experienced is evil, and in flight

---

17. M. Eliade, *Ordeal by Labyrinth: Conversations with Claude-Henri Rocquet* (trans. D. Coltman; Chicago: University of Chicago Press, 1984), p. 125.

18. Otto, *The Idea of the Holy*, p. 18.

from this terrifying power he rushes to Rome. Barclay's unbalanced reaction differs immensely from the response of a contrite Christian such as the young Francis of Assisi in the Church of San Damiano. Indeed, as Franz Wöhrer suggests, this episode in *The Paper Men* 'can be read as a parody of the analogous episode in Bonaventure's *Life of St Francis*, and it seems to have been conceived as such by Golding'.[19]

It is joy; beatific and untranslatable joy that Barclay experiences in this chapter, but initially Barclay himself is unable to comprehend either the magnitude of the contrast, or even to see that what happens in Rome is connected to the revelation in the cathedral on Lipari. Barclay's opening statement in this chapter affirms his inability to comprehend the totality of his experiences: 'This bit can't be connected' (p. 155). This, combined with what follows, may be a reference to these lines in Eliot's 'The Fire Sermon', from *The Waste Land*:

> On Margate Sands.
> I can connect
> Nothing with nothing.

It is not only Golding's title *The Paper Men* which may be indebted to the title of Eliot's poem 'The Hollow Men'; Eliot is a pervasive influence throughout the novel. Barclay's emphasis on the oppressive heat in the desert dream-scape in this chapter is reminiscent of the first section of 'What the Thunder Said', while in both *The Paper Men* and *The Waste Land* eventual relief is expressed metaphorically: in the image of a drained boil in Golding's novel and with the image of rain in Eliot's poem. The reality which brings this relief, however, is in both cases spiritual.

In *The Paper Men*, Rome, too, could join those other famous cities described in *The Waste Land* as 'Unreal'. The entire chapter is one of the most fantastic in the novel, but it is not only Barclay's dreams, nightmares and hallucinations that force the reader to be wary of any reading that is too literal. This is what Barclay sees when he wakes in his hotel room and looks down at the Spanish Steps:

> There was sunlight everywhere, not the heavy light of Rome but a kind of radiance as if the sun were everywhere. I'd never noticed before, but now, I

19. F. Wöhrer, 'Intimate Relationships with the Divine in *The Paper Men*', in F. Regard (ed.), *Fingering Netsukes* (Saint-Etienne: L'Université de Saint-Etienne and Faber and Faber, 1994), p. 159. I am indebted to Professor Wöhrer for his stimulating commments on Bonaventura and Traherne.

saw, looking down, that the steps had the symmetrical curve of a musical instrument, guitar, cello, violin. But this harmonious shape was now embellished and interrupted everywhere by the people and the flowers and the glitter of the jewels strewn among them on the steps. All the people were young and like flowers. I found that he was standing by me on the roof of his house after all, and we went down together and stood among the people with the patterns of jewels and the heaps of flowers all blazing inside and out with the radiance. Then they made music of the steps. They held hands and moved and the movement was music. I saw they were neither male nor female or perhaps they were both and it was of no importance. What mattered was the music they made (pp. 168-69).

Franz Wöhrer notes how reminiscent this passage is of one of the most celebrated passages in Thomas Traherne's *Centuries of Meditation*. Traherne writes, for example:

The Dust and Stones of the Street were as Precious as GOLD. The Gates were at first the End of the World... The Men! O what Venerable and Reverend Creatures did the Aged seem! Immortal Cherubims! And yong Men Glittering and Sparkling Angels and Maids strange Seraphick Pieces of Life and Beauty! Boys and Girles Tumbling in the Street, and Playing, were moving Jewels. I knew not that they were Born or should Die... Eternity was Manifest in the Light of the Day, and som thing infinit Behind evry thing appeared.[20]

Before his vision Barclay sourly comments on the prevalence of guitars among the young, while now he understands that the distinction between the one who plays and that which is played is a false antithesis. Before the vision, Barclay sees that with individual identities and individual instruments the young people make music on the steps; now, after the vision, he sees that individuals and instruments together make music *of* the steps.

W.B. Yeats's poem 'Among School Children' addresses the same issue, rhetorically asking how we can really distinguish the action itself from the being who performs the action:

> O chestnut-tree, great-rooted blossomer,
> Are you the leaf, the blossom or the bole?
> O body swayed to music, O brightening glance,
> How can we know the dancer from the dance?

---

20. Cited in Wöhrer's 'Intimate Relationships', p. 168.

Yeats suggests here that just as a chestnut tree cannot be reduced to an itemized collection of individual components but is a total entity, so too an activity such as dancing is inseparable from the being who dances. There is no antithesis, Yeats concludes, there is only totality; and Barclay's vision grants him the same truth. God, who is undoubtedly present during Barclay's horrifying experience in the cathedral, is also present in Rome, the eternal city, where he takes Barclay by the hand and leads him to a supremely joyous vision.

The covert reference to one of T.S. Eliot's most famous poems that is contained in Barclay's comments upon the language he is forced to employ to describe his experience, clearly establishes a parodic difference between Eliot's poem and the linguistic concerns of Golding's novel. Barclay notes: 'I think that there was a dark, calm sea beyond it, since I have nothing to speak with but with metaphor. Also there were creatures in the sea that sang. For the singing and the song I have no words at all' (p. 161).

The narrator of Eliot's 'The Love Song of J. Alfred Prufrock' says wistfully of 'the creatures in the sea', of whose existence Barclay is similarly aware:

> I have heard the mermaids singing, each to each.
> I do not think that they will sing to me.

In *The Paper Men* there is no suggestion that the creatures of the sea are unwilling to sing to Barclay; there is only Barclay's unequivocal assertion that he does not possess language which would properly describe the singing and the song. Consequently, it becomes apparent that this oblique reference to the older aesthetic model of Eliot's is used to emphasize Golding's persistently reiterated belief throughout *The Paper Men* that language can never adequately portray an experience that is, above all else, *numinous*. Barclay, the novelist, concludes his part within Golding's novel by recognizing, like Rudolf Otto, that we approach God broken-tongued, only through metaphor, only from afar.